JEFF **BORLAND**

T0348170

# MICROECONOMICS

**CASE STUDIES AND APPLICATIONS**

4E

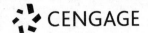

Microeconomics: Case Studies and Applications
4th Edition
Jeff Borland

Head of content management: Dorothy Chiu
Content manager: Rachael Pictor
Content developer: Talia Lewis
Senior project editor: Nathan Katz
Cover designer: Nikita Bansal
Text designer: Ruth O'Connor
Permissions/Photo researcher: Liz McShane
Editor: Greg Alford
Proofreader: James Anderson
Indexer: Julie King
Art direction: Nikita Bansal
Cover: Courtesy Stocksy.com/Lior+Lone
Typeset by Cenveo Publisher Services

Any URLs contained in this publication were checked for currency during the production process. Note, however, that the publisher cannot vouch for the ongoing currency of URLs.

This fourth edition published in 2021

© 2021 Cengage Learning Australia Pty Limited

**Copyright Notice**

This Work is copyright. No part of this Work may be reproduced, stored in a retrieval system, or transmitted in any form or by any means without prior written permission of the Publisher. Except as permitted under the *Copyright Act 1968,* for example any fair dealing for the purposes of private study, research, criticism or review, subject to certain limitations. These limitations include: Restricting the copying to a maximum of one chapter or 10% of this book, whichever is greater; providing an appropriate notice and warning with the copies of the Work disseminated; taking all reasonable steps to limit access to these copies to people authorised to receive these copies; ensuring you hold the appropriate Licences issued by the Copyright Agency Limited ("CAL"), supply a remuneration notice to CAL and pay any required fees. For details of CAL licences and remuneration notices please contact CAL at Level 11, 66 Goulburn Street, Sydney NSW 2000, Tel: (02) 9394 7600, Fax: (02) 9394 7601
Email: info@copyright.com.au
Website: www.copyright.com.au

For product information and technology assistance,
in Australia call **1300 790 853**;
in New Zealand call **0800 449 725**

For permission to use material from this text or product, please email
**aust.permissions@cengage.com**

**National Library of Australia Cataloguing-in-Publication Data**
ISBN: 9780170439268
A catalogue record for this book is available from the National Library of Australia.

**Cengage Learning Australia**
Level 7, 80 Dorcas Street
South Melbourne, Victoria Australia 3205

**Cengage Learning New Zealand**
Unit 4B Rosedale Office Park
331 Rosedale Road, Albany, North Shore 0632, NZ

For learning solutions, visit **cengage.com.au**

Printed in Australia by Ligare Pty Ltd.
1 2 3 4 5 6 7 24 23 22 21 20

# Contents

## SECTION 2

# Preface to the fourth edition

This fourth edition of *Microeconomics: case studies and applications* is a substantial reworking of the third edition. First, it contains new case studies on topics chosen to illustrate a key concept: Uber's surge pricing model as an application of the demand/supply model (2.4); and analysis of a proposal to pay a subsidy to childcare workers in Australia to explain how subsidies work (2.10). Second, all the case studies have been reviewed and most have been updated with new examples. Third, I have taken the opportunity to introduce many new application-oriented questions into the 'Some questions to think about' sections. Fourth, 10 case studies from the third edition have been removed. This has been done to allow the purchase price of the book to hopefully remain affordable for students. The 10 case studies can be accessed online at cengage.com.au/instructors.

Cengage is pleased to provide you with a selection of resources that will help you prepare your lectures and assessments. These teaching tools are accessible via **cengage.com.au/instructors** for Australia or **cengage.co.nz/instructors** for New Zealand. These include:

1  Solutions manual
2  Artwork from the text
3  Gans et al, *Principles of Microeconomics* 8th edition correlation grid
4  Case database.

# Acknowledgements

## First edition

The material in the book has come out of my seven years (so far) of teaching introductory microeconomics at the University of Melbourne. Getting to teach such bright and motivated students, and to work with tutors who are dedicated and clever, provided the inspiration for writing the case studies, and then for keeping on writing them. I can't imagine a more rewarding or enjoyable environment for teaching than that in the Economics and Commerce Faculty at the University of Melbourne.

Throughout my time teaching introductory microeconomics, I'm especially grateful for being able to work with Nahid Khan. Her support and advice, and all-round professionalism in the role of tutorial coordinator, have been a huge part of the pleasure of teaching in the subject. I'm also grateful to Nahid for preparing the original drafts of all the diagrams for the book.

I've been fortunate to have had excellent reviewers who gave feedback on earlier versions of the book. Vivienne Groves read the first drafts of every case study. Her ideas for new case studies and for extra examples, her detailed editorial comments and her advice on organising the book went far beyond the feedback I expected to get, and have enabled me to improve the book in many ways. David Johnston, Stephanie Malon and Helen Mitchell also read the whole book at various stages of its preparation. Each of them went to great effort, making comments that have not only saved me from making several errors, but that significantly improved how the cases are written. At an early stage, Leng Lee read several case studies and gave me comments on writing style that were most useful. I'm grateful as well to colleagues who helped me out with specific examples and references: Stephen King, Andrew Leigh, Ian McDonald and Nikos Nikofarikis. Andrew Leigh also kindly supplied data for Figure 1.4.1 in Case study 1.4.

Cengage Learning has been great to work with on this project. Particular thanks go to Liz Male for her enthusiasm for the project and for being so helpful in guiding the book to publication, to Caroline Hartley for taking up my original suggestion to turn the case material into a book, and to Leanne Poll and Tanya Simmons for their excellent work in editing the book.

Thinking back to my own days as a student, I'm always grateful to my parents, who provided the opportunity for me to study and fostered the love of learning that I hope comes out in the book.

My family, Trish, Tom and Louisa, are constantly encouraging, and their support has made it possible for me to complete a project that has been so time-consuming. An economist probably shouldn't say this, but they are priceless. Thanks guys!

## Fourth edition

I am grateful for the comments and suggestions made by tutors and students in Introductory Microeconomics at the University of Melbourne in the time since the first edition was published. Their feedback has been most valuable in preparing this new edition.

Thanks to Michelle Aarons at Cengage Learning who has been a great supporter of the book. I am grateful to Rachael Pictor and Talia Lewis from Cengage and to Greg Alford for their excellent work in managing publication of this edition – and I want to especially thank Rachael for her understanding as I needed some extra time to complete the revisions.

## Further acknowledgements

The author and Cengage Learning would also like to thank the following reviewers for their incisive and helpful feedback:

Eik Swee – University of Melbourne

David Walker – La Trobe University

Raffaella Belloni – University of the Sunshine Coast

Onur Ates – Macquarie University International College (MUIC), Macquarie University

Ishita Chatterjee – University of Western Australia

Robert Breunig – Australian National University

Jayanath Ananda – Central Queensland University

Dinusha Dharmaratna – Monash College, Monash University.

# About the author

Jeff Borland is Truby Williams Professor in the Department of Economics at the University of Melbourne. He has been teaching microeconomics for 30 years. He is a past winner of the University of Melbourne's Ed Brown Teaching Award, has received a Carrick Citation for Outstanding Contribution to Student Learning and in 2016 was the inaugural winner of the Ross Williams Award for Career Achievement in Teaching in the Faculty of Business and Economics at the University of Melbourne.

# Introduction

Economics is nothing if it doesn't provide us with practical knowledge. The great value of economics is its relevance to the world around us, its capacity to illuminate how the economy and society work and to assist us in making better decisions. Should you buy a car or keep travelling by public transport? What are the best ways to protect the environment? What pricing strategy should your business use? How should you bid at an auction? These questions and many more can be answered using economics. So, if you are going to learn economics, you should learn it in a way that will make it most valuable to you, a way that lets you apply it to answer questions just like these.

How can you do this? Well, economists who want to understand the economy and society develop theories which they apply to analyse the situation in which they're interested. To do the same yourself, to be able to 'think like an economist', you need to understand the main concepts that are used in economics, and you have to be able to apply them. Most textbooks focus on teaching about the concepts. This is sensible, because it's where you need to start. But ultimately, for economics to be useful, you also have to know how to apply the concepts.

That's where this book comes in. Its objective is to help you learn how to apply microeconomic concepts. It does this by example. In each case study you'll find a different application of a core concept or theory in microeconomics. The book begins with a case study (1.1) that shows how the concept of opportunity cost can be applied to measure how much it really costs you to go on a plane trip, and finishes with a case study (7.2) that examines the effectiveness of pay-for-performance schemes.

Seeing how microeconomic concepts can be applied will provide you with the foundation you need to begin to develop your own skills doing this. Another objective of the case studies is to show the different ways in which economics can be valuable. First, it helps us to understand why the economy and society are the way they are. Case studies which apply economic concepts to explain movements in the price of oil (2.3), why airlines sell different classes of tickets (5.8) and why we buy insurance (7.1) are a few examples. Second, using economic concepts can improve our decision making, whether in business or public policy. Examples that illustrate where economics can play this role include a description of how firms can reduce their costs and set prices to earn higher profits (5.3, 5.6 and 5.8) and evaluations of policies that governments can use to deal with problems such as road congestion, carbon emissions and promoting an appropriate level of conservation activity (4.2, 4.3 and 4.5).

A big lesson from the book is that you don't need to get a PhD in economics to be able to answer really important questions about the economy and society. As Herb Stein, adviser to several presidents of the United States, has remarked: 'Most of the economics that is usable for advising on public policy is about at the level of the introductory undergraduate course' (quoted in John McMillan, 2003, 'Market design: the policy uses of theory', *American Economic Review Papers and Proceedings*, vol. 93, p. 139). Likewise, all of the case studies and applications in this book are about important questions, and all of them draw exclusively on concepts that can be taught in an introductory microeconomics subject. So, study hard to develop your skills in economics, because the pay-off can be huge.

In working through the book, you'll find that the case studies are organised into seven sections that cover different topics in microeconomics. Each section begins with an introduction, an overview about the case studies and how they relate to each other. In the individual case studies, there is a range of material to help you learn how to apply economics. The main material is the application of the economic concept. In addition, a 'Theory refresher' provides you with a quick way to revise the key concept or theory that is used in that case study; a set of 'Key lessons' summarises the main points from the case study; 'Some questions to think about' will allow you to test your understanding of the core concept and application; and 'Ideas for further reading' are suggestions for ways to learn more about a topic you may have found particularly interesting.

This book is just one of many that are available today showing how economics can be applied. If, after reading the applications here, you feel you'd like to see more, there are several books I would recommend. Tim Harford's *The Undercover Economist* (2006, Oxford University Press) gives an engaging and insightful introduction to most of the key concepts in microeconomics, and to my mind is the pick of the bunch. Excellent books on markets have been written by John McMillan (*Reinventing the Bazaar*, 2002, W.W. Norton) and John Quiggin (*Economics in Two Lessons: Why Markets Work So Well, and Why They Can Fail So Badly* (2019, Princeton University Press). In his 2007 book *The Economic Naturalist* (Basic Books), Robert Frank shows how microeconomics can be used to answer many puzzling questions about the world. The Nobel Prize winner Jean Tirole describes the many ways that economics can be applied to address the major problems facing societies around the world in his book *Economics for the Common Good* (2017, Princeton University Press). For a sceptical viewpoint on the influence of economics in modern society, Jonathan Aldred's *Licence to be Bad: How Economics Corrupted Us* (2019, Penguin Books) is a good place to start. For Australian perspectives on many important topics in microeconomics (and more), there are Andrew Leigh's *The Economics of Just About Everything* (2014, Allen & Unwin), Ross Gittins' books *Gittins' Guide to Economics* (2006, Allen & Unwin), *Ozonomics* by Andrew Charlton (2007, Random House Australia) and Jason Murphy's book *Incentivology: The Forces that Explain Tremendous Success and Failure* (2019, Hardie Grant Publishing).

Studying economics should be one of the most exciting and valuable experiences you have at university. I hope you find this book contributes to that experience and that it is helpful for learning about economics and for showing why economics is so relevant and important. If you'd like to share any ideas you have about the case studies and applications in the book, or other ideas about economics, please feel welcome to email me (jib@unimelb.edu.au). Good luck with your studies!

# Notes to the lecturer

This book contains 40 case studies and applications of core concepts in microeconomics. It is intended to be used in teaching those core concepts, and to illustrate to students how the concepts can be applied to understand an aspect of economic activity or to guide decision making in business or government. From my experience, showing applications of the concepts can play two roles in teaching economics. First, there are some students for whom seeing the application is the best way for them to understand the concept. Second, there are other students who may have grasped the concept in the abstract but for whom the application is the way of seeing the relevance and importance of the idea. Of course, most textbooks include a number of applications. What distinguishes the applications in this book is their range, the detailed coverage of each application, and the in-depth explanation of how the application can be interpreted using the relevant microeconomic concept or theory.

Each case study presents a different application of a core concept or theory as well as extra material: A 'Theory refresher' section provides a quick way for students to revise a key concept or theory that is important for understanding the application in that case study. The core concept that is applied is listed in the book's table of contents. Also appearing in each case study is a set of 'Key lessons', 'Some questions to think about' and 'Ideas for further reading'.

The book can be used as a teaching resource in your microeconomics subject in a variety of ways:

- Each case study could provide the basis for a section of a lecture presenting a case study or application of the concept being taught in that lecture, with the relevant case study assigned as reading for the lecture.
- Individual case studies could be the main learning resource in tutorials, with students being assigned the text of the case study as prereading, and the section 'Some questions to think about' providing the basis for class discussion.
- Individual case studies and the 'Theory refresher' in each case study could be assigned as a way of revising core concepts taught in lectures.

This book has been written primarily with first-year microeconomics subjects in mind. However, I've deliberately included case studies that vary in the level of understanding of economics they require, with the intention that this will also make the book a valuable resource for teaching second- and third-year subjects. There are almost certainly more case studies and applications in the book than could be covered in a single-semester subject. Indeed, the large number of cases is intended to give you flexibility in choosing topics and in how advanced you want the application of a concept to be. If, for example, you're not teaching a topic such as game theory or international trade, then it's easy to omit the cases on these topics. If you are looking for a straightforward application of a concept such as opportunity cost, you could choose Case study 1.1, whereas if you wanted an application of opportunity cost that requires a little more thought on the part of students, Case study 1.2 could be used. To illustrate how you could put together a package of applications to suit a particular subject, the following table gives a couple of suggested lists of case studies that provide basic and more advanced treatments of core concepts relating to decision making and the theory of perfectly competitive markets.

**Table 0.0.1** Examples of case studies you might choose for particular core concepts

| CONCEPT | BASIC | ADVANCED |
|---|---|---|
| Opportunity cost | 1.1 | 1.2 |
| Marginal benefit/marginal cost | 1.3 | 5.5 |
| Comparative statics | 2.2/2.3 | 2.4 |
| Elasticity | 2.3 | 2.5 |
| Welfare analysis | 2.6 | 2.7 |
| Government regulation and taxation | 2.8 | 2.9/2.10 |

One final note of explanation about the book. I think you'll find that, most of the time, the coverage of core concepts is similar to any introductory microeconomics textbook. The two exceptions are the sections on 'Theory of the firm and managerial economics' and 'Game theory'. The cases on the theory of the firm introduce concepts – such as market power and price discrimination – that are not usually covered (certainly not in detail) in most texts. I've found that by introducing these concepts, I'm able to provide a more comprehensive, engaging and coherent coverage of what economics can contribute to understanding the operation of business and other organisations. The introduction to the section on the theory of the firm describes how I see this material fitting together. The applications of game theory in this book present the theory in a more formal way than most introductory microeconomics textbooks. I've found that students really take to the logic and intuitiveness of game theory and so have no difficulty covering some quite advanced material on this topic.

I hope you find the book a valuable resource. If you have any comments or ideas, please feel welcome to email me (jib@unimelb.edu.au). Happy teaching!

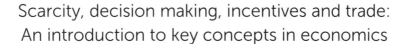

# Scarcity, decision making, incentives and trade: An introduction to key concepts in economics

In the beginning, there was scarcity. If economists had a sacred text, these would undoubtedly be the opening words, because it is scarcity that gives meaning to what economists do.

The central theme of economics is to study the decisions that individuals, organisations and societies make about how to use their available resources. These resources include time and skills, the natural environment, and financial and physical capital such as cash and property. There are many more potential uses for our resources than the available supply; or as an economist would say, resources are scarce. Therefore, we need to make choices about how to allocate our resources between alternative uses. The choices we make can have significant consequences for our wellbeing.

Take the example of your time. Every week you have a fixed number of hours in which you are trying to do a variety of activities – study, work, play sport, see friends and family, watch TV and, of course, sleep. You need to make choices about how to allocate your time between these activities, and this means trade-offs: one more hour working in your part-time job may mean one less hour to spend doing your economics assignment. Because time is scarce, you can't do everything you might like to do. At the same time, how you choose to spend your time is likely to affect your wellbeing. You earn an extra hour's wages from working for longer, but it may also mean a lower mark in that economics subject at the end of the semester. Of course, one extra mark or one hour's wages may not affect you too much. But suppose you choose to work for one more hour each week over the whole year. Now you would be giving up 40 hours, or essentially a whole week, that could have been spent studying. Or think of other decisions about how to use your time, such as whether to study for another degree, or what job you are going to take. These are choices that will have much bigger consequences for your wellbeing.

Saying that we need to choose how to use our available resources raises an important question: How should we make these choices? The core assumption of economics is that decision makers use the benefit–cost principle to make choices. Decision makers compare the benefits and costs of taking an action, and will only choose to take the action if it makes them better off. In a situation where there are multiple actions to choose between, decision makers again compare the benefits and costs of each action, and select the action that makes them best off.

The benefits of an action can be of many kinds. The benefit gained from spending time reading a novel or going to a concert may be the sense of enjoyment or relaxation you obtain. Your regular hour at the gym gives you the benefit of staying fit and healthy, and eating provides nourishment. These examples all suggest different types of benefit for a decision maker, but they have in common the idea of some satisfaction or positive value derived from the activity.

Costs are measured by economists in a particular way, using a concept called opportunity cost. The opportunity cost of an action is the resources used in taking that action valued in their next best alternative use. Case study 1.1 will introduce you to a variety of applications of opportunity cost that illustrate how it is calculated and how it differs from other notions of cost. Case study 1.2 demonstrates how using the concept of opportunity cost can help us to make better decisions about the economic activities in which society should engage. To make this point, we'll consider the example of the value of production by the agricultural sector in the United States. Opportunity cost implies that, in measuring productivity in agriculture, we need to include the environmental damage caused by pesticide use as part of the cost of resources used in agriculture. The case study shows that once this opportunity cost is incorporated, there is a substantial impact on the estimated net value of agricultural production in the United States.

A decision maker can apply the benefit–cost principle by using an approach known as marginal analysis – comparing the marginal addition to benefits and marginal addition to opportunity costs from an action. By only taking an action if the marginal benefit is at least as great as the marginal cost, decision makers can be assured of always choosing actions that will make them as well-off as possible. In Case study 1.3, we apply marginal analysis, the rule of comparing the extra benefits and extra costs associated with taking an action, to show how a student completing high school can decide whether it is optimal to go to university. You'll be happy to know that, for an average student, the benefits of a university degree exceed the costs by a quite considerable amount.

So a decision maker who wants to make the best choice of action will compare the benefits and costs of alternative actions. This means that when the benefits or costs associated with those alternative actions change, the decision maker's optimal choice of action may also change. Higher benefits raise the likelihood that an action will be chosen, while higher costs make it less likely. This is called responding to incentives. The concept of incentives is central to the way that economists seek to understand human behaviour. Using just this one idea – that rational decision makers will want to change their choice of action when there are changes to the benefits and costs of the actions available to them – makes it possible to explain a vast amount of the behaviour and events we see happening around us every day. Case study 1.4 provides an example to illustrate decision makers responding to incentives – and it's an example that may surprise you. Changes to government policies in Australia in the mid-2000s are used to show that even the dates on which births and deaths occur can on occasion be affected by financial incentives.

A common type of decision that individuals and organisations in a modern economy need to make is about being involved in trade. Rational buyers and sellers will only agree to trade when this makes them better off, and hence trade that occurs in an economy must be mutually beneficial. It follows that creating extra opportunities for voluntary trade between buyers and sellers will always improve wellbeing in society. Case study 1.5 illustrates this important idea through the example of facilitating kidney exchanges. In countries such as Australia and the United States, many more people need kidney transplants than there are kidneys currently available. Legal restrictions on trade in human organs mean that this shortage cannot be resolved by those needing kidneys paying for them. Instead, we will see in this case study how introducing the scope for 'trade' in kidneys – essentially between different kidney donors – can expand the number of kidney transplants that can be made and thus go some way to improving this situation.

Much of economics takes it as implicit that decision makers are rational – that they make choices that are consistent with maximising their wellbeing. This is an idea that you may find hard to accept, and you are right to adopt a critical perspective when you see such an important assumption being made. To give you an opportunity to think about this issue in a little more detail, Case study 1.6 asks the question: Are decision makers really rational? By examining two important aspects of rationality – that decision makers should ignore sunk costs and that they can perfectly anticipate the future consequences of actions they take – we find that the answer is mixed. In some (perhaps many) regards, decision makers do appear to act rationally in their decision making. But rationality is not complete, and we are certainly able to find examples of decision making that depart from this principle.

# CASE STUDY 1.1
## WHAT DID THAT REALLY COST YOU?

How much did it cost you to buy your laptop? What about that new car you just purchased, or the flight you have booked? Maybe you are thinking of answering these questions by quoting the price you paid to purchase each item. For an economist, this price is certainly a big part of the cost you will have paid. But it is not the only part. Economists argue that the right way to measure cost is using a concept known as opportunity cost; in this case, the value of all the resources you used in buying these items. Think again about the example of the laptop. Probably you spent several hours researching which model would suit you and where you could get the best price. The principle of opportunity cost says that you should include the value of that time you have spent doing research as part of the cost of buying the laptop.

### THEORY REFRESHER
#### What is opportunity cost?

Economists measure costs using a concept called opportunity cost. The opportunity cost of an action is the resources used in taking that action valued in their next best alternative use. The opportunity cost of an action can be calculated in two steps: first, making a list of all the resources that are used when that action is taken and hence that will not be available in the future for alternative use; and second, estimating the value of each of those resources in their next best alternative use.

As an example, suppose I am running my own business. An important resource used in this activity is my time. The next best use of my time if I was not running my business might be working for another firm, and in this job I think I would earn $100 000 per year. Therefore, the cost of my time spent running the business is $100 000 per year. This amount of forgone earnings becomes part of the opportunity cost of operating my business.

The concept of opportunity cost differs from other notions of cost, such as accounting cost. For example, measures of the accounting cost of operating my business would usually not incorporate the cost of my time spent running the business.

An important aspect of the definition of opportunity cost is to understand that it excludes what are known as 'sunk costs'. Sunk costs are costs incurred prior to the time at which a decision is being made about whether to take some action. Continuing with the example of operating a business, suppose that I have previously bought a piece of specialist machinery for $50 000 that would be worthless if I did not operate my business. This piece of machinery is a sunk cost and should not be included as part of the opportunity cost of operating my business. This is because the cost of the machinery is already paid for, and nothing about this cost changes, depending on whether I continue or cease operating my business today.

It is the problem of scarcity that explains why economists think opportunity cost is the appropriate measure of cost. Scarcity of resources implies that the real cost of an action to society is the resources that are used when that action is taken (and hence are not available for alternative use). Therefore, to properly account for the costs of the action, all resources that are used need to be incorporated into the measure of cost.

In addition to searching for the best product and the best price, even when you know what you want to buy you may need to travel to a store to make the purchase. Of course, businesses are also aware of these costs. And in many markets, trying to reduce your time costs of shopping is an important way in which those businesses are competing to persuade you to buy from them.

A development company building student housing near the University of Wollongong had exactly this idea in mind when it integrated into the development a 'veritable fast-food heaven' including stores such as Red Rooster, KFC and Pizza Hut. As a director of the company explained, 'Students want convenience and they want to live cheaply'. By including fast-food outlets in the apartment building, students' time costs of shopping are reduced, and hence demand by students to live in those apartments is increased. Using the same idea, the developer incorporated 'other add-ons for time-poor students [that] include private internet lines in each bedroom … in-house movies on demand … two 20-metre lap pools and a tennis court' (Chandler 2002).

Even in France, long known for its emphasis on fine dining, the same force is at work. Worker demand for takeaway sandwiches in business districts has leapt in recent years, while local brasseries offering the traditional sit-down lunch have experienced a fall in customers. A major reason for this shift in demand is the lower opportunity costs of time spent buying and eating a sandwich. *The Economist* (2009) made this comment about the shift: 'It leaves them [workers buying lunch] time to do other things, like going shopping during their lunch hour'.

Offering the option to buy on the internet is another way in which businesses are trying to attract you as a customer by reducing your time costs of shopping. Twenty years ago, if you wanted to purchase a plane ticket you would have had to visit a travel agent to investigate the available flight times and to buy the ticket. But today, due to internet sales, the period between deciding you want to take a plane trip and acquiring your ticket may be as short as five minutes. (Businesses also have other reasons for selling on the internet. By eliminating the need for retail outlets, their costs are reduced. Selling on the internet can also expand the market that is accessible to the business.)

There are many products for which it is reasonable to consider the costs of shopping for the product as being negligible. When you want to buy milk, bread or beer, you will know exactly what you want to buy, and for most of us it will only be a short trip to a store to buy that item. But the time costs associated with buying other products may be a substantial component of opportunity cost. At the University of Melbourne, the Commerce Student Society Ball is a popular event. In fact, it's so popular that, as a newspaper article reported, 'students begin to queue the night before in order to snaffle a ticket' (Roginski 2006). Tickets to this event are not cheap, but even so, having to queue for at least 12 hours to get a ticket (not to mention sleeping outside) means that the costs of actually getting to buy a ticket represent a substantial portion of the opportunity cost for many students.

Another time cost associated with buying a product may be the time it takes to consume or use the product. When you make a plane trip, you will spend time flying from the departure point to your destination. There is also the time spent getting to and from airports as well as the time spent checking in and perhaps clearing customs that need to be taken into account. Think about the increased amount of time that must be spent in security screening prior to taking an air flight in many countries as a result of the terrorist attacks that occurred on 11 September 2001. A longer total amount of time taken to make a flight increases the opportunity cost of flying, and hence would be predicted to reduce demand for air travel and increase demand for other types of travel. Consistent with this argument, a jump of over 25 per cent in passengers on Eurostar trains between Britain and continental Europe was observed after tighter security was introduced to airports in the United Kingdom after 9/11 (*The Economist* 2006c).

For some products, it may be quite tough to estimate the value of the time we spend on activities such as shopping and consuming products. In other situations, however, the cost of time can be very explicit. An example is the costs of smoking for Tasmanian Government workers. Concerned about the high numbers of workers leaving their offices to smoke in outside areas, in the early 2000s the government introduced a policy specifying that workers would have to clock in and out for smoking breaks (Allen 2002). Workers thinking about having an extra cigarette therefore need to include in the opportunity cost of smoking the cost of forgone wages for time missing from work.

'Time is money' goes the old saying. Certainly this is correct when we want to calculate opportunity cost. When we spend time shopping for and consuming products, we are using a valuable resource. Hence, we need to include the cost of this time as part of our measure of the opportunity cost of buying any product.

# KEY LESSONS

- Economists measure costs using a concept known as opportunity cost. The opportunity cost of an action is the resources used when that action is taken valued in their next best alternative use.
- The monetary price you pay for a product is an important part of its opportunity cost. But since time is a scarce resource, the costs of time used in shopping for and consuming a product are also part of its opportunity cost. Examples are when we need to take time to compare potential suppliers to find the best price for a product, when we need to spend time queuing to buy a product, or when it takes time to consume or use a product.

# SOME QUESTIONS TO THINK ABOUT

1. Make a list of all the resources that you would use taking a plane trip. How would you value each of these resources in their next best alternative uses?

2. In 2012 the Federal Government in Australia announced that companies with annual turnover of more than $1 billion would shift from paying their taxes on a quarterly basis to a monthly basis (Yeates 2012).

   Consider the following statement: 'The government's new tax payment plan does not change the total amount of tax big companies pay, just the timing. So the opportunity cost of paying tax is not affected by the new policy'. Do you agree with this statement? Explain your answer.

3. Sally Stockbroker has to decide whether to return to university to study for a Master of Business Administration (MBA). The MBA will take three years to complete. Sally knows that the information relevant to calculating opportunity cost is that: (a) MBA fees will cost $20 000 per year; (b) her salary as a stockbroker in every future year of her working life would be $80 000 per year if Sally does not do an MBA; (c) during her time studying, Sally can work as a tutor at the university and earn $10 000 per year; and (d) other costs of studying such as textbooks that Sally would not otherwise incur amount to $5000 per year. At present, Sally has not incurred any of these costs. What is the opportunity cost for Sally of doing an MBA?

4. An article in *The Age* described how Qantas had shelved a project to update its IT system for frequent flyers (O'Sullivan 2013). Qantas had already spent $20 million on the project and its completion was forecast to cost another $40 million.

   What is the opportunity cost to Qantas of completing the IT project? What does this imply about Qantas's beliefs regarding the benefits it would obtain from completing the project?

# REFERENCES

Allen, Lisa (2002), 'Tasmania makes smoking a real drag for workers', *Australian Financial Review*, 6 February, p. 5.

Chandler, Matthew (2002), 'Fast food heaven for busy students', *Australian Financial Review*, 22 January, p. 5.

O'Sullivan, Matt (2013), 'Airline IT victim of cost cuts', *The Age Business Day*, 16 December, p. 23.

Roginski, Alexandra (2006), 'Dipso facto', *The Age*, Education Supplement, 20 February, p. 3.

*The Economist* (2006c), 'Fear of flying', 19 August, p. 22.

*The Economist* (2009), 'Sandwich courses', 7 February, p. 44.

Yeates, Clancy (2012), 'Industry angry over monthly tax plan', *The Age Business Day*, 23 October, p. 1.

# IDEAS FOR FURTHER READING

Introductory textbooks on microeconomics are useful for learning more about opportunity cost. A good place to start is chapter 1 of Joshua Gans, Stephen King, Martin Byford and N. Greg Mankiw's *Principles of Microeconomics* (2018, 7th edn, Cengage Learning).

# CASE STUDY 1.2
## OPPORTUNITY COST AND PRODUCTIVITY IN AGRICULTURE

Greenhouse gas emissions, the depletion of water reserves and the logging of rainforests are examples of environmental damage that can be caused by economic activities such as industry and farming. Dealing effectively with these types of environmental damage is essential for ensuring the continued survival of humankind.

Economists can assist in this task by helping a country to make better choices about the economic activities in which it engages. One way to do this is by developing measures of the costs and benefits of production that incorporate their effects on the environment. This allows decision makers in the country to take explicit account of the environmental consequences of production activities.

---

### THEORY REFRESHER

#### What is productivity?

Economic models of production represent a process whereby a set of inputs are combined to produce output of a good or service. This production process can vary enormously for different industries, or even for different firms producing the same product. Economists measure the *productivity* of a firm or industry, or an economy, as the value of output of goods and services produced divided by the value of inputs used to produce that output. Measuring productivity is a useful tool that allows economists to assess whether the best use is being made of our scarce resources. A higher level of productivity means we are getting more output from our available resources, which is a better outcome from society's point of view.

---

A common approach to judge the value to society of alternative production activities is to compare the levels of productivity between those activities. Productivity in each activity is usually measured by taking into account the inputs used in production including labour that is supplied by workers, physical and financial capital such as the rental costs of machines and factories, and intermediate inputs that will be used to make the final output. There are also, however, other resources that may be used in production that might not immediately come to mind. An example is where the production process causes damage to the environment. Suppose that as a by-product of production there is a resource such as a river or land area that is no longer available for use, or the quality of that resource is lowered. This environmental damage then constitutes a resource cost; that is, some resources are no longer available for use or are of lower quality because of the production activity. This is as much a cost to society as the cost of workers' time or using the owners' capital to operate the business.

Step back for a minute from what we have just said. If you think about it, you will see that in arguing for an 'environmentally sensitive' measure of productivity, we are really saying that we need a measure of productivity that is based on the concept of opportunity cost. A measure of productivity that incorporates a complete list of the resources used in production, such as changes to the natural environment, is a measure that incorporates the opportunity cost of production.

How much difference does it make to measures of productivity if we incorporate the costs of environmental damage caused by a production activity? A study of productivity in the agricultural sector in the United States between 1960 and 1996 was able to answer this question. A conventional measure of productivity was estimated that divided the value of output by the cost of inputs, including as inputs only capital, labour and flows of services from intermediate goods. This was compared with an alternative, environmentally sensitive measure of productivity. That measure included the cost to human health and aquatic life stemming from run-off and the leaching of pesticides used in agriculture, in addition to the same inputs as the conventional measure.

*Figure 1.2.1* shows the evolution of both measures of productivity in US agriculture between 1960 and 1996. Both measures have been converted from their actual values

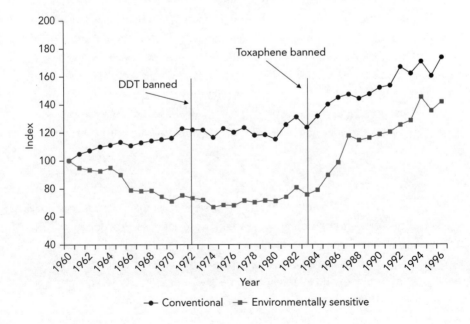

**Figure 1.2.1** Indices of productivity, US crops and livestock, 1960 to 1996

*Source:* compiled from Ball et al. (2004), Table 2.

to equal 100 in 1960 so that it is easy to assess whether productivity rose or fell, and to compare the alternative measures. A movement in a series from, for example, 100 to 105 would mean that productivity had increased by 5 per cent. Generally, societies want to increase the productivity of their economic activities over time. It is this growth in productivity – getting more output from a given amount of resources – that allows improvements in our material wellbeing.

Taking account of the environmental costs of the use of pesticides has a significant effect on conclusions about the value of agricultural activity in the United States. Whereas the conventional measure shows average productivity growth of 1.5 per cent per annum between 1960 and 1996, the environmentally sensitive measure shows average growth of only about 1 per cent per annum. Hence, the environmental costs of pesticide use reduced the increase in productivity in agriculture in the United States that would otherwise have occurred by about one-third, a quite substantial magnitude.

It is also interesting to look at specific time periods in the study. Between 1960 and 1972, the conventional measure of productivity increased, but the environmentally sensitive measure fell by over 25 per cent. This implies that during this period, the amount of damage caused to the environment by pesticide use in agriculture was increasing very rapidly. In 1972, the US Government banned the pesticide DDT (dichlorodiphenyltrichloroethane). Afterwards, for the period to 1983, it can be seen that the conventional and environmentally sensitive productivity measures follow similar paths. This suggests that banning DDT stabilised the amount of environmental damage from pesticide use. Then, in 1983, the insecticide toxaphene was banned. From this time onwards, the environmentally sensitive measure of productivity increases more rapidly than the conventional measure, showing that environmental damage associated with pesticide use was falling. Hence, the actions of the US Government in banning DDT and toxaphene appear to have significantly improved productivity in agriculture measured in terms of the true resource costs of that activity. Notwithstanding this improvement, the gap that still existed between the alternative productivity measures in 1996 implies that the environmental cost from pesticide use remained higher in 1996 than it had been in 1960.

Analysis of productivity in US agriculture has revealed how incorporating the opportunity cost of production into the measurement of productivity can provide a powerful demonstration of the costs of environmental damage. Equally important, having such measures provides a rigorous basis for society to identify production activities that it can engage in to maximise the wellbeing of both current and future generations. Economists have a vital role to play in developing and applying these types of measures, and also in explaining and advocating why costs should always mean opportunity costs.

# KEY LESSONS

- Productivity, the amount of output produced from available inputs, is a measure of the efficiency of resource use in an economy. An economist would argue that the appropriate way to measure productivity is to include as inputs all resources that are unavailable for alternative uses after production; that is, to incorporate the opportunity cost of production as the measure of inputs used.
- Using a measure of productivity that incorporates the opportunity cost of production, such as environmental damage, can offer a very different perspective compared with conventional measures. This is evident from calculating a measure of productivity in US agriculture that takes account of the resource cost of pesticide use.

# SOME QUESTIONS TO THINK ABOUT

1   Can you think of other examples of economic activities that cause environmental damage, where the value of that damage would need to be incorporated into the value of inputs used in production in order to construct a 'true' measure of the productivity of that activity?

2   Simon and Erica give up their jobs in the Economics Department to set up their own consulting firm. To set up the business, they must buy an office for $50 000. Should they choose to cease operating their business at some future date, they know they will be able to sell the office for $40 000. If they had not bought the office, they would have invested the money they spent on the office and earned an annual rate of interest of 10 per cent. They also need to hire a research assistant at a salary of $50 000 per annum. In their first year of business, Simon and Erica expect to earn revenue of $200 000. What is the total opportunity cost to Simon and Erica of setting up their consulting firm for one year?

3   Since 2015, the Victorian government has spent over $2.5 billion removing over 30 train level crossings in Melbourne and replacing them with flyovers or tunnels. Their justification for this policy is the significant delays caused for motorists at the train crossings during peak time. For example, it was estimated in 2015 that the crossing at Koornang Road in Carnegie was closed for up to 87 minutes between 7 am and 9 am (Gordon, 2015). How would you calculate the opportunity cost of time spent by motorists at the level crossings? How would you evaluate whether the Victorian Government is spending its funds wisely by committing to eliminate the level crossings?

# REFERENCES

Ball, Eldon, Lovell, Knox, Luu, Hung & Nehring, Richard (2004), 'Incorporating environmental impacts in the measurement of agricultural productivity growth', *Journal of Agricultural and Resource Economics*, vol. 29, pp. 436–60.

Gordon, Josh (2015), 'Down time for boom gates a big economic cost', *The Age*, 7 May, p. 6.

# IDEAS FOR FURTHER READING

A good introduction to the concept of productivity is provided by Robin Stonecash, Jan Libich, Joshua Gans, Stephen King, Martin Byford and N. Gregory Mankiw's *Principles of Macroeconomics* (2018, 7th edn, Cengage, pp. 171–80).

# CASE STUDY 1.3
## THE BENEFITS AND COSTS OF A UNIVERSITY DEGREE

Is it a good idea to be at university? Perhaps you have asked this question as you dragged yourself out of bed for a 9 a.m. lecture, or as you begin to battle through your first set of assignments and tests. While not denying that it can be painful to have to wake up too early, there is an even more fundamental way in which you might have thought about this question. You are going to spend several years of your life and probably a large amount of money acquiring a university degree (or perhaps degrees). Over that same time, you could have a full-time job, or use the funds you are spending to go to university in many other valuable ways. So how can you be sure that you are doing the right thing?

The decision about whether to attend university is really just another decision like those we make every day throughout our lives. There are benefits and costs to compare in order to make the best choice. Where the comparison reveals that the benefits of attending university exceed the costs, then the optimal decision is to go to university. But where costs are greater than the benefits, not attending will be optimal.

### THEORY REFRESHER

#### Making an optimal decision

Every individual and every organisation in society has objectives that they would like to achieve. Therefore, they need to be sure they are making decisions about how to use the resources available to them in a way that is optimal, that best contributes to achieving those objectives. This can be done by making choices using the benefit–cost principle; that is, based on a comparison of the benefits and costs of different uses of the resources.

The optimal choice of action for a decision maker will maximise their net gain: the benefits they receive minus opportunity cost. This optimal choice can be determined using what is known as marginal analysis. Marginal analysis involves comparing the addition to benefits and the addition to opportunity costs of an action. These are often referred to respectively as the 'marginal benefit' and the 'marginal cost' of that action. The 'golden' rule for optimal decision making is that a decision maker should only take an action if the addition to benefits (marginal benefit) from that action is at least as great as the addition to costs (marginal cost).

Any decision can be made using this approach. One example is a 'yes/no' type of decision such as whether a mining firm should develop a new mine, whether a government should build a new bridge, or whether you should go to university. In these cases, marginal benefit is simply the benefit of doing the activity, and marginal cost is the opportunity cost of doing the activity. A comparison of marginal benefit and marginal cost reveals whether it is optimal to take the action. A different example is decisions about the optimal level of an activity, such as the number of workers a firm should hire, or the amount of money you should invest in the shares of a particular company. For these decisions there is effectively a choice between many possible actions or levels of an activity. Marginal benefit and marginal cost now need to be calculated for each possible action; for example, the marginal benefit and marginal cost of hiring a first worker, a second worker, a third worker and so on. The optimal decision will be to choose to do an extra unit of an activity (such as hiring an extra worker) when the marginal benefit from the extra unit is at least as great as marginal cost, but to choose not to do an extra unit of an activity when marginal cost is greater than marginal benefit.

A range of benefits and costs are associated with the decision to undertake a university degree. A primary source of these benefits and costs relates to labour market activity. During the period of study, you are likely to have to forgo earnings from being in the workforce. You may be able to work part-time, but not full-time as you would if you were not studying. This can be thought of as an opportunity cost of your time spent at university. Other monetary costs and benefits of attending university are more direct – the fees paid to undertake the degree and the monetary costs of student amenities fees, textbooks, transport and possibly housing, all of which may be offset to some degree by receiving a government student allowance. Following the period of study your extra qualification should mean that you will have higher earnings than otherwise, and it may also mean there is a higher likelihood of remaining employed throughout your life. In addition, there may also be non-monetary benefits of attending university, such as the enjoyment you get from studying and learning more about subject areas that interest you, or from making new friends. The benefits and costs of attending university are summarised in *Table 1.3.1*.

Having identified the main benefits and costs of attending university, it's now possible to apply the benefit–cost principle to work out whether attending university is optimal. Marginal benefit can be estimated as the total monetary benefits stemming from attending university, and marginal cost as the total monetary costs. There are quite a few studies that have done this exercise for Australia, and all reach fairly similar conclusions.

**Table 1.3.1** Benefits and costs of acquiring a university degree for a high school graduate

| BENEFITS | COSTS |
| --- | --- |
| Increase in after-tax earnings from labour market activity | Forgone earnings from labour market activity during period of education |
| Higher probability of employment | Fees |
| Non-monetary benefits – intrinsic value of gain in knowledge, social activities and networks | Direct costs minus government student benefits |

One study (Daly et al. 2015) examined the costs and benefits of undertaking a bachelor's degree for a student who was aged 18 years at the commencement of study. The length of degree (time spent studying) was assumed to be between three and five years, depending on the field of study. The forgone earnings during the period of university study were estimated as the average earnings of a high school graduate who did not attend university. The earnings gain after acquiring a university degree was estimated as the average earnings of university graduates at each age from 21 to 64 years minus average earnings for high school graduates over the same time period. It was assumed in the study that the university student was in a Commonwealth-supported (or government-funded) place, and that the required Higher Education Contribution Scheme (HECS) payments were made up-front.

The study's main finding was that, on average, students who are attending university have made the correct decision. Acquiring a bachelor's degree was found to add an average net amount to a graduate's lifetime earnings of about $200 000 for females and $365 000 for males (valued in 2019 dollars). This amounts to a gain of between $4650 and $8500 per annum for every year until retirement. Thinking in investment terms, the net gain can be interpreted as a rate of return on the initial investment of 12 per cent per annum for females and 15 per cent for males for every year spent working. It makes a university degree a very profitable investment indeed.

There are other aspects of the gains from acquiring a university degree worth noting. First, the gains from a university degree appear to vary quite widely by field of study and level of qualification. Estimated returns are relatively high for business and administration (good news if you are reading this case study while doing a business or commerce degree) and engineering, but lower for graduates in the fields of society and culture, and science. Second, HECS does appear to make quite a difference to the size of the gains from attending university. One study (Borland 2002), for example, found that removing HECS payments would increase the rate of return to an average student by about 30 per cent, and switching from up-front to deferred HECS payments increases the return to a university degree by about 15 per cent. Third, delaying the completion of a degree can have a large negative effect on the gains from attending university. So the lesson is to study hard and pass all your subjects!

Thinking about whether to attend university is just one example of the many types of decisions that can (and an economist would argue should) be analysed using the benefit–cost principle. Whether to take a part-time job, what model of computer to buy, when to buy your first car – in every situation, the thing to remember is that making an optimal decision comes down to knowing your objectives and then doing your best to make a comparison of marginal benefit and marginal cost.

## KEY LESSONS

- The 'golden' rule for optimal decision making is that a decision maker should only take an action if the addition to benefits (marginal benefit) from that action is at least as great as the addition to opportunity costs (marginal cost).
- An example of a decision to which this approach can be applied is whether a high school graduate should attend university to acquire a bachelor's degree.
- Analysis of the monetary costs and benefits of acquiring a bachelor's degree in Australia suggests that, on average, students are making the correct choice – benefits significantly outweigh costs. For example, there was an estimated gain of between $4650 and $8500 per annum in lifetime earnings for students commencing a bachelor's degree in 2015.

## SOME QUESTIONS TO THINK ABOUT

1   You own an ice-cream stall at Sandy Beach. You can sell each ice-cream for $2. With extra opening hours for your stall, you believe that you can increase your sales as shown in the table below. For each hour the stall is open, the opportunity cost of your time is $15. For how many hours should you open your stall?

| HOURS OF OPENING | TOTAL SALES OF ICE-CREAMS |
| --- | --- |
| 0 | 0 |
| 1 | 20 |
| 2 | 35 |
| 3 | 45 |
| 4 | 50 |
| 5 | 50 |

2   Suppose you own a small funds-management company. You are trying to decide whether to hire an extra employee. How should you make this decision? What factors should you take into account?

3   An article in *The Economist* (2017) described how theft has declined in most rich countries since the 1990s. Explanations suggested included the ageing population and better policing. The article also noted that criminals appear to respond to the changing value of goods – with a 10 per cent increase in the price of a good being associated on average with a 3.5 per cent rise in the likelihood of it being stolen.

   Use the economic theory of decision making to explain:

   a   Why an ageing population and better policing might be associated with a decrease in theft.

   b   Why the likelihood of an item being stolen would be related to its price.

# REFERENCES

Borland, Jeff (2002), New Estimates of the Private Rate of Return to University Education in Australia, Melbourne Institute of Applied Economic and Social Research, working paper no. 14/02, http://melbourneinstitute.com/downloads/working_paper_series/wp2002n14.pdf, viewed 4 June 2012.

Daly, Anne, Lewis, Phil, Corliss, Michael & Heaslip, Tiffany (2015), 'The private rate of return to a university degree in Australia', *Australian Journal of Education*, 59(1), pp. 97–112.

*The Economist* (2017), 'Lucrative loot', 16 December, p. 49.

# IDEAS FOR FURTHER READING

In addition to the studies by Anne Daly and co-authors, and by Jeff Borland, a recent major review of the benefits and costs of university education in Australia has been undertaken by Andrew Norton and Ittima Cherastidtham (2018, *Mapping Australian Higher Education*, https://grattan.edu.au/wp-content/uploads/2018/09/907-Mapping-Australian-higher-education-2018.pdf, viewed 20 May 2019). For studies that look specifically at the return for economics degrees, see Anne Daly and Phil Lewis (2010), 'The private rate of return to an economics degree: an update', *Economic Papers*, vol. 29, pp. 353–64; and James Bishop and Rochelle Guttmann (2018), 'Does it pay to study economics?', *RBA Bulletin*, September https://www.rba.gov.au/publications/bulletin/2018/sep/pdf/does-it-pay-to-study-economics.pdf, viewed 20 May 2019.

# CASE STUDY 1.4
## DO INCENTIVES REALLY MATTER: CAN ECONOMIC POLICY CHANGE THE TIMING OF BIRTHS AND DEATHS?

Maybe you are convinced, along with University of Chicago economist Steven Levitt, that 'incentives are the cornerstone of modern life' (Levitt & Dubner 2005, p. 13). You are willing to agree that many of the choices we make are influenced by comparing benefits and costs. Whether to go to university, how much time to spend studying versus at work in your part-time job, or whether to live at home or rent a house with friends are decisions that most of us make by thinking about the benefits and costs.

Surely, though, there must be limits to the influence of incentives. There must be some events that don't depend on a decision maker calculating benefits and costs. Like the timing of when we are born and die, for instance. No one could possibly think that these dates depend on incentives. Well, think again. Research by two Australian economists, Joshua Gans and Andrew Leigh, has examined whether the timing of births and deaths in Australia was affected by key government policy changes that altered the monetary benefits and costs associated with birth and death. Their remarkable finding is that the timing of births and deaths does appear to have responded to financial incentives!

---

### THEORY REFRESHER

#### What are incentives?

A rational decision maker will choose whether to take an action, or the optimal level of an action, by taking into account the benefits and costs of the action. Specifically, the rule for optimal decision making is to do an activity or an extra unit of an activity where the marginal benefit is at least as great as the marginal cost, but to not do an activity where the marginal benefit is less than the marginal cost. Changes to the benefit or cost of doing an activity that affect the marginal benefit or marginal cost therefore may change the choice of action made by a decision maker. This is what is known as responding to incentives.

In one study, Gans and Leigh (2006a) examined how the abolition of death duties in Australia on 1 July 1979 affected the timing of deaths. Previously, death duties had been imposed on about 10 per cent of the highest-value estates, and from these estates the government took on average 8 per cent of the value of the estate as a tax payment before the remainder was disbursed to beneficiaries. Abolishing death duties in theory created an incentive for people with high-value estates (or their beneficiaries) to 'shift' the timing of their deaths to after the date of abolition of death duties on 1 July 1979. But of course we know that it's not possible to change the timing of deaths, don't we? Well, you might have thought so. Gans and Leigh's research, however, found otherwise. By comparing the incidence of deaths before and after 1 July 1979 with the same time interval over the preceding 29 years, they were able to conclude that about 50 deaths in 1979 appeared to have been 'shifted' from the week before (mainly the three days before) the policy change to the week after. While this may seem a small amount, it accounts for about 5 per cent of all deaths in the time interval studied. When it is recalled that, on average, only 10 per cent of the population were eligible to pay death duties, the implication is that up to one-half of the estates on which death duties should have been paid were able to avoid the tax by shifting the date of death to after the abolition of death duties. How could this 'shifting' have occurred? Gans and Leigh do not have any direct evidence to answer this question. They speculate that it may reflect deliberate misreporting of the date of death, or that families or medical practitioners had the scope to vary the time of death within small time intervals.

In another study, Gans and Leigh (2006b) examined whether the timing of births in Australia was affected by the introduction of the 'baby bonus' on 1 July 2004. Under this policy, the Australian Government commenced making a payment of $3000 to the family of any child born after 1 July 2004. The policy therefore created an incentive to 'shift' a birth that might otherwise have occurred before 1 July 2004 to after that date in order to receive the bonus.

Similar to their study of the timing of deaths, Gans and Leigh examined births in the time period one month before and one month after the introduction of the baby bonus and compared this with the timing of births in the same period over the preceding 29 years. They found that in 2004, over 1000 births appear to have been 'shifted' from the month before 1 July to after that date, mainly to dates in the week after the policy change. This represents over 10 per cent of all births in these months. *Figure 1.4.1* graphs the daily births for June and July 2004, where the decrease and increase in births prior to and after 1 July are clearly evident.

Gans and Leigh had a few ideas as to how the response in the timing of births to the change in incentives could have come about. Some important information is that the baby bonus policy was only announced a few months prior to its introduction; therefore, any incentive effect could not operate through a deliberate change to the timing of conception. Instead, Gans and Leigh showed that about half of the births that were shifted were delivered by Caesarean section, and about one-third were induced. Hence, potentially five-sixths of the shift in timing of births could be explained by changes in the dates on which obstetricians performed Caesareans or commenced

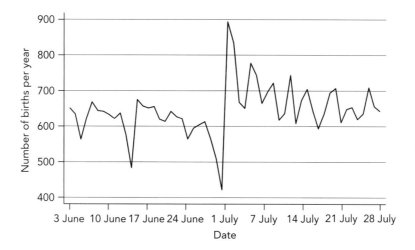

**Figure 1.4.1** Timing of births by day in Australia – June to July 2004

*Note:* Chart shows daily births for June and July 2004, controlling for day-of-week effects.

*Source:* Gans & Leigh (2007), Figure 5.

inducing births compared with the timing in previous years. So where birth date was to some degree discretionary, mothers and families appear to have chosen to delay the timing in order to receive the new baby bonus.

Later studies have confirmed Gans and Leigh's finding on how the baby bonus affected the timing of births – and have also gone on to examine the consequences of parents receiving the cash bonus. The main objective of the baby bonus was to increase fertility and it does seem to have had that effect. Research by Sarah Sinclair and co-authors (2012) found that the policy may have caused more than 100 000 extra births in the five years following its introduction. In addition, extra income from the Baby Bonus appears to have benefitted children whose parents received the bonus – by decreasing their likelihood of being hospitalised, probably as a result of families being able to spend more on heating and private health insurance (Lynch et al., 2019). But the effects of the bonus do not seem to extend much beyond children's early years – John Gaitz and Stefanie Schurer (2017), for example, find that the baby bonus had no appreciable impact on children's learning outcomes once they commenced school.

The research of Joshua Gans and Andrew Leigh confirms the power of incentives to influence our behaviour. It also provides a lesson for governments about designing policies that are intended to affect behaviour in a particular way. Such policies will often have consequences that are unexpected. A highly valuable contribution that economists can make, therefore, is to always be thinking of and offering advice about the multiple ways in which incentives can work.

## KEY LESSONS

- In the economic theory of decision making, individuals make decisions based on the relative benefits and costs of alternative actions. When the benefits or costs of different actions alter, rational decision makers will change the actions they choose. This is what we call responding to incentives.
- Research in Australia has shown that even the timing of births and deaths can respond to incentives – more specifically, to changes in government policy. For example, it appears that decision makers such as obstetricians have the capacity to change the timing of births within small intervals of time, and that this capacity has been used in response to changes in financial incentives that relate to the timing of births.
- Understanding and advising on the diverse ways in which new policies can affect incentives is an important role for economists.

## SOME QUESTIONS TO THINK ABOUT

1   It has been reported that in some cities in Brazil there are large populations of rats that pose a significant public health problem. A proposed solution is to pay a bounty per kilogram of dead rats brought in to city authorities by members of the population of those cities. Would providing monetary incentives assist the government to solve the problem of excessive numbers of rats?

2   There have been growing reports of 'cheating' during National Assessment Program – Literacy and Numeracy (NAPLAN) testing in Australia. The 2018 Report on NAPLAN Test Incidents revealed 68 test incidents including one of cheating where teachers changed students' answers and 20 substantiated security breaches that included instances of opening test materials earlier than allowed and test materials not being kept secure during the test security period (Australian Curriculum Assessment and Reporting Authority, 2019).

    a   Could you regard schools seeking to manipulate their students' test results as an effect on incentives that was unintended when the Australian Government introduced NAPLAN?

    b   How do you think this type of behaviour is likely to be affected as students' performances on NAPLAN tests become a more important way to assess school quality?

3   Do you think that monetary incentives are always successful in motivating behaviour? What might be some limitations or disadvantages of providing monetary incentives?

# REFERENCES

Australian Curriculum Assessment and Reporting Authority (2019), *Report of 2018 NAPLAN Test Incidents*, https://nap.edu.au/docs/default-source/resources/2018-naplan-test-incidents-report.pdf?sfvrsn=2, viewed on 25 May 2019.

Gaitz, John & Schurer, Stefanie (2016), 'Bonus skills: Examining the effect of an unconditional cash transfer on child human capital formation', *IZA Working Paper* no. 10525. Accessed at: http://ftp.iza.org/dp10525.pdf. Viewed on 26 September 2019.

Gans, Joshua & Leigh, Andrew (2006a), 'Did the death of Australian inheritance taxes affect deaths?', *Topics in Economic Policy and Analysis*, vol. 6, article 23.

Gans, Joshua & Leigh, Andrew (2006b), 'Born on the first of July: an un(natural) experiment in birth timing', *Journal of Public Economics*, vol. 93, pp. 246–63.

Gans, Joshua & Leigh, Andrew (2007), 'Unusual days in births and deaths', *Melbourne Review*, vol. 3, pp. 72–9.

Levitt, Steven & Dubner, Stephen (2005), *Freakonomics*, William Morrow.

Lynch, John, Meunier, Aurelie, Pilkington, Rhiannon & Schurer, Stefanie (2019), 'Baby bonuses and early-life health outcomes: Using regression discontinuity to evaluate the causal impact of an unconditional cash transfer', *IZA Working Paper* no. 12230. Accessed at: http://ftp.iza.org/dp12230.pdf. Viewed on 26 September 2019.

Sinclair, Sarah, Boymal, Jonathan & De Silva, Ashton (2012), 'A re-appraisal of the fertility response to the Australian baby bonus', *Economic Record*, 88(S1), pp. 78–87.

# IDEAS FOR FURTHER READING

*Freakonomics*, by Steven Levitt and Stephen Dubner (2005, William Morrow), *The Logic of Life*, by Tim Harford (2008, Little, Brown and Co.), and *Incentivology*, by Jason Murphy (2019, Hardie Grant), include many great examples of how incentives affect behaviour. An excellent overview of Joshua Gans and Andrew Leigh's research is presented in their 2007 article 'Unusual days in births and deaths' (*Melbourne Review*, vol. 3, pp. 72–9).

Economists spend much of their time arguing that mutually beneficial trade – trade that makes both the buyer and seller better off – will improve wellbeing in society. From this perspective, any restrictions that prevent mutually beneficial trades from occurring will lower wellbeing in society; whereas removing those restrictions on trade should make society better off. Removing restrictions might involve creating a market where none previously existed, or expanding the scope of an existing market for buyers and sellers.

### THEORY REFRESHER

#### Trade and wellbeing

Should an individual or organisation engage in trade? To an economist, this is a decision like any other. Decision makers should only be willing to be involved in trade where this makes them better off. Suppose there is one individual who values an item at $10 and another individual who can supply that item at an opportunity cost of $5. At any price between $5 and $10, both individuals would end up better off by trading, and we would expect them to agree to do this. However, if the price was set below $5, the individual who can supply the item will not be made better off by trading and we would expect them to decide not to trade. The same applies to the potential buyer when the price is set above $10. So where trade is voluntary, it will only occur when both parties agree to trade, and this will only happen when both parties are made better off.

## A new market: Kidney exchange

Kidney exchanges provide a striking example of how trade can improve social wellbeing. In this case study, you'll discover how a scheme to allow trade in kidneys has meant that many more people around the world who need kidney transplants to stay alive are able to receive them.

Major kidney disease can generally only be treated via dialysis (cleaning blood mechanically) or by receiving a transplant to replace the diseased kidney. At present, there are two main sources of supply of kidney transplants. One source is cadavers (the bodies of deceased persons), which account for about two-thirds of total transplants.

The other source is live donations, which are usually received from relatives. Live donations of kidneys are possible since most people have two kidneys but can remain healthy with one kidney. Unfortunately, for many years the number of kidneys available for transplant in most developed countries has been much lower than the number required for people with serious kidney disease.

In Australia at the beginning of 2017, there were 12 700 people having treatment for severe kidney disease, but only about 1100 transplants are performed each year (Kidney Health Australia 2017). The problem is even more severe in the United States. In January 2017, 90 000 people needed a kidney transplant in order to deal with a serious kidney disease. However, only 20 500 Americans actually received transplants in that year (Organ Procurement and Transplantation Network 2017). The consequences of this imbalance in the number of people requiring and receiving transplants are long waiting times to obtain a transplant and the deaths of many people on the waiting list for a transplant – it was reported that in 2012 in the United States about 6800 people either died while still on the waiting list for a transplant or were removed from the waiting list because they were too ill to receive a transplant (Sonmez 2013).

When there is excess demand in a market, an economist would usually expect price to increase as a way of inducing an increase in the quantity supplied. But in the case of kidney transplants, this is not possible in most countries. Restrictions on trade in human organs prevent price inducing extra supply. For example, under the US *National Organ Transplant Act* (1984) and under State/Territory legislation in Australia such as Victoria's *Human Tissue Act 1982*, it is a criminal offence to allow organs – even cadaveric organs – to be bought and sold. Trade that could be mutually beneficial, such as where a patient on the transplant waiting list has a willingness to pay an amount for a kidney that is greater than the opportunity cost for a person who could donate a kidney, is therefore prevented. That said, there are a range of ethical reasons why trade in organs is prohibited, and for that reason we can't necessarily conclude that society is worse off because of the restrictions.

So we are not going to get an increase in the quantity of kidneys available for transplant through an increase in price. But what if we could think of a way of allowing more opportunities for kidney exchange without needing to introduce trade involving payment? This could increase the wellbeing of transplant recipients and donors without any adverse ethical implications.

An answer to this question initially came in the mid-1980s from medical practitioners in the United States who noticed that, in some cases, a person who was willing to donate a kidney to a family member could not do so because of an incompatibility; for example, a difference in blood type. The practitioners recognised that if it was possible to find two such pairs of transplant recipients and donors, then mutually beneficial trade might be possible. Each donor could not donate to their own family member, but if they could provide a compatible donation to the other transplant recipient, both pairs would be made better off (see Rapaport 1986). *Figure 1.5.1* illustrates how such a two-way exchange would work.

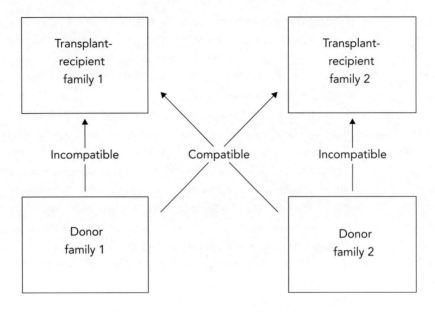

**Figure 1.5.1** Two-way exchange of organs for donation

Unfortunately, although it was understood that the benefits of organising two-way kidney exchanges were potentially large, not much happened for a long time after this idea was initially proposed. By the end of 2004, only about 100 exchange transplants had taken place (Organ Procurement and Transplantation Network 2017). To an economist used to the idea that individuals will respond to incentives – in this case the benefits of two-way kidney exchanges – this may have seemed surprising and troubling. What problem was preventing kidney exchanges? And how could it be fixed?

Enter Alvin Roth, at the time a professor of economics at Harvard University, and a team of co-researchers. They argued that the major problem was a lack of information. As Roth explains:

> When a kidney patient brought a potential donor to his or her doctor to be tested for compatibility, donors who were found to be incompatible with their patient were mostly just sent home … often no medical records were retained to indicate they might be available.

Source: Roth (2007), p. 12.

Roth and his colleagues suggested that what was needed to fix this problem was a central database of incompatible donor–patient pairs that could be used to organise kidney exchanges. They developed the software for a database to identify potential exchanges and it has now been adopted in several locations, including New England

and Ohio. The database stores details of persons requiring a transplant and the characteristics of a person who is willing to donate a kidney on their behalf, allowing the identification of potential two-way exchanges. When two pairs of donors and transplant recipients agree to an exchange, each donor travels to the hospital where the transplant recipient is located, and operations to swap begin simultaneously to prevent either donor backing out after their own family member has received a transplant. The database has significantly expanded the number of kidney exchanges taking place. By the late 2010s there were almost 700 exchanges annually accounting for one-tenth of transplants from living donors (Organ Procurement and Transplantation Network 2017).

Alvin Roth went on from these beginnings to do research that proposed new ways of organising kidney exchanges to facilitate the greatest possible increase in the number of kidney transplants. Exchanges that are three-way, or that end with a donation to a patient on a waiting list in return for priority on the waiting list for that donor's family member, are now being undertaken. Roth is hopeful that ultimately 'there would be about 2000 to 3000 [exchanges] that you might be able to do on an annual basis' (Wessel 2004). Internationally, the idea of kidney exchanges is also spreading. The Australian Paired Kidney Exchange Program was established in January 2009 and started enrolling participants in August 2010. By 2017 over 400 people needing a transplant had received a kidney through this program (ANZDTR 2018, chapter 8).

# Expanding an existing market: Using mobile phones and the internet

Suppose you want to buy some new item – perhaps a computer or a pair of jeans. It makes sense to think that the more suppliers you can choose to buy from, the more likely you are to find a supplier who will sell to you at a price you are willing to pay. Similarly, if you are a supplier, you would expect that the more buyers who are making offers for what you produce, the better are your chances of finding a buyer to whom you are happy to sell. What all this tells us is that the larger the scope of the market in which buyers and sellers can participate, the greater their gains from trade are likely to be.

So being in a big market can be good. But you may be thinking: How can a buyer or seller get to be in a big market? Well, in many developing countries the answer is to buy a mobile phone or to get internet access. There is now an abundance of evidence that mobile phones and internet access are making buyers and sellers better off by allowing them to engage in trade in much broader geographic markets.

In one study, a(nother) Harvard economist, Richard Jensen, examined how the introduction of mobile phones to the coast of the state of Kerala in southern India in the late 1990s affected outcomes in the market for fish in that region. Fishing is a vital part of economic activity in Kerala. Over one million people are employed in the industry and over 70 per cent of the local population eats fish. Before the introduction of mobile phones, fishermen were restricted by transport costs and the perishability of fish to visiting only one market per day, meaning they were unable to discover prices at other markets along the coast. Hence, most of the fishermen sold their catch to their local market. Jensen (2007, p. 892) documents how this caused price variation between the individual markets along the coast, and substantial wastage as fishermen at some oversupplied markets were unable to sell their catches.

All this changed with the introduction of mobile phones. Using the phones while they were still at sea, fishermen were able to communicate with multiple local markets to compare demand and prices, and buyers onshore were able to communicate with a broader set of fishermen. Knowing that there was little demand for his catch at the market at his local village, which would result in a low price if he sold his fish there, a fisherman could determine which other villages had buyers who would purchase his catch at higher prices. Similarly, buyers now had the capacity to generate greater competition between fishermen. Whereas previously a local market might only have had one fisherman selling a particular species of fish, now buyers could contact and seek to trade with fishermen from other locations who had that species among their catch.

By expanding the scope of the market, mobile phones increased the possibilities for mutually advantageous trade between fishermen and buyers in Kerala's coastal markets. The variability in prices between markets fell as supply was able to respond to differences in demand between locations. As well, the greater competition between fishermen caused the average price to fall by about 4 per cent, making consumers better off. You might think that this fall in prices would have made the fishermen worse off. But the opposite happened. By being able to sell their catches at markets where the demand was highest, thereby reducing wastage, fishermen were able to earn average profits that were 8 per cent higher than before the introduction of mobile phones.

Such are the perceived benefits of new technologies like mobile phones and the internet that some market participants have sought to promote their use. One example is ITC Limited, an Indian food-processing company that is a large buyer of soybeans from the state of Madhya Pradesh. The company had initially primarily sourced its soybeans from traders who bought from farmers in local markets and then onsold to ITC. But ITC became concerned that the traders were using their market power to force up the price they charged for the soybeans, as well as to pay relatively low prices to the farmers. ITC's response was to introduce 1700 internet kiosks throughout Madhya Pradesh. As well as displaying prices for soybeans in other villages in the state, the kiosks also posted the price at which ITC was prepared to buy soybeans directly from farmers. An analysis by World Bank economist Aparajita Goyal (2010) found that introduction of the internet kiosks had the effect intended by ITC. Competition between traders was increased, and as a result ITC paid less for its soybeans and farmers received higher payments. In fact, in the areas that had an internet kiosk, it was found that farmers' profits increased by 33 per cent.

There is also evidence that these examples of how technology is increasing the gains achieved from trade represent a more general phenomenon. In a 2008 study of the determinants of economic growth across 120 countries, World Bank economist Christine Zhen-Wei Qiang found that in developing countries a 10 per cent increase in the rate of mobile phone adoption was associated with extra growth in GDP per capita of 0.8 per cent, and that a 10 per cent increase in broadband internet use was associated with extra growth of 1.1 per cent (Qiang 2009). Based on these and other research findings, the World Economic Forum is now promoting mobile phones as a major mechanism for economic development (Granryd, 2018).

## Economic design

The work that Alvin Roth has done on kidney exchange, and the ideas about using new communications technologies to improve the functioning of markets that are being explored by development economists, are part of an exciting new area of economics known as economic design. This area is all about how we can best design the institutions and rules that are used to govern trade in an economy. Other examples of how economists are trying to help design better institutions include creating new types of auctions for selling government assets such as the spectrum for mobile phone services, suggesting how markets for carbon emission permits should be organised and proposing innovative market-based mechanisms for promoting conservation activity. Economic design is economics at its best, showing not only how to understand but also how to improve the way in which our society works.

## KEY LESSONS

- Mutually beneficial trade – trade that makes both a buyer and a seller better off – will improve wellbeing in society. Restrictions that prevent such trade occurring will therefore lower wellbeing.
- Opportunities for trade of kidneys have been expanded by creating a database of potential kidney donors who are physiologically incompatible with the person they would like to receive a transplant but who can be matched with another recipient. This increased scope for trade has improved the wellbeing of donors and kidney transplant recipients.
- Mobile phones have allowed fishermen in southern India to sell into a larger number of local markets, thereby expanding the scope for mutually advantageous trade. Greater scope for trade has improved the wellbeing of both fishermen and buyers.

## SOME QUESTIONS TO THINK ABOUT

1   Draw a diagram showing how a three-way kidney exchange would work. Can you think of reasons why it may be difficult to have exchanges that are larger than three-way?

2   Do you think restrictions on the legal trading of human organs are likely to completely halt such trade?

3   An article in *The Economist* (2013) described how pre-paid mobile-airtime minutes are used as a de facto currency in Kenya – being able to be transferred between phones, exchanged for cash, or bartered for goods and services. The value of airtime minutes does not depend on a government's stability or ability to hold down inflation, and has the advantage of being able to be purchased and sent immediately and anonymously. Many telecoms firms in Africa transfer airtime minutes free of charge, and hence the mobile minutes are especially useful for settling small debts.

   a   In what ways can pre-paid mobile airtime be used in trade in Kenya?

   b   Why might the mobile airtime be preferred to available substitutes? In what way could the use of mobile airtime be argued to be increasing the gains from trade?

## REFERENCES

Australia and New Zealand Dialysis and Transplant Registry (ANZDTR) (2018), *41st Annual Report* (Canberra), https://www.anzdata.org.au/report/anzdata-41st-annual-report-2018-anzdata/, viewed 24 May 2019.

Goyal, Aparajita (2010), 'Information, direct access to farmers, and rural market performance in Central India', *American Economic Journal: Applied Economics*, vol. 2(3), pp. 22–45.

Granryd, Mats (2018), 'More than just a phone: Mobile's impact on sustainable development'. Accessed at: https://www.weforum.org/agenda/2018/09/more-than-just-a-phone-mobile-s-impact-on-sustainable-development/, viewed 26 September 2019.

Jensen, Robert (2007), 'The digital provide: information (technology), market performance and welfare in the South Indian fisheries sector', *Quarterly Journal of Economics*, vol. 122, pp. 879–924.

Kidney Health Australia (2019), 'Fast facts on CKD in Australia', https://kidney.org.au/cms_uploads/docs/kidney-health-australia-kidney-fast-facts-fact-sheet.pdf, viewed 24 May 2019.

Organ Procurement and Transplantation Network (2017), OPTN/SRTR 2017 Annual Data Report: Kidney, https://srtr.transplant.hrsa.gov/annual_reports/2017/Kidney.aspx#KI_57_tx_counts_type_1_b64, viewed 24 May 2019.

Qiang, Christine Zhen-Wei (2009), Telecommunications and Economic Growth, World Bank, mimeo.

Rapaport, Felix (1986), 'The case for a living emotionally related international kidney donor exchange registry', *Transplantation Proceedings*, vol. 18, pp. 5–9.

Roth, Alvin (2007), 'What have we learned from market design?', Hahn Lecture to the Royal Economic Society Meetings, University of Warwick.

Sonmez, Tayfun (2013), 'Kidney exchange policy', **www.tayfunsonmez.net/wp-content/uploads/2013/11/KidneyExchange-policy.pdf**

*The Economist* (2013), 'Airtime is money', 19 January, p. 66.

Wessel, David (2004), 'Renal donors swap recipients if blood types don't match', *The Wall Street Journal*, 17 June, p. B1.

# IDEAS FOR FURTHER READING

Many of the important references and articles on kidney exchange are available at Alvin Roth's website (web.stanford.edu/~alroth/). The website also includes some excellent introductory articles on economic design, such as his 2007 Hahn Lecture, 'What have we learned from market design?' For overviews of research on the effects of mobile phones and the internet on how markets function, see the articles 'Worth a hill of soyabeans' (*The Economist*, 2010, 9 January, p. 69) and 'The mother of invention' (*The Economist*, 2009, 26 September, pp. 8–10).

Articles in the *For the Student* section of the *Australian Economic Review* contain reviews on economic design written for students. These include Simon Loertscher and Tom Wilkening's 'Auctions and economic design' (2011, *Australian Economic Review*, vol. 44, pp. 347–54) and Georgy Artemov, Sven Feldmann and Simon Loertscher's 'Matching and economic design' (2012, *Australian Economic Review*, vol. 45, pp. 134–41).

# CASE STUDY 1.6
## ARE WE ALWAYS RATIONAL?

Nothing is more fundamental to modern economic theory than the assumption that decision makers act rationally. Almost every economic model makes the assumption that individuals or organisations make choices rationally. But an assumption is just that. What do we know about how decisions are actually made? Should we be worried if we find that decision makers don't seem to behave rationally?

---

### THEORY REFRESHER

#### What is rationality?

A rational decision maker has a well-defined objective, knows the consequences of alternative actions and chooses actions that are consistent with achieving the objective (or, in other words, chooses the action that maximises wellbeing).

As an example, a firm with the objective to maximise profits, which makes every decision regarding what products to sell, how to produce those products and what price to charge in a way that is consistent with profit maximisation, would be considered rational.

---

There are many aspects to rational decision making that could be investigated. Here, we will look at two particular aspects. First, a rational decision maker should take into account the opportunity costs of any action, but should ignore sunk costs. Sunk costs are costs that are incurred prior to the time at which a decision is being made about whether to take an action. As these costs have already been incurred, they do not affect the benefits and costs associated with the choice of action that is being contemplated, and thus should not be taken into account. A question we can therefore ask relating to rationality is whether decision makers do ignore sunk costs. Second, rational decision making requires the capacity to correctly forecast the consequences of alternative choices. For decision makers to choose actions that are going to make them as well-off as possible, it is necessary to know the benefits and costs that will be associated with each alternative action. Often, these benefits and costs may not occur until some time in the future, and a rational decision maker needs to be able to precisely evaluate these future consequences. Another question about rationality that can therefore be asked is whether decision makers possess this capacity to know the future consequences of their actions.

Studies that have sought to answer these questions reveal a mixed story. In many regards, individuals and organisations do make decisions in a way that is consistent with rationality. At the same time, it would be silly to claim that decision making is always rational, or even that it is not possible to find systematic departures from rational behaviour.

A variety of studies have set out to show that decision makers don't ignore sunk costs. Major business flops such as the Concorde and the NASA shuttle program, the development of which continued despite being clearly unviable, are often cited as examples of how businesses are motivated to complete projects that have already cost them a lot of money despite those costs being sunk. One rather different study on sunk costs looked at players drafted to play in the US National Basketball Association competition. It found that even after players had been in the competition for several years, at which stage information on the order in which they had been drafted should have been irrelevant (or sunk) as an indicator of their abilities, those who had been drafted using higher picks still got more playing time and were less likely to be traded (Staw & Hoang 1995). A later study, again on NBA players, but using player salary as a measure of their anticipated quality, confirmed the sunk cost effect on playing time (Hinton & Sun 2019). Continuing the theme, it has even been suggested that the US invasion of Iraq in March 2003 only came about because the US Government, feeling it had invested so much money in preparing for war, thought it had to invade to justify this expense. This was regardless of Saddam Hussein appearing ready to agree to extensive weapons inspections and to the placement of NATO troops in Iraq.

Each of these examples can reasonably be interpreted as showing an instance where a decision maker did not ignore sunk costs. But this does not necessarily imply the decision makers' behaviour was irrational. Take the example of the Concorde. Continued development of the aeroplane may not have been rational for its manufacturers, European Aeronautic Defence and Space (EADS) and BAE Systems, which were going to lose money on the project, yet for the project managers it may have been perfectly rational. Closing down the project would have meant the loss of the jobs and reputations of those managers, whereas delaying closure of the project allowed them to retain their jobs and keep alive the small hope that the aeroplane might become commercially viable. Similarly, for basketball team managers, giving more playing time to a player drafted with a higher pick maintains the illusion that the player is of higher quality than other basketballers, therefore confirming the manager's ability to judge talent. So while we can find many examples of how sunk costs seem to have been ignored, it is more difficult to draw a conclusion on whether this meant that decision making was irrational.

Or at least this was the case until Daniel Friedman, a professor of economics at the University of California Santa Cruz, and several of his colleagues provided a new and more powerful test of whether decision makers irrationally ignore sunk costs. This test applies an approach known as experimental economics, where human subjects make choices in simulated environments that have been created by a researcher to learn about those choices.

To test for sunk-cost effects on decision making, the economists used a game they called the 'Treasure Hunt'. The participants in this experiment visit a sequence of 'islands'. On each island there are 20 sites where the participants can 'dig' for buried treasure, and at each site where treasure is found, a 'reward' is paid. The number of sites with treasure on any island is between two and 18. Each participant has a fixed total number of sites where they are allowed to dig, but on each island they can dig as many sites as they like. Switching between islands imposes a travel cost on a participant that may be either 'high' or 'low'. The size of the travel cost, however, is independent of the amount of treasure on the next island the participant visits.

The central idea of this game is that once a participant reaches a new island, the cost they paid to get to that island is sunk. Hence, for a rational participant, the number of sites they search on an island should be independent of the cost they paid to reach that island. So what happened when participants played the game? Used to suggestions that decision makers do take sunk costs into account, the economists described their findings as a 'surprise'. Most of the evidence suggested that decision makers searched optimally for treasure by ignoring sunk costs. They chose the same number of sites to dig at on islands regardless of whether they were low-cost or high-cost to visit (Friedman et al. 2007, p. 80).

So far, so good. Examining decision making where sunk costs are involved does not seem to reveal significant evidence of departures from rationality. What about the second aspect of a decision maker needing to have the capacity to forecast the consequences of alternative choices? Here it has to be acknowledged that the evidence for rationality is weaker.

A novel perspective on our ability to forecast the consequences of the actions we take comes from a study of gym memberships in the United States. Potential users of gyms included in the study were able to choose between three methods of payment: a monthly contract, an annual contract or a pay-per-visit option. The annual contract was automatically cancelled and had to be renewed to continue, whereas the monthly contract was automatically renewed and had to be cancelled to be stopped. Analysing the payment options chosen by gym users, Stefano Della Vigna and Ulrike Malmendier, economists at (respectively) the University of California at Berkeley and Stanford, found several troubling facts.

Most worrying were two findings that related to the users who purchased a monthly contract. First, on the basis of the number of visits they actually made to the gym, it was found that 80 per cent of gym members who chose the monthly contract would actually have paid less if they had chosen the pay-per-visit option. Second, monthly members were about 20 per cent less likely to cancel their contract after 12 months than users with an annual contract. This was despite monthly members having greater opportunities to cancel, and visiting the gym much less often than annual members.

How can this seemingly perverse behaviour be explained? Della Vigna and Malmendier suggested that it primarily represented a failure of rational decision making:

> Consumers over-estimate … their future self-control or their future efficiency in pursuing costly activities. This leads to over-estimation of attendance and of cancellation in automatically renewed contracts … In a simple yet economically significant decision – enrolment and attendance in a health club – consumers deviate systematically from the optimal contractual choice.

Source: Della Vigna & Malmendier (2006), pp. 695–6.

The bottom line is that gym users with monthly contracts did not seem to be able to forecast the future consequences of the different choices available to them. Most gym users who purchased monthly contracts overestimated the number of future visits they would make to the gym at the time they chose their payment method. This explains why they chose a payment method that would have been cheaper per visit if they had made more visits to the gym, yet in practice worked out to be more expensive for them. Not only this, but gym users on monthly contracts also overestimated the likelihood that they would cancel their contract in the future when it became optimal to do this. It is this overconfidence that explains why gym users on a monthly contract were even less likely to cancel the contract than users on annual contracts, although they paid more for the option to be able to cancel their contract on a monthly basis.

Should we be concerned about having economic models in which the assumption of rationality is central, knowing there is evidence that decision making will not always be rational? There are several responses to this question. One response is to say that it certainly doesn't mean we need to throw away our economic models. As long as a sufficient proportion of the population is behaving in a manner that is close to rational, then our models can still be valuable for predicting what will happen in the economy and for guiding decision making. Moreover, if decision makers make choices that are not rational but there is no systematic bias in their mistakes, then on average the decisions that are made are likely to correspond to the economic theory. Another response is that many instances of irrational decision making may be short-lived and corrected relatively quickly. For example, an investor who pays more for a company's shares than is justified by forecasts of the company's future profitability will quickly learn, from losing money on those shares, that a change in behaviour is needed. A third response is that evidence of behaviour that is not rational may provide us with ways of developing better models that are consistent with such behaviour. One example is models of how firms should choose prices or aspects of long-term contracts such as cancellation clauses to maximise their profits, taking into account overconfidence by consumers. This is part of the work being done in a new field known as behavioural economics. A final response is that evidence that there are departures from rational decision making shows us that, as economists, we need to always think critically about the assumptions we make in our models, and how this affects the value of those models.

## KEY LESSONS

- Rationality in decision making is the central assumption in most economic models.
- Empirical analysis of decision making provides mixed evidence on the existence of rationality. Many aspects of decision making do seem to conform to rationality, but there are also significant departures.
- Evidence that decision making may not always be rational does not mean we should give up using economic models that assume rationality. It does, however, provide an opportunity for developing better models, and shows that we need to take a critical approach to evaluating our models.

## SOME QUESTIONS TO THINK ABOUT

1   Can you think of an experiment you could use to test whether decision makers ignore or take into account sunk costs?
2   Often we have a limited amount of time and limited mental capacity for processing all the information necessary to make an optimal decision. Bounded rationality is the idea that decision makers in such situations will behave rationally given the set of constraints on their decision making. Do you think this is a good way of representing the limits on rational decision making? Can you think of examples for which this would be a good model for representing decision making?
3   Suppose that a study of restaurants showed that the mark-up (price minus cost) on the second-cheapest type of bottle or glass of white or red wine listed on the menu was higher than for any other wines. What type of decision making by patrons of restaurants would make this pricing practice optimal for the restaurant? What does it imply about the rationality of decision making by patrons of restaurants?

## REFERENCES

Della Vigna, Stefano & Malmendier, Ulrike (2006), 'Paying not to go to the gym', *American Economic Review*, vol. 96, pp. 694–719.

Friedman, Daniel, Pommerenke, Kai, Lukose, Rajan, Milam, Garrett & Huberman, Bernado (2007), 'Searching for the sunk cost fallacy', *Experimental Economics*, vol. 10, pp. 79–104.

Hinton, Alexander & Sun, Yiguo (2019), 'The sunk-cost fallacy in the National Basketball Association: Evidence using player salary and playing time', *Empirical Economics*, https://doi.org/10.1007/s00181-019-01641-4.

Staw, Barry & Hoang, Ha (1995), 'Sunk costs in the NBA: why draft order affects playing time and survival in professional basketball', *Administrative Science Quarterly*, vol. 40, pp. 474–94.

# IDEAS FOR FURTHER READING

An excellent introduction to the concept of rationality is provided in chapter 1 of Tim Harford's book *The Logic of Life* (2008, Little, Brown and Co.). A great short review of the new field of behavioural economics, which emphasises the role of psychology and behavioural influences on how we make decisions, is provided in Ian McDonald's article 'Behavioural economics' (2008, *Australian Economic Review*, 41, pp. 222–8). *Nudge*, by Richard Thaler and Cass Sunstein (2008, Yale University Press), reviews at greater length what is known about the biases that affect human decision making, and presents a variety of case studies that examine how public policy should be made. Dan Ariely gives a highly entertaining account of his experimental psychology research on human decision making in *Predictably Irrational* (2008, HarperCollins). One of the pioneers of behavioural economics, Daniel Kahneman, brought together many of his contributions in *Thinking, Fast and Slow* (2011, Princeton University Press). *The Age* columnist Ross Gittins and I debate what the field of behavioural economics adds to the discipline of economics in articles published in the *Australian Economic Review* (Ross Gittins, 2012, 'Using psychology to improve economic policy', Vol. 45, pp. 379–85; Jeff Borland, 2012, 'I want to be an economist: A rejoinder to Ross Gittins', Vol. 45, pp. 386–94).

# Demand, supply and equilibrium
# in competitive markets

These days, the concepts of demand and supply are part of our everyday thinking. Media reports and conversations with family and friends will have given you some understanding of how demand and supply determine prices, even without studying economics. So familiar are we with these concepts that it can be difficult to appreciate what a great achievement the model of demand and supply really is.

Up until the early twentieth century, economists had been quite confused about how to explain prices. Some emphasised the role of demand, thinking prices mainly reflected how much satisfaction or benefit consumers received from different goods. Others attributed the primary role to supply, and saw prices as being determined by costs of production. Only with Alfred Marshall's path-breaking work *Principles of Economics* (1890) was there a recognition that market prices should be thought of as reflecting both demand and supply. The model of demand and supply, the idea that prices depend on the 'two blades of the pair of scissors', as Marshall expressed it, has become fundamental to our understanding of markets. It is arguably the most valuable contribution to knowledge that economists have made.

The case studies in this section are all about demand and supply, and the theory of perfectly competitive markets. The cases have two main objectives: first, to describe how the model of demand, supply and equilibrium is used to represent the workings of a perfectly competitive market; second, to illustrate the many ways in which the model can be applied to help us understand economic activity and to guide decision making in business and government.

The initial case study (2.1) introduces the model of a perfectly competitive market. This is followed by case studies (2.2 to 2.5) showing how the model can be used to understand what happens in competitive markets – especially the prices at which trade occurs and the quantities of goods and services traded. A group of case studies (2.6 to 2.10) then demonstrate the ways in which the competitive market model can be used to measure wellbeing in society and to evaluate the consequences of government policies.

A market is where trade of an item between groups of buyers and sellers takes place. The necessity for trade arises where individuals in a society specialise in production activities, and so need to trade to obtain all the goods and services that they want to consume.

A perfectly competitive market is a special type of market where it is assumed that all buyers and sellers are trading exactly the same product, and where there are so many buyers and sellers (each, therefore, accounting for such a small share of trade in the market) that no individual buyer or seller has any influence over the price at which trade occurs.

The model of a perfectly competitive market consists of three main components: market demand, market supply and equilibrium. The concepts of market demand and market supply are used to represent the behaviour of buyers and sellers in the market, respectively. In Case study 2.1, you'll see how an understanding of demand (and the same applies for supply) requires a knowledge of the many factors that might potentially affect demand. Examples are given to show that consumers' incomes, the price and availability of substitute products, fashion and the cost of the time spent buying a product may all influence demand. Equilibrium is the way in which economists characterise or predict the outcome in a market. It is defined as the price and quantity traded in a market at which quantity demanded equals quantity supplied.

A major application of the perfectly competitive market model is to explain how prices can change over time in a market, or why they might vary between markets. The ability to use the model in this way is an essential skill for an economist. Case studies 2.2, 2.3 and 2.4 give examples of how to use the model to understand observed changes in prices for three very different products – fish, oil, and Uber rides! For each product, changes to demand and/or supply are shown to be able to explain price changes that happen.

As well as telling us about the direction of change in price or quantity traded that we should expect in a market due to a change in demand or supply, the model of a perfectly competitive market can guide our thinking about the magnitude of those changes. In the model, it is the degree of responsiveness of demand and supply to changes in price that will determine the relative size of the changes in price and quantity traded. The responsiveness of demand and supply to changes in price are referred to, respectively, as the own-price elasticity of demand and own-price elasticity of supply. Case study 2.5 uses an analysis of an issue of great global significance – deciding which policies are the most effective in reducing the use of child labour in developing countries – to show how elasticity matters. You'll see that the extent to which alternative policies can reduce child labour depends on the size of elasticities of demand for and supply of child labour.

A valuable application of the perfectly competitive market model is to measure and understand the determinants of wellbeing in a society. In Case study 2.6 the model is applied to ask how wellbeing in Australia would be affected by allowing mining activity in high-quality environmental areas such as Kakadu National Park. Primarily this involves using the model to calculate measures of the changes to society's wellbeing caused by mining activity. It is shown that a socially optimal decision about environmental preservation depends on a comparison of a measure of the loss to consumers from not preserving the environmental areas with a measure of the gain to producers from mining on the land. Case study 2.7 shows a different way in which the perfectly competitive market model can be applied to study wellbeing. It uses the concept of efficiency to try to convince you that ticket scalping can make society better off. This may seem controversial, but you'll see that to an economist, scalping is just another form of trade that improves the wellbeing of both buyers and sellers.

A fundamental proposition in economics is that in a perfectly competitive market, the equilibrium quantity traded of a good or service will be efficient; that is, it is the best possible outcome for society. Hence, it follows that any restrictions that prevent the market from reaching that equilibrium will lower society's wellbeing. Some government regulations that cause the quantity traded in a market to depart from the competitive equilibrium level have just this effect.

Case studies 2.8 to 2.10 illustrate how the perfectly competitive market model can be adapted to study the effects of government regulation on prices and quantity traded in a market, and hence on society's wellbeing. Case study 2.8 examines the consequences of the US Government imposing a maximum limit on bonus payments to banking executives following the Global Financial Crisis in the late 2000s. As much as we might feel that the executives deserved to take a pay cut for their role in the crisis, it is shown that the policy of restricting pay may only make us worse off – by reducing the supply of talented executives who want to work at firms where pay is regulated. Case study 2.9 analyses the alcopop tax on pre-mixed drinks, introduced by the Australian Government in 2008 as a way of decreasing binge drinking by young people. The model of a perfectly competitive market with an indirect tax is used to predict the size of the decrease in alcohol consumption due to the alcopop tax that the government could have anticipated. As well as taxing activities that they want to stop, governments can also make payments to promote activities or to benefit members of society who they regard as deserving. Case study 2.10 considers the proposal made during the 2019 Federal election in Australia for a subsidy to be paid to childcare workers in Australia to supplement their earnings. In this application, we'll use the model of a perfectly competitive market with a subsidy to examine claims that the subsidy would not have ended up in the pockets of childcare workers.

# CASE STUDY 2.1
## WHAT DETERMINES DEMAND?

Turn to the section on market demand in an introductory microeconomics textbook. What you're most likely to find is a detailed treatment of how you should represent the effect of a change in price compared to how to represent the effect of other determinants of demand. This is important, of course. Often what is missing from the textbooks, however, is any sense of what are those other determinants of demand. Yet knowing why demand might change is critical for being able to apply the perfectly competitive market model, be it to explain a movement in prices that has occurred or to predict future prices. Hence, it's worth trying to identify these mysterious other factors that can change market demand.

A bit of investigation reveals a wide variety of potential determinants of demand. As a starting point, factors that generally receive attention in textbooks, such as the prices of substitutes and complements, and consumers' incomes, do appear to affect demand.

An analysis of increasing demand for camels in the Indian state of Rajasthan concluded that as 'the cost of running gas-guzzling tractors soars, even-toed ungulates [camels] are making a comeback ... "It's excellent for the camel population if the price of oil continues to go up because demand for camels will also go up," says Ilse Kohler-Rollefson of the League for Pastoral Peoples' (Johnson 2008). What is being suggested is that the increasing price of running tractors (due to higher oil prices) is causing an increase in demand for camels, which are a substitute for tractors on farms. This is exactly what would be predicted in any textbook – that an increase in the price of the substitute, tractors, will cause an increase in demand for camels.

Alternatively, changes in demand for a product may be explained by changes in the demand for complementary goods. One example is the effect of internet retailing on demand for parcel postage services. Such is the increase in demand for air freight generated by online shopping that Qantas added an extra Boeing 737 freighter to its fleet to transport parcels for Australian Post (Freed 2016). Other examples are the decrease in demand for auto-teller banking machines as we use less cash (Yeates 2017); growth in demand for student accommodation with increasing numbers of international students at Australian universities (Cummins 2017); and more demand for ocean-going cruise vessels in response to a boom in the cruise industry (*The Economist* 2015a).

Consumer incomes also matter for demand. In China, a growing middle class has meant higher expenditure on items such as international travel and premium goods and cosmetic products (*The Economist* 2015b, 2016). The mid-2010s saw sales of cosmetics and sportswear goods growing by over 10 per cent per year; and an extra 10 million overseas trips being taken each year. Provided that these are all regarded as 'normal' goods, this is again what textbooks would tell us – that an increase in income will increase demand for international travel and premium goods.

Many other factors can affect demand. One is what economists call a 'taste change'. This just means that consumers' preferences for a good or service can alter, and that this will cause a change in demand. A possible reason why consumers' tastes or preferences may change is fashion. Take the examples of the recent rise in demand for vinyl records and collectable trainers and sneakers (*The Economist*, 2017a, 2017b). Or think about the growth in demand for gluten-free food, four-wheel-drive vehicles, and tourism to sites where Australian soldiers once fought, all of which largely seems driven by fashion. Tastes may also change because consumers discover new information about a product that causes them to value it differently. An example is the growth in demand for bottled water in China. It has been suggested that 'Hygiene and health concerns have stoked demand' (*The Economist* 2015c).

Demand for a product can be affected by the introduction of new substitutes. To the extent that a new product better matches what some consumers want, we'd expect those consumers to switch from the product they presently buy; in other words, the availability of new substitutes would be expected to decrease demand for existing products. Some recent examples are declining numbers of visitors to national parks due to a growing range of alternative recreation opportunities; the switch by children from time spent reading to playing computer games; and the impact of Uber and other ride-sharing services on the demand for public transport (*The Economist* 2006, 2013, 2018).

Apart from the price paid to the supplier to buy the product, there may be other aspects of the opportunity cost of consuming a product that affect demand. An example is the cost of the time spent buying a product or consuming it. It would be expected that the scope to buy airline tickets on the internet should increase demand, because of a reduction in the amount of time spent buying the tickets. Or take the example of cigars. With bans on smoking in indoor venues, demand for cigars has shifted away from full-size cigars, which take at least 45 minutes to smoke, to minis, which only require three to five minutes to puff through – 'a better choice for those forced out into the cold from formerly ash-friendly venues such as pubs and gentlemen's clubs' (*The Economist* 2011).

---

## THEORY REFRESHER

### Demand and supply

The model of a perfectly competitive market involves three main elements:

1. a representation of the buyers in the market, referred to as market demand
2. a representation of the suppliers in the market, referred to as market supply
3. a rule for determining the market outcome from trade between buyers and sellers, known as equilibrium.

Market demand and market supply are used to represent the aggregate behaviour of (respectively) all buyers and all suppliers in a market.

An important distinction is made between the effect of price and the effect of other influences on the behaviour of buyers and suppliers. The 'Law of demand' specifies that there is an inverse relation between price and quantity demanded, and the 'Law of supply' specifies that there is a positive relation between price and quantity supplied. Graphically, these Laws are represented in the demand and supply curves, which show the relation between price and (respectively) the quantity demanded and quantity supplied of a product. Changes in the price of a product are said to cause 'movements along the curve', as shown for the case of demand in *Figure 2.1.1*.

Other possible influences on demand include the price of substitute or complementary products, consumers' incomes and size of population. Graphically, changes in any other determinant of demand (apart from price) are represented as causing an increase or decrease in demand at each given price, so that there is a shift in the demand curve. For example, where consumers' incomes increase (and the product we are considering is a normal good), it is assumed that demand will increase. This is represented by an outward shift of the demand curve, showing that at any given price a larger quantity of the product is now demanded. This is illustrated in *Figure 2.1.1*.

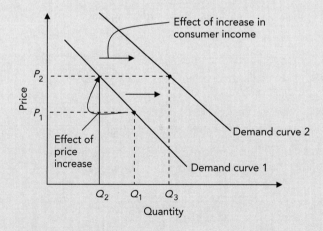

**Figure 2.1.1** Movement along and shift in the demand curve

Other possible influences on supply are the cost of production and number of suppliers. Changes in any other determinant of supply (apart from price) are represented as causing an increase or decrease in supply at each given price, so that there is a shift in the supply curve.

# KEY LESSON

- Demand for goods and services can be influenced by many factors. Sometimes these are the types of factors described in your textbook, such as changes in the price of substitute or complementary goods, or changes in consumer incomes. But there are many other influences that may matter, such as changes in consumer tastes or preferences, changes in the opportunity cost of buying or consuming a good, and changes in the availability of substitutes.

# SOME QUESTIONS TO THINK ABOUT

1 How would you represent each of the following?
   a The effect on demand for furniture produced by a furniture company changing its products from being already assembled to requiring buyers to assemble them.
   b The effect of extra road congestion on demand for travel by train.
   c The effect on demand for texting of the increased popularity of TV shows with viewer voting such as *The Voice*.
   d The effect on demand for DVDs of TV shows if the same TV shows become available from streaming services.
2 Can you think of factors apart from those described in the examples above that might affect demand?

# REFERENCES

Cummins, Carolyn (2017), 'Rising demand for uni housing helps boost investment class', *The Age*, 27 September, p. 25.

Freed, Jamie (2016), 'Online shopping boosts air freight for Australia Post, Qantas', *The Age*, 2 May, p. 23.

Johnson, Jo (2008), 'Camel demand soars as oil price makes tractors too costly to run', *Financial Times Weekend*, May 3–4, p. 1.

*The Economist* (2006), 'Catching up', 23 December, p. 87.

*The Economist* (2011), 'Up in smoke', 10 December, p. 56.

*The Economist* (2013), 'Why go outside when you have an iPhone?', 17 August, p. 31.

*The Economist* (2015a), 'Riding the wave', 27 June, p. 55.

*The Economist* (2015b), 'Treasure hunt', 28 March, pp. 29–30.

*The Economist* (2015c), 'Spring tide', 28 February, p. 57.

*The Economist* (2016), 'From noodles to poodles', 2 July, p. 61.

*The Economist* (2017a), 'Vinyl gets its groove back', 20 May, p. 55.

*The Economist* (2017b), 'Sole trading', 27 May, p. 54.

*The Economist* (2018), 'Missing the bus', 23 June, pp. 52–3.

Yeates, Clancy (2017), 'ATMs declining as we use less cash', *The Age*, 8 December, p. 23.

## IDEAS FOR FURTHER READING

Some interesting Australian studies of the determinants of demand for individual products have examined questions such as how anti-smoking policies affect the demand for tobacco (Peter Bardsley and Nilss Olekalns, 1999, 'Cigarette and tobacco consumption: have anti-smoking policies made a difference?', *Economic Record*, vol. 75, pp. 225–40), whether alcohol and cannabis are substitutes or complements (Lisa Cameron and Jenny Williams, 2001, 'Cannabis, alcohol and cigarettes: substitutes or complements?', *Economic Record*, vol. 77, pp. 19–34), and how weather conditions affect attendance at the Melbourne Cup (Paresh Kumar Narayan and Russell Smyth, 2004, 'The race that stops a nation: the demand for the Melbourne Cup', *Economic Record*, vol. 80, pp. 193–207).

In the 1850s, a lobster meal would have cost less than US$4 in today's money for a diner in San Francisco. The price of the same meal in California in 2005 was about US$30. On the other side of the United States, in Virginia, the wholesale price for a bushel of blue crabs was US$10 in 2006. But a year before, the price had ranged from US$40 to US$85. Don't think that having prices all over the place is just some weird American phenomenon. Prices for whole lobsters in Australia in the summer of 2003 were reported to have 'crashed' from more than $100 to less than $50, even though prices usually rise in the holiday season. At the same time, the price of Tasmanian farmed salmon increased by 20 per cent, whereas a kilogram of prawns, which had been selling for over $40 in major Australian cities one year previously, was now priced at only $20 (Strutt & Hepworth 2002; *The Economist* 2005, 2006; Wisenthal 2003).

If you wanted proof that markets make no sense, that what happens to prices is as random as the toss of a coin, surely these examples demonstrate exactly that proposition. Or so you might think. It turns out, in fact, that nothing could be further from the truth. What may at first seem a jumble of numbers is, when viewed through the lens of the model of competitive markets, the logical consequence of changes to demand and supply.

---

### THEORY REFRESHER

#### Comparative statics

How can we use the model of perfectly competitive markets to understand why prices and quantities traded in a market change over time or differ between markets? The answer is 'comparative statics'. Comparative statics is a method applied to understand why market prices change – by studying predicted changes in equilibrium that occur when there are changes in demand or supply. Since our method of predicting market outcomes is to use the concept of equilibrium, it follows that studying changes in the equilibrium is how we analyse why prices and quantity traded in a market might have changed.

The method is called 'static' because it involves a comparison of the new and old equilibria, and abstracts from the process of change by which the economy moves from the old to new equilibrium.

The price of lobsters is a good place to begin. In a fascinating research project, Glenn Jones, an oceanographer from Texas A&M University, studied menus of seafood restaurants in the United States dating from 1850 to the 2000s. Among a range of other findings, he showed that there was a dramatic increase in the price of lobster meals. The initial price 150 years ago was so low that

> it was fed to inmates in prison and children in orphanages. Farmers even fertilised their fields with it, and servants would bargain with their employers to be given it no more than twice or thrice a week.

> Source: *The Economist* (2005), p. 76.

This is certainly a far cry from lobster's current status as a luxury good. What Jones' research also showed was that it was the influence of demand and supply that explained the increase in price that had occurred. Overharvesting of lobsters diminished supply, and demand increased as live lobsters grew in status as a restaurant food. Both the decrease in supply and increase in demand would have been predicted to increase the price of lobster. This is illustrated in *Figure 2.2.1*. The steady increase over time in menu prices also indicates that the influence of changes to demand and supply was gradual, rather than occurring suddenly at a point in time. Of course, without having more details on the magnitudes of changes in supply and demand, it is not possible to claim that these changes perfectly explain all of the increase in restaurant prices for lobster. But just knowing that the higher price is consistent with changes to demand and supply that have occurred means that we don't need to treat the market for lobsters as a mystery.

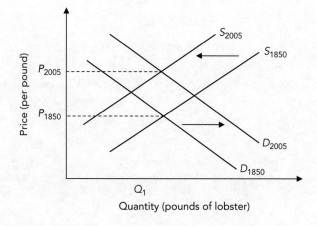

**Figure 2.2.1** Explaining the increase in the price of lobsters

Changes to other seafood prices can also be explained by changes to demand and supply. The decline in the price of blue crabs in Virginia after 2005 appears to have resulted from an increase in supply ('the first crab catch ... [in 2005] was the biggest in more than a decade') and a decrease in demand due to greater availability of a cheap substitute ('the American market has been flooded with imported crab, most of it from Asia') (*The Economist* 2006). In Australia, the falling price of lobsters in the early 2000s was attributed to a decline in international demand for Australian lobsters and an increase in supply of about 20 per cent between seasons, while the rising price of salmon occurred because of industry consolidation that restricted supply (Wisenthal 2003). Finally, it's been suggested that the fall in the price of Australian prawns was the result of the increased availability of imported prawns from China and Vietnam due to reduced tourism in those areas during the period in which Severe Acute Respiratory Syndrome (SARS) was present there (Strutt & Hepworth 2002).

None of this is to say that changes to demand and supply can explain everything that occurs in markets. It does suggest, however, that when thinking about the likely causes of changes to prices in a competitive market, it pays to first understand what has happened to demand and supply in that market. On many occasions, this approach will allow you to make sense of what otherwise may seem rather puzzling movements up and down in prices.

## KEY LESSONS

■ The prices of a variety of types of seafood have changed dramatically over both short and long timespans in the United States and Australia.

■ The changes in prices that have occurred can be explained by changes in demand for and/or supply of each type of seafood.

■ The demand and supply framework is a useful starting point when trying to explain the causes of changes to prices in a competitive market.

## SOME QUESTIONS TO THINK ABOUT

1   Describe what happens to the equilibrium price and quantity traded of soft drink in response to each of the following. Explain your answer using a diagram.

   a   global warming makes for longer and hotter Australian summers

   b   new health concerns about the preservative content in soft drinks

   c   an increase in the price of sugar used to produce soft drinks

   d   a decrease in the price of petrol

2   An article in *The Economist* (2019) described several main changes that have occurred in the market for chicken meat in recent years: higher incomes of consumers; new evidence that eating red meat may be associated with an

increased risk of colon cancer; and the increased use of antibiotics making it cheaper to raise chickens.

    a   What do you think will be the effect of these changes on the demand for and supply of chicken meat?

    b   What affect would those changes in demand and supply have on the market price and quantity traded of chicken meat?

    c   The article also described how consumers in the United States prefer white meat from chicken breasts and Asian consumers prefer dark meat from the legs and wings. What effect do you think these preferences would have on the relative price of chicken breasts and chicken legs in the United States and Asia?

3   Adverse weather conditions – a combination of frost and drought – affected wheat crops in eastern Australian in 2018; with forecasts being for reductions in crop sizes of 40 to 50 per cent (Phelan 2018).

    a   How do you think the decrease in crop size would affect the market price and quantity traded of wheat?

    b   At the same time as forecasting smaller crops, industry groups also predicted higher prices of some types of food? Why might higher prices of food occur, and which types of food would be likely to be most affected?

# REFERENCES

Phelan, Liam (2018), 'Food price warning as wheat plummets', *The Age*, 5 December, p. 27.

Strutt, Sam & Hepworth, Annabel (2002), 'Prices soar as seafood supplies shrink', *Australian Financial Review*, 11 November, p. 3.

*The Economist* (2005), 'When lobster was fertiliser', 29 October, p. 76.

*The Economist* (2006), 'A glut of claws', 27 May, p. 35.

*The Economist* (2019), 'Ruling the roost', 19 January, pp. 59–61.

Wisenthal, Stephen (2003), 'Caught between a rock lobster and a hard place', *Australian Financial Review*, 31 December, p. 2.

# IDEAS FOR FURTHER READING

The demand/supply model was introduced by Alfred Marshall. You can read about him in Steven Pressman's book *Fifty Major Economists* (2002, Routledge, pp. 64–8). Robert Frank presents a variety of interesting applications of the demand/supply model in chapter 2 of *The Economic Naturalist* (2007, Basic Books).

## CASE STUDY 2.3
## EXPLAINING CHANGES IN THE PRICE OF OIL: NOT SO SLIPPERY WHEN YOU USE SUPPLY AND DEMAND

In his classic history of the oil industry, Daniel Yergin (1991, p. xv) accurately describes it as 'the world's biggest and most pervasive business'. Ever since it emerged as a global commodity in the early twentieth century, oil has been front-page news. Much of that news has concerned gyrations in the price of crude oil. In the months following late 2018 it was a US$20 decrease in the price of a barrel of crude oil that captured attention. For the three years prior to that, however, it was a US$50 increase that had everyone talking. Going back even further, from mid-2014 to early 2016 the price fell from about US $110 to US$30. For the decade before, the opposite trend had been highlighted. *Figure 2.3.1* shows the evolution of the crude oil price from 1990 to the present.

**Figure 2.3.1** Crude oil price, Brent, $US/bbl

*Source:* World Bank Commodity Price Data (The Pink Sheet), pubdocs.worldbank.org > CMO-Historical-Data-Monthly. Licensed under a Creative Commons Attribution 4.0 International License (CC BY 4.0). Link to license: https://creativecommons.org/licenses/by/4.0/

With such large swings in the price of oil, and with those price changes having a big impact on global economic activity, trying to predict the price of oil has become an industry itself. In this case study, you'll see that with your knowledge of the theory of perfectly competitive markets, you are in a position to contribute to the industry – by making your own judgements about how oil prices will change.

If you have done much reading on the global oil market you might be a bit doubtful about this claim. Expressions like 'cartel', 'market power' and 'multinational' are commonly used when the global oil market is discussed. So how can we use the theory of perfectly competitive markets to understand the oil market? Well, it's certainly the case that the global oil market doesn't exactly fit our description of a perfectly competitive market. Nevertheless, applying the theory of perfectly competitive markets can take us a long way towards understanding price movements in the oil market. The theory of perfectly competitive markets emphasises the role of changes in market demand and market supply in explaining price changes. It turns out that thinking about the global oil market in this way, using changes in demand and supply to predict or explain price changes, can provide many important insights.

This case study contains three main illustrations of the power of the theory of perfectly competitive markets to assist in understanding outcomes in the global oil market. First, the theory can be applied to explain changes in the price of oil. Second, the theory – together with knowledge of the concept of price elasticity – can be used to predict the magnitude of changes in the price of oil. Third, the theory can identify spillover effects on other markets from changes in the price of oil.

## What causes changes in the price of oil?

The theory of perfectly competitive markets provides an organising framework for understanding why price changes happen. The framework classifies potential causes of price changes as changes in supply, changes in demand, or changes in both.

Let's begin with supply. Commentaries on the global oil market since late 2018 have linked the falling price of oil to large increases in the supply of oil due to extra output from fracking and from gains in efficiency from fracking (*The Economist* 2018a; Latimer 2019). This is exactly what would be predicted in the demand/supply model of a perfectly competitive market. An increase in market supply causes a shift to a new equilibrium with a lower equilibrium price and a higher quantity traded.

At other times it is demand factors that have been regarded as the main driver of the price of crude oil. A major example was the contraction in global economic activity that happened in the Global Financial Crisis, which was associated with a large decrease in the crude oil price (*The Economist* 2014). Again, this is exactly the effect that is predicted by the theory of perfectly competitive markets. A decrease in market demand causes a shift to a new equilibrium with a lower price and smaller quantity traded.

Sometimes there are events that cause a change in both demand and supply. An example in the global oil market occurred in early 2012. An article in *The Economist* (2012) described fears that Iran might commence military activity in the Strait of Hormuz, cutting off supplies to global markets. Any future decrease in supply would be expected to cause an increase in prices at that future time. Hence, oil buyers in March 2012 believed that the price of oil at the future date would be higher than they had previously thought. This caused some buyers to shift their demand from that future date to March 2012 in order to take advantage of the current price of oil now being relatively cheaper compared to the expected future price. Similarly, suppliers in March 2012 now expected a higher future price for oil than they had previously thought. This caused some suppliers to shift supply from the present to the future in order to take advantage of the higher expected future price. In summary, a higher expected future price caused an increase in demand by buyers and a decrease in supply by oil producers in March 2012. Hence, the price of crude oil would be predicted to increase. This is indeed what happened, with the price of a barrel of oil jumping by $20. These changes in demand and supply, and the resulting effect on the equilibrium price, are displayed graphically in *Figure 2.3.2*.

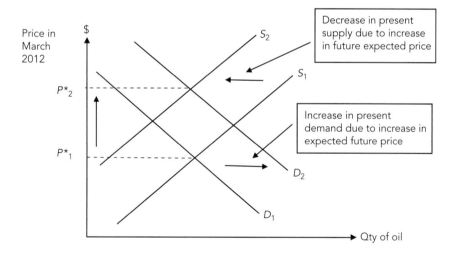

**Figure 2.3.2** The effect on the price of oil in March 2012 of an increase in the expected future price

## How much will the price of oil change?

As well as wanting to forecast the direction of change in the price of a product such as oil, often it's important to be able to say something about the likely magnitude of change in price. You'll have noticed from the history of the crude oil price presented in *Figure 2.3.1* that some large swings in price have occurred. What would account for the large price changes over time? One possible explanation is that there have been large changes in demand or supply. The other main explanation relates to the price elasticities of demand and supply.

In an analysis of changes in the oil price from the mid to late 2000s, the economist James Smith (2009, pp. 154–5) argued that '... in the short-run, price elasticities of supply and demand are extremely small, so that even seemingly small shocks [to demand or supply] may have large effects'. Essentially Smith is making two points. First, he is saying that the demand for and supply of oil are highly price inelastic in the short run. Second, he is saying that, since the demand for and supply of oil are highly price inelastic, it follows that large changes in the price of oil will occur when demand or supply change.

Why would the demand for and supply of oil be price inelastic? On the demand side, much of the consumption of oil is related to the use of particular technologies for travel, home heating and the production of energy. Hence, it is only by changing these technologies that it is possible for consumers to make a large change to their use of oil. Making changes to these technologies will take some time. Therefore, the short-run change in the quantity demanded of oil in response to a change in price is likely to be relatively small. For example, motorists may want to respond to a substantial increase in the price of oil by reducing their consumption of petrol, yet to do this it may be necessary to switch to a smaller car, which will only happen when the cars they currently own are worn out. On the supply side, making large-scale adjustments to the quantity of oil supplied in response to a price change is also likely to take some time. Adjusting the rate of extraction from existing wells and establishing new wells to increase supply is a long-term task involving exploration and major construction activity.

So, it is reasonable to think that the demand for and supply of oil are indeed price inelastic in the short run. Does it follow that changes in demand or supply will cause large movements in the equilibrium price? To test the argument, we'll do a thought experiment. The purpose of the experiment is to ask: How does the size of increase in price of oil due to an increase in demand vary between cases where the supply of oil is relatively price elastic and relatively price inelastic? The experiment is depicted graphically in *Figure 2.3.3*. The figure displays the effect of an increase in demand on the equilibrium price of oil for two different supply curves, one which is relatively price inelastic and the other which is relatively price elastic.

The outcome of our experiment is that the increase in price is much larger for the case where supply is relatively price inelastic than where it is relatively price elastic. An increase in demand causes a shift in the market outcome up the supply curve to a new equilibrium. Where the supply of oil is relatively price inelastic the shift to the new equilibrium will involve a relatively larger increase in the price of oil. This can be seen in *Figure 2.3.3*. In the former case price increases from $P_1^*$ to $P_{2inelastic}^*$; and in the latter case price increases from $P_1^*$ to $P_{2elastic}^*$.

So, looking at the size of changes to the price of oil has demonstrated a second application of the theory of perfectly competitive markets. Using the theory together

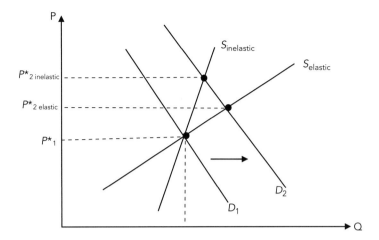

**Figure 2.3.3** Predicting the size of change in the price of oil

with knowledge of the price elasticity of the demand for and supply of oil has allowed us to predict the size of price changes that will occur in the market.

## Consequences of changes to the price of oil

Spillover effects between markets happen when there are goods that are substitutes or complements, or where a good is an input to production of another good or service. In that situation, a change in the price of one good will cause a change in demand for the other good. A third application of the theory of perfectly competitive markets is to analyse these spillover effects.

Where two goods are substitutes, an increase in the price of one good will cause an increase in the market demand for the other. By contrast, when two goods are complements, an increase in the price of one good causes a decrease in the market demand for the other. Where a good is an input for production of another good, a change in its price will change supply of the other good – for example, an increase in the price of the input good will cause a decrease in supply of the good for which it is an input.

| THEORY REFRESHER |
| --- |
| **Spillover effects between markets** |
| A change in the equilibrium price of a good or service will often have spillover effects on other markets. This can happen where the good or service that experiences a change in price is a substitute or complement to some other good or service, or is an input to the production of another good or service. |

To illustrate how spillover effects can occur between markets, take the example of two goods that are substitutes. Specifically, consider the case of sunscreen lotion and sunhats, which can be regarded as substitutes for protection from UV rays. Assume that the markets for both goods are perfectly competitive. Suppose that initially both markets are in equilibrium. Then a new type of fabric is discovered that is cheaper to manufacture than existing fabrics that provide UV protection used in production of sunhats.

The direct effect of the discovery of the new type of fabric will be to increase the market supply of sunhats. That increase in market supply will cause a decrease in the equilibrium price and increase in the equilibrium quantity traded of sunhats. This is shown below in the left-hand panel of *Figure 2.3.4*.

Because of this adjustment in the market for sunhats, a spillover effect on the market for sunscreen will follow. Sunhats and sunscreen are substitutes, hence a decrease in the price of sunhats will cause a decrease in market demand for sunscreen. The size of the decrease in market demand for sunscreen will depend on the amount by which the price of sunhats decreases (bigger fall in price of sunhats causes a larger decrease in demand for sunscreen, other things equal); and the degree of substitutability between sunhats and sunscreen (a higher degree of substitutability causes a larger decrease in demand for sunscreen, other things equal). The effect of the decrease in market demand for sunscreen will be to decrease the equilibrium price and reduce the equilibrium quantity traded of sunscreen. This is shown in the right-hand panel of *Figure 2.3.4*.

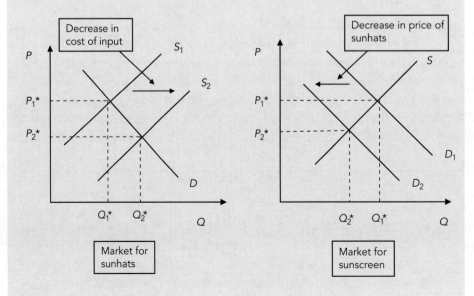

**Figure 2.3.4** Spillover effect between markets for sunhats and sunscreen

It is easy to think of goods that are substitutes and complements for oil. Gas, for example, is a substitute for oil – since they are alternative energy sources and fuels for home heating. Therefore, the decrease in the price of oil that happened in 2014 and 2015 would be predicted to have decreased the demand for gas as buyers switched from the now relatively more expensive option of gas towards the relatively cheaper option of oil (Cauchi 2014).

Oil is an input for the production of many of the items we consume on a daily basis. As one example, 20 per cent of the cost of supplying grains comes from oil, which is used to operate production machinery and transport equipment. Rapid growth in the price of oil in the 2000s is estimated to have increased the price of corn and soybeans in the United States by 30 to 40 per cent (*The Economist* 2015). This is exactly the effect predicted by the theory of perfectly competitive markets: An increase in the price of an input causes a decrease in the supply of a good – with the result being an increase in its equilibrium price. At times when the price of oil has been decreasing, such as in 2016, an opposite effect has been observed – with, for example, the lower price of oil contributing to cheaper fares for air travel (*The Economist* 2016).

## KEY LESSONS

- The theory of perfectly competitive markets emphasises the role of changes in market demand and market supply in explaining changes to market prices.
- The theory therefore provides a valuable organising framework for examining the causes of changes in the price of a good such as oil, where market-level demand and supply are important influences on the price.
- The theory, together with information on the price elasticities of demand and supply, is able to explain why changes in the price of oil in response to changes in demand and supply have been large.
- Changes in the price of a good or service often cause spillover effects on the demand for or supply of another good or service. An example is how the 2014–2015 decrease in the world price of oil reduced the demand for gas.

## SOME QUESTIONS TO THINK ABOUT

1   An article in *The Economist* (2007a) described changes in the market for helium:

> Alas, expected new sources of the stuff have failed to materialise just as high-tech industries that rely on it are booming.

Use the demand/supply model of a perfectly competitive market to predict the effects on the equilibrium price of helium from the changes in demand and supply described.

2   An article in *The Economist* (2018a) described how despite an agreement by OPEC and Russia to increase output by up to 1m barrels a day (b/d), the price of crude oil increased. The increased in price was instead attributed to supply outages in Libya and Venezuela. At the same time, the Trump administration in the United States was pressuring allies to cut oil imports from Iran to zero, or risk punishment for violating American sanctions.

Use the demand/supply model to explain how the increase in the price of oil can be explained by:

a   supply outages in Libya and Venezuela; and

b   future decreases in oil exports by Iran.

3   For each of the following scenarios, what would be the effect on the equilibrium price and quantity traded in each of the markets described?

a   Wheat is an input to bread. Both wheat and bread are traded in perfectly competitive markets. Bans on pesticides increase the cost of production of wheat. What will be the effects on the equilibrium price and quantity traded of wheat and bread?

b   Bicycles and bike helmets can be considered to be complements. A decrease in the price of aluminium makes it cheaper to manufacture bicycles. Markets for bicycles and bike helmets can both be assumed to be perfectly competitive. What will be the effects on the equilibrium price and quantity traded of bicycles and bicycle helmets?

4   An article in *The Economist* (2018b) described concerns that soaring demand for cobalt would cause a substantial increase in its price. Discuss potential reasons why an increase in demand for cobalt could cause a substantial rise in its equilibrium price?

# REFERENCES

Cauchi, Stephen (2014), 'Depressed oil prices; happy motorists', *The Age Business Day*, 20 October, p. 23.

Latimer, Cole (2019), 'US oil gush to keep lid on petrol prices', *The Age Business*, 13 March, p. 29.

Smith, James (2009), 'World oil: Market or mayhem?', *Journal of Economic Perspectives*, Summer, pp. 154–5.

*The Economist* (2007a), 'Inflated', 5 May, p. 66.

*The Economist* (2007b), 'Year of the golden pig', 9 June, p. 30.

*The Economist* (2012), 'Rollercoaster', 7 July, p. 63.

*The Economist* (2014), 'Oil and trouble', 4 October, pp. 75–6.

*The Economist* (2015), 'Oily food', 10 October, pp. 68–9.

*The Economist* (2016), 'Don't get carried away', 23 January, p. 60.

*The Economist* (2018a), 'Donald v the OPEC dons', 7 July, p. 57.

*The Economist* (2018b), 'Battery farming', 1 December, p. 58.

World Bank Commodity Price Data (The Pink Sheet), http://econ.worldbank.org/
WBSITE/EXTERNAL/EXTDEC/EXTDECPROSPECTS/0,,contentMDK:21574907~
menuPK:7859231~pagePK:64165401~piPK:64165026~theSitePK:476883,00.html,
viewed 17 September 2019.

Yergin, Daniel (1991), *The Prize: The Epic Quest for Oil, Power and Money*, Free Press.

# IDEAS FOR FURTHER READING

Daniel Yergin's book *The Prize* (1991, Free Press) is a Pulitzer prize-winning account of the history of the global oil industry. Christiane Baumeister and Lutz Kilian analyse historical movements in oil prices in their article 'Forty years of oil price fluctuations: Why the price of oil may still surprise us' (2016, *Journal of Economic Perspectives*, 30(1), pp. 139–60).

Using the concepts of demand and supply can help us understand why the prices of goods and services we buy change over time. Making this connection can even be taken as the start and end of the story of price changes. Where an increase or decrease in price is explained by a change in demand or supply, then surely the price change is justified. Reasoning in this way may appear entirely legitimate to an economist schooled in the theory of perfectly competitive markets. However, it's important to realise that not everyone accepts that having an explanation for price changes makes them justified.

The ride-sharing app Uber is a notable example. At times when the quantity of rides demanded is anticipated or observed to be substantially in excess of supply from drivers currently working, Uber increases the price it charges to customers and the wage paid to its drivers – what has become known as surge pricing. Uber argues that the practice of surge pricing allows it to do a better job of matching riders and drivers – thereby making everyone better off. However, there have also been vocal critics – who believe, for example, that varying the price is unfair and exploits riders at times of high demand.

In this case study, you'll start out by learning how Uber's surge pricing works – and how it depends on demand and supply. We'll then consider the arguments that have been made for and against surge pricing. These arguments illustrate that the way economists think about wellbeing may differ from other perspectives prevalent in the community.

## What is surge pricing?

To understand the motivation for surge pricing, it's important to begin with two facts about the ride-sharing market. First, the demand for ride-sharing services varies widely over time; for example, by day of the week and by time of day, or across the year depending on the timing of major entertainment events. Second, drivers who use ride-sharing apps can choose their own work hours: How much they work and when they work. And it's entirely possible that times when drivers want to drive may not be the times when passengers want to travel.

What this means is that the ride-sharing market can be unbalanced. At times, the quantity of rides demanded may exceed the quantity of rides that can be supplied by available drivers, with the result being long waiting times for passengers. Of course, when we say that quantity demanded exceeds quantity supplied, we need to add: at the prevailing price. This is where surge pricing comes in.

Surge pricing is the way that Uber tries to deal with the imbalance between demand and supply. Anticipating or having observed a spike in the quantity of rides demanded, Uber is able to estimate how many extra drivers are required so that waiting times for passengers do not increase excessively. By applying data on how drivers using its app respond to increases in their rate of pay, Uber can raise the price it charges customers and the payment it makes to drivers, in order to induce extra drivers to supply rides. This increase in the price of a ride at times of high demand is what is referred to as surge pricing.

An example of surge pricing happened following a sell-out concert by Ariana Grande at Madison Square Garden in March 2015 (Hall et al. 2016). In the 90 minutes after the concert, Uber app openings by potential riders increased four-fold above the normal level, and rides requested almost doubled. The quantity of rides demanded in the vicinity of Madison Square Garden therefore far exceeded the quantity of rides available, meaning that surge pricing was implemented. During the same period as the spike in demand, the price of rides went as high as 1.8 times what would have been charged if demand had remained at the normal level. The surge pricing had its desired effect, with the number of available drivers in the vicinity of Madison Square Garden at some points doubling compared to during normal times. With the quantity of rides available increasing to match the rise in the quantity of rides demanded, there was little change in waiting time for a ride: on average the waiting time was about 2½ minutes.

---

### THEORY REFRESHER

#### Where can we apply the demand/supply model?

The theory of perfectly competitive markets is a versatile approach that can usefully be applied to understand price and quantity outcomes in a variety of markets. Three main types of markets are:

1 product markets, where goods such as food, clothing and durable items (for example, televisions and cars) are traded
2 labour markets, where businesses buy labour services from workers
3 financial markets, where various types of financial assets such as money, bonds and shares are traded.

Each of these types of markets can be analysed using the demand/supply model. All that is necessary is to adopt the appropriate specification of demand and supply, and to relabel the price and quantity traded to represent how those outcomes are defined in each type of market. *Table 2.4.1* provides general examples of how this would be done.

**Table 2.4.1** Examples of market analysis

|  | PRODUCT | LABOUR | FINANCIAL (e.g. SHARES) |
|---|---|---|---|
| Demand | Demand for good | Demand for labour | Demand for financial asset |
| Supply | Supply of good | Supply of labour | Supply of financial asset |
| Price | Price per unit of good | Wage rate per hour of labour | Price per share |
| Quantity | Number of units of good traded | Hours of labour time traded | Quantity (or value) of shares traded |

# Can surge pricing make riders and drivers better off?

If you are thinking that the idea of surge pricing sounds quite familiar, you'd be right. What Uber is doing in response to the increase in demand for rides is nothing more than the way we would expect a competitive market to evolve in the same circumstance. Where quantity demanded of a good or service exceeds quantity supplied, we identify a market as being in shortage – and we expect that the response to the shortage will be for the market price to increase. Moreover, that the market price increases when otherwise a shortage would exist is seen as making buyers and sellers in the market better off.

To explain how this happens, it's useful to begin with the situation where a shortage exists. This is shown for the case of a perfectly competitive market in *Figure 2.4.1*. It is assumed that the level of demand can be either low or high; and that supply remains fixed. When demand is 'low' the market is in equilibrium at 'Base price' and with quantity traded equal to $Q_1$. But when demand is 'high', at the 'Base price' there is a shortage. Quantity demanded exceeds quantity supplied; and there are $(Q_2 - Q_1)$ buyers who would like to buy the product being traded but cannot.

Now suppose that when demand is 'high' the price rises to equal 'Surge price'. This is shown in *Figure 2.4.2*. With the higher price will come an increase in quantity supplied – either extra suppliers are induced to enter the market or existing suppliers increase the quantities they supply. The increase in quantity supplied allows extra buyers to purchase the product. Overall, the quantity traded increases from $Q_1$ to $Q_3$. Importantly, all the extra units traded bring together buyers and sellers who would not have traded at the 'Base price'; yet all those extra buyers have higher willingness to pay than the

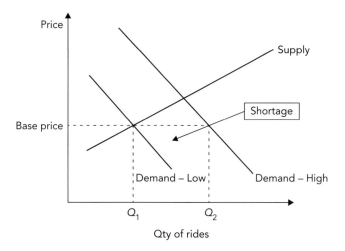

**Figure 2.4.1** Shortage in the market for ride-sharing

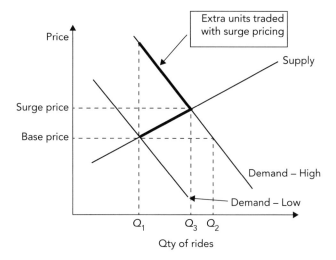

**Figure 2.4.2** The application of surge pricing in the market for ride-sharing

opportunity cost of the suppliers who they are trading with. In this way the 'Surge price' expands the amount of trade, and hence increases the overall wellbeing of market participants.

Perhaps it seems to you that we should be ending this case study here. We've seen how surge pricing works, and we've seen how it improves the wellbeing of market participants. What more can there be to say? Well, it turns out that there is quite a bit more to say. Despite the apparent boon that surge pricing constitutes for market participants, it has attracted trenchant criticism (Irwin 2017).

## The opposition to surge pricing

When it comes to listing criticisms of Uber's surge pricing, it is a matter of: Where to start? Sources of discontent include the excessive size of price increases that can happen with surge pricing; not knowing how the surge price is calculated; and the uncertainty that surge pricing imposes on riders and drivers (Prytz 2018). But the major complaint levelled against Uber's surge pricing is that it is unfair. Increasing the price for rides at times of high demand is regarded by many as akin to Uber exploiting its customers. No business likes to get criticism like this. But Uber probably shouldn't take it too personally. Because the feeling that surge pricing is unfair draws on beliefs about price setting by business that are deep rooted in the human psyche.

In a famous series of experiments in the 1980s, the Nobel Prize-winning economists Daniel Kahneman and Richard Thaler, together with a co-author Jack Knetsch, set out to determine what consumers regarded as fair price-setting behaviour by businesses. In one experiment they presented the following scenario (Kahneman et al., 1986, p. 729):

> A hardware store has been selling snow shovels for $15. The morning after a large snowstorm, the store raises the price to $20.

Participants in the experiment were asked to rate this behaviour as: (i) completely fair; (ii) acceptable; (iii) unfair; or (iv) very unfair. Over 80 per cent believed that the hardware store's behaviour was unfair or very unfair. Yet in other scenarios where the profits or existence of a business were threatened, participants thought it was reasonable to increase prices (or cut wages of employees). The conclusion that the authors drew from these experiments was that the community has a strongly negative attitude to price rises that are made by business in response to higher demand – especially where the increase in demand has not come about by any action of the business.

Studying Uber's surge pricing is a lesson in the practical value of the demand/supply model. But the opposition to surge pricing provides an equally important lesson about using economic concepts and models. The standard ways that economists judge a business practice or government policy, with concepts such as gains from trade and wellbeing, are not universally shared. For that reason, it is important to develop an appreciation of alternative perspectives, and to be willing to use them together with standard approaches when we analyse economic activity.

## KEY LESSONS

- Market intermediaries, such as Uber, are using information on demand and supply to adjust prices for the services they offer – in the same way as we would expect a perfectly competitive market to operate.

- An example is surge pricing, where in times of high demand Uber increases the price it charges to customers and the payment it makes to drivers.
- Just as the wellbeing of market participants is improved when the market price increases in response to a shortage, surge pricing at times of high demand can be argued to make drivers and riders better off by increasing the volume of rides completed.
- Major concerns are expressed about aspects of surge pricing – such as being an unfair exploitation of riders.

## EXTRA NOTES

* The author, Jeff Borland, is co-author of a research paper on the labour market for Uber drivers in Australia using prepared data supplied by Uber. He did not receive any payment from Uber for that research work nor for any activity undertaken for them.

## SOME QUESTIONS TO THINK ABOUT

1   Can you think of other markets where the idea of surge pricing (adjusting price upwards when there are abnormal increases in quantity demanded) might usefully be applied? Would the same criticisms be likely to arise as have been made of Uber's surge pricing?
2   Explain why variability in the price of Uber rides due to surge pricing is likely to be moderated where travellers have readily available substitutes such as public transport or other ride-sharing apps.

## REFERENCES

Hall, Jonathan, Kendrick, Cory & Nosko, Chris (2016), 'The effect of Uber's surge pricing: A case study', https://www.valuewalk.com/2015/09/uber-surge-pricing/, viewed 3 October 2019.

Irwin, Neil (2017), 'Why surge prices make us so mad. What Springsteen, Home Depot and a Nobel Prize winner know', *New York Times*, 14 October, https://www.nytimes.com/2017/10/14/upshot/why-surge-prices-make-us-so-mad-what-springsteen-home-depot-and-a-nobel-winner-know.html, viewed 8 October 2019.

Kahneman, Daniel, Knetsch, Jack & Thaler, Richard (1986), 'Fairness as a constraint on profit seeking: Entitlements in the market', *American Economic Review*, 76(4), pp. 728–41.

Prytz, Anna (2018), '$70 for 4 km: Commuter shock at Uber surge pricing during train chaos', *The Age*, 3 May, https://www.theage.com.au/national/victoria/70-for-4km-commuter-shock-at-uber-surge-pricing-during-train-chaos-20180503-p4zd2s.html, viewed 8 October 2019.

## IDEAS FOR FURTHER READING

*The Economist* (2016) reviews Uber's pricing policy in 'A fare shake' (14 May, p. 64). A more recent article (2019) assesses Uber's long-term prospects ('Can Uber ever make money?', 27 April, p. 58). Opposed views on the labour market for Uber drivers are presented in articles by Jonathan Hall and Alan Krueger (2018), 'An analysis of the labor market for Uber's driver-partners in the United States', *Industrial and Labor Relations Review*, 71(3), pp. 705–32; and Janine Berg and Hannah Johnston (2019), 'Too good to be true: A comment on Hall and Krueger's analysis of the labor market for Uber's driver-partners', *Industrial and Labor Relations Review*, 72(1), pp. 32–68.

Going on recent estimates, there are 152 million children aged five to 17 years in the global workforce today, including 73 million working in hazardous conditions. While the number of children in the workforce around the world has declined by about one-third since the start of the century, in many regions the incidence of child labour remains high – for example, over 21 per cent in Sub-Saharan Africa and around 10 per cent in Asia and the Pacific (ILO 2017).

The existence of child labour is first a human rights issue. As an example, an article on the banana industry in Ecuador has described conditions where:

> children as young as eight are forced to work 12-hour days on plantations where they are exposed to toxic chemicals and sexual harassment … based on interviews with 45 children … 40 said they had to continue working while toxic fungicides were sprayed from crop-dusters flying overhead. The children were paid an average wage of $3.50 a day, or less than 60% of the amount that is paid to an adult worker.

Source: *The Economist* (2002), p. 42.

A second adverse consequence of child labour is the creation of 'poverty traps'. Children taken out of schooling at an early age will not acquire a high level of skill or human capital, and hence are likely to remain in low-income jobs throughout their lives. Countries with high rates of child labour therefore have lower rates of educational attainment which in the long run translates into lower rates of economic growth.

It seems generally accepted that the main cause of child labour is poverty. Children from families with low incomes are more likely to be in paid employment. At the national level, the proportion of children working is also correlated with income levels; for example, as countries become richer, rates of child labour decrease, as has happened in China since the 1970s and in Vietnam in the 1990s.

Two main types of policies to reduce the use of child labour have been proposed. The first type, 'supply-side' policies, seeks to reduce the supply of child labour. Examples are schemes that offer rewards to children who attend school (for example, providing a midday meal or incentive payments for attendance) and programs that improve credit markets so that parents are able to borrow funds that allow them to keep their children in school. The second type, 'demand-side' policies, is intended to reduce demand for child labour by employers. Examples are bans on child labour, with fines for employers who do not comply, and international campaigns to boycott products made using child labour.

With different policies having been proposed to address the problem of child labour, the question arises as to which type of policy will work best. To examine this question, we can consider the effect of two specific policies: First, an incentive payment to children who remain in school; and, second, a ban by developed countries on imports produced using child labour. The incentive payment policy should reduce supply of child labour by raising the financial returns to families from having their children remain in school. The import ban policy is intended to reduce demand for child labour since businesses will not want their products to be prohibited from being sold in developed countries.

The effects of these policies on the use of child labour can be studied by examining how they change the market equilibrium. The difference in the equilibrium quantity of child labour employed prior to and after the introduction of a policy shows the impact of each policy. By comparing the size of the impacts on the equilibrium quantity, it is possible to see which policy is more effective in reducing the use of child labour.

Our particular focus will be on how the impact of each type of policy is affected by the relative size of the wage elasticities of demand for child labour and supply of child labour. These elasticities measure the responsiveness of labour demand and labour supply to a change in the wage rate. (Usually we refer to the price elasticity of demand or supply. But since the 'price' of labour is the wage, when we describe elasticity of labour demand or labour supply, it is more common to refer to the wage elasticity.)

---

### THEORY REFRESHER

#### What is elasticity?

Elasticity is how economists measure the responsiveness of demand and supply to their determinants. Knowing the elasticity of demand (supply) with respect to a determinant such as price tells you: (i) whether that determinant has a positive or negative effect on demand (supply), and (ii) the size of the effect.

The measure of elasticity used most often is the own-price elasticity of demand. This measure shows the percentage change in quantity demanded of a good when there is a 1 per cent increase in the price of the good. For example, knowing that the own-price elasticity of demand for petrol is −0.5 tells you that there is a negative relation between price and quantity demanded, and that a 1 per cent increase in the price of petrol causes a 0.5 per cent decrease in the quantity demanded of petrol. Own-price elasticity of demand is classified as being either price elastic or price inelastic. Where a change in price causes a more than proportionate change in quantity demanded, we say that demand is own-price elastic. Where a change in price causes a less than proportionate change in quantity demanded, then demand is said to be own-price inelastic. For example, if the own-price elasticity of demand for petrol is −0.5, this would mean that demand for petrol would be classified as own-price inelastic.

The own-price elasticity of demand for a product will depend upon its characteristics. For example, we would expect demand for a necessary good with few substitutes, such as medicine to treat a serious illness, to be price inelastic, whereas demand for a luxury good that has many substitutes would be price elastic.

A measure of the own-price elasticity of supply can be similarly defined as the percentage change in quantity supplied of a good when there is a 1 per cent increase in the price of that good. Where a change in price causes a more than proportionate change in quantity supplied, we again say that supply is own-price elastic; and where a change in price causes a less than proportionate change in quantity supplied, then supply is own-price inelastic.

To understand how elasticity matters, we need to make assumptions about the wage elasticities of demand for and supply of child labour. Suppose that we think of labour demand as being relatively wage elastic. This implies that an increase in the wage of a child worker will cause a relatively large decrease in demand for child labour. This seems a reasonable assumption where substitutes such as young adults are readily available to replace children. Suppose also that supply of child labour is relatively wage inelastic; that is, a decrease in the wage of child workers would cause a relatively small decrease in the supply of child labour. Where poverty imposes the need to earn income, and other potential sources of income are not readily available, it seems plausible that the supply of labour by children would be relatively wage inelastic. Examples of labour demand and labour supply curves that are consistent with these assumptions on elasticities are shown in *Figure 2.5.1*.

Our particular interest is to examine how the relative size of the wage elasticities of labour demand and labour supply affect the impact of the different types of policies. Therefore, we'd like to carry out our analysis in a way that makes it possible to attribute any difference we find in the effects of the policies to the effects of the wage elasticities. For that reason, we'll assume that the demand-side policy will shift the demand curve by exactly the same amount that the supply-side policy shifts the supply curve. Making this assumption rules out different effects of the policies due to the policies shifting demand

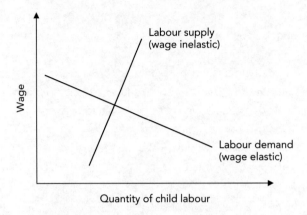

**Figure 2.5.1** Illustrating our assumptions on elasticities of labour demand and labour
supply

and supply by different magnitudes. Instead, any differences in the effects of the policies
must be due to the assumptions we have made about the elasticities of labour demand
and labour supply.

Changes in the equilibrium quantity of child labour used following the introduction
of each type of policy are shown in **Figures 2.5.2** and **2.5.3**. In each diagram, $Q_1$
represents the employment of child labour prior to the policy being introduced, and $Q_2$
is the quantity of child labour employed once the policy has been introduced.

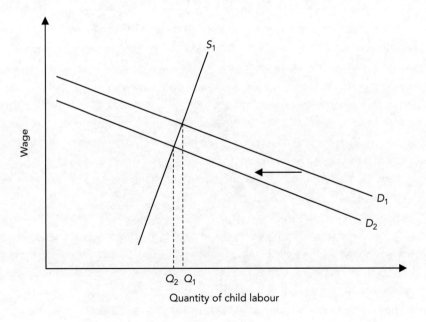

**Figure 2.5.2** Demand-side policy

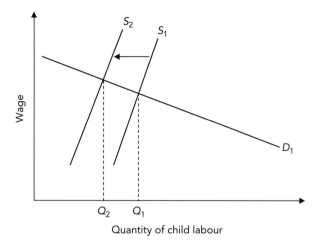

**Figure 2.5.3** Supply-side policy

The demand-side policy has a relatively small effect on the equilibrium amount of child labour employed. This can be seen from the small decrease in quantity from $Q_1$ to $Q_2$ in **Figure 2.5.2**. It is the degree of elasticity of labour supply with respect to wages that explains this effect on employment. The demand-side policy decreases labour demand (from $D_1$ to $D_2$ in **Figure 2.5.2**), which causes a shift along the labour supply curve to a new equilibrium. Because labour supply is relatively wage inelastic, the shift in demand mainly results in a decrease in wages and has little effect on the quantity of child labour employed.

In contrast, there is a much larger reduction in the equilibrium quantity of child labour when the supply-side policy is used. Here, it is the degree of elasticity of labour demand with respect to wages that explains this result. The supply-side policy reduces the supply of child labour (from $S_1$ to $S_2$ in **Figure 2.5.3**), which causes a shift up the labour demand curve to a new equilibrium. Because labour demand is relatively wage elastic, this mainly results in a decrease in the quantity of labour employed, with little effect on wages.

Hence, our analysis predicts that supply-side policies have a greater effect in reducing child labour than demand-side policies. This conclusion is, of course, conditional on labour supply being relatively wage inelastic and labour demand being relatively wage elastic, and on the assumption that the policies shift the labour demand and labour supply curves by equal amounts. There is a range of other factors that it would be necessary to take into account before deciding on the best policy for reducing child labour. For example, a criticism of demand-side policies such as product bans is that they may simply shift child labour involvement in the production of those banned goods to other undesirable activities, whereas supply-side policies, as well as reducing the use of child labour, may have additional valuable features, such as where free school lunches increase the benefits of schooling by making students better able to learn.

## KEY LESSONS

- Two main types of policies to reduce the use of child labour in developing economies have been proposed. Supply-side policies seek to reduce the supply of child labour, and demand-side policies are intended to reduce demand for child labour by employers.
- A policymaker would want to choose the type of policy that could achieve the largest decrease in the use of child labour. A potentially important influence on the effect of each type of policy on the use of child labour is the relative size of the wage elasticities of labour demand and labour supply.
- Where labour demand is relatively wage elastic and labour supply is relatively wage inelastic, and both types of policy shift the demand or supply curve by the same magnitude, supply-side policies will be more effective in reducing the use of child labour.

## SOME QUESTIONS TO THINK ABOUT

1. For each of the following goods, which good would you expect to have the higher degree of own-price elasticity of demand? Why?
   a   car-repair manuals – mystery novels
   b   soft drink – water
   c   pharmaceutical drugs for heart conditions – personal fitness trainers
2. What is the relative efficacy of demand-side and supply-side policies if labour demand is relatively wage inelastic and labour supply is relatively wage elastic? How would you explain this finding?
3. Alan Accountant and Edwina Economist are debating the optimal policy for government to apply to reduce illicit drug use. Alan says: 'We know that the demand for illicit drugs is own-price inelastic, and that the supply of those drugs is own-price elastic. Therefore, the government will have most impact in reducing illicit drug use if it puts more emphasis on policies that reduce supply rather than policies that reduce demand'. Edwina says: 'I agree with your description of the price elasticity of demand for and supply of illicit drugs. But you have made the wrong policy recommendation. The government can have most impact in reducing illicit drug use if it puts more emphasis on policies that reduce demand rather than policies that reduce supply.'

   Who is correct, Alan or Edwina?

# REFERENCES

International Labour Organization (2017), 'Global estimates of child labour', https://
www.ilo.org/wcmsp5/groups/public/—dgreports/—dcomm/documents/
publication/wcms_575499.pdf, viewed 17 September 2019.
*The Economist* (2002), 'Banana skins', 27 April, p. 42.

# IDEAS FOR FURTHER READING

Articles by Eric Edmonds (2008, 'Child labor', chapter 58 in J. Strauss and T. Paul Schultz (eds), *Handbook of Development Economics Volume IV*, Elsevier) and by Esteban Ortiz-Ospina and Max Roser (2019), 'Child labor' (https://ourworldindata.org/child-labor, viewed 17 September 2019) survey evidence of the causes and consequences of child labour. A recent episode that received attention – of child labour being used in horrendous conditions to mine cobalt in the Congo – is described in an article by Siddharth Kara in 'Is your phone tainted by the misery of 35,000 children in Congo's mines?' (*The Guardian*, 12 October 2018, https://www.theguardian.com/global-development/2018/oct/12/phone-misery-children-congo-cobalt-mines-drc, viewed 1 October 2019).

The study of child labour is an example of the field of economics known as development economics – essentially the study of the economies of developing countries. To find out more about this area, visit web pages devoted to prominent researchers in development economics such as Esther Duflo (http://economics.mit.edu/faculty/eduflo) and Michael Kremer (https://scholar.harvard.edu/kremer).

Ultimately, the questions that most interest economists are about standards of living and wellbeing. What is the level of material wellbeing in a country? Why does material wellbeing differ between countries? How do governments affect wellbeing? Much of the practical relevance of economics lies in helping to answer these questions.

To answer questions about wellbeing of course means that we need a way to measure it. Economists do this by defining a society's level of wellbeing as the net gains that consumers and producers obtain by engaging in consumption, production and trade.

---

### THEORY REFRESHER

#### Surplus and the net gain from trade

Economists measure society's wellbeing from engaging in trade as the net gain in wellbeing to consumers and producers compared to the situation that would exist if they did not trade. For consumers in a market, this net gain is defined as 'consumer surplus'. This is the difference between the amount that consumers would have been willing to pay for whatever quantity of the product they obtain through trade and the amount that they actually are required to pay. For suppliers in a market, the net gain is defined as 'producer surplus'. This is the difference between the amount that suppliers receive as payment for the quantity of the product they supply and the minimum amount they would have been willing to accept to supply that quantity. The total net gain in wellbeing to society from trade in a market, referred to as total surplus, is the sum of consumer surplus and producer surplus.

Consumers' willingness to pay for a product is represented by the market demand curve. The minimum price at which suppliers are willing to supply a product is represented by the market supply curve. The market price represents the amount that consumers pay, and that suppliers will receive, from engaging in trade. Consumer surplus is therefore equal to the area under the demand curve and above the market price; and producer surplus is the area below the market price and above the supply curve. These areas are shown in *Figure 2.6.1*. Society's total surplus from trade, consumer surplus plus producer surplus, is the sum of the two areas; that is, the area under the demand curve and above the supply curve for the quantity traded of the good or service.

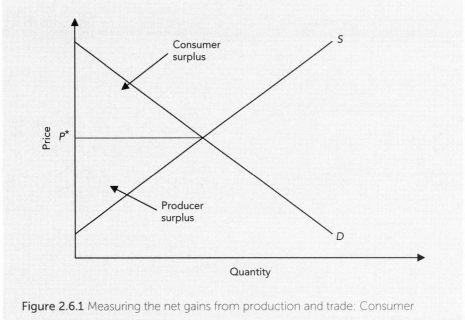

**Figure 2.6.1** Measuring the net gains from production and trade: Consumer surplus and producer surplus

A major application of the measures of wellbeing occurred in Australia in the 1990s. At that time, the Australian Government had to decide whether mining activity should be allowed within the Kakadu Conservation Zone (KCZ), an area of 50 sq km within Kakadu National Park in the Northern Territory. Allowing mining would mean that the valuable deposits of gold, platinum and palladium in the KCZ could be extracted. But this would come at the cost of damage to the environment in the KCZ, especially the headwaters of the South Alligator River. Whether allowing mining in the KCZ would be socially optimal therefore depended on a comparison of the benefits and costs to Australian society. Supposing the value of mineral resources was greater than the costs of environmental damage, it would be optimal to allow mining to proceed, but otherwise mining should not be allowed.

In order to decide whether allowing mining in the KCZ would be socially optimal, the government needed measures of the benefits and costs of mining. This is where consumer surplus and producer surplus came in. Benefits from extra mining activity could be measured as the gain in producer surplus, and costs of mining as the loss in consumer surplus from the reduced quality of environment at the KCZ. *Figure 2.6.2* shows these measures of surplus.

The gain in producer surplus from mining activity in the KCZ was calculated using geological data to estimate the volume of output, forecasts of prices of the minerals to be extracted from the KCZ and data on the costs of production. Using this approach, the gain in producer surplus was estimated to be $102 million.

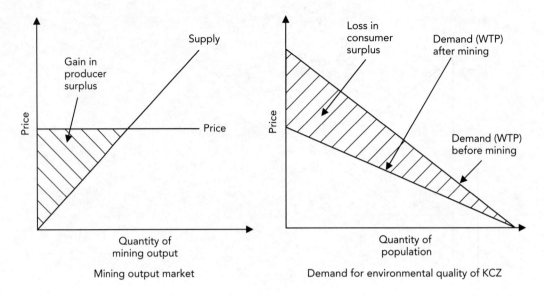

**Figure 2.6.2** Changes to producer surplus and consumer surplus from mining activity in the KCZ

Measurement of the loss in consumer surplus was done by comparing the value that the Australian population placed on the environmental quality of the KCZ with and without the mining activity. Information on the value placed on environmental quality in the KCZ was therefore needed to calculate the loss in consumer surplus. Obtaining this information was not straightforward. Measuring the loss resulting from a lower quality of environment in the KCZ could not be done, for example, by observing the price of environmental quality, because there is no market in which 'environmental quality' is traded. Hence, the Australian Government used an alternative approach, a method known as contingent valuation (CV). This method uses surveys to elicit respondents' willingness to pay for some good, service, or program. Valuations revealed by respondents are 'contingent', as they depend on a constructed or simulated market that is described in the survey. The CV method is most often applied as a way of obtaining society's valuations of items that will not or cannot be traded in markets.

Survey respondents randomly chosen from throughout Australia were asked to state the size of payment they would be willing to make out of their take-home pay to retain the KCZ in its current state; that is, to prevent environmental damage from mining activity. This hypothetical payment was interpreted as being a measure of the loss that each respondent would experience due to environmental damage to the KCZ. This is represented as the vertical gap between the demand curves in *Figure 2.6.2*. Surveys were undertaken face-to-face so that respondents could be given a detailed description of the current state of the KCZ and how it would be affected by mining. This included maps and photographs.

How much value did society place on preventing damage to the KCZ? *Figure 2.6.3* provides data on the distribution of survey responses on willingness to pay for preventing environmental damage in the KCZ. It shows that over 35 per cent of respondents were willing to pay more than $250 per annum to avoid the damage to the KCZ that would be caused by the proposed mining activity, and almost 70 per cent were willing to pay at least $2 per annum. The willingness to pay of the median member of the Australian population was between $50 and $100.

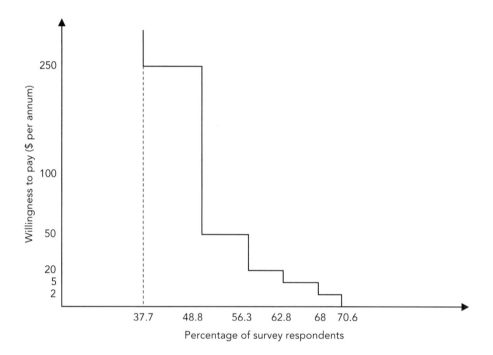

**Figure 2.6.3** Willingness to pay to avoid environmental damage to the KCZ

*Source:* Carson, Wilks & Imber (1994).

It is probably not surprising that people planning to visit Kakadu would be willing to make a large contribution to avoid the environmental damage caused by mining. But as only a small proportion of the Australian population is ever likely to visit Kakadu, how do we explain the relatively large amounts that survey respondents indicated they would be willing to pay? A possible explanation for why even those in the population who were not planning to visit Kakadu were willing to pay for its preservation is known as 'existence value'. This is the idea that we can gain satisfaction from the knowledge that areas within Australia with high environmental value exist and are being maintained in their current states.

Using the survey data, the loss in consumer surplus from environmental damage to the KCZ was calculated by assuming that the median willingness to pay to prevent damage to the KCZ was representative of the loss imposed on each Australian household. Aggregating over all households, the loss in consumer surplus from environmental damage to Kakadu from mining activity was therefore estimated to be $435 million. A comparison of producer surplus and consumer surplus, $102 million against $435 million, revealed that going ahead with mining activity in the KCZ would reduce the level of wellbeing in Australia. Hence, the socially optimal decision was to not proceed with mining activity at Kakadu. This was also the decision that was made at the time by the Australian Government.

## KEY LESSONS

- Estimating wellbeing in a society can be done using a measure of the net gain in wellbeing that households and producers obtain by engaging in consumption, production and trade.
- The consumer surplus and producer surplus measures of wellbeing can be applied to evaluate the effects of government policy on society's wellbeing.
- An important application of these measures was the Australian Government assessing whether or not to allow mining activity in the KCZ in the early 1990s. This was done by comparing the gain in producer surplus from the extra mining activity with the loss in consumer surplus from reduced environmental quality in the KCZ.

## SOME QUESTIONS TO THINK ABOUT

1 What are some other examples of types of goods or services for which you might need to apply a CV method in order to estimate willingness to pay? What do you think might be some of the main criticisms of the CV method?

2 There are five potential suppliers of a car wash service. Sally, Simon, Sonia, Stewart and Sam are each willing to provide one car wash. Their respective opportunity costs are $1, $3, $5, $7 and $9. There are five potential consumers of the car wash service. Cate, Colin, Chloe, Chris and Cassie are each willing to purchase one car wash. The respective amounts they are willing to pay are $16, $13, $10, $7 and $4. Trade of car washes occurs in a perfectly competitive market. What will be the consumer surplus and producer surplus in the competitive market equilibrium?

3 Use the concepts of consumer surplus and producer surplus to describe how the creation of kidney exchange markets (case study 1.5) has improved the wellbeing of participants in those markets.

## REFERENCE

Carson, Richard, Wilks, Leanne & Imber, David (1994), 'Valuing the preservation of Australia's Kakadu zone', Oxford Economic Papers, vol. 46, pp. 727–49.

# IDEAS FOR FURTHER READING

For excellent discussions of the strengths and weaknesses of the contingent valuation methodology, see articles by Richard Carson (2012, 'Contingent valuation: A practical alternative when prices aren't available', *Journal of Economic Perspectives*, 26(4), pp. 27–42) and Jerry Hausman (2012, 'Contingent valuation: From dubious to hopeless', *Journal of Economic Perspectives*, 26(4), pp. 43–56).

What are the occupations we love to hate? According to most surveys on this topic, the occupations with the lowest prestige are politician, real estate agent and – the worst of the worst – used car salesman. If it were up to Sir Bob Geldof, though, another group would be rated below all these occupations – ticket scalpers.

In 2005, Sir Bob organised the Live8 concert in England with the objective of raising funds to provide food and other aid for poor countries. Tickets to the concert were randomly assigned to people who had entered a lottery. When Sir Bob found out that some of the lucky winners were seeking to sell their tickets on eBay, he was none too pleased, accusing them of 'sick profiteering' and also describing eBay as an 'electronic pimp' (*The Economist* 2005, p. 50). Scalpers, it must be said, do not have a lot of friends. Reselling of football tickets has been illegal in the United Kingdom since 1994, while in the United States, more than a dozen states have had legal restrictions on scalping for over a decade (*The Economist* 2006, p. 65). In Australia, the Victorian government has the power to nominate 'declared events' for which it is illegal to resell tickets for more than 10 per cent above face value (Preiss & Cherney 2018).

Not everyone, however, thinks that scalping is bad. And you guessed it, economists are at the head of this group. For them, ticket scalping is just another way of improving wellbeing through voluntary trade.

The argument for how scalping can improve wellbeing is pretty straightforward. In order for the original owner of a ticket to an event and a buyer of that ticket to be willing to trade, we know that they must both be made better off by doing this. As both buyer and seller are better off, therefore society is better off.

We can illustrate this argument using the example of the Rose Bowl, a major end-of-season game for US college football. In 2006, tickets to this event were officially sold for US$175, but were subsequently reported to have been resold, or scalped, on the internet for as much as US$3000 (*The Economist* 2006, p. 65). Because trade occurred, we know that the buyer must have valued the ticket to the Rose Bowl at more than US$3000, and the original ticket owner at less than US$3000. For example, perhaps the original owner of the Rose Bowl ticket valued going to the event at $500 and the buyer valued attending the event at $5000. Through scalping, the resource of the ticket to the Rose Bowl, which would have provided a benefit of US$500 to society, if the ticket was retained by the original owner, instead now provides a benefit of US$5000. Total surplus to society has been increased by the difference between the values that the buyer and the original owner place on the ticket; that is, US$4500.

The same intuition can be applied in the case of Sir Bob's Live8 concert. *Figure 2.7.1* shows how we might think about this example. A fixed quantity of tickets, $\bar{Q}$, was available for the concert. These tickets were to be assigned at a zero price to individuals wanting to attend the concert. Hence, we would expect that all individuals who had a value of attending the concert greater than zero would enter the lottery. (This ignores any cost of entering the lottery, such as the time taken to process an application on the internet, but this was negligible.) Suppose that the number of individuals who have a willingness to pay to attend the concert of zero or greater equals $Q^*$. This includes some consumers who have a relatively high willingness to pay (segment A of the demand curve in *Figure 2.7.1*) and other consumers with a lower willingness to pay (segment B on the demand curve). Suppose that when the price is zero, demand exceeds supply, so that $Q^*$ is greater than $\bar{Q}$. With excess demand, the concert organisers must have some way of rationing the available supply of tickets between all those wanting to attend. In the case of the Live8 concert, this was done by a lottery. Each of the $Q^*$ individuals was therefore given an equal probability of $\bar{Q}/Q^*$ of attending the concert. For example, where $\bar{Q} = 5000$ and $Q^* = 10\ 000$, each individual would have a one-half chance of being assigned a ticket in the lottery. Allocating tickets by lottery implies that an individual at any point on the demand curve has an equal likelihood of receiving a ticket.

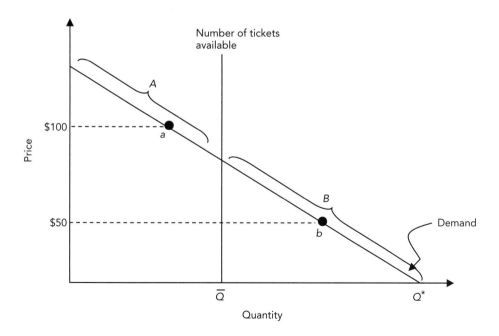

**Figure 2.7.1** Demand for tickets at the Live8 concert

The problem is that this is not an efficient allocation. An efficient allocation requires assigning the tickets in a way that maximises the total surplus to society. For the example of the Live8 concert, total surplus equals consumer surplus. Once the decision has been made to make available $\bar{Q}$ tickets, consumer surplus is maximised only if the tickets are allocated to the $\bar{Q}$ individuals who value them most highly; that is, the individuals in segment A on the demand curve in *Figure 2.7.1*.

---

### THEORY REFRESHER

#### What is efficiency?

Efficiency is where: (i) the quantity of a good or service traded in a market; and (ii) allocation of production and consumption of that good or service between (respectively) suppliers and buyers, are such that society's wellbeing is maximised. Society's wellbeing is measured as the total surplus that buyers and sellers gain from engaging in consumption, production and trade. Hence, efficiency implies that the total surplus to society is maximised.

Efficiency provides a benchmark for the best possible market outcome that can be achieved for society. An important example of an efficient outcome is the equilibrium in a perfectly competitive market. The total surplus that society can achieve from trade in a perfectly competitive market is maximised at the equilibrium. At the total quantity traded in equilibrium, all units of the good or service are being traded for which a consumer has a greater willingness to pay than the opportunity cost for a supplier to provide that unit. Equilibrium also has the property that units of the good or service that are traded are provided by suppliers with the lowest opportunity cost of supplying those units, and bought by consumers with the highest valuation or willingness to pay for those units.

---

It is because the lottery system caused an inefficient allocation of tickets to the Live8 concert that scalping could make society better off. Suppose there is an individual who has been allocated a ticket from the lottery who values attending the concert at $50, and another individual who would get $100 of value from attending the concert but has not been allocated a ticket. These individuals are represented respectively as points b and a on the demand curve in *Figure 2.7.1*. The individual who has been allocated a ticket can offer to sell that ticket to the individual who has not been allocated a ticket. At any price between $50 and $100, they would both be willing to trade. For example, at a price of $75, each will obtain a net gain of $25 and be made better off. When both individuals are better off, it follows that society is made better off. Total surplus from the trade is $50. In this way, as a commentary on the Live8 concert noted, scalping is 'increasing economic efficiency by reallocating resources from those who value them little to those who value them a lot' (*The Economist* 2005, p. 50).

As well, it is not just these two individuals who should be able to trade. Using exactly the same argument, anyone who is in segment B of the demand curve in *Figure 2.7.1* and who has been allocated a ticket should be able to trade with a person in segment A who has not been allocated a ticket. Therefore, if there is sufficient scope for scalping to occur, eventually trade would achieve an efficient distribution of tickets, where all tickets are in the hands of the $\bar{Q}$ individuals who value them most highly.

Despite the efficiency gains from allowing scalping, there may, however, be other reasons why ticket scalping should concern us. First, as well as efficiency, a government or event promoter may also care about equity. Willingness to pay for tickets would be expected to be related to income. Hence, allocating tickets just to those who value them most highly may mean allocating tickets only to the rich. So, by enforcing the allocation of tickets by lottery, every member of society is given an opportunity to attend events such as the Live8 concert. (Of course, a counter-argument is that low-income members of society, who attach a low value to attending the concert and are allocated tickets, are made even better off if they can sell them for a higher price.) Second, there may be other aspects of efficiency that we need to take into account. Giving out free tickets to events such as the Live8 concert may produce extra publicity or goodwill that will ultimately generate a higher amount of donations. Or perhaps governments feel they are promoting a materialistic culture by allowing scalping and want to avoid this effect. Having one of these explanations regarding equity or some other aspect of efficiency is what you would need to convince an economist that bans on ticket scalping are justified. Otherwise, scalping is simply another way that trade can improve wellbeing.

## KEY LESSONS

- Ticket scalping is an example of voluntary trade between a buyer and a seller. Such trade will only occur where both buyer and seller are made better off. This implies that the activity of scalping is improving society's wellbeing.
- Bans on ticket scalping will reduce society's wellbeing where there is not some other rationale for such a restriction. This rationale might be the adverse equity implications of allowing scalping, or other indirect efficiency consequences such as reducing public goodwill towards an event where scalping is allowed to occur.

## SOME QUESTIONS TO THINK ABOUT

1   Consider the system for selling tickets for the Commerce Students' Society (CSS) Ball at the University of Melbourne. There is a pre-announced time (usually early on a Monday morning) at which tickets go on sale, and a pre-announced price per ticket. To obtain tickets, you must be at the venue when ticket sales begin, which means you are likely to have to queue the night before tickets go on sale.

a   Do you think such a system is likely to leave scope for welfare-improving trade between students who have obtained tickets and students who have not obtained tickets?

b   Do you think the scope for ticket scalping would increase or decrease if the CSS shifted to an alternative system where there is a pre-announced time at which tickets are made available for sale via the internet?

c   If there is excess demand at the price at which the CSS sells tickets to the ball, as evidenced by the long queues and people's willingness to sleep overnight outside in the cold, why do you think the CSS doesn't increase ticket prices?

2   Suppose that all tickets to an upcoming Ashes Test series between England and Australia have been sold or otherwise allocated. Suppose as well that you don't own any tickets. Assuming that ticket scalping is legal, can you think of ways in which it might be possible for you to make money from scalping, even though you don't own any tickets?

3   Can you think of a way to sell tickets to concerts and sporting events that would mean that consumers who valued attending those events most highly are assigned tickets, hence removing the scope for ticket scalping?

# REFERENCES

Preiss, Benjamin & Cherny, Daniel (2018), 'All AFL finals to be protected by anti-scalping laws', *The Age*, 9 May, https://www.theage.com.au/sport/afl/all-afl-finals-to-be-protected-by-anti-scalping-laws-20180509-p4zeby.html, viewed 17 September 2019.

*The Economist* (2005), 'Fair trade', 18 June, p. 50.

*The Economist* (2006), 'Free-market fleecing', 7 January, p. 65.

# IDEAS FOR FURTHER READING

Restrictions on ticket scalping are one example of how impediments to trade can adversely affect wellbeing in a society. The 'value of trade and markets' is a popular theme in many books – see chapter 2 of John McMillan's *Reinventing the Bazaar* (2002, W.W. Norton) and chapter 3 of Tim Harford's *The Undercover Economist* (2006, Oxford University Press). Paul Crosy and Jordi McKenzie provide a thorough introduction to the economics of scalping in an article in *The Conversation* ('The economics of ticket scalping', 11 September 2017, https://theconversation.com/the-economics-of-ticket-scalping-83434, viewed 1 October 2019).

A constant refrain in the aftermath of the Global Financial Crisis (GFC) was the need to punish those responsible; and in the minds of most people, right at the top of the list were Wall Street financiers. Edolphus Towns, the Democrat Chair of the US House of Representatives Oversight Committee, was typical of those expressing concern when he told Congress in 2009 that Americans didn't resent seeing someone make a lot of money, but they did resent executives at financial institutions which were bailed out by the government still being paid high salaries.

Calls to regulate the pay of banking sector executives reflected two main concerns. First, there was a feeling that the executives needed to take their share of the pain caused by the GFC. Second, high compensation was argued to be a source of the excessive risk-taking by banks that had caused the GFC.

To bail out the banking sector, it had been necessary for the US Government to make large payments and loans to banks and other financial institutions, and the source of these payments was taxpayer funds. Justice therefore seemed to demand that banking executives' compensation should be reined in. Yet, as *The Economist* (2009a) noted, this was not happening. Banks making losses, such as Citigroup and Bank of America, were still paying large bonuses; and, somewhat incredibly, Merrill Lynch made cash payments to staff worth over 100 per cent of its remaining capital. If it was only shareholders paying for this behaviour, it might merely have raised eyebrows. But these were the same banks that had been bailed out by taxpayers; the bonuses were coming out of subsidies provided by taxpayers. In the absence of a willingness by the banking sector to self-regulate compensation paid to executives, it seemed to many that this regulation needed to be provided by government.

High executive pay in the banking sector was also seen as a source of the financial market instability that had created the GFC. The GFC had many causes, but undoubtedly a primary reason was excessive risk-taking within the banking sector. One of the explanations for why these risks were taken was that the returns were so high. Taking risks meant you could get paid a lot of money. Like Howie Hubler, the man in charge of subprime mortgages at Morgan Stanley, who was reputed to be earning US$25 million a year. As a result of his risk-taking, Morgan Stanley is estimated to have lost US$9.2 billion, the single largest trading loss in the history of Wall Street (Lewis 2010). University of Chicago economist Raghuram Rajan said of the incentives for fund managers in the lead-up to the GFC:

> If she [a fund manager] wants to attract substantial inflows of new money, which is the key to being paid large amounts, she has to give the appearance of superior performance … What then is a manager to do? The answer for many is to take on tail risk … Suppose a financial manager decides to write earthquake insurance policies but does not tell her investors. As she writes policies and collects premiums, she will increase her firm's earnings. Moreover, because earthquakes occur rarely, no claims will be made for a long time. If a manager does not set aside reserves for the eventual payouts that will be needed, she will be feted as the new Warren Buffett: all the premiums she collects will be seen as pure returns.

Source: Rajan (2010), p. 138.

So, the thinking went, to reduce the risk-taking behaviour that had brought on the biggest financial crisis since the Great Depression, the scope for bankers to earn such high pay had to be limited.

No doubt partly motivated by public concerns, US President Barack Obama and the US Congress moved in the late 2000s to introduce new regulations controlling the compensation of banking sector executives. For the top five executives plus the next 20 highest-paid employees of any organisation that had received taxpayer funds through the Troubled Asset Relief Program (TARP), the US Treasury assumed the right to limit bonus payments (Davies 2009). (Bonus payments are in principle not part of a worker's guaranteed pay, and are only paid ex-post to workers as a reward for good performance.) For example, in 2009 the US Treasury knocked back proposed bonus payments by AIG and Citigroup (Jenkins et al. 2009).

You might think this would have made everyone happy. But no. Despite there being general support for the regulation of bankers' pay, the way in which the US Government decided to regulate pay did not win widespread approval. Analysis of the Obama administration's policy of imposing an upper limit on bonus payments suggested two main potential adverse consequences. First, there were concerns that the regulation might restrict the supply of talented executives to the banking sector. Second, whether the policy could even be implemented was questionable.

The US Treasury's right to regulate the bonus pay of banking executives was confined to those firms that had received government funding under TARP. Hence, other firms in the finance sector, or companies in other industries, could continue to make unrestricted bonus payments. This raised the possibility that more talented executives at the regulated banking firms would move to work elsewhere – specifically, firms where they could get higher pay. Hence, the regulated banking firms would be left with a less talented group of executives. Exactly those businesses that most needed good management would then see the quality of their executives falling due to the government regulation of pay.

The idea that limiting banking executives' pay might affect the supply of executives may sound familiar to you. That's because setting an upper limit on what banking executives are paid is just another example of the policy of setting a maximum price in a market. And when we analyse how setting a maximum price affects outcomes in a perfectly competitive market, we reach the conclusion that its main effect is to reduce the quantity traded. This is exactly the consequence of regulation of the pay of banking executives that was identified.

## THEORY REFRESHER

### How does a price ceiling affect market outcomes?

A price ceiling is a government regulation that specifies a maximum price above which trade in a market is not allowed to occur. Common examples are rent controls that specify a maximum price for rental accommodation and price controls imposed during wartime to restrict inflation.

Where a specified price ceiling is below the equilibrium price at which trade would otherwise occur, we would expect that the market price will now be equal to that maximum price. At the price ceiling, the quantity traded in the market will equal the quantity supplied. This quantity will be below the equilibrium quantity. (This depends, of course, on the maximum price being below the equilibrium price – if the maximum price is above the equilibrium price, then it will not affect the market outcome.)

The effect of a price ceiling on the market price and quantity traded is shown in *Figure 2.8.1*. Imposing the maximum price causes a reduction in the quantity traded to $Q_{Max}P$.

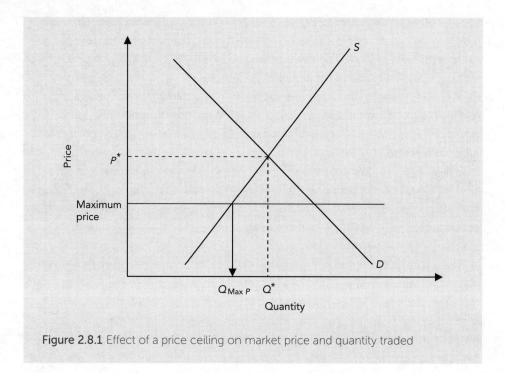

**Figure 2.8.1** Effect of a price ceiling on market price and quantity traded

Some commentators therefore saw imposing an upper limit on pay for executives as a problem, as it would reduce the supply of executives to firms where the pay limit applied. Other commentators, however, did not see this as a problem. This wasn't because they disagreed that imposing a maximum price could reduce supply. Instead, they just didn't believe that the pay of bankers would be restricted by the Obama administration's policy. In their view, there were so many ways for banking firms to avoid the policy that attempts by the US Treasury to impose an upper limit on pay for executives would inevitably fail.

A major component of the Obama administration's regulation of executives' pay was to limit bonus payments. But bonus payments are only one part of an executive's total pay. This meant that the regulated banking firms could offset the effect of the limit on bonus payments by increasing other components of the executives' total pay packages. Some attempts were made to limit these other components of pay, including a restriction on offering executives at the regulated firms more than US$25 000 in benefits such as country club memberships and company cars (Davies 2009). Nevertheless, changing the structure of compensation to undo the effects of the government-imposed limits on bonuses did seem to happen. One report, for example, described how the 'trend is to increase base pay in light of the reduced bonuses' (Kelly & Enrich 2009). Forced to reduce the size of bonus payments for good performance, regulated banking firms made up for this by paying higher guaranteed annual salaries.

Getting around limits on pay or prices in this way is nothing new. Another occasion on which the United States sought to regulate CEOs' pay was in the 1990s 'when Bill Clinton signed a law restricting the tax deductibility of executive pay to $1 million. This merely prompted a burst of creativity. Perks were devised that got around the cap' (*The Economist* 2009b).

The imposition of maximum prices has also commonly been used during wartime in an attempt to stem price inflation, which might otherwise have occurred due to shortages of consumer goods. A consequence was the creation of 'black markets', where producers and buyers made unauthorised trades at prices above the legal maximum.

A notorious example of the effect of imposing a price ceiling is rent control in New York, where 'black markets and bribery thrive' (*The Economist* 2003). Having a regulated rental price that is below the market equilibrium price implies there will be an excess demand for rental housing. Hence, rental property owners must have some means of rationing supply, and one method is to ask existing or prospective tenants for extra 'side-payments'.

None of this is to say that we shouldn't worry about the pay of executives in the banking sector. After the GFC, it can hardly be argued that the system is not broken. So, if setting a maximum limit on executive pay isn't the answer, then what can governments do? Well, several suggestions have been made. One proposal was to impose a super payroll tax on high salaries (*The Economist* 2009b). This would raise the cost to firms of paying high salaries and enable the government to recover some of the public funds provided to the banking sector. A second proposal, intended to more directly address the sources of high executive pay, was to give shareholders a greater role in pay-setting (*The Economist* 2009c). This proposal derived from a belief that excessive pay for executives has occurred where management and company boards are insufficiently accountable for their decisions. A third proposal suggested banks should be forced to repay public funds by requiring them to make payments into an insurance account that would be used to fund future bank bailouts (*The Economist* 2009a).

## KEY LESSONS

- A frequently expressed concern following the GFC was that the pay of US banking sector executives needed to be regulated – partly to prevent them from unfairly benefiting from taxpayer-funded bailouts, and partly to reduce excessive risk-taking in the banking sector.
- Notwithstanding the general desire for regulating bankers' pay, proposals to do this by setting a maximum limit on bonus payments were seen as potentially flawed. This was because the limit could be easily avoided, and where it was effective, it would cause a decline in the supply of talented executives to banking firms where pay was regulated.

■ In other instances where price ceilings have been applied by governments, such as rent controls in New York or wartime price controls, it has also been observed that market participants will try to undo the effects of the price ceilings, and that price ceilings can reduce supply to the market.

## SOME QUESTIONS TO THINK ABOUT

1  An article in *The Economist* (2003) described how two-thirds of New York's two million rental apartments are subject to some form of price restraint, with a city board setting allowable rent increases for those apartments each year. It is well known that economists oppose such price controls – regarding them as the cause of reduced supply and market inefficiencies. Less known is that economists also think these policies are likely to do more harm than good for the population they are intended to help – that of low-income households.

    a  Why might policymakers in New York think that rent control would assist low-income households?

    b  How could a policy that lowers the price of rental accommodation actually make low-income households worse off?

    c  Can you suggest a better policy for improving access to housing for low-income households?

2  Suppose demand for and supply of labour in Australia are:

$$\text{Demand} = 2000 - 50W; \text{Supply} = 1000 + 50W$$

(where demand and supply are expressed in total hours worked, and $W$ = hourly wage rate (dollars)).

    a  What would be the equilibrium hourly wage rate and quantity of labour employed in the absence of any government intervention in the market?

    b  Suppose that the Australian Government imposes a minimum wage of $15 per hour for workers. What will be the effect on the market outcome? How does this relate to arguments by business in Australia that minimum wages reduce employment?

    c  Explain how the effect on the quantity of labour employed due to the introduction of the minimum wage will depend on whether the own-wage elasticity of demand is elastic or inelastic. How might your answer to this question be related to the argument in *The Economist* (2013) that the introduction of Britain's minimum wage in 1999 had no notable impact on jobs?

    d  Are there other effects of a minimum wage that need to be taken into account to judge whether it provides a net gain to society?

# REFERENCES

Davies, Anne (2009), 'Obama cuts Wall Street salaries', *The Age*, 23 October, p. 13.

Jenkins, P., Murphy, M., Guerrara, F. & Braithwaite, T. (2009), 'A revival of fortunes', *Financial Times*, 17/18 October, p. 8.

Kelly, Kate & Enrich, David (2009), 'Companies study ways to beat salary caps', *The Australian*, business section, 18 March, p. 19.

Lewis, Michael (2010), *The Big Short: Inside the Doomsday Machine*, W.W. Norton.

Rajan, Raghuram (2010), *Fault Lines,* Princeton University Press.

*The Economist* (2003), 'The great Manhattan rip-off', 7 June, p. 69.

*The Economist* (2009a), 'Compensation claim', 24 October, pp. 17–18.

*The Economist* (2009b), 'Cui bono?', 12 December, pp. 56–7.

*The Economist* (2009c), 'Paying the piper', 7 February, pp. 56–57.

*The Economist* (2013), 'Trickle up economics', 13 February, p. 34.

# IDEAS FOR FURTHER READING

The Productivity Commission report on *Executive Remuneration* (2010) provides an overview of the evolution of executive pay in Australia and makes recommendations on how to regulate such pay. There are many excellent accounts of the GFC. Andrew Ross Sorkin's book *Too Big to Fail* (2009, Penguin) is a blow-by-blow retelling of the main events of the crisis in 2008. *After the Music Stopped: The Financial Crisis, the Response and the Work Ahead* by Alan Blinder (2013, Penguin) is about why the crisis occurred and the policy responses that followed. The account which goes the furthest in seeking to understand the origins of the GFC is by Raghuram Rajan, *Fault Lines* (2010, Princeton University Press). Alex Edmans, Xavier Gabaix and Dirk Jenter review evidence on CEO pay in their article 'Executive compensation: A survey of theory and evidence' (2017, National Bureau of Economic Research Working Paper no. 23596).

At midnight on 26 April 2008, the Australian Government increased the rate of tax on pre-mixed 'alcopop' drinks by 70 per cent. The government justified the increase as being part of its attempt to 'tackle binge drinking among teenagers' (Gordon & Harrison 2008). Not everyone, however, accepted that the extra tax would achieve its objective. Opposition parties argued that the consumption of alcopop drinks was unlikely to decrease, and that any decrease would be offset by increased consumption of other alcoholic drinks.

So, should the government have introduced the tax on alcopops? Was this just window-dressing or were policymakers justified in thinking that the tax could reduce alcohol consumption? Well, even before assessing how the tax actually affected drinking behaviour, as an economist you would have been able to advise on these questions. The theory of how an indirect tax affects price and the quantity traded in a perfectly competitive market would have given you everything you needed to provide the advice.

---

### THEORY REFRESHER

#### How does an indirect tax affect market outcomes?

Indirect taxes are taxes imposed on the trade of goods and services in markets. Suppliers or consumers are required to make a payment to the government for each unit of the good or service traded. A quantity tax is an indirect tax where the amount that must be paid is fixed per unit traded. A value tax is where the amount of tax that must be paid is a percentage of the price at which the product is traded.

Where an indirect tax is applied to a good or service, it introduces a wedge between the price that is paid by consumers and the price that is received by suppliers – the size of the wedge is equal to the tax payment to the government.

The relation between the price paid by consumers and the price received by suppliers can be expressed as:

$$\text{Quantity tax: } P_D = P_S + t$$

$$\text{Value tax: } P_D = P_S(1 + t)$$

where $P_D$ and $P_S$ are the prices paid by consumers and the prices received by suppliers, respectively.

How does the imposition of an indirect tax affect market outcomes? The best way to answer this question is to consider a specific example that can provide general lessons about the effect of an indirect tax. In the example given, it is assumed that the government imposes a quantity tax that is a fixed amount per unit of a good sold that it requires suppliers to remit to the government.

The key to understanding the effect of an indirect tax is to recognise that imposing the tax increases the amount that suppliers need to be paid by consumers to be willing to supply the good. When the government introduces an indirect tax, nothing changes in regard to the opportunity cost of production for suppliers. Whatever it cost suppliers to produce the good before the tax, it will still cost the same after the tax. So when they are required to pay the government a tax per unit of the good they sell, suppliers will only be willing to continue to supply the good if they receive an increase in price equal to the amount of the tax. For example, if suppliers were willing to supply each unit of a good for $8 before the tax was imposed, and the government has imposed a tax of $2 per unit, then after the imposition of the tax the supplier will need to be paid $10 by consumers to be willing to supply.

*Figure 2.9.1* demonstrates how the indirect tax affects the market quantity traded. The left-hand panel shows the case where suppliers pay the tax. The market supply curve (S) represents the willingness to supply of suppliers, and S(tax) shows the amounts that suppliers need to receive from consumers to be willing to supply after imposition of the tax. Equilibrium before the tax is imposed is at the intersection of market demand (D) and market supply (S). Imposing the tax shifts the equilibrium to the intersection of the S(tax) and market demand curves. Hence, the market quantity traded decreases from $Q^*$ to $Q_{tax}$.

We have therefore derived a *first general result*: imposing an indirect tax will reduce the quantity traded of the good or service being taxed. One way to understand this result is to think of the indirect tax as an increase in the opportunity cost of trading the product being taxed. It is this higher cost of trade that reduces the amount of trade.

Once the quantity traded has been determined, it is also possible to establish the prices for consumers and suppliers. The total price paid by consumers, $P_D$, can be read off the demand curve $D$ at the quantity traded $Q_{tax}$. Similarly, the price received by suppliers, $P_S$, can be read off the supply curve S at the quantity traded $Q_{tax}$. The total gap between $P_D$ and $P_S$ is equal to the tax per unit of the good traded. The shaded region in the graph shows the total amount of tax paid to the government, equal to $Q_{tax} (P_D - P_S)$.

It can be seen that the price paid by consumers is increased due to the tax ($P_D > P*$) and the price received by suppliers is reduced ($P_S < P*$). This is a *second general result*: imposing an indirect tax raises the price paid by consumers and lowers the price received by suppliers. The relative sizes of the increase in price for consumers and the decrease in price for suppliers is referred to as the *incidence* of the tax.

There is one other important point to be made about how an indirect tax affects market outcomes. The example that has just been worked through made the assumption that suppliers pay the indirect tax to the government. The alternative would be to assume that it is the consumers who are required to pay the tax. A *third general result* is that changing this assumption of who pays the indirect tax to the government would not change any of the results that have been described. Imposing the same indirect tax will cause the same decrease in quantity traded and have the same effect on prices, regardless of who pays the tax. This equivalence can be seen in the right-hand panel of **Figure 2.9.1**, which represents the market outcome where the indirect tax is paid by consumers.

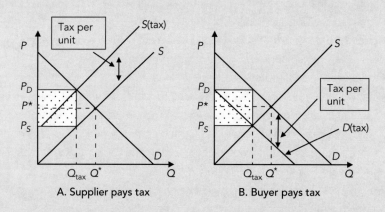

**Figure 2.9.1** How an indirect tax affects the market price and quantity traded

From the theory, we can say that increasing the rate of an indirect tax on a product will decrease the quantity traded. A higher tax raises the cost to buyers and sellers of trading the product, and hence a smaller quantity is traded. Your advice to the government could therefore have been that introducing the alcopop tax would lower consumption of pre-mixed drinks.

Of course, just saying that the tax will reduce the consumption of pre-mixed drinks does not take us very far. The success or failure of the policy would be judged according to whether it caused a small or large decrease in the consumption of alcopops and other alcoholic drinks. What we really need to know is: By how much will the tax cause the consumption of pre-mixed drinks to fall, and how much substitution will there be of other alcoholic drinks?

To address the first question, let's begin by thinking about the size of the effect of the alcopop tax on the consumption of pre-mixed drinks. Does it cause a small or large decrease? The answer to this question will partly depend on the size of the tax increase. Other things being equal, a bigger tax will cause a larger decrease in consumption. The other main determinant of the size of the effect of the tax will be the own-price elasticities of demand and supply.

Take the own-price elasticity of demand. We can examine how it influences the effect of the tax by considering what happens in alternative scenarios: Where the own-price elasticity of demand is inelastic and where it is elastic. This is done in *Figure 2.9.2*. In each diagram it is assumed that a per-unit tax is imposed on suppliers. S and S(tax) are the quantities supplied before and after the tax, respectively. The gap between the two supply curves is equal to the amount of the per-unit tax. The same supply curves are drawn in each diagram, so that it is only the own-price elasticity of demand that differs.

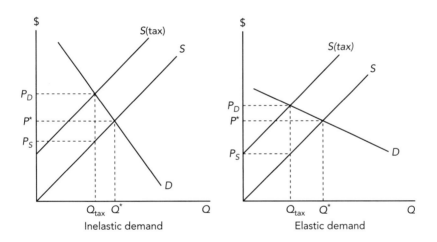

**Figure 2.9.2** How the effect of an indirect tax on market price and quantity traded depends on the own-price elasticity of demand

The main conclusion we can draw from the comparison in *Figure 2.9.2* is that the higher the degree of own-price elasticity of demand, the larger will be the decrease in consumption. This conclusion can be explained as follows: Increasing the tax raises the price that consumers must pay. The higher the own-price elasticity of demand is, the more that this price increase will translate into a decline in quantity traded.

We have therefore reached a point where we can say something about the effect of the alcopop tax. The size of the effect of the tax on consumption of pre-mixed drinks will depend on the own-price elasticity of demand, with more elastic demand meaning that the consumption of pre-mixed drinks will decrease by a larger amount.

By putting yourself in the shoes of the policymaker you are advising, you can imagine what their next question might be: What is the own-price elasticity of demand for pre-mixed drinks? It is possible there will be evidence from empirical analysis of the demand for pre-mixed drinks that you could use to reply to this question. But if there isn't, you could go back to first principles to make a response. By thinking about each of the possible determinants of the own-price elasticity of demand, you may be able to make an informed prediction of whether you would expect demand for pre-mixed drinks to be price elastic or inelastic.

The main determinants of the own-price elasticity of demand for pre-mixed drinks are: (i) the availability of substitutes; (ii) the extent to which pre-mixed drinks are a necessary or discretionary good; (iii) the share of income spent on pre-mixed drinks; and (iv) the time horizon required to adjust consumption behaviour to the tax. Suppose, for example, that you think there are close substitutes for pre-mixed drinks, and that it is relatively easy for consumers to adjust their behaviour quickly to the tax (since alcohol is not a durable good). Both these factors would tend to make the demand for alcopops more price elastic. Hence, you could tell the policymaker that you expect the demand for pre-mixed drinks to be own-price elastic, with the consequence that the alcopop tax will cause a relatively large decrease in the consumption of pre-mixed drinks.

As well as learning that the size of the effect of an indirect tax on quantity consumed depends on the own-price elasticity of demand, you might have noticed from *Figure 2.9.2* that the degree of elasticity also affects the incidence of the tax. The general result in regard to the incidence of the tax is that the higher the degree of the own-price elasticity of demand, the smaller is the share of the tax paid by consumers and the larger is the share of the tax borne by suppliers. It is also important to note that the analysis here has only considered the effect of the own-price elasticity of demand, and that a similar analysis could be undertaken showing how the size of the effect of the indirect tax will depend on the own-price elasticity of supply.

Now we can turn our attention to the final question: How will consumption of other alcoholic drinks be affected when the alcopop tax is imposed? A higher price for pre-mixed drinks is likely to cause consumers to shift towards other types of alcoholic drinks that they regard as substitutes. The extent to which this occurs will depend on how substitutable those other drinks are seen as being for pre-mixed drinks. The greater the substitutability, the greater will be the increase in consumption of other alcoholic drinks as the quantity demanded of pre-mixed drinks declines.

Judging the degree of substitutability between pre-mixed drinks and other alcoholic drinks would probably require some market research. In one regard, as both pre-mixed drinks and other drinks have alcoholic content, they might be seen as close substitutes. However, in other ways, such as taste or image, there may be more distance between pre-mixed drinks and other alcoholic beverages such as beer or wine.

We've given our advice on the alcopops tax to the policymakers. As it turns out, we can also check how good our advice has been. A study of alcohol consumption in

Australia compared the consumption of pre-mixed drinks and of other types of alcoholic beverages between the period immediately after introduction of the alcopop tax in 2008 and the period in 2007 prior to introduction of the tax. The findings from this study by Tanya Chikritzhs and her co-authors are summarised in *Table 2.9.1*.

**Table 2.9.1** Number of standard drinks consumed May to July, 2007 and 2008, by beverage type

| BEVERAGE TYPE | STANDARD DRINKS CONSUMED IN 2007 (IN MILLIONS) | STANDARD DRINKS CONSUMED IN 2008 (IN MILLIONS) | CHANGE (IN MILLIONS) | CHANGE (%) |
|---|---|---|---|---|
| Ready-to-drink spirits (including alcopops) | 348 | 257 | −91 | −26.1 |
| Beer | 886 | 899 | +13 | +1.5 |
| Other spirits and wine | 1110 | 1124 | +14 | +1.2 |
| Total | 2344 | 2280 | −64 | −2.7 |

*Source:* Chikritzhs et al. (2009), 'The 'alcopops' tax: heading in the right direction', *Medical Journal of Australia*, 2 March, pp. 293–4. © Copyright 2009 The Medical Journal of Australia – reproduced with permission. The Medical Journal of Australia does not accept responsibility for any errors in translation.

Three main features of the changes in demand for alcoholic beverages are evident in *Table 2.9.1*. First, there was a relatively large decline in the consumption of pre-mixed drinks. The timing of this change makes it most likely that it was due to the alcopops tax. Since a large proportion of the consumption of alcopops was known to involve teenagers, it also seems reasonable to think that the higher tax succeeded in reducing consumption by teenagers. Second, the consumption of other alcoholic beverages increased. This may represent the effect of consumers substituting other types of alcoholic beverages that had become relatively cheaper compared to pre-mixed drinks. However, extra factors such as increasing consumer incomes may also account for some part of this increase in demand. Third, there was a decline in the total consumption of alcohol measured by standard drinks. Given that this decline was driven by the fall in consumption of pre-mixed drinks, and that this seems to have happened mainly because of the alcopop tax, we could conclude that the government's policy achieved its objective.

Subsequent analysis also investigated whether the alcopops tax was able to reduce rates of alcohol-related harm for young people. A study of emergency department hospitalisations in New South Wales from 1998 to 2011 found that the alcopops tax was associated with a significant decrease in admissions due to acute alcohol problems, especially for females aged 18 to 24 years (Gale et al. 2015). Hence, it does seem that the alcopops tax, by causing reduced consumption of pre-mixed drinks, was able to decrease the incidence of binge drinking, just as the policymakers intended.

## KEY LESSONS

■ The alcopop tax on pre-mixed drinks was intended to reduce alcohol consumption by teenagers in Australia. Predicting whether it would achieve this objective depended on the expected size of the effect of the tax on consumption of pre-mixed drinks, and the extent of substitution to other alcoholic beverages caused by the alcopop tax.

■ The size of the effect of the alcopop tax on consumption of pre-mixed drinks can be predicted from the size of the tax and from the own-price elasticities of demand and supply. For example, the higher the own-price elasticity of demand, the larger will be the decrease in consumption of the product being taxed.

■ The effect of the alcopop tax on the consumption of other alcoholic beverages can be predicted from information on how substitutable those drinks are perceived to be for pre-mixed drinks.

## SOME QUESTIONS TO THINK ABOUT

1   The following statistics appeared in an article in *The Age*:

> Sales of nicotine patches and gum increased more than 30 per cent following the federal government's 25 per cent tax hike on cigarettes, pharmacists say. And calls to Victoria's Quitline doubled after the April 30 rise pushed the cost of a pack up from $14 to $16.50.

> Source: (Hagan 2010).

a   Use the demand/supply model to show how the higher tax on cigarettes will affect the market outcome in the market for cigarettes.

b   Show how the effect of the tax will depend on the own-price elasticity of demand for cigarettes.

c   Why has the higher cigarette tax caused sales of nicotine patches and gum to increase by more than 30 per cent?

2   In early 2018 the Australian Government proposed introducing a tax of $5 on every parcel posted from overseas containing purchases of less than $1000. The tax was intended to partially recoup costs of security screening of those parcels by the government (Bagshaw 2018). Assume that the market for the retail supply of books in Australia is: (i) perfectly competitive; and (ii) contains some online suppliers who operate internationally and ship purchases made by Australian buyers into the country, and other suppliers who are based in Australia and operate out of shops.

a   Use the demand/supply model to show how the imposition of a parcel tax would affect an international supplier of books to Australia, such as amazon.com.

b   Use the demand/supply model to show the short-run impact of the imposition of a parcel tax on a local supplier of books. How might the long-run impact differ from the short-run impact?

# REFERENCES

Bagshaw, Eryk (2018), 'Push is on to pass a parcel tax', *The Age*, 22 March, p. 2.

Chikritzhs, Tanya, Dietze, Paul, Allsop, Steven, Daube, Michael, Hall, Wayne & Kypri, Kypros (2009), 'The "alcopops" tax: heading in the right direction', *Medical Journal of Australia*, 2 March, pp. 293–4. © Copyright 2009. The Medical Journal of Australia – reproduced with permission. The *Medical Journal of Australia* does not accept responsibility for any errors in translation.

Gale, Marianne, Muscatello, David, Dinh, Michael, Byrnes, Joshua, Shakeshaft, Anthony, Hayden, Andrew, Macintyre, Chandini Raina, Haber, Paul, Cretikos, Michelle & Morton, Patricia (2015), 'Alcopops, taxation and harm: a segmented time series analysis of emergency department hospitalisations', *BMC Public Health*, 15: 468.

Gordon, Josh & Harrison, Dan (2008), 'Booze blitz', *The Age*, 27 April, p. 1.

Hagan, Kate (2010), 'Cigarette tax rise sends puffers over to patches', *The Age*, 10 June, p. 3.

# IDEAS FOR FURTHER READING

A good introduction to the analytics of indirect taxes is provided in *Principles of Microeconomics* by Joshua Gans, Stephen King, Martin Byford and Gregory Mankiw (2017, Cengage Learning, pp. 131–5). The analysis of the effects of taxation is part of the field of public finance. Good textbooks covering this field include Harvey Rosen and Ted Gayer's *Public Finance* (2013, 10th edn, McGraw-Hill/Irwin) and Jonathan Gruber's *Public Finance and Public Policy* (2015, 5th edn, Worth Publishers).

Many people think that childcare workers in Australia aren't paid enough. Most qualified childcare workers earn only about $44 000 per year, just one-half of full-time earnings for an average employee (Smith 2019). Agreement extends to a major explanation for why they are underpaid – gender pay discrimination. The gap in pay between males and females in Australia was supposed to have been eradicated by the equal pay decisions handed down by the Arbitration Commission over 50 years ago. Putting equal pay into practice, however, has proved difficult to achieve in jobs which are female-dominated – since it has been almost impossible to find male occupations to benchmark those jobs against. Early childhood education is certainly a female-dominated occupation, with 97 per cent of workers being women. And in early 2018 the body that governs wage-setting in Australia, the Fair Work Commission, rejected the latest application by unions for a substantial pay rise for childcare workers – using exactly the reason that the unions had not provided a suitable male-dominated occupation against which the value of work done by childcare workers could be compared (Marin-Guzman 2018).

## Pay equity: The Labor Party proposals

So, with no progress towards pay equity for childcare workers in 50 years, will it ever be possible to improve their wages? One of Australia's major political parties, the Labor Party, thinks so, and in the run-up to the 2019 Federal election, made two proposals for achieving pay equity for childcare workers.

The first proposal sought to directly address what has in recent times been the road block to pay equity. The Labor Party announced a suite of policy reforms intended to make it more straightforward for the Fair Work Commission to consider pay equity cases relating to female-dominated occupations. The proposed reforms included legislating to make pay equity a main objective of the regulation of wage-setting in Australia; and establishing a new senior-level role in the Fair Work Commission which would have responsibility for conducting pay equity reviews (Wood 2019). Making these types of reforms to Australia's wage-setting institutions is the conventional way for changes in wage-setting practices to be made – and it aroused little comment during the election.

The same cannot be said for the Labor Party's second proposal. It was announced that a Labor Government, if elected, would pay a subsidy to increase by 20 per cent the wages of 100 000 childcare workers. The criticisms of this proposal flowed thick and fast – questioning who would be the 100 000 workers to get the wage rise (out of the 192 000 workers in the sector); claiming that with a cost of $20 billion over eight years the policy was far too expensive to afford; and concern that the policy would cause shortages of labour in other care occupations such as aged care (Bagshaw & McCauley 2019).

Another, and arguably the most fundamental, criticism of the subsidy policy asked the question: Would the childcare workers who were supposed to be paid the subsidy actually receive it? This might seem a strange question to ask. Surely, if the subsidy was paid to the workers, they would get to keep it. Well, maybe. But what happens if the owners of childcare centres can respond to the introduction of the subsidy by lowering the wage they pay to their workers? Childcare workers would then gain from the government subsidy – only to see that partly reversed by a decrease in the wage paid to them by their employers. Put another way, childcare workers would not be receiving the whole amount of the subsidy intended for them.

---

### THEORY REFRESHER

#### How does a subsidy affect market outcomes?

A subsidy is a payment associated with trade of a good or service in a market. The payment is made by the government to suppliers or consumers for each unit of the good or service traded. Governments choose to pay subsidies for a wide range of goods and services – some current examples are rebates paid to purchasers of solar panels in Victoria; caps on the price of pharmaceutical drugs that are part of the Pharmaceutical Benefits Scheme; and the Fuel Tax Credit scheme which removes the fuel excise tax for consumers who use diesel fuel for transport on non-public roads.

How does the payment of a subsidy affect market outcomes? The starting point for answering this question is to understand how a subsidy introduces a difference in the price paid by consumers and the price received by suppliers. Formally, the relation between the price paid by consumers and the price received by suppliers can be expressed as:

$$P_S = P_D + S$$

where $P_D$ and $P_S$ are respectively the prices paid by consumers and received by suppliers.

Suppose that the subsidy for a good is paid by the government to consumers. Nothing changes with regard to the value consumers get from the good when the subsidy is introduced. Whatever the good was worth to consumers prior to the subsidy, it will still be worth the same afterwards. So, when they receive a subsidy per unit of the good they buy, consumers will be willing to pay the amount the good is worth to them plus the subsidy. For example, if the most that consumers are willing to pay to buy a unit of a good is $10, and a subsidy of $2 is paid by the government for each unit sold, it implies that the maximum total amount that consumers will be willing to pay, and hence the amount received by suppliers, is $12.

Now that we have described how a subsidy introduces a wedge between prices paid by consumers and received by suppliers, we can go on to study its effect on market outcomes. By increasing the price that consumers are willing to pay to suppliers for a good, a subsidy causes an increase in market demand. This increase in market demand causes an increase in the quantity traded. Hence, we have derived a *first general result*: Paying a subsidy will increase the quantity traded of the good to which the subsidy is attached.

*Figure 2.10.1* demonstrates graphically how the subsidy affects the market quantity traded. The left-hand panel shows the case where consumers receive the subsidy. The market demand curve $D$ represents the total willingness to pay of consumers, and $D$(subsidy) shows the amounts that consumers are willing to pay to suppliers (or the amounts that suppliers receive from consumers) after provision of the subsidy. Equilibrium prior to the subsidy is at the intersection of market demand, $D$, and market supply, $S$. Providing the subsidy shifts the equilibrium to the intersection of the $D$(subsidy) and market supply curves. Hence the market quantity traded increases from $Q^*$ to $Q_{subsidy}$.

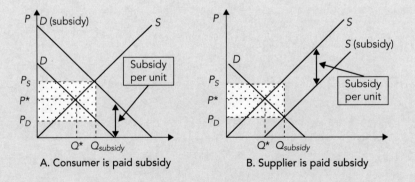

Figure 2.10.1 How a subsidy affects the market price and quantity traded

Once the quantity traded has been determined, it is also possible to establish the prices for consumers and suppliers. The price received by suppliers, $P_S$, can be read off the supply curve $S$ at the quantity traded $Q_{subsidy}$. The price paid by consumers, $P_D$, can be read off the demand curve $D$ at the quantity traded

$Q_{subsidy}$. The total gap between $P_D$ and $P_S$ is equal to the subsidy per unit of the good traded. The shaded region in the graph shows the total amount of subsidy paid by the government to consumers, equal to $Q_{subsidy}*(P_D - P_S)$.

The price received by suppliers is increased due to the subsidy ($P_S > P^*$), and the price received by suppliers is reduced ($P_D < P^*$). This is a *second general result*: Providing a subsidy raises the price received by suppliers and decreases the price paid by consumers (compared to equilibrium without payment of a subsidy). The relative sizes of the increase in price to suppliers and decrease in price for consumers is referred to as the incidence of the subsidy.

There is one other important point about how a subsidy affects market outcomes. The example that has just been worked was based on the assumption that the government paid the subsidy to consumers. The alternative would be to assume that it was suppliers who were paid the subsidy. A *third general result* is that changing this assumption of who receives the subsidy from the government would not change any of the results that have been described. Providing the same subsidy will cause the same increase in quantity traded and the same effect on prices, regardless of who the subsidy is paid to. This equivalence can be seen in the right-hand panel of **Figure 2.10.1**, which represents the market outcome where the subsidy is paid to suppliers.

The Labor Party did not win the 2019 Federal election in Australia, so we won't get the opportunity to find out how paying the subsidy to childcare workers affects their wage. What we can do, however, is to use the model of a perfectly competitive market with a subsidy to predict what would have happened. The question of how much of the subsidy would end up in the pockets of childcare workers is exactly what we refer to in the model as the incidence of the subsidy. From the model we also know that the incidence of a subsidy will depend on the elasticities of demand and supply with respect to the wage.

## Predicting the incidence of the subsidy

We can study the likely impact of the subsidy on the total wage paid to childcare workers by predicting the incidence of the subsidy; and to do that, we need to make assumptions about the responsiveness of demand for and supply of childcare workers to changes in the wage paid to them.

Let's begin with the elasticity of demand for childcare workers. The number of early years educators is regulated – with, for example, minimum standards for how many educators are needed for given class sizes of children being specified in National Quality

Standards (ACECQA 2019). Hence, we might expect demand to be relatively inelastic in response to changes in wages of childcare workers.

What about the elasticity of supply of childcare workers to changes in wages? In the time following introduction of the subsidy, there would be the scope for a relatively rapid increase in supply of early years educators. The pool of potential workers in caring occupations is large, requirements for training as an early years educator make entry to the occupation feasible for most of that pool of potential workers, and the training can be completed in six months. Hence, the supply of childcare workers is likely to be relatively elastic with regard to wages.

Having made our assumptions about the wage elasticities of demand for and supply of childcare workers, we can now go on to predict the incidence of the subsidy. A graphical representation of how the introduction of a subsidy will change the market equilibrium is shown in **Figure 2.10.2**. Note that $w_D$ denotes the wage paid by employers and $w_S$ denotes the wage received by workers. The incidence of the subsidy that is predicted is striking. Most of the subsidy would be received by the owners of childcare centres – via being able to decrease the wage that they pay to childcare workers.

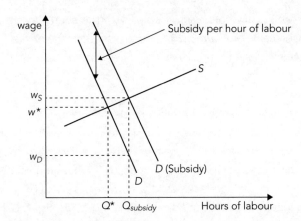

**Figure 2.10.2** Incidence of subsidy for childcare workers

A numerical example can illustrate this finding on the incidence of the subsidy. Suppose prior to the introduction of the subsidy that owners of childcare centres pay a wage of $20 per hour to childcare workers. Then the government introduces a subsidy of $5 per hour for childcare workers. Our analysis predicts that most of this subsidy will go to owners of childcare centres. Childcare workers will be better off with payment of the subsidy – perhaps their total hourly wage including the subsidy will increase to $20.50. But owners of childcare centres are made even better off – now needing to pay only $15.50 per hour, with the rest of the childcare workers' total wage coming from the government subsidy.

What explains this result? When the government introduces the subsidy there is an increase in the quantity demanded of childcare workers. To induce an increase in the quantity supplied of childcare workers, it is necessary for the total wage paid to childcare workers to rise. But because supply of childcare workers is relatively responsive to changes in the wage, it is possible to hire the extra workers needed without much increase in their total wage. In other words, the childcare centre owners are able to almost fully capture the subsidy by lowering the component of the total wage that they pay.

In a competitive market, therefore, there is a problem with paying a subsidy and expecting that it will all go to a chosen group – buyers or sellers. In fact, as in the example of childcare workers, the subsidy may go mainly to the opposite group for whom it was intended.

Of course, our finding on the incidence of a subsidy for childcare workers depends on a critical assumption – that owners of childcare centres can reduce the wage they pay to workers in response to the government making available the subsidy. If instead childcare centre owners are restricted in how much they can reduce the wage they pay, more of the subsidy may go to the childcare workers. It turns out that this is a highly relevant consideration in the labour market for childcare workers. Most are paid according to minimum wage rates (known as modern awards) that are specified by the Fair Work Commission. Hence, owners of childcare centres may be prevented legally from reducing their workers' wages below what they currently pay. To see how imposing this constraint on owners affects the market outcome, *Figure 2.10.3* shows the case where owners are not able to make any reduction to the wage they were paying prior to the subsidy. Our result on the predicted incidence of the subsidy is completely reversed. Owners of childcare centres must pay a wage equal to the equilibrium wage prior to the subsidy, $w^*$. Therefore, the entire amount of the subsidy is received by the childcare workers.

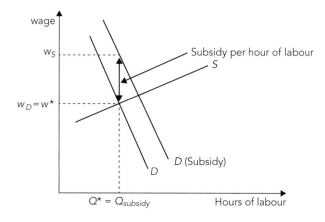

**Figure 2.10.3** Incidence of subsidy for childcare workers with minimum wage

At the end of our analysis we can conclude that the Labor Party's subsidy for childcare workers would most likely have ended up with them – thereby achieving the goal of raising their earnings. The way we have got to this conclusion – by using the model of perfect competition to study the incidence of a subsidy – is another demonstration of how far it's possible to go with the tools you are learning in your introductory microeconomics class. In this case, we've been able to shed light on what was a major policy debate in Australia's 2019 Federal election. This application has also illustrated another important lesson. We always need to give thought to, and incorporate into our model, what we regard as the essential elements of the situation we are studying. Here, our conclusion on the impact of a subsidy for childcare workers turned out to depend critically on knowing that most childcare workers are paid a regulated minimum wage – so there would be little scope for owners of childcare centres to capture the subsidy by reducing their wages.

## KEY LESSONS

- The introduction of a subsidy in a perfectly competitive market will, in general, cause an increase in the price received by suppliers and a decrease in the price paid by buyers. The relative gain (sizes of the changes in prices) for suppliers and buyers is referred to as the incidence of the subsidy.

- The incidence of a subsidy will vary depending on the relative own-price elasticities of demand and supply for the product being traded. Hence, by making assumptions about these elasticities, it is possible to predict the incidence of a subsidy for any good or service.

- Making an accurate prediction of the incidence of a subsidy (or any policy intervention) requires incorporating into our model all the essential elements of the situation being studied. For example, in analysis of the proposed subsidy for childcare workers, it was important to take into account that most childcare workers are currently paid a regulated minimum wage.

## SOME QUESTIONS TO THINK ABOUT

1   Analyse the incidence of a subsidy paid to childcare workers for a scenario where:
   (i)   the demand for childcare workers is relatively elastic with respect to wages
   (ii)  the supply of childcare workers is relatively inelastic with respect to wages.
         Explain the result you find.

2  Analyse the incidence of a subsidy paid to childcare workers and the impact of the subsidy on the market outcome for a scenario where:

(i)  the demand for childcare workers is relatively inelastic with respect to wages

(ii)  the supply of childcare workers is relatively elastic with respect to wages

(iii) there is a maximum amount by which childcare centre owners are allowed to decrease the wage they pay following the introduction of the wage subsidy. Explain the result you find.

# REFERENCES

Australian Children's Education and Care Quality Authority (ACECQA) (2019), *National Quality Standard*, https://www.acecqa.gov.au/nqf/national-quality-standard, viewed 4 October 2019.

Bagshaw, Eryk & Dana McCauley (2019), 'Attack on childcare pay rise', *The Age*, 2 May, pp. 1, 9.

Marin-Guzman, David (2018), 'Unions lose equal pay case for childcare workers', *Australian Financial Review*, 6 February, https://www.afr.com/policy/economy/unions-lose-equal-pay-case-for-childcare-workers-20180206-h0ue7a, viewed 4 October 2019.

Smith, Warwick (2019), 'Labor wants to pay childcare wages itself. A perfect storm makes it not such a bad idea', 9 May, https://theconversation.com/labor-wants-to-pay-childcare-wages-itself-a-perfect-storm-makes-it-not-such-a-bad-idea-116272, viewed 4 October 2019.

Wood, Danielle (2019), 'When it pays to be big on details', *The Age*, 3 May, p. 21.

# IDEAS FOR FURTHER READING

A good survey of the recent history of equal pay in Australia is provided by Leonora Risse in her article '50 years after Australia's historic "equal pay" decision, the legacy of "women's work" remains' (*The Conversation*, 19 June, https://theconversation.com/50-years-after-australias-historic-equal-pay-decision-the-legacy-of-womens-work-remains-118761, viewed 8 October 2019). For an introduction to the concept of subsidy, see pages 137–41 in Joshua Gans, Stephen King, Martin Byford and N. Gregory Mankiw (2018), *Principles of Microeconomics* (Cengage).

# International trade

International trade, where consumers and suppliers in different countries engage in trade, today accounts for a large share of global economic activity. In fact, the degree to which countries trade with each other is about as high as it has been in the past several hundred years. From *Figure 3.0.1*, you can see that in 1960 in Australia, the share of international trade in gross domestic product (GDP) was only 25 per cent, but by the 2010s this had grown to 40 per cent. Australia's experience has been close to the norm, with the average share of international trade in GDP for all countries increasing from 25 per cent to almost 60 per cent between 1960 and 2017. In China, which is also shown in *Figure 3.0.1*, the growth in international trade was even more dramatic, rising from less than 10 per cent in the 1960s to over 60 per cent in the late 2000s, before decreasing back to about 40 per cent at present. The importance of international trade to economic activity makes it essential for anyone working in business or government to know why countries trade, what determines the extent to which they trade and the likely consequences of trade. These are all topics that you'll learn about in the case studies in this section.

As inextricably linked to economic activity as it may seem, there is nothing inevitable about international trade. Japan during the Edo period of the nineteenth century, Franco's Spain and current-day North Korea are just a few examples of countries that have chosen to go it alone. So why would a country engage in international trade?

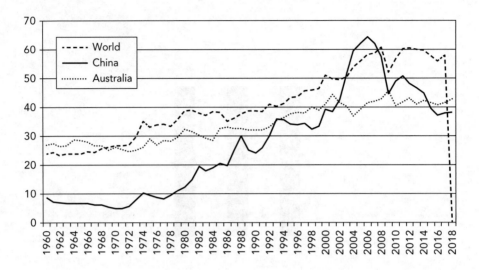

**Figure 3.0.1** Trade as a percentage of GDP, 1960 to 2017

*Source:* World Bank national accounts data, and OECD National Accounts data files,
28 October 2019, https://datacatalog.worldbank.org/public-licenses#cc-by.
Licensed under a Creative Commons Attribution 4.0 International License (CC BY 4.0).
Link to license: https://creativecommons.org/licenses/by/4.0/

This question is answered in Case study 3.1. Trade allows a country to specialise its
production, yet still consume a wide variety of goods and services. The advantage of
specialisation in production is that it enables countries to make the best use of their
scarce resources. By specialising in producing those goods and services at which it is
most efficient, and trading to buy other products, a country maximises its material
wellbeing. Data on what countries produce does show that they specialise in producing
goods and services which they can supply at relatively low cost; although looking at
costs is more useful for predicting the very broad industries in which a country is likely to
specialise in than predicting the specific goods and services it produces.

Despite the prediction from economic theory that there will be an overall
improvement in wellbeing when countries engage in international trade, many countries
seek to limit this type of trade. Case study 3.2 describes how countries have sought to
limit international trade. It describes the myriad methods that can be used to protect
against imports, including tariffs on imports, import quotas and anti-dumping measures,
and analyses the consequences for a country's wellbeing.

The remarkable growth in international trade that has occurred in the past 40 years is
part of what is generally described as an era of globalisation. Globalisation, as you'll
probably be aware, has been the subject of much criticism. Economic theory predicts
that, by allowing countries to obtain many goods and services at a lower price than
previously, globalisation should have improved wellbeing. Yet it is claimed by its critics
that globalisation has made many people, especially those in developing countries,

worse off. Case study 3.3 addresses this apparent paradox. Notwithstanding the criticisms of globalisation that have been made, you'll find that there is evidence of many people in developing countries being made better off by globalisation. Furthermore, problems that have been associated with globalisation are argued to reflect shortcomings of the process of trade reform and legal and political systems in developing countries, rather than revealing a flaw in the economic theory of international trade.

# CASE STUDY 3.1
## WHY DO WE TRADE?

Trade between countries has been a constant of world history. From the simple exchange of horses, tea and slaves between China, Central Asia and Europe around 200 CE, right through to the present, when Barbie dolls are assembled in Japan with parts shipped in gigantic container boats from six different countries, trade has been a major part of human activity. Historians have found many motivations for why countries engage in trade – to achieve strategic or military objectives, to acquire new lands, or even as a way of disseminating religious beliefs. For an economist, there is another reason why trade happens. An economist explains international trade as the natural corollary of countries specialising in production. Because each country produces only a subset of the goods and services which its population wants to consume, it is necessary to trade with other countries to obtain those products.

This is an explanation of sorts, but it also shifts the question to: Why do countries specialise in production? The answer is that specialisation turns out to be efficient. Specialisation means that a country can get the greatest amount of output possible from its available resources, yet by trading is still able to consume a wide range of goods and services. Together, specialisation and openness to trade allow a country's population to maximise its material wellbeing. However, not just any pattern of specialisation by countries will achieve this outcome. Countries must specialise in production activities that they can undertake using relatively fewer resources than other countries would need to do the same production. The more formal expression of this idea is to say that countries should specialise in production activities in which they have a comparative advantage.

## THEORY REFRESHER

### Absolute advantage, comparative advantage and the returns to specialisation

Absolute advantage and comparative advantage are concepts that are used by economists to describe the relative efficiency of suppliers in producing a good or service. A country that uses a smaller amount of inputs to produce a given quantity of a product than another country is defined as having an absolute advantage in supplying that product. A country that has a smaller opportunity cost of supplying a given quantity of a product than another country is defined as having a comparative advantage in supplying that product.

For example, suppose that Australia and the United States can each produce steel and sugar. To keep this as simple as possible, we assume that production of either good requires only one input: labour. The amounts of each good that can be produced using one hour of labour in each country are shown in **Table 3.1.1**.

**Table 3.1.1** Output from one hour of labour

| COUNTRY | STEEL (TONNES PER HOUR OF LABOUR) | SUGAR (TONNES PER HOUR OF LABOUR) |
| --- | --- | --- |
| Australia | 4 | 6 |
| United States | 2 | 1 |

We can see that Australia uses less labour input than the United States to produce either 1 tonne of steel or 1 tonne of sugar. For example, in Australia one-quarter of an hour of labour is required to produce a tonne of steel, compared to one-half an hour in the United States. Hence, Australia is defined as having an absolute advantage in both activities. We can also work out for this example the production activity in which each country has a comparative advantage. Using the information from **Table 3.1.1**, it's possible to derive the opportunity cost of producing a tonne of steel or a tonne of sugar in Australia and the United States. In each case, the opportunity cost of producing a tonne of one product is the amount of the other product that must therefore be forgone. For example, in Australia an hour of labour can be used to produce either 4 tonnes of steel or 6 tonnes of sugar. Hence, Australia's opportunity cost of producing 4 tonnes of steel is 6 tonnes of sugar; or, in other words, the opportunity cost of producing a tonne of steel in Australia is 1½ tonnes of sugar. Doing the same exercise for each product in each country, we obtain the information on opportunity cost shown in **Table 3.1.2**.

**Table 3.1.2** Opportunity cost of producing steel and sugar

| COUNTRY | STEEL (TONNES) | SUGAR (TONNES) |
| --- | --- | --- |
| Australia | 1½ | ⅔ |
| United States | ½ | 2 |

The United States has a lower opportunity cost of producing steel than Australia, whereas the opposite holds for sugar. This implies that the comparative advantage of the United States will be in producing steel, and Australia's comparative advantage is in producing sugar. Notice that even though Australia had an absolute advantage in both production activities, the United States and Australia each has a comparative advantage in one of the activities.

Efficiency requires that each country should specialise in the activity in which it has a comparative advantage. By assigning production of a good or service to the country that uses the least resources to produce that good or service, the total value of what is produced from available resources will be maximised.

Suppose that both Australia and the United States have 10 hours of labour time available. Applying the principle of specialisation, we can represent graphically the total amount of output that the two countries could produce, as in *Figure 3.1.1*.

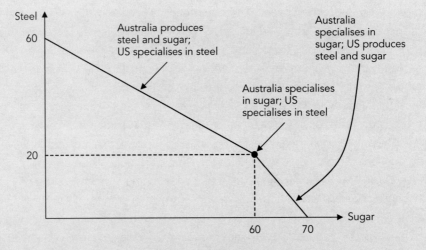

**Figure 3.1.1** Possible combinations of output when both countries specialise in the activities in which they have a comparative advantage.

The diagram in *Figure 3.1.1* shows that when both countries specialise completely in the activity in which they have a comparative advantage, the total output is 20 tonnes of steel and 60 tonnes of sugar. It also shows what happens to output of steel and sugar if one country allocates labour time to the production activity in which it does not have a comparative advantage while the other country specialises in the activity in which it has a comparative advantage. For example, the upper segment of the diagram shows what happens if the

United States specialises in steel production, and labour time from Australia is used to produce both steel and sugar.

To demonstrate the benefits of specialisation, we can compare the output that can be produced when the two countries specialise with what happens when both allocate labour to production of steel and sugar. For example, suppose each country devotes five hours to the production of steel and five hours to the production of sugar. Australia then produces 20 tonnes of steel and 30 tonnes of sugar, and the United States produces 10 tonnes of steel and 5 tonnes of sugar. In total, there are 30 tonnes of steel and 35 tonnes of sugar. Now suppose instead that we use labour exclusively from Australia to produce the 35 tonnes of sugar. This will take $5\frac{5}{6}$ hours of labour (equal to 35 tonnes divided by 6 tonnes per hour). That leaves $4\frac{1}{6}$ hours of labour from Australia that can be used for steel production, so that $16\frac{2}{3}$ tonnes of steel would be produced by the leftover Australian labour (equal to $4\frac{1}{6}$ hours multiplied by 4 tonnes per hour). As well, there are 10 hours of labour from the United States that can be applied to produce 20 tonnes of steel. Therefore, specialisation has allowed us to produce the same amount of sugar, but also $36\frac{2}{3}$ tonnes of steel, which is more than the amount of steel produced when the countries do not specialise. This is shown graphically in *Figure 3.1.2*. The general point is that any way of allocating labour that does not follow the principle of specialisation will produce less total output than when labour is assigned to production activities using that principle.

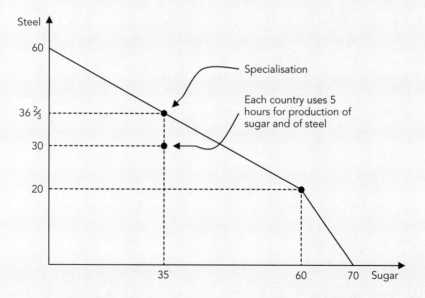

**Figure 3.1.2** Comparison of combinations of output when both countries specialise compared with not specialising.

Because specialisation in a country's areas of comparative advantage makes it better off, we might expect that this is what any country will be doing. But is this what happens? Do countries choose to specialise in producing goods and services in which they have a comparative advantage?

One way to identify production activities in which we think a country may have a comparative advantage is to consider activities that require as inputs resources in which the country is relatively abundant. When a country has an abundant supply of a resource, other things being equal, this should be associated with a relatively low opportunity cost of using that resource. So, we'd expect the country to have a comparative advantage in production activities that require intensive use of that resource. For example, a country that has a large land area might be expected to have a relatively low opportunity cost of using land, and hence to have a comparative advantage in land-intensive agricultural activity; meanwhile, a country with a large population of low-skill workers could have a comparative advantage in types of manufacturing industry that require a relatively high usage of low-skill labour. To test whether countries specialise in production activities in which they have a comparative advantage, one approach is therefore to examine whether they are specialising in activities that require intensive use of resources with which they are relatively abundantly endowed.

A limited test of this idea was undertaken by James Harrigan and Egon Zakrajsek, two economists working at the US Federal Reserve. Using data for 28 countries, they examined the correlation between the types of manufacturing activities in which countries engaged and the resource endowments of those countries. They concluded that the idea of comparative advantage – that countries specialise in production activities intensive in inputs with which they were most endowed – does a reasonable job of predicting what countries produce.

To illustrate Harrigan and Zakrajsek's general findings (2000, p. 20), we'll use an example with data from three countries. *Table 3.1.3* shows the relative resource endowments and output for selected manufacturing industry sectors for Australia, Japan and Taiwan. Australia is relatively abundant in capital, high-education workers and crop land compared to Japan and Taiwan, whereas those countries are relatively abundant in workers with low levels of education. Between Japan and Taiwan, Japan has a greater endowment of capital and high-education workers, whereas Taiwan is more abundant in low-education workers. These differences in resources are certainly reflected in the extent to which the countries have chosen to engage in different manufacturing activities. Taiwan, which is abundant in low-skill labour, specialised to a much greater degree than either Australia or Japan in the production of textiles, an activity that is intensive in low-skill labour. In contrast, Australia and Japan, with greater relative endowments of capital, are more specialised than Taiwan in activities that require a large capital investment – fabricated metals and transport equipment, respectively. And although the theory does not explain everything, such as Taiwan being more specialised in transport equipment than Australia, if the analysis was expanded to include agricultural

**Table 3.1.3** Relative resource abundance and specialisation in manufacturing industry

|  | AUSTRALIA | JAPAN | TAIWAN |
| --- | --- | --- | --- |
| Country's resources (relative to mean; 100 = mean) |  |  |  |
| Capital | 139 | 99 | 61 |
| High-education workers | 155 | 120 | 72 |
| Low-education workers | 55 | 84 | 123 |
| Crop land | 1240 | 1 | 3 |
| Output by sector (relative to mean; mean = 100) |  |  |  |
| Textiles | 45 | 75 | 205 |
| Fabricated metals | 104 | 143 | 95 |
| Transport equipment | 96 | 165 | 116 |

*Source:* Harrigan & Zakrajsek (2000), Tables 2 and 3.

activity, we'd also find that, consistent with its much larger endowment of crop land, Australia is more heavily engaged in most types of agriculture than either Japan or Taiwan.

Confirmation that countries specialise in production activities within broad industry categories, that require inputs with which they are abundantly endowed, provides some evidence that comparative advantage is important. Beyond this, however, it can be difficult to identify what a country's comparative advantage is, and hence hard to test whether comparative advantage matters.

As an example, the development economists Ricardo Hausman and Dani Rodrik cite India's success in information technology (IT), which they ascribe to 'the time-zone difference that allows processing to be done in Bangalore before the west coast of the US is back at work in the morning, the linkages with the Indian diaspora in Silicon Valley, [and] the facility with the English language' (2002, p. 23). After the Indian success in IT, it was easy to see that these factors were important, yet beforehand it was unlikely anyone would have nominated them as a source of comparative advantage.

A further complication is that the production activities in which a country has a comparative advantage will depend on what it is already producing. By specialising in the production of a good or service, a country is likely to learn about potential improvements in the production process for that good or service. Hence, it becomes more efficient in that production activity and in doing so acquires a comparative advantage. Recent research on international trade in pharmaceutical drugs supports this idea. Countries which for demographic reasons have a higher demand for a particular type of drug (for example, countries with older populations have higher demand for blood pressure drugs) are found to be more likely to be net exporters of that drug (Costinot et al. 2018). These countries are unlikely to have a greater innate ability to produce the drug than other countries. Instead, it's much more likely that by producing more of the drug, the countries have found ways to produce it more cheaply. So, there are certainly plenty of reasons to think that countries are specialising in production activities in which they have a comparative advantage, and that this is a major source of international trade. But it also seems we need to have a careful approach to thinking about comparative advantage. It's important to recognise that it may be difficult to identify what will be a country's sources of comparative advantage, and that comparative advantage may evolve over time according to what is already being produced in a country.

## KEY LESSONS

- International trade allows a country to consume a wide range of goods and services, while at the same time choosing to specialise in a narrower set of production activities. Specialising in production activities in which it has a comparative advantage means that a country is able to create the greatest value from its available resources, thereby maximising its population's material wellbeing.

- Countries do appear to specialise in production activities within the broad industry categories that require intensive use of inputs with which they are relatively abundantly endowed. They can therefore be considered to be engaging in activities that involve the lowest opportunity cost or in which they have a comparative advantage. Beyond this, it can be difficult to say more about the effects of comparative advantage on production. Sources of comparative advantage are often idiosyncratic, and the production activities in which a country has comparative advantage may depend on what it already produces.

## SOME QUESTIONS TO THINK ABOUT

1   Ben and Louise are colleagues in the Economics Department. They each have two main activities – writing research papers and preparing lectures. For Ben, it takes five hours to write a research paper and two hours to prepare a lecture. For Louise, it takes 10 hours to write a research paper and two hours to prepare a lecture. Ben and Louise each have 40 hours per week to spend on their work for the Economics Department.

Who has an absolute advantage in writing research papers and who has an absolute advantage in preparing lectures? Who has a comparative advantage in writing research papers? What about preparing lectures?

2   Suppose that Australia, New Zealand and India can each produce two goods: steel and wool. The production of each good requires only one input: labour. In Australia, a worker can produce either six bales of wool in one hour or 3 tonnes of steel in one hour. In New Zealand, a worker can produce either one bale of wool in one hour or 2 tonnes of steel in one hour. In India, a worker can produce either three bales of wool in one hour or 2 tonnes of steel in one hour.

For each pair of countries, which country has a comparative advantage in the production of steel? How about wool?

3   An article in *The Economist* (2016) describes the decline of the steel industry in Britain and its rise in China and other developing economies. Two points noted in the article are the higher wages in Britain than China and the huge volume of output of steel in China – as much in the two previous years as had been produced in Britain since 1900.

Do you think the concept of comparative advantage can be applied to explain the changing pattern of steel production between Britain and China?

# REFERENCES

Costinot, Arnaud, Donaldson, David, Kyle, Margaret & Williams, Heidi (2019), 'The More We Die, The More We Sell? A Simple Test of the Home Market Effect', *Quarterly Journal of Economics*, Vol. 134(2), May, pp. 843–94.

Harrigan, James & Zakrajsek, Egon (2000), *Factor Supplies and Specialization in the World Economy*, National Bureau of Economic Research, working paper no. 7848.

Hausman, Ricardo & Rodrik, Dani (2002), *Economic Development as Self-discovery*, National Bureau of Economic Research, working paper no. 8952.

*The Economist* (2016), 'Through the Mill', 9 April, pp. 56–7.

# IDEAS FOR FURTHER READING

The concept of comparative advantage is usually attributed to the economist David Ricardo. You can read more about him in Steven Pressman's book, *Fifty Major Economists* (2002, Routledge, pp. 35–8). Tim Harford provides an excellent introduction to why countries engage in trade in chapter 8 of his book *The Undercover Economist* (2006, Oxford University Press). Jeffrey Frieden provides a highly readable history of international trade in the twentieth century in *Global Capitalism: Its Fall and Rise in the Twentieth Century* (2006, W.W. Norton).

The legendary New Zealand finance minister Roger Douglas once remarked: 'It is possible to grow bananas on Mount Cook. But is it worth spending the money it takes to do so?' (quoted in King 2003, p. 490). Douglas' remark highlights the choice every country must make about what to produce itself and what to import, and the significant consequences for national wellbeing. Growing bananas on Mount Cook would cost a great deal of money, and since bananas can be imported relatively cheaply, it would only be sustainable by protecting the Mount Cook bananas from imports, at a significant cost to consumers in New Zealand. Thus far, New Zealand has avoided the temptation to grow bananas on Mount Cook. Many other countries, however, do have local producers engaged in equally bizarre ventures, strongly supported by their governments. Around the world, it seems that every country has a product it just has to buy from its own suppliers. As notable as the products that countries choose to protect against imports are the myriad ways in which they seek to implement that protection.

The first policy of choice in stopping imports is the tariff. A tariff is a tax imposed on imports of a specified product. It can be imposed as a fixed amount of tax per unit imported or as a percentage of the price of each unit imported. Australia is one country that has used tariffs extensively to protect against imports. In the early 1970s, Australia's tariffs on imports of manufactured goods were higher than those of any other developed economy, with the exception of New Zealand (Anderson & Garnaut 1987, p. 7). Tariff rates on clothing and footwear averaged 220 per cent, so that, for example, when you bought a pair of imported running shoes that cost $160, you were paying $110 to the government. Other highly protected manufacturing sectors were textiles and transport equipment, especially passenger motor vehicles (Anderson & Garnaut 1987, p. 11). From the 1980s onwards, however, Australian governments undertook policy reforms that achieved substantial reductions in import protection. The average rate of tariff protection of manufacturing products, which had been over 70 per cent in the 1930s and remained at around 25 to 30 per cent in the 1980s, had decreased to below 10 per cent by the mid-2000s and to about 4 per cent a decade later. Protection of specific products such as passenger motor vehicles fell from over 50 per cent in the 1980s to about 10 per cent in the 2010s (Lloyd 2007; Productivity Commission 2017, p. 36). A major impetus to the policy of reducing tariffs was concern that import protection was having a serious adverse effect on the productivity of the Australian economy (Kenwood 1995, pp. 79–82).

Tariff levels in Australia might have been high by international standards, but it has not been alone in using them as a method of protecting against imports. The US–China trade war of recent years has seen both countries imposing and raising tariffs on each other's products. The US began in March 2018 by imposing tariffs on Chinese steel and aluminium, and subsequently substantially broadening the scope of protection, including the announcement of higher tariffs on an extra $200 billion of goods from China (*The Economist* 2019). In the meantime, China has retaliated, targeting its tariffs on US imports on politically sensitive goods such as soyabeans and aircraft (*The Economist* 2018).

Next on the list of ways to protect against imports is an import quota. Imposing an import quota restricts the quantity of a product that can be imported to a country. A notable application of import quotas occurred in Myanmar, where imports of cars were restricted to just 4500 in 2004 (*The Economist* 2005). With such a limited quota, prices of cars in Myanmar skyrocketed – a 1993 Toyota saloon that could have been bought from a Japanese wholesaler for US$1000 sold for up to US$75 000, and a new Toyota LandCruiser retailed for six times its regular price at US$300 000. Higher prices make the right to supply quota-restricted imports a valuable asset, and this was especially so in Myanmar, where there was such a pronounced effect on prices. In Myanmar, an army-owned monopoly, the Union of Myanmar Economic Holdings Limited, was able to sell the right to import a single car for about US$100 000!

To examine more formally how Myanmar's import quota affected the market for cars and national wellbeing, we can use a version of the demand/supply model that allows for international trade. Suppose, as seems reasonable, that as a small country, Myanmar is a price-taker on the world market for cars and pays the world price for each car it imports, and that there are no car manufacturers in Myanmar, so the only source of cars is imports. This scenario is represented in **Figure 3.2.1**, where $D_{\text{Myanmar}}$ and $S_{\text{Myanmar}}^{\text{free-trade}}$ show the demand and supply curves respectively for cars in Myanmar with free trade. In the absence of any restrictions on international trade, the market outcome will be socially optimal. Trade occurs at the world price, and hence consumers in Myanmar buy cars so long as their willingness to pay is greater than the world price. In **Figure 3.2.1**, this outcome is shown as the quantity traded, $Q^*$, and the price, $P^*$.

What happens when Myanmar imposes an import quota? Now the supply of cars will be restricted to the amount of the quota, $Q_{\text{quota}}$. In **Figure 3.2.1**, this is represented by the supply curve $S_{\text{Myanmar}}^{\text{importquota}}$, which becomes vertical at the quantity of cars at which the quota is set. The new market outcome is at the intersection of this supply curve, $S_{\text{Myanmar}}^{\text{importquota}}$, and the demand curve. With the quota, consumers pay a higher price, $P_{\text{quota}}$, for a car, and importers earn a surplus on each car imported equal to the difference between $P_{\text{quota}}$ and $P^*$ (world price). These effects reflect exactly what occurred in Myanmar.

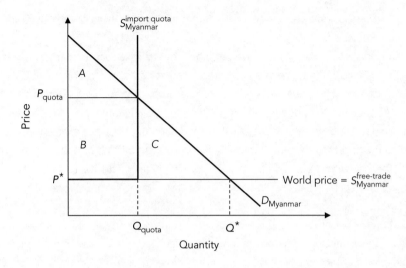

**Figure 3.2.1** Demand/supply model of international trade in cars to Myanmar

We can also evaluate how the import quota affected wellbeing in Myanmar. Consumers were made worse off by paying a higher price and consuming a smaller quantity of cars, whereas importers were made better off by earning a surplus on each car imported. Overall, the negative effect for consumers outweighed the positive effect for importers, so that society was made worse off. We can show this formally by seeing how the society's total surplus from trade is affected by the import quota. This is done using measures of surplus for consumers and importers in the demand/supply model shown in *Figure 3.2.1*. In *Table 3.2.1*, the labelled areas from the demand/supply model are used to demonstrate that total surplus, and hence overall wellbeing, is lower when an import quota is introduced. Wellbeing is decreased by the amount C, which corresponds to the reduction in quantity traded below the equilibrium quantity.

**Table 3.2.1** Welfare effects of import quota

|  | FREE TRADE | WITH IMPORT QUOTA | CHANGE |
|---|---|---|---|
| Consumer surplus | A + B + C | A | −B −C |
| Import licence holder |  | B | +B |
| Total surplus | A + B + C | A + B | −C |

In this example of a country protecting against imports, interestingly, the justification for protection was not that there were local car manufacturers in Myanmar who would benefit from the import quota. Instead, the fact that it was the army which owned the rights to import licences and thereby received the benefits from the import quota probably goes a long way to explaining why this policy existed.

Subsidies to domestic producers that compete with importers are another way of seeking to protect against imports. The subsidy effectively increases the price received by local suppliers compared with the price received by importers. Hence, it allows local producers to remain as suppliers in a market even where they have higher costs of production than international producers.

Agricultural products are a favourite target for governments when it comes to handing out subsidies. For the European Union, it has been noted that, 'according to the OECD, total assistance to rich country farmers was $311 billion in 2001 ... In 2000, the EU provided $913 for each cow' (Wolf 2004, p. 215). With expenditure of over US$20 billion in 2005, the United States spent less on farm subsidies than Europe, but still more than its spending on foreign aid and nearly twice what it spent subsidising poor children to go to college. Amazingly, over 70 per cent of the subsidy payments went to just 10 per cent of farms, most of which are large commercial businesses (*The Economist* 2006, p. 39).

National pride seems to be at stake when it comes to a country having its own airline – and paying subsidies has been a way to make that happen. A recent study found that the airlines owned by the Gulf States – Emirates, Etihad and Qatar – have received benefits such as hand-outs, loans without interest and free land that have been worth $42 billion over past decades (*The Economist* 2015).

Claiming quarantine and safety concerns about imports can give a country the moral high ground in protecting against imports. Although the 1994 North American Free Trade Agreement between the United States and Mexico was supposed to pave the way for Mexican suppliers to provide trucking services in the United States, this did not happen. Initially claiming that Mexican trucks had 'lower safety and environmental standards than their American counterparts', and then seeking to overturn a decision to allow a trial of 100 Mexican trucks in the United States by arguing that 'the lorries would be full of drugs and illegal immigrants', the Teamsters Union, which represents American truck drivers, has been very effective in using safety as a way of restricting import competition (*The Economist* 2007a). At various times there have also been complaints by international producers that Australia has made false allegations about disease in imports of products such as salmon and apples in order to force the government to impose restrictions on those imports (Colebatch 2004; Guerrera 2007). Similarly, restrictions on imports of cheese supposedly imposed on health grounds have been estimated to reduce the volume of international trade in cheese by 7 per cent (*The Economist* 2017a). During the 2010s the Australian Government has prevented the Chinese firm Huawei from bidding to be a supplier for the National Broadband Network and the 5G mobile phone network, citing national security concerns based on perceived links between Huawei and China's military (Battersby 2012; Hartcher 2018). Of course, when the introduction of an imported product could cause harm to consumers or compromise the quality of output produced in a country, restricting imports may be entirely justified on welfare grounds. Examples are bans that were placed on imports of toys from China found to have used highly toxic paint (Doherty 2008; see also MacLaren 2004); and measures by China to restrict imports of recyclable waste following the discovery of hazardous substances in the waste (*The Economist* 2017b).

'Anti-dumping' measures provide a justification for protection against imports for governments looking for something a little out of the ordinary. Dumping occurs when suppliers seek to sell imports in a country at a price below the cost of production. This will lose them money, but if it succeeds in driving that country's suppliers out of business, so that in the long term the only source of supply is from imports, it may be a profitable strategy. Assessing whether international suppliers are dumping or whether they just have much lower costs of production than local producers is a difficult exercise. This has not, however, stopped many countries from claiming that dumping is occurring, and using it as a justification for imposing protection against imports. As one article noted, 'sunglasses, hairbrushes, picks, hoes, nuts and bolts – this is just a sampling of the goods China is alleged to have dumped on the markets of manufacturing rivals such as Brazil, Argentina and South Africa in recent years' (*The Economist* 2007b). Using the same approach, the United States imposed tariffs of up to 20 per cent on imports of paper from China, claiming that those suppliers were receiving unfair subsidies (*The Economist* 2007c).

Governments around the world have shown infinite inventiveness in their approaches to protecting domestic producers against imports. Unfortunately, this inventiveness is not doing much for overall wellbeing in their countries. Domestic producers and their workers may be made better off, but growing bananas on Mount Cook, paying US$300 000 for a Toyota LandCruiser or giving over US$900 for each cow in the European Union can only make society as a whole worse off.

## THEORY REFRESHER

### The welfare cost of protection against imports

A country that introduces or increases protection against imports will cause a reduction in its volume of imports. These imports would only have been coming to the country when they provided a cheaper source of supply than was available from that country's producers. Hence, the shift away from imports and towards supply by local producers will mean that the price of the product being protected increases for consumers and producers in the country that imposes the protection.

An increase in the price of the import-competing product could occur directly, such as where a tariff raises the price paid by consumers, and this higher price is also received by local producers. Or it may increase the price indirectly, such as where subsidies paid to local producers are financed by tax payments by consumers. A higher price will increase supply by local producers in the country that imposes protection. This is because there will be some local producers who could not profitably supply the product previously, but for whom the price (or price plus subsidy) will now be sufficiently high to cover their opportunity costs. The other effect will be to decrease demand by consumers.

As an example, suppose the price had previously been $10, in which case any producer with an opportunity cost above $10 would not have operated. But after the imposition of an import tariff of $2, the price paid to producers in the country that imposes protection increases to $12, so that any local producer with an opportunity cost of between $10 and $12 will now be willing to supply the product. Furthermore, any consumer with a willingness to pay between $10 and $12 would previously have bought the product, but now will choose not to.

The introduction of import protection will generally decrease society's overall wellbeing. Consumers are made unambiguously worse off. This occurs because of the higher price (or price plus taxes) paid, as well as a decrease in the quantity consumed. By contrast, local producers are unambiguously better off. They supply a higher quantity of output and receive a higher price for that output. The effect on the total surplus from trade can be calculated by comparing the negative effect on consumers' wellbeing with the positive effect for producers. Making this comparison shows that total surplus will always decrease. This reduction in total surplus is an example of what is referred to as a deadweight loss, a reduction in the total surplus from trade compared with the efficient or socially optimal outcome.

The decrease in society's wellbeing reflects two effects of import protection. First, resources are wasted due to excessive production by local producers. A part of its supply of a product that a country could have obtained from importers is instead supplied by local producers. These producers have higher costs than the price at which the product could have been imported. Hence, society is using more of its resources than necessary in obtaining the product. Second, the decrease in wellbeing will also reflect that consumption by local consumers is below the optimal level. Due to the higher price (or extra tax payments), some consumers will reduce their consumption of the product. If the product had not increased in price, these same consumers would have had a willingness to pay more than the price, and therefore would have bought the product and been better off.

# KEY LESSONS

- Countries have adopted a wide variety of approaches to protect their own producers against imports. Some examples are tariffs, import quotas, import subsidies, anti-dumping measures and quarantine or safety regulations.
- The effects of international trade, and of each of the aforementioned types of government interventions, can be studied using the demand/supply model adapted to allow for international trade.
- Import protection reduces society's overall level of wellbeing. A country's producers or other groups, such as importers, can be made better off by being protected, but this is outweighed by the negative effect on consumers in the same country. The reduction in overall wellbeing reflects a waste of resources due to having more of a product supplied by the country's producers than is efficient, and having less of the product consumed than is efficient.

# SOME QUESTIONS TO THINK ABOUT

1   In the Australian labour market there is demand for and supply of low-skill labour as follows:

$$Q_D = 10\,000 - 500w$$
$$Q_S = 500w$$

(where $Q_D$ = quantity of hours of low-skill labour demanded by Australian firms, $Q_S$ = quantity of hours of labour supplied by Australian low-skill workers, and $w$ = wage rate per hour of low-skill labour).

a   What will be the equilibrium wage rate and total hours of low-skill labour?
    Suppose now that Australian businesses can 'import' any quantity of low-skill labour they want via a special government visa scheme for temporary low-skill immigrants. The cost of each hour of 'imported' labour will be $5 per hour.

b   What will be the effect of the scope to 'import' low-skill labour on:
    i    the equilibrium wage rate for low-skill labour in Australia?
    ii   the total hours of low-skill labour supplied by Australian workers?
    iii  total hours of low-skill labour demanded by Australian firms?
    iv   quantity of low-skill labour imported?

c   Using a diagram, show the effect of introducing the scope to 'import' low-skill labour on:
    i    surplus for Australian low-skill workers
    ii   surplus for Australian firms
    iii  total surplus to Australian low-skill workers and firms.

    d   Discuss briefly how your answer to part (c) would change if the government imposed a tax of $5 per hour on any hour of low-skill labour that was 'imported' by an Australian firm.

2   In the third quarter of 2015 Indonesia reduced the quota of live cattle imports allowed from Australia from 250 000 to 50 000. An article on this episode described how it had led to 'soaring beef prices and butchers in Jakarta and Bandung walking off their jobs in protest' (Topsfield 2015).

    a   Use the demand/supply model with international trade to show the effect that reducing the number of import permits for Australian beef has on outcomes in the beef market in Indonesia. Can the model explain why the price of beef in Jakarta would have sky-rocketed? Who is made better off by the reduced number of permits? Who is made worse off?

    b   Use the demand/supply model with international trade to show the effect that reducing the number of import permits for Australian beef to Indonesia will have on outcomes in the market for beef in Australia. Who is made better off by the reduced number of permits? Who is made worse off? Can your model explain why live cattle exports to Indonesia would have decreased?

# REFERENCES

Anderson, Kym & Garnaut, Ross (1987), *Australian Protectionism: Extent, Causes and Effects*, Allen and Unwin.

Battersby, Lucy (2012), 'China company ban puts trade relations "at risk"', *The Age*, 27 March, p. 3.

Colebatch, Tim (2004), 'Bans on foreign foods to be lifted', *The Age*, 20 February, p. 1.

Doherty, Ben (2008), 'Toy cars with asbestos parts illegally imported', *The Age*, 14 January, p. 3.

Guerrera, Orietta (2007), 'NZ apple anger goes to WTO', *The Age*, 21 August, Business section, p. 2.

Hartcher, Peter (2018), 'China 5G ban "model for others"', 22 September, p. 4.

Kenwood, Albert (1995), *Australian Economic Institutions since Federation*, Oxford University Press.

King, Michael (2003), *The Penguin History of New Zealand*, Penguin Books.

Lloyd, Peter (2007), '100 years of tariff protection in Australia', Department of Economics, University of Melbourne, research paper no. 1023.

Productivity Commission (2017), *Trade and Assistance Review 2016–17*, Annual Report Series, Canberra.

MacLaren, Donald (2004), 'The high price of a toxic diet', *Australian Financial Review*, 5 April, p. 23.

*The Economist* (2005), 'On yer bike', 18 June, p. 26.

*The Economist* (2006), 'Uncle Sam's treat', 9 September, p. 39.

*The Economist* (2007a), 'Free trade and fireballs', 15 September, p. 47.

*The Economist* (2007b), 'Mangling trade', 30 June, p. 78.

*The Economist* (2007c), 'The trade two-step', 7 April, pp. 32–3.

*The Economist* (2013), 'Chicken and eggs', 24 August, p. 36.

*The Economist* (2015), 'Flights of hypocrisy', 25 April, p. 12.

*The Economist* (2017a), 'Curd your enthusiasm', 2 December, p. 65.

*The Economist* (2017b), 'Anti-dumping', 5 August, p. 22.

*The Economist* (2018), 'Blow for blow', 7 April, p. 63.

*The Economist* (2019), 'Speaking softly', 11 May, pp. 58–9.

Topsfield, Jewel (2015), 'Indonesia to seek new beef imports', *The Age*, 20 September, p. 9.

Wolf, Martin (2004), *Why Globalization Works*, Yale University Press.

## IDEAS FOR FURTHER READING

Brief histories of protection against imports of agricultural and manufacturing products into Australia are provided in A.G. Kenwood's *Australian Economic Institutions since Federation* (1995, Oxford University Press, chapters 3 and 4) and Kym Anderson and Ross Garnaut's *Australian Protectionism* (1987, Allen and Unwin).

Globalisation presents us with a seeming paradox. The rapid growth in international trade and in flows of capital between countries that has occurred as part of globalisation should – according to economic theory – have increased our wellbeing. Yet, in practice there is much controversy regarding the effects of globalisation. Criticism ranges from the very public protests that regularly accompany meetings of the International Monetary Fund and G20 to the pronouncements of economists such as the Nobel prize winner Joseph Stiglitz:

> If, in too many instances, the benefits of globalisation have been less than its advocates claim, the price paid has been greater, as the environment has been destroyed, as political processes have been corrupted, and as the rapid pace of change has not allowed time for cultural adaption.

Source: Stiglitz (2002), p. 8.

Economists define globalisation as closer integration or interconnectedness between countries. This closer integration can include growth in international trade and capital flows, increases in population mobility, standardisation of culture and more widespread transmission of ideas. Decreasing costs of transportation and communication, and the removal of barriers to international trade imposed by governments, are regarded as having been the major causes of the recent era of globalisation.

The consequences of globalisation are straightforward, according to economic theory. Growth in the volume of international trade, which allows countries to obtain many goods and services at a lower cost, should have improved global wellbeing. With all the criticism, though, you would be right to wonder if this is what has happened. Or, has economic theory got it all wrong?

## THEORY REFRESHER

### How does globalisation occur?

For an illustration of the process of globalisation, consider the effects of removing a barrier to international trade. Suppose a country accounts for a small share of world trade of a product. Suppose also that it has imposed a tariff on imports of that product. This implies that the price paid by consumers and received by producers in that country will be equal to the world price of the product plus the tariff. The quantity demanded by local consumers and the quantity supplied by local producers will then be determined by this price. Imports will make up the gap between what consumers demand and the quantity that local producers are willing to supply. This is shown in **Figure 3.3.1**, where local supply and demand are determined at the intersections of the supply and demand curves with the 'World price + tariff' line, and the quantity of imports with a tariff is equal to 'Imports – with tariff'. What happens if the tariff is removed? The price at which trade occurs now decreases to equal the world price. Local producers will therefore want to supply a smaller quantity and local consumers will want to buy a larger quantity. Hence, imports will increase. This is shown in **Figure 3.3.1** as the quantity 'Imports – no tariff'. Removal of a barrier to international trade has prompted an increase in the volume of international trade. Aggregated over many countries and many products, this is exactly how globalisation has happened.

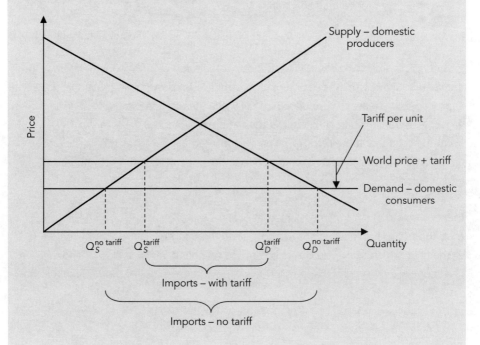

**Figure 3.3.1** Effects of removal of an import tariff on the volume of international trade

Notwithstanding the protests and concerns of some leading economists, there is in fact much evidence that globalisation has had many of the effects predicted by economic theory. In the globalisation era, countries such as China, which have experienced the largest increases in exposure to international trade, have had the highest rates of economic growth. The globalisation era has also coincided with a significant decrease in global poverty, largely due to the higher rates of economic growth in China and India. According to World Bank data, between 1981 and 2015 the proportion of the world's population in poverty decreased from 42 per cent to 10 per cent (see **Table 3.3.1**). Finally, there is evidence that increased international trade has improved working conditions and environmental standards in developing countries. This effect largely occurs through increases in income as a result of greater international trade; for example, Wolf (2004, p. 189) cites a study showing that once per-capita income in a country reaches about US$5000, the country will commence improving its environmental standards.

**Table 3.3.1** Regional incidence of income poverty (share of people living on less than $1.90 per day, %)

| REGIONS | 1981 | 1990 | 2005 | 2015 |
|---|---|---|---|---|
| Middle East and North Africa | | 6.2 | 3.1 | 4.2 |
| South Asia | 55.7 | 47.3 | 33.7 | |
| Sub Saharan Africa | | 54.7 | 50.8 | 41.4 |
| Latin America and Caribbean | 13.5 | 14.8 | 9.9 | 3.9 |
| Central Asia | 80.5 | 61.3 | 18.9 | 2.3 |
| China | | 66.2 | 18.5 | 0.7 |
| World | 42.1 | 35.9 | 20.7 | 10.0 |

*Source:* (World Bank 2019).

## THEORY REFRESHER

### The effects of globalisation on wellbeing

How is wellbeing in a society affected by globalisation? To examine this question, we can again use the effects of removing a barrier to international trade, such as an import tariff, as an example of the process of globalisation. Removal of a tariff will reduce the price at which a product is traded – from the world price plus tariff, to just the world price. This decrease in price will cause an increase in demand by local consumers, a decrease in supply by local suppliers and hence a higher quantity of imports. From these effects on the market outcome, we can characterise how the wellbeing of consumers and producers is affected. Local consumers, who can buy at a lower price and are consuming a higher quantity, are made better off. Local producers, who receive a lower price and are supplying a lower quantity, are made worse off. The government, which loses the tariff revenue, is also made worse off. Overall, the positive effect for consumers outweighs the negative effects for producers and the government, so that society is made better off. We can show this argument formally by seeing how the total surplus from trade is affected by the removal of the tariff. This is done using measures of surplus for consumers, producers and the government from the demand/supply model shown in *Figure 3.3.2*. *Table 3.3.2* documents how the removal of the tariff affects the wellbeing of each group and society as a whole.

In *Figure 3.3.2*, a larger area corresponds to a larger amount of surplus. Hence, from the 'Change' column in *Table 3.3.2*, we can see that consumer surplus increases, producer surplus and government revenue decrease, and the total surplus increases. Globalisation, therefore, improves society's overall wellbeing, even though local producers and their workers will be made worse off.

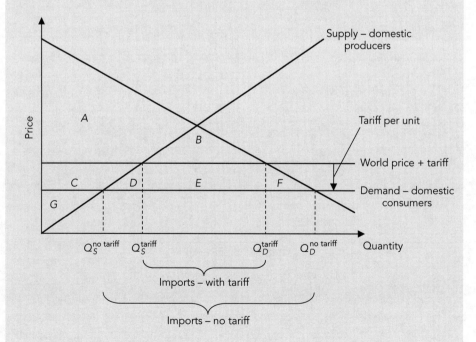

**Figure 3.3.2** Effects of removal of an import tariff on national wellbeing

**Table 3.3.2** Effects of tariff removal on the wellbeing of each group and on society as a whole

|  | WITH TARIFF | AFTER REMOVAL OF TARIFF | CHANGE |
|---|---|---|---|
| Consumer surplus | A + B | A + B + C + D + E + F | +C +D +E +F |
| Producer surplus | C + G | G | −C |
| Government | E |  | −E |
| Total surplus | A + B + C + E + G | A + B + C + D + E + F + G | +D +F |

So why the opposition to globalisation? There are several key reasons. What must be emphasised, however, is that none of these reasons is inconsistent with the predictions of economic theory about the impacts of globalisation.

First, economic theory does predict that some groups, such as producers and workers who are affected by greater competition from imports, will be made worse off by growth in international trade. Evidence that this has occurred during the recent phase of globalisation has come from studies of how workers in developed countries have been affected by the growth in imports of manufactured goods from China since the early 1990s. For example, research for the United States has found that this growth in imports could have caused the loss of 500 000 jobs in manufacturing, with those job losses being concentrated on lower skill workers and bringing long-term income reductions for those workers (Autor 2018). It is not surprising, therefore, that producers and workers in industries that face heavy import competition are often vocal opponents of trade reform. President Trump's trade war with China can in large part be attributed to that opposition – as he seeks to implement trade policies to assist workers disadvantaged by globalisation who supported him in the 2016 election (*The Economist* 2018).

Second, it can be argued that the process of international trade reform has at times favoured developed economies over developing economies. Especially during its initial stages, trade reform brought asymmetric reductions in trade barriers; that is, a greater decrease in barriers to trade between developed economies than between developed and developing economies. Hence, the benefits of early trade reform went mainly to the already relatively rich developed economies. Not all the blame, however, can be put on developed economies. The other important feature of trade reform has been a failure by developing economies to lower barriers to trading with each other.

For example, in 2017 South Asia imposed an average level of tariff restriction on imports from Latin America of 17.8 per cent; which was reciprocated by Latin America having an average level of 10.6 per cent on imports from South Asia (UNCTAD 2019, Table 1). So just as economic theory predicts, trade reform does appear to improve wellbeing. What is needed, however, is a fairer process of trade reform to share the benefits from reform more evenly than has occurred thus far.

Finally, the era of globalisation has been associated with rapid growth in international borrowing by developing economies. Often, the funds that were borrowed have been squandered by corrupt regimes, and the requirement to repay the loans has then imposed massive costs on the populations of those developing countries. More generally, studies of international financial market integration have found 'no robust proof that financial globalisation helped countries to grow more quickly' (*The Economist* 2006, p. 82).

Here again, there is nothing to contradict economic theory. It is not that financial integration cannot improve wellbeing. Instead, the message is about what is needed for this to happen. The experience of financial integration suggests that the existence of global markets is not sufficient to ensure improvements in wellbeing. Good governments and appropriate legal frameworks are also required. For example, Professor Noreena Hertz from the University of Cambridge has proposed legal reforms to reduce the incentive for governments and banks in developed economies to make loans to developing countries with corrupt governments (2004, pp. 178–84). The main idea of the reforms is that the debts owed by developing countries would be deemed illegitimate if a loan is made to a country without a democratically elected government, when the loan is not used in the interests of the population, and when the lender should have known that the loan would not be used to benefit the population.

What of the future? For the present, it appears that the pace of reform of international trade has slowed, and may even be going backwards. The trade negotiations known as the Doha Round commenced in 2001. These negotiations put priority on increasing access for agricultural producers in developing countries to markets in rich countries. However, now many years later, having almost collapsed on several occasions, little has come from the Doha Round. Lobbying against lower trade barriers by agricultural producers in developed countries, such as the US and Japan, and the complexity of negotiating trade reform with 155 countries have been largely to blame (*The Economist* 2012). In the absence of progress on multilateral trade liberalisation, some countries have turned to more limited (most often, bilateral) trade agreements. Free trade agreements that Australia signed with South Korea and Japan in the early 2010s are examples (Martin 2013). These preferential agreements have been viewed by some as a positive, much better than doing nothing when multilateral trade reform is being stymied; but others are wary, arguing that they mainly change who countries trade with rather than increasing the total volume of international trade (*The Economist* 2019). Then, of course, there is the growing trade war between the

United States and China and the decision by the UK to leave the European Union. Both episodes are moves away from trade liberalisation. Moreover, both episodes may also signal an end to the political consensus on the value of trade liberalisation that has been such a large part of the international political environment since World War II (*The Economist* 2019; Tooze 2018, pp. 591–97).

# KEY LESSONS

- The expansion of international trade, by allowing countries access to goods and services at the least possible cost, is predicted to improve global wellbeing. The recent phase of globalisation, which has involved significant growth in international trade, should therefore have increased global wellbeing. Yet there is much controversy regarding the effects of globalisation.
- Analysis of the effects of globalisation does reveal some important benefits. For example, there have been large decreases in world poverty and inequality in the era of globalisation.
- But globalisation has not made everyone better off. Some workers in developed economies have lost their jobs as a result of competition from cheaper imported versions of the goods they produced. And on a larger scale, many developing economies do not seem to have benefited from trade liberalisation.
- The fact that globalisation has not made everyone better off does not, however, mean that the economic theory is wrong. For example, the reason some developing economies have not benefited from reform is not that trade reform does not bring benefits, but that the process of reform thus far has brought much greater reductions in trade barriers for developed rather than developing economies.

# SOME QUESTIONS TO THINK ABOUT

1   A report (Kwek & Binsted 2014) has described how:

> Australian suppliers are set to benefit from the spike in the world wheat price as concerns about the crisis in Ukraine … and fears about US winter wheat production raise the price of the commodity … Wheat prices have surged 13 per cent this year …

Explain how, and the magnitude by which, Australian suppliers will benefit from the increase in the world price of wheat.

2   In the late 2010s, Australia temporarily switched from being an exporter to an importer of wheat. A report at the time (Robinson 2019) stated that the reason for the switch was a decrease in production of wheat in Australia due to El Niño weather conditions.

a   Use the demand/supply model with international trade to show how a country could switch from being an exporter to an importer of a product due to a decrease in its own supply of that product.

b   What do you predict would happen to the wellbeing of consumers and suppliers in Australia due to the decrease in supply? What is the effect on overall wellbeing?

c   How does the scope to switch from being an exporter to an importer of a product in response to a change in local supply affect wellbeing?

# REFERENCES

Autor, David (2018), 'Trade and labor markets: Lessons from China's rise', *IZA World of Labor*, 431.

Hertz, Noreena (2004), *The Debt Threat*, Harper Business.

Kwek, Glenda & Binsted, Tim (2014), 'Wheat price rises but drought saps hope', *The Age*, 18 March, p. 24.

Martin, Peter (2013), 'Korean deal sorted, now big one looms', *The Age Business Day*, 6 December, p. 23.

Robinson, Ashley (2019), 'Drought forces wheat grain imports', *The Age*, 16 May, p. 35.

Stiglitz, Joseph (2002), *Globalization and Its Discontents*, W.W. Norton.

*The Economist* (2006), 'Third thoughts on foreign capital', 18 November, p. 82.

*The Economist* (2012), 'Goodbye Doha, hello Bali', 8 September, p. 12.

*The Economist* (2018), 'Faction and friction', 17 March, p. 70.

*The Economist* (2019), 'Going it alone', 5 January, pp. 51–2.

Tooze, Adam (2018), *Crashed: How a Decade of Financial Crises Changed the World*, Viking.

United Nations Conference on Trade and Development (UNCTAD) (2019), *Key Statistics and Trends in Trade Policy 2018*, United Nations.

Wolf, Martin (2004), *Why Globalization Works*, Yale University Press.

World Bank (2019), *Poverty and Equity Databank*, https://databank.worldbank.org/reports.aspx?source=poverty-and-equity-database#, viewed 30 November 2019.

# IDEAS FOR FURTHER READING

Nayan Chanda's book *Bound Together* (2007, Yale University Press) is an excellent history of globalisation. Alternative perspectives on the effects of globalisation are presented by Joseph Stiglitz in *Globalization and Its Discontents* (2002, W.W. Norton), Martin Wolf in *Why Globalization Works* (2004, Yale University Press). A highly readable account of how globalisation has affected Australia is provided by Andrew Leigh in *Choosing Openness* (2017, Penguin Books). A dissenting view on the evolution of globalisation is provided by Pankaj Ghemawat in his article 'Why the world isn't flat' (2007, *Foreign Policy*, no. 159, pp. 54–60). The Harvard economist Dani Rodrik provides an insightful overview of recent developments in trade policy in 'What do trade agreements really do?', *Journal of Economic Perspectives* (2018, 23(2): 73–90).

# IV

## Market failure and government policy

Do traffic jams mean it is taking you longer and longer to drive to university? Are you concerned that we don't pay enough attention to the environment? Do you worry about the amount of junk food being consumed? For an economist, it is no surprise that you would be worried about these questions. They are examples of what is known as *market failure*, situations where the outcome of economic activity is not optimal for society. In this section, we'll look at how market failure can happen in the economy and, importantly, how we may be able to prevent it from occurring.

Market failure exists when the equilibrium outcome in a market is not efficient. Our definition of an efficient market outcome is where the total wellbeing society gains from trade in that market is maximised. Market failure therefore implies that the level of society's wellbeing is not being maximised. An important consequence of market failure concerns the role of government in the economy. Through policies designed to remedy the market failure, there is now potential for government to improve society's wellbeing.

There are a variety of possible causes of market failure in an economy. These include external effects from consumption or production activities, the existence of public goods, imperfectly competitive markets and information asymmetries between buyers and sellers in a market.

The case studies in this section present examples of market failure due to externalities and public goods. In each case study you will learn about one or more examples of these sources of market failure, and how government policy can assist in solving the market failure and thus improve society's wellbeing. Together, the cases illustrate that externalities and public goods are common in modern economies, and show you how knowledge of market failure and policy remedies allow economists to make a major contribution to the improvement of society's wellbeing.

Case study 4.1 introduces a wide variety of examples of externalities, both from market activity and from within business organisations. Plastic shopping bags, the flatulence of dairy cows, junk food and the value of bees are just some of the examples. Each example begins with a description of the externality and then explains various solutions that have been proposed for dealing with that externality.

The other case studies on externalities focus on specific examples and are designed to give you a more detailed understanding of possible policy solutions. Case study 4.2 is about what for many motorists is the daily frustration of road congestion. You'll see how road congestion can be interpreted as an example of market failure, and how tax-based solutions such as road tolls can potentially deal with the negative externality that causes the market failure. Case study 4.3 addresses why it might be a good idea to have policies for dealing with pollution that allow rights to emit pollution to be traded. An example is the carbon emissions market that was proposed for Australia. You'll find out how this policy, by directly regulating the total quantity of pollution emitted, can deal with the market failure of excessive emission of pollution, and also how allowing trade in pollution permits can ensure that each business in an economy emits an efficient quantity of pollution. Case study 4.4 explains why so much effort is put into getting people vaccinated against influenza each winter. Not only does the individual who is vaccinated benefit, but other members of society who might otherwise have been infected by that individual are also made better off. So being vaccinated is an activity that provides a positive external effect. An interesting aspect of vaccination is that the size of this external effect is likely to differ according to a person's age, which has important implications for the policies that governments should adopt to promote vaccination.

The case studies on public goods illustrate how the supply of these goods is likely to be less than is optimal for society, and describes some recommendations made by economists to improve outcomes in markets for public goods. Case study 4.5 uses conservation activity on private land as an example of a public good. It describes how the problem of undersupply of conservation activity has been dealt with in Victoria through an innovative scheme known as the Bush Tender. The scheme provides government financing to promote conservation activity, and uses a market-based mechanism to achieve an efficient assignment of funds between landowners. In Case study 4.6, we look at why, even though you may feel that there are too many boy bands (or whatever is your least favourite type of band or musician), an economist worries that there is not enough variety in the market for pop music. You'll learn that goods which can be easily copied, such as sound recordings or movies, are regarded as public goods, and how it is therefore likely that they will be undersupplied. Assignment by government of exclusive property rights, such as copyright or patents that legally prohibit copying, is shown to be a possible policy solution.

# CASE STUDY 4.1
## EXTERNALITIES ARE EVERYWHERE

Externalities really are everywhere. Once you know how to recognise an externality, you'll find it is a rare week in which an issue that relates to externalities is not prominent in the media. Overuse of our scarce water resources, environmental damage caused by greenhouse gas emissions or plastic shopping bags, and the problems orchard owners experience in having their fruit trees pollinated are just a few examples of how external effects can affect wellbeing in society. The responsibility for solving the problems caused by these external effects is likely to fall on the government. It's not only governments, however, that need to be concerned with external effects. Within organisations, externalities can also be a problem, such as when different divisions of the same company take actions that harm each other. So the bottom line is simple. Whether you are involved in government or business, you need to know about externalities and how to deal with them.

## THEORY REFRESHER

### What is an externality?

An external effect exists where: (i) a decision-maker's choice of action has effects on the wellbeing of other members of society; and (ii) those effects are not reflected in the costs or benefits of the action to the decision-maker. External effects are often described as being an 'unpriced' effect of a decision maker's actions on the other members of society. An external effect that improves the wellbeing of other members of society is defined as positive, and when the external effect reduces the wellbeing of other members of society it is defined as negative.

Externalities are a source of market failure. This can be seen by comparing the definitions of market equilibrium and efficiency, and recognising that the existence of an externality implies that these conditions cannot both hold. Market equilibrium is the level of an activity where the private marginal benefits (PMB) equal the private marginal costs (PMC) associated with the activity. An efficient outcome is the level of the activity where the social marginal benefits (SMB) equal the social marginal costs (SMC) associated with the activity. The existence of an externality implies that private decision makers are not taking into account some costs or benefits to society of their actions, and that therefore social benefit differs from private benefit or social cost differs from private cost (or both). Hence, the existence of an external effect implies that the market equilibrium will always differ from the efficient outcome. Where there is a negative externality, the level of the activity or amount of trade will be more than the efficient level. A positive externality implies that the level of the activity or amount of trade will be less than the efficient level.

How externalities are associated with market failure can be shown graphically. This is done in *Figure 4.1.1*. Suppose there is a negative externality. This can be represented as a situation where the SMC of some activity, such as tree clearing, is above the PMC. The difference between SMC and PMC is the size of the negative external effect. PMB from the activity is the same as SMB; that is, here, the effect of the negative externality is represented solely through the cost curves. The market outcome will be at the intersection of PMB and PMC at $Q^*$, whereas the efficient level is at the intersection of SMB and SMC at $Q^{**}$. Since $Q^*$ is greater than $Q^{**}$, we can conclude that the existence of a negative externality implies that the market level of the activity is greater than the efficient level. The case of a positive externality can be represented in a similar way.

Possible policy solutions to the existence of externalities are to 'internalise' the externality via a tax or subsidy, to facilitate trade between the parties causing and affected by the externality, or through direct regulation.

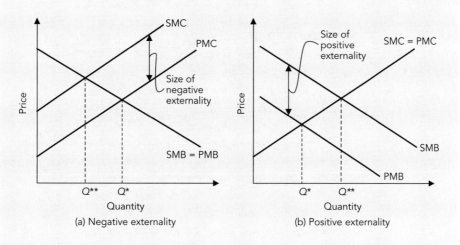

**Figure 4.1.1** Market failure and externalities

# Some examples of external effects and possible solutions

## Emission of greenhouse gases

Production of some goods causes the emission of greenhouse gases. For example, in New Zealand, the emission by livestock of methane and nitrous oxide accounts for half of that country's emissions (*Australian Financial Review* 2003). Greenhouse gases are suspected of being a major cause of climate change and hence constitute a cost to society. This is an unpriced effect of livestock production, since costs of production for livestock producers do not incorporate the costs of climate change. It represents a negative external effect, and hence the level of livestock production is greater than the efficient level.

One policy remedy that has been proposed is to tax activities that produce greenhouse gases:

> New Zealand farmers are being asked to cough up $NZ8.4 million a year to help reduce greenhouse gas effects caused by flatulence of their millions of sheep and cattle ... On current livestock numbers of about 46 million sheep and 9 million cows, the levy will be about NZ9c per sheep and about NZ72c per cow.

> Source: *Australian Financial Review* (2003), p. 20.

The rationale for imposing a tax on livestock is to seek to reduce the level of livestock production in the direction of the efficient level by raising the costs of producing livestock.

## Education: good citizen effect

When you get a degree, you don't just increase your future earnings, you also provide a variety of benefits to the rest of society. As one commentator has written:

> the returns to education extend well beyond increases in graduate earnings. Education ... also yields additional indirect benefits through processes such as stimulating physical capital investments and the development and adoption of new technology ... Other social benefits of investing in education include reduced levels of criminal activity, more informed public debate, improved social cohesion, and more sophisticated voting behaviour.

> Source: Watson (2002), p. 5.

When someone is trying to decide whether to invest time and money in a university education, we would expect them to take into account the benefits that they will personally receive, such as higher earnings. But they are not likely to take into account any benefits to the rest of society from them obtaining a degree. In this way, the benefits to society are an unpriced or external effect of an individual deciding to acquire extra education. As the effect improves the wellbeing of society, it is a positive externality.

Hence, the level of education that individuals choose to acquire is likely to be less than the efficient level.

Possible solutions to this type of external effect are a compulsory schooling law that requires all children to attend school until they reach a specified minimum age, and government subsidies for the provision of education that reduce the cost of schooling and thereby increase the incentives to stay at school longer. By increasing levels of education, both policies should improve society's wellbeing.

## Environmental effects of plastic shopping bags

The use of plastic bags by shoppers causes significant damage. Of the 3.9 billion bags used each year in Australia, it has been estimated that 30 million may end up as litter (Productivity Commission 2006, p. 207). Some of the bags will be part of the 10 million tonnes of plastics that enter the world's oceans each year, causing damage to marine life (*The Economist* 2018a). These are unpriced effects since the cost of shopping bags to shoppers does not reflect the costs of the environmental damage caused by their use. It constitutes a negative external effect.

Possible remedies to deal with the problems caused by plastic shopping bags that have been proposed are a ban or a tax on the use of plastic bags. In Australia, it is the former policy that has been preferred, with all states and territories except New South Wales having policies to phase out the use of lightweight plastic bags (Comack 2016). Not everyone agrees with the policy of banning the bags. One argument is that the environmental cost of manufacturing substitute bags, such as a cotton tote bag, is so high as to undo any benefit from the policy. Another argument is that the policy penalises everyone who uses plastic bags rather than the small proportion of users whose actions cause litter; implying that a much better approach is to have policies that are targeted at reducing littering (Productivity Commission 2006, pp. 216–17).

## Bees

Bees are essential for pollinating food-based crops that are not self-pollinating. Without bees, it has been estimated that the United States 'would lose about $15 billion in crops – almonds, citrus fruits, pears, cucumbers and apples' (*The Economist* 2007, p. 87). In Australia as well, 'one in three mouthfuls of food we eat is the result of insect pollination' (Cornish 2007). Bees have therefore often been described as a classic example of a positive externality. Owners of bees provide a significant benefit to crop farmers that is 'unpriced'. Their importance has meant that a decline in the number of bees in Australia, Europe and the United States has caused great concern (Battersby 2008). What is now referred to as 'colony collapse disorder' (CCD), where whole hives of bees die for no apparent reason, has been the subject of intense investigation since the mid-2000s. Current thinking attributes a major role in CCD to the increasing use of a class of farming pesticides known as neonicotinoids (*The Economist* 2012a). These pesticides have been banned in several regions in Europe.

## Space junk

Outer space is getting crowded. A report in *The Economist* (2009) documented how, 'of the 18 000 tracked objects travelling around the Earth that are larger than 10 cm (4 inches), only about 900 are active satellites. The rest is debris – everything from fragments of paint to entire dead satellites and bits of old rockets'. The problem with all this space junk is that it is dangerous. Should a working satellite collide with a piece of space junk, it would be wiped out, thereby putting at risk mobile phone systems, television broadcasts, weather forecasts and surveillance systems that rely on such satellites.

Each time a government or private organisation launches a new satellite, it increases the amount of space debris that will exist in future years once that satellite is out of commission. More debris increases the probability that a collision with an active satellite will happen, with a consequent adverse effect on the owner and users of that satellite. This higher risk of collision between an active satellite and space junk is an unpriced effect of a government or private organisation deciding to launch a new satellite. The satellite launcher might take into account the likelihood of a collision in the future with another of its own satellites and the consequent effect on its wellbeing, but would not be concerned about collisions with active satellites owned by other organisations. With this negative externality, the amount of satellites launched will be greater than is efficient.

One proposed solution to reduce the number of new satellites is a scheme of insurance, whereby organisations launching satellites would be required to make payments against the possibility that the 'life spans' of their satellites turn out to be shorter than expected. This proposal is akin to a tax where the required payment would be larger the shorter a satellite's life span, and hence the longer the time it will spend as debris. This addresses market failure by giving organisations an incentive to launch satellites that will have the longest possible life spans, hence reducing the number of satellites that need to be launched in the future. An alternative proposal is to ban activities that needlessly increase the amount of space debris – for example, a moratorium on anti-satellite tests, where satellites are launched and then destroyed by missiles, simply for the purpose of testing the missile technology.

## Junk food

Eating junk food, such as those French fries or that can of Coke you didn't really need, may bring about feelings of guilt as you contemplate the effect on your waistline. The effects, however, are likely to go beyond your waistline. By contributing to what is often described today as an 'obesity epidemic', junk food is causing an increase in society's medical costs. A study by PWC concluded that the cost of obesity in Australia in 2011–12 was over $8 billion, with about one-half being direct costs such as medical expenses and one-half indirect costs including the value of lost output (PWC 2015).

While individual consumers should take into account any adverse effects of the consumption of junk food on their own future health, we don't expect that they will take into account the costs of extra health care that will be paid for by other members of society. So, there is an unpriced effect of the consumption of junk food. Since this is a negative externality, it follows that the amount of junk food consumed will be above the socially optimal level.

The adverse consequences of obesity have led to proposals intended to reduce consumption of junk food, such as bans on some types of junk food, or the imposition of extra taxes on junk food. In recent times, the attention of policymakers has focused on sugary drinks – with the United Kingdom introducing a tax on drinks with over 5 mg of sugar per 100 ml (*The Economist* 2018b); and governments in Australia being urged to take the same action (Duckett & Swerissen 2016). Despite concerns about obesity, taxing sugary drinks has not been universally supported. One problem is that the link between consuming sugary drinks and costs to society is less direct than for other behaviours that are regulated, such as smoking. Regulating the consumption may therefore have unintended consequences. For example, even people who, because they exercise regularly, do not experience obesity and hence do not impose extra medical costs on society would have to pay more for sugary drinks (Freebairn 2010). A second potential problem is the suggestion that consumers will respond to the tax by substituting to other sources of sugar, such as alcohol (*The Economist* 2018c). A third problem is that a tax on sugary drinks is regressive, as low-income households spend a larger share of their income on this item (*The Economist* 2019).

## Air quality in India and China

Being the world champion of air pollution is a title that in the past 250 years has usually gone to a country undergoing rapid industrialisation. In the eighteenth century it was England; today it is China and India. Industrialisation brings many benefits to a country – but air pollution is certainly not one of them. Recent studies have estimated that the life spans of northern Chinese are 5.5 years shorter on average because of air pollution; and that the 660 million Indians most exposed to air pollution could live for three extra years if that pollution was reduced to meet national standards (*The Economist* 2015a). China's Prime Minister Li Keqiang declared war on air pollution in 2014, and India has also made moves to improve its air quality (*The Economist* 2015b).

Air pollution in China and India comes from several main sources. These include fumes from paraffin-fuelled stoves and from motor vehicles, smoke from diesel-powered generators and coal-fired power stations, and emissions from steel mills and factories. Whatever the source, we can be pretty sure that the individual or business causing the air pollution made the decision about how much pollution to emit taking into account the effect on their own wellbeing, but not the impact on the rest of the population living in that region. Hence, that impact on the rest of the population is an unpriced effect of their activity. Because air pollution lowers the wellbeing of the other members of society, we say that it is a negative externality – and it follows that the volume of air pollution will be greater than the socially optimal level.

Aware of the serious costs it is imposing on their countries, governments in China and India have introduced policies intended to reduce air pollution. Both countries have favoured direct regulation. China, for example, has ordered mass closures of businesses that are the worst polluters and banned the use of coal-powered heating in public buildings (*The Economist* 2018d). These policies seem to be working, with substantial decreases in concentrations of air pollutants in major cities such as Beijing during the 2010s (*The Economist* 2017a). India has introduced new emissions standards for motor vehicles and sought to reduce driving in major cities. But these policies do not deal with what remains a major source of air pollution in India – the burn-off of stubble from crops by farmers after harvest season (*The Economist* 2016).

## Overfishing

Declining fish stocks in oceans and freshwater locations are a concern in many parts of the world. The decline can be attributed to an externality problem. Where a fisher catches a fish, this reduces the total stock available for other fishers, and also reduces the future stock of fish as fewer fish are available to breed. Although a fisher will take account of the effect of the reduction of stock on their own future capacity to catch fish, we would not expect them to take account of the effect on other fishers. Hence, this is a negative external effect. The quantity of fish caught in any time period will be greater than the efficient quantity.

A United Nations Food and Agriculture Organisation report has estimated that in 2013 32 per cent of the world's fish stocks were being exploited beyond their sustainable limit, a three-fold increase on the 1970s. By allowing stocks to rise to their optimal levels it would be possible to raise the value of ocean fishing by $32 billion per year (*The Economist* 2017b).

The good news is that there has been increasing recognition of the costs of overfishing, accompanied by new policy solutions to restore depleted fish stocks. Policy solutions applied in Australia have involved direct regulation, establishing a scheme whereby only fishers assigned licences are allowed to fish for specified quantities of each fish species, and creating sanctuary zones where no fishing is allowed (Darby 2007). Another approach is to seek to create incentives for fishers to avoid overfishing. For example, Chile has sought to manage the stock of sea snails off its Pacific coastline by assigning groups of fishers defined areas of seabed, giving them exclusive long-term rights to fish in that area (*The Economist* 2012c). Making the fishers effectively the owners of an area of seabed gives them a greater incentive to take into account the consequences of their actions on the long-term fish stock in that area. For such a policy to work, however, it requires effective enforcement by government – and where that enforcement is absent, as it has been in Indonesia's marine protected areas, the effects on fish stocks are limited (*The Economist* 2017b).

Using the World Trade Organisation to reduce government subsidies paid to fishers, currently worth $30 billion a year, has also been proposed as a way to reduce incentives for overfishing (*The Economist* 2017b).

## The multidivision firm

External effects do not just occur in markets. They can also be important within organisations. An example is where an organisation has multiple divisions that operate with autonomy. Suppose that a business has two divisions, each of which has been given the objective of maximising profits from its own activities. If one of the divisions can take some action that will increase its own profits, but at the expense of lower profits for the other unit, this can be thought of as a negative externality. The cost to the organisation is that its overall profits are not maximised.

In Michael Lewis' wonderful account of his time as a trader for Salomon Brothers, *Liar's Poker*, he describes how, by paying traders on the basis of the profits earned by the division for which they worked, an incentive was created for traders to steal profits from other divisions (1989, pp. 144–8; see also Milgrom & Roberts 1992, pp. 9–12). Lewis tells how the manager of mortgage trading, Mark Smith, who was losing money on bonds he was holding,

> began by telling people that all along his bonds had meant to be bundled together with the bonds held by the mortgage arbitrage group … He then informed the mortgage arbitrage traders that their profitable IO (interest-only) bonds belonged in his trading account … Smith was stealing profits from other traders.

Source: Lewis (1989), p. 147.

Salomon Brothers subsequently sought to solve these externality problems by reforming its compensation scheme for traders in a way that tied payments to the long-term market value of the whole firm. Linking payment to firm performance was intended to give traders an incentive to worry about Salomon Brothers' overall profitability rather than just the profits of their own division.

A professional sporting competition is another example of a multidivision firm. In this example, the sporting league is the 'firm' and individual clubs are the divisions within the firm. In his book *Reinventing the Bazaar*, John McMillan describes how external effects may also arise in this type of organisation (2002, pp. 129–34). The league wants to maximise the performance of its sporting competition, including maintaining high levels of fan interest. An important influence on fan interest is the extent of competitive balance between teams, with fans preferring a more even competition. The objective of each individual club, however, is to maximise its own winning percentage, which it will seek to do regardless of the implications for other clubs or for competitive balance.

Hence, where each club pursues its own self-interest, there is no guarantee of an even competition. For this reason, the sporting league may need to intervene to ensure a satisfactory level of competitive balance. This can include implementing measures such as redistributing revenue between teams (from rich to poor clubs) and instituting a salary cap to limit the amount that any club can pay in player salaries.

## Network effects

A network externality exists when the value of one person using a product increases with the number of other people using the same product. An example of a product associated with network externalities is the mobile phone. As the economist John Kay has noted, 'there is no point in being the only person with a telephone, and the more people that have them the more valuable an individual phone becomes' (2003, p. 252).

Other examples of products where network externalities exist are computer systems or games, and some websites. If you are the only one using an Apple computer or playing games on a Sony PlayStation, you will not be as well off as if you are using the same computer system or games platform as everyone else, in which case you can more easily share computer files or games. Similarly, the value of a website that seeks to match buyers and sellers, such as a job vacancy and application website, will depend on the number of other users. If a business posts a job vacancy advertisement on a website, the value of posting the advertisement will increase with the number of potential employees who search the website. Equally, if a jobseeker looks for a new job on a website, the value of their search will be greater the larger the number of firms that post job vacancies on that website.

The main lesson for a business operating in a market where network externalities exist is the importance of securing early widespread adoption of its product. The higher the market share of its product, the greater its value to buyers. Hence, future sales of the product will significantly depend on its current market share. If a business is able to attract a sufficiently large market share, its product may even become so highly preferred by consumers that ultimately other suppliers will be forced to exit the market, leaving it as the sole supplier.

# KEY LESSONS

- External effects are ubiquitous in society and arise in ways that are relevant both to government and business.
- Proposals for dealing with external effects in society generally involve seeking to face decision makers with the costs or benefits of those external effects. This might involve a tax or subsidy on the good or activity that is the source of the external effect, or mandating a maximum or minimum quantity of an activity.
- Strategies for business to deal with external effects may involve reorganising the structure of the business or seeking to secure the rapid adoption of new products.

# SOME QUESTIONS TO THINK ABOUT

1   Do you think that there would be external effects associated with any of the following and, if so, what would be the nature of the external effect in each case? Can you think of policies that might deal with each external effect; that is, improve social wellbeing?

a   driving a four-wheel drive vehicle

b   a hotel that is located next to an apartment building and plays loud music late at night

c   water from a uranium mine leaking into Kakadu National Park.

2   Larry the land-clearer is considering how many hectares of trees to clear from his property. From selling the cut-down trees, he will obtain a private marginal benefit:

$$PMB = 120 - 2Q, \text{ where } Q = \text{hectares of cleared land.}$$

His $PMC = Q$. The social marginal benefit from tree-clearing is the same as the private marginal benefit (that is, $PMB = SMB$). However, with respect to social marginal cost, in addition to the PMC that Larry incurs, each hectare of cleared land causes a cost of 30 to neighbouring landowners through increasing the salinity content of their land.

a   How many hectares of land will be cleared in the market outcome? What is the efficient amount of land to be cleared?

b   Discuss possible policy solutions for ensuring that Larry clears an area of land that is efficient. What are the strengths and weaknesses of the solutions you have proposed?

3   The Australian Greens policy on poker machines states:

> Australians are the world's most prolific gamblers. We spend an impressive $1200 per capita every year on bets. Of the $19 billion gambled by Australians every year, 60% (or $12 billion) goes into poker machines. About 4% of the adult population, or 600 000 people, play pokies at least weekly. Up to 15% of the people who gamble weekly are considered 'problem gamblers' who have difficulty controlling their play and expenditure. These problem gamblers account for about 40% of all pokies losses …
>
> Under the Greens' policy, all Australian poker machines will have the following limitations:
>
> • A maximum bet limit of $1 per spin.
> • A load-up limit of $20 …

> Source: (Australian Greens 2014)

a   Do you think there is an externality-related argument to support government regulation of poker machines?

b   Do you think the $1 maximum bet limit is the best policy for addressing any externality?

# REFERENCES

*Australian Financial Review* (2003), 'Flatulence tax for NZ farmers', 21 June, p. 20.

Australian Greens (2014), 'Australia needs a $1 bet limit on poker machines', http://greens.org.au/, viewed 21 March 2014.

Battersby, Luke (2008), 'Beekeepers face mighty challenge from tiny foe', *The Age*, 15 June, p. 3.

Comack, Lucy (2016), 'Australia falling behind third world on global map of plastic bag bans', *Sydney Morning Herald*, 9 April.

Cornish, Richard (2007), 'Attack of the bee killers', *The Age*, Epicure, 14 August, p. 5.

Darby, Andrew (2007), 'Rough justice: over-fishing's net effect', *The Age*, 6 July, p. 3.

Duckett, Stephen & Swerissen, Hal (2016), *A Sugary Drinks Tax*, https://grattan.edu.au/wp-content/uploads/2016/11/880-A-sugary-drinks-tax.pdf, viewed 25 September 2019.

Freebairn, John (2010), 'Taxation and obesity', *Australian Economic Review*, vol. 43, pp. 54–62.

Kay, John (2003), *The Truth about Markets: Their Genius, Their Limits, Their Follies*, Allen Lane.

Lewis, Michael (1989), *Liar's Poker*, W.W. Norton.

McMillan, John (2002), *Reinventing the Bazaar: A Natural History of Markets*, W.W. Norton.

Milgrom, Paul & Roberts, John (1992), *Economics, Organization and Management*, Prentice-Hall.

Price Waterhouse Coopers (PWC) (2015), *Weighing the Cost of Obesity: A Case for Action*, https://www.pwc.com.au/pdf/weighing-the-cost-of-obesity-final.pdf, viewed 25 September 2019.

Productivity Commission (2006), *Waste Management*, inquiry report no. 28.

*The Economist* (2007), 'A sticky ending', 8 September, p. 87.

*The Economist* (2009), 'Flying blind', 21 February, p. 4.

*The Economist* (2012a), 'Subtle poison', 31 March, pp. 85–6.

*The Economist* (2012b), 'Lost property', 25 February, pp. 57–8.

*The Economist* (2015a), 'Breathe uneasy', 7 February, p. 26.

*The Economist* (2015b), 'The cost of unclean air', 7 February, pp. 29–30.

*The Economist* (2016), 'Worse than Beijing', 12 November, p. 24.

*The Economist* (2017a), 'Awry in the sky', 16 December, pp. 27–8.

*The Economist* (2017b), 'All the fish in the sea', 27 May, pp.18–20.

*The Economist* (2018a), 'Too much of a good thing', 3 March, pp. 49–52.

*The Economist* (2018b), 'Sweet talk', 7 April, p. 51.

*The Economist* (2018c), 'The taxes of sin', 28 July, pp. 42–3.

*The Economist* (2018d), 'Towards a greener future', 6 January, pp. 51–3.

*The Economist* (2019), 'Soda stream', 25 May, p. 73.

Urban Institute (2009), 'Reducing obesity: policy strategies from the tobacco wars',
www.urban.org/publications/411926.html, viewed 10 April 2012.

Watson, Louise (2002), *Social transformation and economic growth: the critical role of universities*, National Institute of Social Sciences, Australian National University, September.

# IDEAS FOR FURTHER READING

Tim Harford provides a nice introduction to externalities in chapter 4 of *The Undercover Economist* (2006, Little, Brown and Co.). Another useful introduction is provided by *The Economist* ('The lives of others', 19 August 2019, pp. 55–6). You'll find many interesting illustrations of the concept of externalities in chapter 5 of Robert Frank's *The Economic Naturalist* (2007, Basic Books). An excellent overview of the case for a tax on sugary drinks is provided by Hunt Allcott, Benjamin Lockwood and Dmitry Taubinsky in their article on 'Should we tax sugar-sweetened beverages? An overview of theory and evidence' (2019, *Journal of Economic Perspectives*, 33(3), 202–27. The strengths and weaknesses of a sugary drinks tax for Australia are debated in the Grattan Institute report on *A Sugary Drinks Tax* by Stephen Duckett and Hal Swerissen and the response by Jonathan Pincus ('Grattan Institute's case for sugar tax is not proven', *Australian Economic Review*, 51(1), pp. 41–51).

# CASE STUDY 4.2
## HOW CAN WE UNJAM TRAFFIC JAMS?

The traffic jam has become a regular part of the experience of living in many major cities of the world. But it is not an experience you will find those cities boasting about. For the cities' residents, traffic congestion brings many unpleasant consequences: Longer travelling time and greater fuel usage, as well as the psychological cost for motorists of frustration from seeing pedestrians walking faster than their cars are travelling. Governments at local and national levels are therefore seeking ways in which they can reduce the number of cars and other vehicles on their roads.

In Britain, the European traffic jam champion, the average commuter spent over an hour per day travelling to and from work in 2013/14, up by 15 per cent from three decades previously (UK Department for Transport 2016). Most other countries in western Europe were not far behind, with commuters in France, Italy and Spain spending similar amounts of time travelling each day (OECD 2016). In the United States, the cost of traffic congestion, measured in terms of wasted time and fuel, has been estimated to be US$53 billion in 2017 just for New York and Los Angeles (*The Economist* 2018a). Increases in population and rising income levels making cars more affordable has also seen congestion problems in many developing countries rapidly become much worse (*The Economist* 2018a).

Australian motorists have not been immune from growing car traffic. In Melbourne, morning and evening peak-hour periods now last for 3.5 hours and average travel times increased by 1.4 minutes for every 10 km from 2005 to 2014 (Carey 2016). The costs of traffic congestion in Australia are estimated at between $5 billion and $15 billion per year (Clarke & Prentice 2009).

Of course, saying that there is a large volume of traffic and saying that there is too much traffic are quite different statements. To determine whether there is too much car traffic, we need to know how the actual volume of traffic compares with the efficient level of traffic for society.

To an economist, for the volume of traffic to differ from the efficient level, there must be some source of market failure. In fact, finding market failure in this situation is not difficult. Car travel causes a variety of negative external effects, one of which is exactly the congestion problems that have just been described. When you decide to travel by car, you increase the total volume of car traffic on the roads at that time. Since a greater amount of traffic will cause longer travelling times, your decision to travel by car will increase the amount of time that other motorists will have to spend travelling, albeit by a small amount. But when you decide whether and how to travel, you will only consider your own travelling time. You won't take into account the effect that your decision to travel by car has on the travelling time of other motorists. In this way, your behaviour adversely affects other motorists and is an 'unpriced' negative consequence of your decision to travel by car. Apart from congestion effects, other negative externalities associated with car travel are the creation of air pollution, injuries caused to other travellers, such as pedestrians or cyclists, and the costs of public road and traffic control infrastructure.

Having established the existence of a negative externality from car travel, we have our answer to the question of whether there is too much traffic. Knowing there is a negative externality allows us to conclude that the volume of traffic will be above the level that society regards as efficient. This is shown graphically in *Figure 4.2.1*. Individual drivers decide how many kilometres to travel by car, taking into account their private marginal benefits (PMB) and private marginal costs (PMC). Hence, the individual optimum, or 'market' outcome, will be for $Q^*$ kilometres to be travelled by car. However, due to the costs of increased travelling time imposed by each driver on other motorists, the marginal cost to society (SMC) from each kilometre travelled will be greater than the cost to the individual drivers. The efficient level of travel for society, which reflects the SMC and marginal benefits to society (SMB), is therefore at $Q^{**}$.

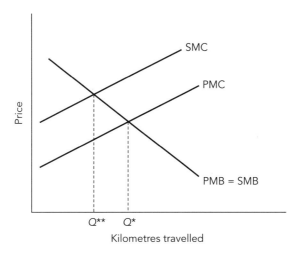

**Figure 4.2.1** Negative externality associated with car travel

The market failure associated with car travel provides a rationale for government intervention. By implementing policies that reduce the volume of car travel to the efficient level, the government can improve a society's wellbeing.

---

**THEORY REFRESHER**

**Dealing with externalities using Pigovian taxes and subsidies**

The existence of an externality implies that in an unregulated market the level of an activity, such as the quantity of a good or service traded, will differ from the efficient level. To improve society's wellbeing, government can therefore adopt policies that shift the level of the activity to the efficient level.

Taxes provide one way of altering the level of an activity undertaken. Taxing an activity raises the costs of doing that activity, and so will reduce the level undertaken. Therefore, the application of a tax can be an appropriate policy for dealing with market failure due to a negative externality. More particularly, by choosing the tax on the activity to be equal to the size of the negative externality, the opportunity cost of doing the activity for individuals in society is made exactly the same as the cost to society. Hence, the 'market' outcome will be equivalent to the efficient outcome. This policy solution is generally attributed to the English economist Arthur Pigou (1877–1959).

A subsidy can be applied in a similar way to deal with market failure due to a positive externality. Providing a subsidy to an activity raises the benefits from doing that activity and hence will increase the level undertaken.

---

Tax policies could be used as one way of reducing car travel. By imposing a tax on car travel, the opportunity cost for individuals choosing to travel by car is thereby increased, with the expected consequence that there will be a decrease in the volume of car traffic. This is illustrated in *Figure 4.2.2*. Imposing a tax (here it is assumed that the tax is per kilometre travelled) increases the marginal cost to individuals of travelling by car. The total opportunity cost to an individual motorist now consists of PMC plus the tax. Therefore, individual motorists will choose to reduce their amount of car travel.

There are a variety of tax-related policies for dealing with traffic congestion. One type of policy that is often referred to as a 'congestion tax' imposes a charge on motorists entering the central business district of a city within specified hours each day. For example, in 2003, London introduced a charge of £5 for cars entering specified city areas between 7 a.m. and 6.30 p.m. on weekdays. The system was initially policed by a set of video cameras that scanned the rear licence plates of cars entering the city areas, and is now a 'tag-and-beacon' system where cars are fitted with electronic tags that are read by roadside detectors. Imposing a congestion tax has been largely successful, reducing the number of cars entering London by a quarter (*The Economist* 2017a). A related idea, also intended to reduce traffic within the central business district of a city, is to increase the cost of parking in that area. This could involve introducing parking fees for public parking spaces that were previously free (*The Economist* 2017b), or imposing

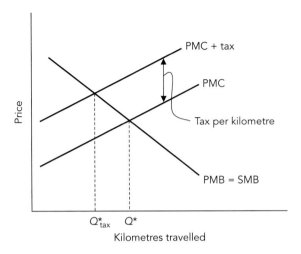

**Figure 4.2.2** Impact of tax on volume of car travel

a tax on private parking operators to cause them to raise their charges. For example, in 2006, the Victorian Government introduced an $820-per-parking-spot levy on 52 000 long-stay car parking spaces provide by private operators in Melbourne (Clarke & Prentice 2009, p. 44). The concept of a congestion tax can also be broadened to encompass charging motorists to travel on any roads, not just in the central business district. An example would be toll roads where motorists pay a charge for travelling between specified points. In advanced toll systems, such as in Singapore, it is possible to have charges that vary by distance driven, time of day, location and type of vehicle (*The Economist* 2017a).

Some commentators, however, have suggested possible problems with tax-type policies for dealing with congestion. One problem is potential spillover effects, where creating toll roads has the consequence of directing higher volumes of traffic onto neighbouring streets and roads. Another issue is that charging for car travel may be politically unpopular. The specific details of tax-type solutions, therefore, need to be designed to deal with these problems.

Other policies for changing motorists' incentives also exist. An example is car pool lanes, where cars with multiple occupants are allowed to travel in an exclusive lane. Encouraging car pooling should reduce the volume of car traffic. The experience in American cities, however, casts doubt on the effectiveness of this policy. California's car pool lanes are 'often virtually empty', as most drivers appear to prefer the flexibility of travelling alone (*The Economist* 2005, p. 35).

Another policy approach is direct regulation, where government seeks to enforce the efficient level of an activity. Restrictions on the types of vehicles allowed to travel on roads at specified times and bans on parking within specified areas are examples of attempts to reduce the amount of car traffic by directly regulating the quantity of traffic.

Responses to traffic congestion in most Australian cities mainly involve supply-based responses; that is, building bigger or extra roads. But as options for expanding the supply of road networks become limited or increasingly expensive, and the environmental costs of car travel come to the fore, there may be a greater role for policies that seek to manage demand (Terrill & Emslie 2016). This will provide new opportunities for the application of policies such as congestion charges and toll roads.

## KEY LESSONS

- Car travel is associated with a variety of negative external effects. One of these effects is that when any individual travels by car, the total volume of car traffic on the roads at that time is increased. This extra traffic congestion is an 'unpriced' consequence of the decision to travel by car. The existence of this negative externality associated with car travel allows us to conclude that the volume of traffic is likely to be above the efficient level.
- Possible solutions are tax-related policies that seek to reduce the volume of car traffic, and direct regulation of car travel.

## SOME QUESTIONS TO THINK ABOUT

1   A variety of tax-related policies are available to address the problem of traffic congestion. These include congestion tax, parking tax, toll roads, or even a tax on petrol. What problems might exist with each of these policies? How would you choose which tax is most appropriate to use to reduce traffic congestion?

2   An article in *The Age* stated:

> Motorists who use the East West Link in the peak hours could pay a higher toll than those who drive on the planned road outside the rush hour. In what would be a first for Melbourne motorists, a 'variable toll' could be set as a way to manage peak hour traffic flows on the link road …

Source: (Carey & Lucas 2014).

Explain why a government policy of setting a variable price for road travel depending on the time of day of travel might increase society's wellbeing.

3   A recent article in *The Economist* (2018b) described how the use of ride-hailing firms like Uber and Lyft has led to extra road congestion in cities such as London and New York. New York responded to this problem in 2018 by placing a one-year moratorium on issuing new licences for ride-hailing cars. But *The*

*Economist* article suggested that a better way for big cities to reduce traffic jams is to implement road pricing. It also suggested that cities with existing congestion charge policies should stop undermining them by offering concessions to green vehicles – that both low-emission cars and petrol-guzzlers needed to pay congestion charges.

a   Use the SMB/SMC diagram to show how (i) the moratorium on issuing new ride-hailing licences and (ii) the congestion tax could reduce traffic and hence improve society's wellbeing.

b   Do you agree that a congestion charge is a better way to regulate traffic than the moratorium on new licences for ride-hailing services?

c   Do you agree that the problems of traffic and pollution need to be treated separately? How could this be done?

# REFERENCES

Carey, Adam & Lucas, Clay (2014), 'Higher price proposed for peak-hour tollway trip', *The Age*, 4 March, p. 2.

Carey, Adam (2016), 'Are we there yet?', *The Age*, 20 February, pp. 6–7.

Clarke, Harry & Prentice, David (2009), *A Conceptual Framework for the Reform of Taxes Related to Roads and Transport*, report prepared for the Henry Review of Taxation in Australia, http://www.treasury.gov.au, viewed 10 April 2012.

Organisation for Economic Cooperation and Development (2016), 'Time spent travelling to and from work', mimeo, https://www.oecd.org/els/family/LMF2_6_Time_spent_travelling_to_and_from_work.pdf, viewed 24 September 2019.

Terrill, Marion & Emslie, Owain (2016), 'The road out of gridlock', *The Age*, 11 September, p. 14.

*The Economist* (2005), 'America's great headache', 4 June, pp. 34–5.

*The Economist* (2006), 'Jambusters', 7 January, p. 57.

*The Economist* (2017a), 'The price of jam', 5 August, pp. 45–6.

*The Economist* (2017b), 'Aparkalypse now', 8 April, p. 10.

*The Economist* (2018a), 'The slow and the furious', 8 September, pp. 49–50.

*The Economist* (2018b), 'Rules of the road', 25 August, p. 9.

United Kingdom Department of Transport (2016), *Commuting Trends in England 1988–2015*, https://assets.publishing.service.gov.uk/government/uploads/system/uploads/attachment_data/file/657839/commuting-in-england-1988-2015.pdf, viewed 24 September 2019.

# IDEAS FOR FURTHER READING

Tim Harford provides a nice introduction to externalities, including traffic congestion, in chapter 4 of *The Undercover Economist* (2006, Little, Brown and Co.). Ian Parry, Margaret Walls and Winston Harrington review policies for dealing with car-related externalities in their 2007 article 'Automobile externalities and policies' (*Journal of Economic Literature*, vol. 45, pp. 373–99). You can read more about Arthur Pigou in Steven Pressman's book *Fifty Major Economists* (2002, Routledge, pp. 95–9).

Graeme Davison's book *Car Wars* (2004, Allen and Unwin) tells the story of how car travel took over the city of Melbourne. A major overview of traffic congestion in Melbourne and Sydney is provided in a 2017 Grattan Institute report on 'Stuck in Traffic?' by Marion Terrill (https://grattan.edu.au/report/stuck-in-traffic/, viewed 24 September 2019).

# CASE STUDY 4.3
## WHY WOULD WE WANT TO TRADE POLLUTION?

Trade in pollution may seem a strange idea. Yet it is an idea that is taking hold around the world as countries seek to address the problems of climate change and the excessive emission of pollutants.

In 2005, the European Union Emissions Trading Scheme was introduced as part of an attempt by countries in Europe to meet their obligations to reduce carbon emissions under the Kyoto Protocol. That market currently covers over 14 000 energy-intensive plants across 31 countries and trades allowances to produce about 40 per cent of the total carbon emitted in the European Union (Dechezleprêtre et al. 2018). Other examples of trading schemes are the UK Landfill Allowance Trading Scheme and permit systems for the emission of sulphur dioxide (the cause of acid rain) in the United States and China (*The Economist* 2015).

The 2006 Stern report on the economics of climate change, which was commissioned by the British Government, estimated that climate change could cost the world economy between 5 and 20 per cent of global output, and supported tradeable pollution permits as a possible method for controlling emissions of carbon dioxide.

Australia moved towards adopting an emissions trading scheme in the early 2010s. The *Clean Energy Act 2011* introduced a tax on carbon emissions of $23 per tonne from 1 July 2012. The tax was imposed on about 500 businesses in Australia that were emitting more than 25 000 tonnes of $CO_2e$ (carbon dioxide equivalent) per year (Clean Energy Regulator 2015). The carbon tax was to be transformed into an emissions trading scheme on 1 July 2015. Before this could happen, however, the carbon pricing mechanism in Australia was abolished through the repeal of the *Clean Energy Act 2011* (Clean Energy Regulator 2015).

What is meant by a system of trading pollution or pollution permits? Essentially, such a system incorporates two main components. First, there is direct regulation of the total quantity of the pollutant that can be emitted. This is done by requiring businesses in a geographic region, such as a city or country, to own a 'permit' in order to be allowed to emit a specified quantity of the pollutant. By issuing a fixed total quantity of permits, a government can restrict the total quantity of pollution emitted to this amount. Second, following an initial allocation of permits between firms in the economy, these firms are offered the opportunity to trade their permits with each other. The scope for firms to trade permits means that they can vary the amount of pollutants they emit by buying or selling permits.

---

### THEORY REFRESHER

#### What is direct regulation?

Direct regulation is where a policymaker, such as the government, specifies a maximum or minimum allowable level of an activity. An example of direct regulation is when a government specifies maximum allowable driving speeds on roads, or that children must remain at school at least until they reach a minimum age.

When there is an externality associated with an activity, market failure is manifested in either too low or too high a level of that activity compared with the efficient outcome. Direct regulation seeks to solve this problem by 'forcing' the level of the activity to be at the efficient level. For example, if a government believed that the efficient level of usage of plastic shopping bags was zero, it could force this outcome by banning their use. Potential problems with the application of direct regulation are that a government must know the efficient level of an activity in order to set the allowable level correctly, and that enforcing the regulation may be costly.

---

Regulating the number of permits to emit a pollutant makes it possible for a government to constrain the total amount of pollution to what it believes is an efficient level. In practical terms, this usually involves seeking to reduce the total emission of pollution from current levels to a lower efficient quantity of pollution. This is referred to as abatement of pollution. Pollution abatement will have benefits to society by, for example, improving air quality and decreasing the extent of climate change. The costs to society from pollution abatement will include the costs of adopting new production technologies that emit less pollution and perhaps costs of lower levels of output.

To determine the optimal amount by which a society should reduce its emission of pollution, we can think in terms of the social marginal benefit (SMB) and social marginal cost (SMC) of pollution abatement. This may take a little effort to grasp. It is different from how we would usually think of SMB and SMC. In most cases, we are concerned with the SMB and SMC of doing an extra unit of an activity or trading an extra unit of a good or service. Here, we are thinking of the SMB and SMC of doing one less unit of the activity of emitting pollution.

It is standard to assume that the SMB from each extra unit of pollution abatement decreases with the quantity by which pollution has already been reduced. This is equivalent to saying that the greatest benefit to society comes from the initial units by which pollution is reduced from its current level. The SMC of pollution abatement is assumed to increase with the amount by which pollution is reduced. This means that the cost to society of reducing pollution by some amount is lower for the initial units by which pollution is reduced than for subsequent units. These assumptions on SMB and SMC are illustrated in *Figure 4.3.1*. The 'zero' point on the horizontal axis represents the current level of emission of pollutants. Moving to the right along the horizontal axis represents the amount of pollution abatement, with larger amounts further to the right.

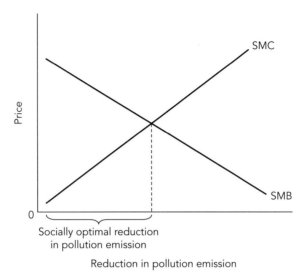

**Figure 4.3.1** Comparing the SMB and SMC of pollution abatement to calculate an efficient level

The efficient amount of pollution abatement is where SMB and SMC are equal – at the intersection of the SMB and SMC curves. At a zero level of abatement the SMB of doing a unit of abatement is above the SMC. Hence society's wellbeing is increased by doing that unit of abatement. The same argument can be made for every extra unit of abatement up to the level where SMB and SMC intersect. Doing each of those extra units of abatement adds more to society's wellbeing than the cost to society of reducing pollution by that unit. However, for units of abatement greater than the level where SMB and SMC intersect, the addition to society's wellbeing from each extra unit is less than the cost to society. Therefore, it reduces society's wellbeing to do units of abatement beyond the level where SMB and SMC intersect. It follows that society's wellbeing is maximised at the level of abatement where SMB and SMC intersect.

To achieve the efficient amount of pollution abatement, pollution permits would need to be issued for an amount equal to the current level of emission minus the efficient level of pollution abatement. For example, if the current level of emission of a pollutant is 100 tonnes and the efficient level of abatement is 40 tonnes, the government should issue permits for 60 tonnes of the pollutant to be emitted.

So, the total amount of pollution emission can be regulated to be at the efficient level by the total number of permits issued. But then why allow firms to trade their permits? What does society gain from this trade?

Efficiency requires that society expend the least possible amount of resources in reducing pollution emission to the target level. Hence, where firms differ in their marginal costs of pollution abatement, achieving the efficient outcome will require firms that can reduce their emission of pollution more cheaply to undertake a larger amount of pollution abatement. Assigning property rights and allowing trade in permits will achieve this outcome: Firms emit different amounts of pollution that relate to their costs of pollution abatement.

Differences in abatement costs between firms are likely to be large, and so allowing for firms to emit amounts of pollution that vary according to their costs of abatement is important for getting the socially optimal outcome. For example, it has been estimated that firms can differ in their costs of reducing emission of sulphur dioxide from $60 to $1200 per tonne of gas emitted (*The Economist* 2002).

To better understand why allowing trade in permits will achieve an efficient distribution of pollution emission between firms, we'll consider a numerical example, represented using **Figure 4.3.2**. The total amount by which it is socially efficient to reduce pollution is represented by the length of the horizontal axis. We assume there are two firms in the economy. The amount of pollution abatement undertaken by firm 1 is measured rightwards on the horizontal axis and the amount of abatement by firm 2 is measured leftwards. For example, the point at the far right of the horizontal axis would imply that all the pollution abatement is being done by firm 1.

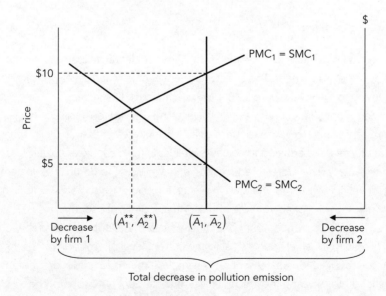

**Figure 4.3.2** Effect of differences in PMC and SMC on pollution abatement

Suppose, as is shown in **Figure 4.3.2**, that firm 1 has a higher SMC of reducing pollution than firm 2. With this difference in costs of abatement, an allocation that was at

($\bar{A}_1$, $\bar{A}_2$), where each firm reduces pollution by an equal amount, would not be efficient. This is because at that allocation, it is costing firm 1 $10 for the last unit by which it reduced its pollution, compared with $5 for the last unit by which firm 2 reduced its pollution. By making firm 2 reduce its pollution by one more unit, and allowing firm 1 to emit one more unit of pollution, society would save $10 and have an extra cost of $5; that is, a net gain of $5 for reducing pollution by the same total amount.

This example illustrates a general principle. Whenever the marginal cost of pollution abatement differs between firms, it will be possible to reduce the cost to society of achieving pollution abatement by having a firm with lower marginal costs reduce its pollution by one more unit, and having a firm with higher marginal costs increase its pollution by one unit. Hence, the efficient distribution of pollution abatement between firms is where each firm reduces its emission of pollution by an amount such that their marginal costs of pollution abatement are equalised. It follows that in the example in **Figure 4.3.2** the efficient amount of pollution reduction is at ($A_1$**, $A_2$**), where firm 2 reduces its emission of pollution by more than firm 1.

You might think this means that all a government has to do is to give each firm an amount of permits that corresponds to its SMC of abatement. But knowing enough about individual firms' costs to calculate the efficient amount of pollution abatement for each firm will almost certainly be well beyond the information that a government has available. For example, in the European Union Emissions Trading Scheme, permits had to be allocated to 13 000 businesses. Working out the optimal level of emissions for each business would have been a Herculean task and, most likely, would have produced badly flawed results. In fact, even knowing the total amount of pollution abatement required is difficult for a government. It now seems to be accepted that in the initial phase of the European Union Emissions Trading Scheme, regulators overestimated the amount of carbon dioxide being emitted in Europe. As a consequence, too many permits were allocated to achieve the amount of pollution abatement that had been intended (*The Economist* 2015).

With a permit trading system, governments do not need to worry about how they initially distribute permits among firms. Regardless of the initial allocation of permits, the scope for trade should lead to each firm emitting an amount of pollution that is efficient. We can understand this point by looking again at the numerical example in **Figure 4.3.2**. Suppose that the initial allocation of pollution permits is at the point considered to be where each firm is required to reduce its pollution by the same amount ($\bar{A}_1$, $\bar{A}_2$). At that allocation, firm 1 is willing to pay up to $10 to be allowed to increase its emission of pollution by one unit, because this is how much it would cost the firm to decrease its emission of pollution by that unit. At the same time, firm 2 needs to be paid at least $5 to be willing to decrease its emission of pollution by one extra unit. This is the cost to firm 2 of one extra unit of pollution abatement. Hence, there is scope for mutually beneficial trade. Firm 2 can offer to sell one permit to firm 1 at some price between $5 and $10, say $7.50, and the offer will be accepted.

Both firms are thereby made better off. Firm 1 values the right to emit an extra unit of pollution at $10 and obtains this right for $7.50; and firm 2 is paid $7.50 for reducing its pollution by one unit which costs it $5. Notice that this trade is also efficient as it moves the distribution of pollution emission between firms closer to the efficient outcome. Firm 1 does less abatement and firm 2 does more. The same scope for mutually beneficial trade created by firm 2 offering to sell permits to firm 1 will exist so long as the amount of pollution reduction by both firms is such that their marginal costs differ. Hence, we would expect trade to continue until the amount of pollution reduction by each firm is $(A_1^{**}, A_2^{**})$. Trade in permits between the firms, which they would both have a private incentive to undertake, will therefore result in the efficient distribution of pollution abatement between firms.

## KEY LESSONS

- The level of emission of pollutants in a competitive market is likely to be greater than the efficient level. This is because producers do not take into account the social costs of pollution in making a decision on the level of the production activity that is causing the pollution.
- A pollution permit system has been proposed as one method of achieving an efficient level of pollution emission. This system involves regulation of the total emission of pollution through the number of permits issued and allowing trade in permits between firms that emit pollution.
- The rationale for trade in pollution permits is to ensure that each firm emits the efficient level of pollution. Mutually beneficial trade between firms should ensure that firms with lower marginal costs of pollution abatement will decrease pollution emission by more than firms with higher marginal costs of pollution abatement.
- To implement a pollution permit system, a government needs to know the efficient aggregate quantity of pollution emission to allow, but it does not need to know information on the costs of pollution abatement for each individual firm in the economy.

## SOME QUESTIONS TO THINK ABOUT

1   Consider the example shown in *Figure 4.3.2*. Suppose the PMC and SMC of reducing pollution decreases for firm 1. How would this affect the efficient distribution of reduction of pollution emission between the firms? Suppose that the allocation prior to the reduction in costs for firm 1 was $(A_1^{**}, A_2^{**})$. Would the trading system allow the distribution of reduction in pollution between firms to shift to the new, efficient distribution?

2   Some commentators have suggested that a tax on businesses per tonne of carbon they emit is a better way of reducing carbon emissions than a permit or emissions trading system. What would be the reasons for preferring one approach over the other?

3   The 2000s were a period of low rainfall in eastern Australia. One report (*The Economist* 2003) described how the mouth of the Murray River, Australia's main river, had dried up for only the second time in the 215 years of European settlement. Should reductions in the flow of the river continue, rising salt levels are likely to make Adelaide's water supply, drawn from the Murray, undrinkable.

   One policy proposal was for a set of systems whereby the governments of the three states bordering the Murray River (Victoria, NSW and South Australia) (a) determined the total amount of water that users in their state could take from the Murray River system, and (b) facilitated the trade of water rights between users.

   a   How can direct regulation of the amount of water taken from the Murray River improve social wellbeing?

   b   How might allowing trade between users of water improve social wellbeing compared with a system where water users are given the right to use a specified amount of water and are not allowed to trade?

   c   Why might allowing each state to have a separate system for determining water rights and the trading of those rights limit the potential benefits of the regulation of water rights?

# REFERENCES

Clean Energy Regulator (2015), 'About the carbon pricing mechanism', http://www.cleanenergyregulator.gov.au/Infohub/CPM/About-the-mechanism

Dechezleprêtre, Antoine, Nachtigall, Daniel & Venmans, Frank (2018), 'The joint impact of the European Union Emissions Trading System on carbon emissions and economic performance', OECD Economics Department Working Paper no. 1515, http://www.oecd.org/officialdocuments/publicdisplaydocumentpdf/?cote=ECO/WKP(2018)63&docLanguage=En, viewed 24 September 2019.

*The Economist* (2002), 'A great leap forward', 11 May, p. 77.

*The Economist* (2003), 'Drying out', 12 July, p. 2.

*The Economist* (2015), 'The best is the enemy of the green', 5 December, p. 72.

# IDEAS FOR FURTHER READING

A readable introduction to climate change science is provided by Solomon Hsiang and Robert Kopp in their article 'An economist's guide to climate change science' (2018, *Journal of Economic Perspectives*, 32(4), 3–32). *Sunburnt Country: The History and*

*Future of Climate Change in Australia* by Joelle Gergis (2018, Melbourne University Publishing) is an excellent account of how climate change has and will affect Australia.

The main report on climate change and policy responses in Australia is the Garnaut report. The updated version of Ross Garnaut's report is *The Garnaut Review 2011: Australia in the Global Response to Climate Change* (Cambridge University Press). Some of these issues are discussed by a lead author of the 2014 Intergovernmental Panel on Climate Change report, Frank Jotzo, in 'Economics and policy of climate change' (chapter 8 in Jan Libich, 2015, *Real-World Economics and Policy: Insights from Leading Australian Economists*, Cengage). A paper by Lawrence Goulder and Andrew Schein (2013, 'Carbon taxes versus cap and trade: A critical review', National Bureau of Economic Research, Working Paper no. 19338) provides an excellent introduction to and evaluation of emissions trading schemes.

# CASE STUDY 4.4
# GETTING VACCINATED AGAINST INFLUENZA: THERE IS A 'WIN–WIN' IN ECONOMICS

Influenza is the illness that keeps coming back. It was responsible for the worst pandemic in history, the Spanish influenza disaster of 1918–20, in which over 20 million people died. Today, the world's influenza seasons remain deadly, killing up to 650 000 people each year (World Health Organization 2019). The economic burden of influenza is also substantial, with one study estimating the cost to the United States alone to be in the vicinity of US$11 billion per annum (Putri et al. 2018).

The main medical intervention to prevent influenza is giving people the annual jab in the arm to immunise them against that year's strain(s). Experimental vaccines were created in the 1930s and were first approved for human use by the US military in the Second World War (Artenstein 2010). Nowadays, production of the influenza vaccine occurs on a mass scale, with over 400 million doses manufactured for each cycle of winter seasons. While research on a vaccine that will last forever is underway, at present acquiring maximum protection still requires getting a dose of the latest vaccination, targeted at this year's anticipated strains of influenza (Du et al. 2010).

Whether to be vaccinated is a decision that each of us makes every time winter rolls around. Of course, nobody wants to catch influenza, and by having the injection we get the benefit that this is less likely to happen. However, vaccination is far from universal, implying that many people believe the costs of the immunisation outweigh the expected benefits. This wouldn't be a problem if having influenza was just an event that happened to an individual, with no consequences for other members of society. But it's not. Influenza is a contagious disease. When one member of society gets influenza, it makes it more likely that other members will become ill.

---

### THEORY REFRESHER

For a 'Theory refresher' on 'Externalities are everywhere', see Case study 4.1.

---

This is where economics comes into the picture. You may think it strange to suggest that economists would have anything to say about medicine and influenza. In fact, the choice of whether to be vaccinated is, for an economist, a perfect example of the existence of an externality.

Because influenza is contagious, someone who is vaccinated not only reduces the likelihood that they will catch influenza, they also lower the likelihood of their friends and relatives becoming ill. This raises the wellbeing of those friends and relatives, but it is not an effect that would necessarily be taken into account by the individual in deciding whether to have the vaccination. Getting immunised therefore can be thought of as an activity that produces a positive externality. Since an individual fails to take into account the benefit to other members of society, it follows that the proportion of society choosing to have a vaccination will be less than is socially optimal.

The existence of market failure – a vaccination rate that is less than is socially optimal – introduces the scope for government to intervene to improve wellbeing. This would happen by the government implementing policies that increase the proportion of the population being vaccinated. To be able to do this, to design a policy that will be most effective in improving wellbeing, there is an essential piece of information for the government to know: That the size of the positive externality associated with having an influenza vaccination will vary by the age of the individual being vaccinated.

Why does the size of the externality vary in this way? Well, if you think about it for a minute, it will probably be obvious. Children have more extensive social networks, and therefore they have greater opportunity to spread flu than adults (*The Economist* 2007; Gorlick 2010). So, when an influenza injection is given to a child, the spillover effect of reducing the incidence of flu in the rest of the population is larger than when an adult is vaccinated. Since vaccinating children has greater scope to reduce the proportion of the population who catch influenza, the size of the positive external effect of having children vaccinated is greater than for the older population. A larger positive external effect for children than adults implies that the extent of market failure is larger for children than for adults. Differences in the size of positive externality from vaccination between children and adults has an important implication for policy-makers. It follows that socially optimal vaccination rates and the extent of market failure will differ between children and adults.

*Figure 4.4.1* demonstrates this conclusion graphically, using a model that represents the privately optimal and socially optimal outcomes. To simplify the analysis, the population is considered to consist of two equally sized age groups, children and adults. There are three important features of the diagrams. First, adults are assumed to have a higher private marginal benefit (PMB) from vaccination than children. As the incidence of death from influenza is much higher for adults than for children, it makes sense to think that the private benefit from vaccination increases with age. For example, in Australia in 2017, 92% of deaths from influenza were among the population aged 65 years and over (De Castro et al. 2019). Second, the size of the positive external effect associated with vaccination is assumed to be higher for children than for adults. This assumption fits with the discussion above about how children are more likely to spread influenza than adults. Third, vaccinations for children and adults are assumed to have the same private marginal cost (PMC) and social marginal cost (SMC).

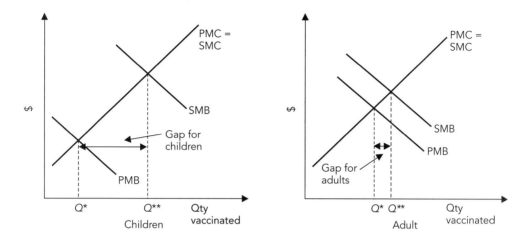

**Figure 4.4.1** The gap between socially optimal and privately optimal numbers of children and adults vaccinated

The main lesson from **Figure 4.4.1** is how the extent of market failure varies between adults and children. In each diagram, the gap between the socially optimal and privately optimal outcomes is measured by the distance between $Q^{**}$ and $Q^*$. Because $(Q^{**}_{children} - Q^*_{children})$ is a greater distance than $(Q^{**}_{adult} - Q^*_{adult})$, we can conclude that the size of the gap between the socially optimal and privately optimal outcomes is larger for children than for adults. This result provides a strong message for policymakers. To address market failure, vaccination rates need to be increased more for children than adults.

One other point to note from the diagrams is that the privately optimal vaccination rate for adults exceeds that for children ($Q^*_{adult} > Q^*_{child}$). This reflects the higher private benefit from vaccination for adults than children. This pattern is consistent with evidence that a much higher proportion of the older population in countries such as Australia and the United States are vaccinated than younger age groups (*The Economist* 2012).

Our analysis of the vaccination decision has identified that not enough people are likely to get a flu injection; and that this problem will be particularly pronounced for children. The next step, then, is to think about how a government can get more of the population to be vaccinated. A variety of policies might help. A first possibility is direct regulation: mandating an annual influenza vaccination. This might be required for the whole population, or the policy could seek to address the differential extent of market failure between age groups by only requiring that children receive influenza vaccinations. A second possibility is to introduce a subsidy which lowers the cost of vaccination.

By decreasing the cost (PMC) of being vaccinated, the subsidy induces a larger proportion of the population to choose to get vaccinated. Ideally, the subsidy would be designed so that the reduction in cost reflects the size of the gap between social benefit and private benefit for different age groups. Larger positive external effects from vaccination for children than for adults would imply a larger subsidy for children than for adults. A third option is an education campaign about the benefits of vaccination. This may provide better information to individuals who currently underestimate the private benefits of being vaccinated. Also, education about the benefits to society that stem from vaccination might cause some individuals to 'internalise' those benefits to society when they make their vaccination decision.

In countries such as Australia, it is the subsidy and education policies that have been most commonly adopted. Influenza vaccination is provided free of charge in Australia to population groups regarded as being at risk of a poor health outcome should they catch influenza, such as persons aged over 65 years. As an example of education-oriented policies, Australia takes part in the World Health Organization's Immunisation Awareness Week program, which in 2012 had as a focus to raise immunisation rates among adolescents (Victorian Department of Health 2012).

In recent years though, there has also been a move to make use of direct regulation. The 'no jab, no play' policy introduced in 2017 seeks to induce more parents to immunise their children by:

(i) withholding government child-related welfare payments from parents of children under 20 years of age who are not fully immunised or on a recognised catch-up schedule

(ii) imposing fines on childcare centres that admit unvaccinated children (Commonwealth Department of Health 2017).

None of these policies is likely to work perfectly. A criticism of direct regulation, for example, is that it hardens attitudes against vaccination; and it has been suggested that eventually people stop listening to advertising campaigns (*The Economist* 2016). The good news though is that we may not need to achieve universal vaccination to reach the social optimum. Once a sufficiently large proportion of the population is vaccinated, then the negative spillover effects from others remaining unvaccinated would be small. In fact, it has been estimated that a vaccination rate of about 77 per cent among the younger population would be sufficient to eradicate influenza (*The Economist* 2007).

## KEY LESSONS

- The decision to have an influenza vaccination is associated with a positive externality, as someone who is vaccinated not only lowers the likelihood that they will catch influenza, they also lower the likelihood of their friends and relatives becoming ill. The existence of a positive externality associated with influenza vaccination implies that the proportion of society choosing to have an influenza vaccination will be less than is socially optimal.

- Vaccinating children has greater scope to reduce the spread of influenza, so the size of the positive external effect of having children vaccinated is greater than for the older population. The larger positive external effect for children implies that the extent of market failure is larger for children than for adults; that is, achieving the socially optimal outcome will require increasing the vaccination rate for children by a larger amount than for adults.

- Government can alleviate market failure by seeking to increase the vaccination rate. This might occur via direct regulation, providing a subsidy for influenza vaccinations, or by an education campaign.

# SOME QUESTIONS TO THINK ABOUT

1  Ingrid Inventor has invented a new product, the Cosmic Communicator, which is strapped to the user's head and allows them to send their thoughts to another person. However, for this to happen, the receiver of the thoughts must also own a Cosmic Communicator and have it strapped to their own head. Alan Accountant says: 'These Cosmic Communicators are great. Everyone will have a private marginal benefit of owning one that is greater than the private marginal cost of supply. So, the market outcome will be efficient.' But Edwina Economist has a different opinion: 'The private marginal benefit of a Cosmic Communicator is less than the social marginal benefit. Therefore, the government should subsidise this product to ensure that a socially optimal quantity is supplied.'

    Consider the statements made by Alan Accountant and Edwina Economist. State whether you believe each statement is correct or incorrect.

2  Suppose that there are two producers in an economy: An apiary and an apple orchard. The apiary is located next door to the orchard, and bees that fly into the orchard pollinate the apple crop; that is, the apiary provides an external benefit to the apple orchard. Suppose also that the apiary's MB and MC can be expressed as follows (where $Q$ = quantity of honey produced by the apiary):

$$PMB = 100 - Q$$
$$SMB = 120 - Q$$
$$PMC = SMC = 20$$

a  What quantity of honey will the apiary produce if it chooses the level that is privately optimal (market outcome)? What is the size of the positive external effect? What is the socially optimal quantity of honey to produce? Draw a diagram representing these outcomes.

b Is it possible for the government to intervene to ensure that the apiary produces a socially optimal quantity of output? How could it achieve this objective with a tax/subsidy? Could it do so by using direct regulation?

# REFERENCES

Artenstein, Andrew (2010), 'Influenza', in A. Artenstein (ed.), *Vaccines: a Biography*, Springer, pp. 191–205.

Commonwealth Department of Health (2017), 'Clinical update: No jab, no play', https://www.health.gov.au/news/clinical-update-no-jab-no-pay, viewed 24 September 2019.

De Castro, Magali, Leeb, Alan & Van Buynder (2019), 'Seasonal influenza immunisation for older adults in Australia: Vaccine options for 2019', *Australian Nursing and Midwifery Journal*, https://anmj.org.au/seasonal-influenza-immunisation-for-older-adults-in-australia-vaccine-options-for-2019/, viewed 24 September 2019.

Du, Lanying, Zhou, Yusen & Jiang, Shibo (2010), 'Research and development of universal flu vaccines', *Microbes and Infection*, vol. 12, pp. 280–6.

Gorlick, Adam (2010), 'Stanford research fellow follows spread of flu in high school', *Stanford Report*, http://news.stanford.edu/news/2010/december/track-flu-spread-121410.html, viewed 24 January 2011.

Putri, W., Muscatello, D., Stockwall, M. & Newall, A. (2018), 'Economic burden of seasonal influenza in the United States', *Vaccine*, 36(27), 3960–66.

*The Economist* (2007), 'Pricking consciences', 17 March, p. 86.

*The Economist* (2012), 'Herd at risk', 5 May 2012, p. 39.

*The Economist* (2016), 'A jab in time', 26 March, pp. 55–6.

Victorian Department of Health (2012), 'Immunisation', www.health.vic.gov.au/immunisation, viewed 3 May 2012.

World Health Organization (2019), 'Estimate of respiratory deaths due to seasonal influenza', https://www.who.int/influenza/surveillance_monitoring/bod/en/, viewed 24 September 2019.

# IDEAS FOR FURTHER READING

John Barry's book *The Great Influenza* (2004, Penguin) is an authoritative account of the 1918 Spanish influenza pandemic. A move by the Australian Government to mandate vaccination for children against diseases such as measles is described by Mark Kenny and Julia Medew (2015, 'Vaccinate children or lose benefits', *The Age*, 11 April, p. 12). Concern over declining child vaccination rates in the United States is discussed in *The Economist* (31 January 2015, 'Of vaccines and vacuous starlets', p. 31). Good textbook introductions to the field of health economics are provided by Charles Phelps (1997, *Health Economics*, Addison-Wesley) and Sherman Folland, Allen Goodman and Miron Stano (2001, *The Economics of Health and Healthcare*, Prentice-Hall).

# CASE STUDY 4.5
## THE BUSH TENDER SCHEME AND CONSERVATION ACTIVITY

The Bush Tender scheme is an innovative policy approach introduced by the Victorian Government in 2001 to reduce environmental degradation and improve biodiversity conservation on privately owned land. Conservation activity undertaken by landowners has a major impact on the quality of the natural environment. In Victoria, for example, about 15 per cent of threatened vegetation types are located solely on private land and, more generally, about 1 million hectares of native vegetation in Victoria is on private land. Conservation activity is, however, usually regarded as a public good, and hence there is concern that less than the efficient level of this activity will be undertaken.

---

### THEORY REFRESHER

#### What is a public good?

A public good is a good that is both non-rivalrous, so that consumption by one member of society does not diminish the consumption possibilities for another member, and non-excludable, so that once the good is supplied to one member of a society, it is available to all members.

In a competitive market, the quantity of a public good traded is generally expected to be less than the efficient level. Hence, public goods are a source of market failure. One reason that the quantity of public goods is less than the efficient level is an externality effect – each member of society ignores the benefit other members of society receive when they supply a public good. Another reason is the 'free-rider' effect, whereby each member of society has an incentive to understate their true valuation of a public good in order to have other members of society contribute a larger share to the costs of production.

Possible policies to increase the provision of public goods to the efficient level are to have the government finance provision of extra amounts of the good, or to seek to 'create' excludability and hence increase incentives for supply by assigning ownership of the good to some individual or group in society.

---

Conservation activity meets the definition of a public good. It is non-rivalrous, in that one person enjoying the benefit from a better natural environment does not reduce the capacity of others to obtain the same benefit. It also seems reasonable to regard conservation activity as being non-excludable. Because the land on which the conservation activity occurs is privately owned, it might seem that no-one apart from the owners would be able to directly experience the vegetation and animal species on that land, and therefore the benefits of the conservation activity will be excludable. But an important source of benefit that is often argued to derive from the environment is 'existence value', the value that members of society derive from knowing that a wide range of vegetation and animal species has been preserved. Existence value is non-excludable since it is not possible to prevent any member of a society from enjoying the knowledge that a high-quality natural environment exists. A further source of non-excludability is that there are likely to be spillover benefits from conservation activity on private land to neighbouring public land, such as the effect of eradicating rabbits.

A variety of policies for increasing the level of conservation activity could be contemplated. It might be possible to include important vegetation on private land within the national reserve system. Such an approach, however, would be costly to administer and is unlikely to be sufficiently flexible to take advantage of local knowledge on conservation activity. An alternative would be to subsidise the cost of buying products that are used as inputs to conservation activity. But for such an approach to yield an efficient outcome would require the government to have a detailed knowledge of the costs of conservation activity to individual landowners.

The Bush Tender scheme is an alternative policy intended to achieve an efficient level of conservation activity in a way that takes advantage of local knowledge and is sensitive to differences in the costs and benefits of conservation activity between different regions. As the scheme's originator, Gary Stoneham, an economist who at the time of launching the endeavour worked at the Victorian Department of Natural Resources and Environment, explains:

> We ask farmers to tell us how much it would cost them to improve the biodiversity on their land ... that includes fencing certain areas, not running stock on the area, controlling weeds, not removing fallen logs ... Those willing to offer a lower price will have a higher chance of succeeding.

Source: Macken (2002), p. 81.

More formally, in the first stage of the Bush Tender, landowners make proposals for conservation activity, such as fencing or weed control, that they would be willing to undertake, and nominate the amount of money they would need to be paid to do that activity. In the second stage, the government allocates funding to the winning bidders. Bidders are ranked according to the Biodiversity Benefits Index formula: BBI = (BSS × HSS)/(Bid). BSS is a Biodiversity Significance Score that rates the conservation value of a site, and HSS is a Habitat Service Score that measures the amount of biodiversity improvement offered by a landowner. The HSS and BSS scores are assigned by officers from the Victorian Government who inspect each site. Bid is the amount of money that the landowner nominates they need to be paid to undertake the conservation activity. The overall BBI score is the ratio of the value of environmental improvement from a proposal to the cost of the proposal. Hence, it can be thought of as the ratio of social benefit to social cost for each proposal. Proposals are funded from the highest BBI downwards, until the government budget allocated to the scheme is exhausted.

The Bush Tender scheme has three major strengths. First, by assigning government funds to promote extra conservation activity, it partially overcomes the 'public good' problem of less than the efficient amount of this activity being undertaken. Second, the scheme maximises the social benefit that is obtained from the extra funds allocated for conservation activity. This is because by assigning funds to proposals on the basis of the ratio of social benefit to social cost (from highest downwards), each dollar spent is always assigned to the project that provides the greatest marginal net gain to society. For example, suppose that the government has allocated $3000 to the Bush Tender scheme and that there are three proposals with (BSS × HSS)/Bid amounts that are respectively (2000/1000), (3000/2000) and (3000/3000). These projects therefore have BBI ratios of 2, 1.5 and 1. Hence, under the Bush Tender scheme, the government would choose to fund the first and second proposals, and thereby achieve total social benefit of 5000. No other combination can achieve as high a level of social benefit with the available funds. Third, by using a market-type mechanism, the scheme overcomes the administrative or information problems that arise with other policy approaches. Creating competition between landowners for funding, where the likelihood of making a successful tender depends inversely on the bid amount, means that the Bush Tender scheme provides an incentive for landowners to truthfully report their costs. For the initial Bush Tender trial, it was estimated that adopting a tender-based approach to allocating funds achieved costs that were lower by over $2 million than if landowners had each been paid a uniform amount for conservation activity (Stoneham et al. 2003, p. 495).

The Bush Tender scheme was first introduced as a trial in 2001 in two regions in Victoria, with $400 000 being allocated across 73 sites covering 3200 hectares of vegetation. In 2008, the Victorian Government announced the expansion of the Bush Tender scheme as part of its 'Our environment, Our future' program (Crowe 2008). The success of Bush Tender has also meant that a variety of other tender-based schemes for promoting conservation activity have been implemented in Australia; by one count 32 schemes commenced prior to 2012 extending across all states (Rolfe et al. 2017, Table 1). A notable example is the Emissions Reduction Fund implemented by the Commonwealth Government to fund projects to reduce greenhouse gas emissions as a part of its Direct Action climate policy (Muthuswamy 2015).

## KEY LESSONS

- Conservation activity is a public good and so there is a concern that less than the efficient level of this activity will be undertaken.
- The Bush Tender scheme seeks to improve incentives for conservation activity on private land. Extra government funding is provided for conservation activity, and a market-type mechanism (auction) is used to allocate the funds between landowners who submit bids to undertake conservation activity on their land.
- The use of the market or auction system for allocating funds means that by assigning funds to proposals from landowners on the basis of the ratio of the social benefit to the social cost of each proposal (from highest downwards), the government maximises the net gain obtained from the funds allocated for the scheme.

## SOME QUESTIONS TO THINK ABOUT

1   What do you think would be the main problems for government in seeking to implement the Bush Tender scheme?
2   What are the advantages of the Bush Tender scheme compared to other possible policy solutions for promoting conservation activity on private land?

## REFERENCES

Crowe, Michael (2008), *BushTender: rethinking investment for native vegetation outcomes, the application of auctions for securing private land management agreements*, Department of Sustainability and Environment, Melbourne.

Macken, Julie (2002), 'Saving the great outdoors', *Australian Financial Review*, 21 June, p. 81.

Muthuswamy, Gujji (2015), 'Explainer: How does today's Direct Action reverse auction work?', *The Conversation*, **https://theconversation.com/explainer-how-does-todays-direct-action-reverse-auction-work-40152**, viewed 11 May 2015.

Rolfe, John, Whitten, Stuart & Windle, Jill (2017), 'The Australian experience in using tenders for conservation', *Land Use Policy*, 63, pp. 611–20.

Stoneham, Gary, Chaudhri, Vivek, Ha, Arthur & Strappazzon, Loris (2003), 'Auctions for conservation contracts: an empirical examination of Victoria's Bush Tender Trial', *Australian Journal of Agricultural Economics*, vol. 47, pp. 477–500.

## IDEAS FOR FURTHER READING

You can read more about the Bush Tender scheme in the article by Gary Stoneham and colleagues titled 'Auctions for conservation contracts: an empirical examination of Victoria's

Bush Tender Trial' (2003, *Australian Journal of Agricultural Economics*, vol. 47, pp. 477–500). The Victorian Government Bush Tender website (**https://www.environment.vic.gov.au/ innovative-market-approaches/bushtender**) is another good source of information. A recent article by John Rolfe, Stuart Whitten and Jill Windle gives an overview of the use of tenders to achieve conservation objectives in Australia (2017, 'The Australian experience in using tenders for conservation', *Land Use Policy*, 63, 611–20).

# CASE STUDY 4.6
## WHY IS COPYING BAD?

No doubt you have become used to hearing your teachers say that you should not copy. Taking the work of a fellow student or copying from a published work without appropriate attribution is considered unacceptable. If you have ever paused to think about why this is, you will understand that it is a matter of ethics. In our society, we consider it morally wrong to claim that work is our own when it is not.

For an economist, there is another equally important reason why we should worry about copying. Allowing copying reduces incentives to engage in production of the goods that are being copied. In this way, copying may restrict many types of invention and innovation that are important to economic development.

Think of some of the blockbuster movies you've seen in the past few years, the films that are expensive to produce. The *Avengers Endgame* movie released in 2019 cost US$355 million to make, the combined budgets for the three Hobbit movies were over US$600 million (in 2019 dollars), and each of the *Pirates of the Caribbean* movies cost more than US$250 million to make. For the producers of those movies to have been willing to make them, they must have expected that the revenue from cinema and pay-TV or streaming plus DVD sales would exceed the movie's production costs. Now think about how you saw those movies. If you saw them at the cinema or on a streaming service you are paying for, or bought DVDs issued by the producers, you contributed to their revenue. But if you accessed the movie through an illegal streaming site or copy, you didn't contribute to the producers' revenue. Of course, just one person not paying to view a movie is not going to affect the producers' total revenue much, or affect their decision to make a movie. If, however, enough viewers of a movie can avoid paying, producers may expect that their revenue will be reduced by such a large amount that the costs of making the movie will actually exceed revenues. In this situation, they will decide not to make the movie. The scope for copying would thereby have diminished the economic incentives to engage in making movies.

The potential adverse consequence of not paying to view a movie for the economic incentive to produce movies is common to a variety of goods. Other examples include sound recordings, books, product designs and knowledge of the formulae to manufacture pharmaceutical drugs.

Products that can be copied will generally be public goods. The scope for copying a good means that it is non-rivalrous. Copying allows consumption by any number of consumers without diminishing the opportunity for other consumers to also consume the same good. For example, an audience of viewers can watch a movie and simultaneously another audience can be watching a different copy of the same movie.

As well, the possibility of copying means that it can be difficult to exclude consumers from consuming a good. The producer of a movie may be able to control the sale of movie tickets and authorised copies of the movie, but it is difficult (or impossible in the absence of legal sanctions) to prevent buyers of authorised copies of the movie from then making copies that they provide to other consumers.

The copying of a product introduces a gap between the benefit that society derives from the product and the amount that the original supplier receives as payment. This is because some consumers who benefit from the product are using copies for which they have not made a payment to the supplier. It is possible, therefore, for the benefit society receives from a product to exceed its cost of production, yet no supplier will be willing to supply the product since its revenue from sales will be less than the cost of production. For example, suppose the estimated cost of making a movie is $1 million and the total benefit to viewers from being able to watch the movie will be $2 million, but due to unauthorised streaming and copying the producers only expect to receive $500 000 in sales revenue. The producers would then decide not to make the movie. This is a situation of market failure. It is efficient for the product to be supplied; however, this will not occur as the market outcome. It is an example of how public goods are undersupplied in a market economy.

For any society, it is obviously a major concern that other public goods, such as books or knowledge of the formulae to produce pharmaceutical drugs, might not be supplied due to the scope for parties other than the original producer to copy that item and use it without payment. Hence, policymakers have sought to develop remedies to this problem. The main type of policy solution has been to introduce legal restrictions on the scope for parties other than the original producer of certain products to derive commercial advantage from those products.

Copyright is one example of this type of legal remedy. With the capacity to be applied to products such as sound recordings, movies and books, it assigns sole right to the copyright owner to make copies or sell copies of the product for a specified period after its initial publication. Patents are another example. Generally applied to knowledge-based products, such as the formulae for pharmaceutical drugs or software designs, a patent gives the owner exclusive rights to derive commercial advantage from that knowledge for some specified period – for example, 15 years.

These remedies can be thought of as creating excludability. For example, in the absence of copyright, there is no impediment to anyone who wants to watch a movie from watching a pirated or illegally streamed version. But with copyright, this is deemed illegal. Hence, in theory, copyright makes it necessary for any movie viewer to make a payment to the original producer, because every viewer must either pay at the cinema or via a legal streaming service or else buy their own copy of the DVD. Thus, consumers can be excluded from viewing the movie unless they make a payment to the producer. When all viewers of the movie are making a payment, the revenue that the producer receives will reflect the benefit that society receives from the movie. Hence, we would expect that any movie for which the benefit to society exceeds its cost of production will be made.

---

**THEORY REFRESHER**

**What are property rights?**

Property rights are the rights given to a member or members of a society to use and control a good or asset. For example, an individual who owns a business has the right to operate that business in the way he or she desires (subject to laws and regulations) and owns the stream of profits that comes from operation of the business.

The system of property rights in a society (designating who is able to have property rights in any good or asset, and the rights and obligations that are associated with being assigned property rights) is generally decided on by government. The existence of a system of well-defined and secure property rights is a critical determinant of a society's wellbeing. Continuing the example of owning a business, it is the right of the owner to its stream of profits that provides the incentive to make that business as successful as possible. Thus, one group of economists has argued that: 'Of primary importance to economic outcomes are the institutions in society such as property rights ... Without property rights, individuals will not have the incentive to invest in physical or human capital or adopt more efficient technologies' (Acemoglu et al. 2004, pp. 1–2).

Institutions such as copyright and patents can be thought of as methods of assigning property rights. For example, copyright assigns the exclusive right to derive commercial advantage from a book or sound recording to its original producer. It is this prospect of exclusive ownership of a product by its developer that provides the appropriate incentives for potential suppliers of books and sound recordings to create new products.

---

Copyright can therefore solve the problem of market failure. This only happens, however, so long as consumers act in accordance with the legal restrictions on copying. In the 2000s the advent of peer-to-peer file sharing became a major threat to copyright. By making it easier to obtain copies of sound recordings and movies without the permission of the copyright owner, file-sharing services reduced the extent of 'excludability' provided by copyright. On one estimate, 6 billion songs were illegally downloaded on file-sharing networks each year (Recording Industry Association of America 2015); and in the United States retail music sales dropped from $14.6 billion in 1999 to $6.7 billion in 2014 (*The Economist* 2018). Australians were a big part of illegal downloading activity – being the world's leading illegal downloaders of music on a per capita basis, and accounting for $1.3 billion of the annual cost of illegal movie downloads (Knott 2014).

The movie and sound recording industries responded in several ways to the threat to copyright. One approach was to seek to enforce copyright legislation by taking legal action against counterfeiters and individuals engaging in copying. But this proved slow and expensive, and had limited success in reducing copying. For example, an initial decision by the Australian Federal Court in 2015 ordering internet service providers to hand over the names and addresses of customers alleged to have illegally downloaded the movie *Dallas Buyers Club*, thereby allowing those customers to be charged for their downloads, was subsequently reversed due to the Court's concern that the makers of the *Dallas Buyers Club* were asking for an excessive payment (Francis 2015; Ockenden 2015). Another approach was to convince governments to strengthen copyright; such as the Australian anti-piracy laws which allowed the Federal Court to order internet service providers to prevent their customers accessing content from sites assessed to have the purpose to infringe copyright (Biggs & Grubb 2015). However, court action can be a slow and cumbersome remedy and the laws could be avoided by accessing blocked websites using a virtual private network.

Eventually, movie and sound recording producers recognised that they had to change the ways in which movies and music were being sold in order to reduce the incentive to engage in copying. The beginning of this shift was the development of the iTunes store, where music could be legally downloaded for a payment (*The Economist* 2009). It was streaming services, however, that have made the most difference. Bundling thousands of songs (or hundreds of movies) together and offering access on demand – without the requirement to purchase a copy – has increased the willingness of consumers to pay for legal access to songs and movies (*The Economist* 2016a). In 2016 it was estimated that revenue to music streaming services in the United States reached $2 billion, at least partly undoing the fall over the previous 15 years (*The Economist* 2016b). Movie streaming services, such as Netflix, have had similar success.

The evolution of the sound recording and movie industries has an important lesson about how market failure gets resolved. Government regulations such as copyright have an important role to play. But there are sometimes limits to their impact. When this happens, overcoming market failure may require suppliers to find new ways to create excludability for their products.

## KEY LESSONS

- Products that can be copied, such as movies, sounds recordings and knowledge, are public goods. Hence, these types of products are likely to be undersupplied in a competitive market compared to the efficient level.
- The main type of policy solution to market failure due to copying has been to introduce legal restrictions on the scope for parties other than the original producer to make copies or to derive commercial advantage from a product.
- Peer-to-peer file sharing, which increased the extent of copying of movies and sound recordings, was a major threat to copyright. Attempts to use or reform

copyright to deal with file sharing had limited success. Instead, overcoming this threat has required producers to find new ways to supply movies and sound recordings that consumers are willing to pay for.

## SOME QUESTIONS TO THINK ABOUT

1   Are there similar consequences of the scope for digitalisation for copying of written works as for the file sharing of sound recordings and movies?

2   The government of LeisureLand is considering whether to build a new public swimming pool. The social cost of building the pool is known to be $100. There are five citizens of LeisureLand who might use the pool and who have private valuations of the pool as follows: Astrid ($10), Ben ($40), Cate ($50), Dan ($75) and Ed ($75). Is it socially optimal for the swimming pool to be built? Will this happen in a competitive market? What policy solutions could the government of LeisureLand use to get the socially optimal outcome?

3   Counterfeiting is on the rise, according to a report in *The Economist* (2016c). The article describes how the Italian shoe-maker Ferragamo has been forced to install a radio-frequency identification tag in each pair of shoes it sells so that genuine shoes can be distinguished from a recent flood of fakes.

   a   Can brand names and the design of goods such as Ferragamo, Porsche cars and Louis Vuitton luxury goods be considered public goods?

   b   What is the motivation for intellectual property laws that seek to restrict commercial use of brand names and designs to the originators of those brand names and designs?

   c   Can you think of reasons why counterfeiting activity might have increased recently?

## REFERENCES

Acemoglu, Daron, Johnson, Simon & Robinson, James (2004), *Institutions as the Fundamental Cause of Long-run Growth*, National Bureau of Economic Research, working paper no. 10481.

Biggs, Tim & Grubb, Ben (2015), 'Is this the end of online piracy?', *The Age*, 28 June, p. 14.

Francis, Heath (2015), 'Pirates risk paying court costs', *The Age*, 9 April, p. 10.

Harris, Andrew (2011), 'Get on board, me hearties', *The Age*, business section, 17 March, p. 6.

Knott, Matthew (2014), 'Brandis keen to break our illegal downloading', *The Age*, 15 February, p. 3.

Ockenden, Will (2015), 'Dallas Buyers Club: Federal Court backs ISPs in row over illegal downloads', http://www.abc.net.au/news/2015–08-14/iinet-dallas-buyers-club/6697314, viewed 6 October 2015.

Recording Industry Association of America (2015), 'For students doing reports', http://
www.riaa.com/faq.php, viewed 11 May 2015.

*The Economist* (2009), 'Singing a different tune', 14 November, p. 67.

*The Economist* (2016a), 'When life gives you lemons', 7 May, p. 65.

*The Economist* (2016b), 'Change of tune', 8 October, p. 61.

*The Economist* (2016c), 'Stamping it out', 23 April, pp. 51–2.

*The Economist* (2018), 'Float of a celestial jutebox', 13 January, pp. 53–4.

## IDEAS FOR FURTHER READING

A great overview of the sound recording industry is *Rockonomics* by Alan Krueger (2019, Penguin Random House).

## Theory of the firm and managerial economics

Almost every activity we do involves an organisation. The businesses or government departments that we work for are organisations. We spend our leisure time involved in sport, religion, or volunteer activities where we are members of organisations such as clubs and churches. And if we want to join a political party, that's another organisation. Not only do we work for or belong to these organisations, but at many stages most of us will also take on roles in managing them. Doing a good job as a manager will be vital for ensuring that your organisation makes a valuable contribution to society.

With organisations playing such an important role in the economy and in society more generally, it shouldn't be surprising that economists spend a lot of time thinking about them. What are the main decisions organisations need to make? What strategies are available to them to achieve their objectives? How can their performance be improved? These are a few of the key questions addressed by economists that we'll take up in this section.

To an economist, an organisation is fundamentally a decision-making unit. Any organisation has an objective, and it will want to make decisions about its activities to achieve that objective. Mostly, economists have been concerned with organisations that have the objective of profit maximisation; for example, sole proprietor businesses, partnerships, or limited liability companies. Much of what economics has to say is, however, relevant to other types of organisations; for example, not-for-profit bodies such as Oxfam or Greenpeace, and government departments and agencies.

The main activity of a profit-maximising firm is production. Production is the process whereby a set of inputs such as labour, capital equipment and intermediate goods are transformed into output that the firm will seek to sell to buyers. For example, the process of making a car involves using as inputs workers, capital equipment and various materials such as steel, plastic and aluminium.

When we say that a firm's objective is profit maximisation, what is meant is that the firm will try to make the size of its economic profits – equal to total revenue minus total opportunity costs – as large as possible. This definition identifies revenue and costs as the key components of profits. It motivates the way that economists usually analyse a profit-maximising firm, dealing separately with costs and revenue.

Through the case studies in this section, you'll see how economics makes two main contributions to the study of costs, revenue and profit-maximising firms. First, it provides a set of approaches to help us understand how firms operate and the main factors that will determine their profits. These approaches can be used to ask questions such as: How do a firm's costs vary with the quantity of output it produces? How much competition does a firm face? And why do different firms in the same market set prices at different levels? Second, economics can assist a firm's managers to make decisions to improve its profitability. It does this by highlighting the most important decisions that a firm has to make, and by suggesting strategies that firms can use to achieve maximum profits. Drawing out these lessons for managers is a major theme of the case studies in this section.

## Costs

All organisations need to worry about costs. Costs directly affect whether a business that wants to maximise its profits achieves its objective. Costs are also important for a not-for-profit organisation or government department, as they determine the amount of services that can be provided from the organisation's available budget. Whatever type of organisation we are talking about, where it is possible to operate with lower costs, the organisation's overall performance will improve (provided, of course, that other aspects of performance such as the quantity or quality of output are not adversely affected).

It might seem obvious that costs are important, but this isn't always evident from the limited coverage that the topic receives in many management texts and popular books on economics. So, Case study 5.1 sets out to make the point that costs do matter. It presents a variety of examples, from the collapse of a major airline in Australia to the difficulties faced by independent car-repair garages in competing with dealer garages, that illustrate how changes to costs or the mismanagement of costs can have major effects on an organisation's performance.

Case study 5.2 shows how the measures of costs used by economists can be useful for understanding an organisation's costs of supply. The concepts of average cost, fixed cost and variable cost are applied to describe the costs for a university to supply different courses. You'll see how using these measures of costs can, for example, explain differences between the costs of supplying medical and commerce degrees. You'll also learn that to understand an organisation's costs, it is always necessary to begin by understanding its method of production.

The nexus between an organisation's method of production and its costs is taken up in more detail in Case study 5.3, which addresses how an organisation can reduce its costs. In this case, we'll examine several examples where organisations have been able to lower their costs by achieving higher productivity; that is, finding new ways to produce that allow the same amount of output to be produced using fewer inputs. The general importance and relevance of the concepts of costs and productivity are shown by choosing examples from a diverse range of areas: professional sport, farming, the retail sector and airlines. One of the examples is about a baseball team manager, Billy Beane, who found a whole new way to produce 'wins' for his team, and in doing so became the subject of a best-selling book.

## Revenue

Total revenue is what a firm is paid by buyers for its output. It can be calculated by adding up the amounts that the firm gets from selling each unit of output; or where it sells every unit of output at the same price, it is just the firm's quantity of output multiplied by that price. Hence, a firm's revenue will depend on the quantity of output it sells and on the price(s) at which it sells that output.

Two key decisions made by a firm determine the amount of revenue it earns: First, what to produce and, second, what price to set. Once a firm chooses what it will produce, it has determined the market in which it will be a supplier. This will in turn determine the demand for the firm's product. Knowing demand, the firm's choice of price will then determine its total revenue. (Think of the firm as first choosing its demand curve and next choosing the specific price on the demand curve at which it will operate. When we know the demand curve, and the price, we can work out quantity demanded, and hence total revenue.) Much of what economists have to say about a firm's revenue therefore comes back to the decisions that a firm makes about product choice and pricing strategy. These are the two major issues that are addressed in the case studies on revenue in this section.

When a firm chooses its product, it chooses the market in which it will be competing. The most important characteristic of a market is the degree of competition. It is this characteristic that will determine what price the firm can set and hence its profits.

Economists use several stylised types of markets to represent different degrees of competition. A perfectly competitive market, where there are many buyers and sellers who trade an identical product, is the benchmark for the greatest degree of competition that is possible. A monopoly, with a single supplier, represents the lowest possible degree of competition in a market. An intermediate case is imperfect competition, where it is assumed there are many suppliers selling products that are similar but which are differentiated in some way such as by quality or brand name. These alternative representations of markets can be used to show how differences in the degree of competition will affect a firm's revenue and profits.

The relation between price and competition can be explained using a concept known as market power. A firm's market power is its capacity to increase the price for its output to a level that is above what would exist in a perfectly competitive market, without losing all its customers. A firm's market power depends on the degree of competition in the market in which it operates; that is, on the number of other suppliers in the market and on the degree of substitutability of the products they are selling.

Case study 5.4 introduces the concept of market power and describes how it is related to the degree of competition in a market. Examples from many different markets, including the voices for *The Simpsons* characters, bottled water and the global supply of cobalt, are used to illustrate how a firm's market power will depend on the number of competitors in its market, and on the extent to which the product it sells is differentiated from those of its competitors.

Two case studies then demonstrate how the model of a profit-maximising firm can be applied to understand market outcomes – first, in a perfectly competitive market; and second, where the market is imperfectly competitive and firms within the market differ in their market power.

Case study 5.5 introduces the golden rule for profit maximisation by a firm – that it should choose a price or quantity of output at which its marginal revenue equals its marginal cost of supply. Treating the mining industry as a competitive market, and assuming that firms in the industry operate using this rule, it is possible to evaluate the consequences of a proposal by the Australian Government to introduce a mineral resource rent tax.

Case study 5.6 demonstrates that firms in an imperfectly competitive market which differ in their market power will have different profit-maximising prices. More specifically, firms with greater market power will be able to set higher prices. You'll see how differences in market power seem a likely explanation for price differences between brand-name and generic versions of pharmaceutical drugs, between different universities supplying similar courses and between the retail prices of petrol in different regions. Differences in market power can even explain why sausage rolls are more expensive at the Sydney University cafeteria than at nearby bakeries.

The degree of competition in a market also matters because it affects how the market evolves over time. An important aspect of competitive markets is the scope for new firms to enter and compete with existing suppliers. Case study 5.7 describes how the scope for entry by new firms into competitive markets will cause a natural dynamic that involves innovation and imitation. Firms that successfully engage in product innovation – developing a new product that does not have close substitutes and attracts a large number of customers – are likely to earn positive profits. The existence of firms making positive economic profits will attract new entrants to that market. New entrants will seek to 'imitate' the existing firms, supplying the same type of product in order to attract the same profits. Those existing suppliers, whose profits are being eroded by imitation, may then seek to innovate again in order to maintain their profits, and so on. This case study provides a wide range of examples of competitive markets, from the wine grape market in Australia to the global market for ship-building, where this process of innovation and imitation can be seen to have occurred.

For firms that have market power, a key area of competitive strategy is pricing. One way for a firm to use prices to achieve higher profits is by engaging in price discrimination, charging different prices to different customers. Price discrimination can allow firms to better target prices at the amounts that different customers are willing to pay and hence to earn higher sales revenue, compared with the situation where the same price is charged to all customers.

In Case study 5.8 we'll study a type of price discrimination where a firm is able to sell alternative versions of the same product at different prices. For example, by having a high-price/high-quality product that is preferred by customers with a high willingness to pay, and a low-price/low-quality product that is preferred by customers with a low willingness to pay, a firm can earn revenue from both groups of customers that reflects their different valuations. To illustrate this approach to pricing, we'll examine two main examples: the different classes of flights that are available to airline passengers and the sale of different quality packages of radio broadcast rights for Australian Rules football matches.

It's not only firms that are affected by the prices they charge. If firms are selling at higher prices, it must mean that consumers are paying higher prices. A market with less competition, where a firm can charge a higher price, may therefore be good for the firm but it is bad for consumers. For this reason, governments worry a lot about balancing the interests of business and consumers. They sometimes do this by making sure there is a sufficient degree of competition in markets or, in other situations where this is not possible, by directly regulating the activities of firms in markets with limited competition.

Case study 5.9 describes how the Australian Government has regulated the prices of pharmaceutical drugs, which are generally supplied by firms that, through a patent, have been given a legal monopoly. We'll use welfare analysis to show that the regulation has brought about a big increase in the wellbeing of Australian society. Described as 'ingenious' by some commentators, the regulation, known as the Pharmaceutical Benefits Scheme, is a great example of the clever design of government policy.

# CASE STUDY 5.1
## ARE COSTS IMPORTANT?

Costs are not the sexiest part of doing economics. Ask any lecturer in a microeconomics subject what is the hardest topic to teach and they will be sure to nominate costs. Have a look at the range of new pop economics books – if you can find a single mention of costs, you'll be doing well: *Freakonomics*, *The Naked Economist*, *The Armchair Economist* – even *The Undercover Economist* doesn't go undercover enough to say anything about costs. Most troubling of all is the fact that there are economics textbooks written for managers that say nothing about costs. This is troubling because costs might not be sexy, but they certainly matter.

You don't need to tell this to the 15 000 employees of Ansett Airlines who lost their jobs when the business, which had been one of Australia's two main domestic airlines, went bankrupt in March 2002. The simple story of Ansett is of a firm that mismanaged its costs. Ansett's great problem was that it developed what has been described as a 'Noah's Ark fleet' of planes (Easdown & Wilms 2002, p. 83). Its fleet was old and included just about every type of passenger jet. Older planes are more expensive to operate as they are less efficient and incur higher landing charges and greater maintenance costs. As well, pilots, flight attendants, ground staff and maintenance crew had to be trained separately for each different plane. Training a pilot to fly a new type of plane, for example, cost about $1 million at the time (Low 2002).

The reason why Ansett acquired such a mixed fleet of planes was attributed partly to its strategy of growing by taking over smaller competitors that each used different types of planes, as well as to the lack of a coherent acquisition strategy in the 1980s and early 1990s. One description of the approach of Ansett's then CEO, Sir Peter Abeles, to buying new planes has it that:

> Abeles would attend the air show in Paris, sip the offered champagne in the hospitality tents and buy airplanes. Nobody would know what he had done till he got back, when he would tell someone: 'By the way, we're now flying a new brand of airplane.'

> Source: (Easdown & Wilms 2002, p. 87).

For many years, entry to the domestic aviation market in Australia had been regulated by the government, and the competition between Ansett and the other incumbent supplier, Australian Airlines, was not intense. Therefore, even though it had high costs, Ansett had been able to operate profitably. As Bruce Low, at the time an equity analyst with ABN Amro, explained: 'Whenever costs got too high, they were able just to put fares up' (2002). At the beginning of the 1990s, however, entry to the market was opened up and the existing suppliers suddenly faced competition from new airlines such as Compass. Compass did not last long, but the threat of entry by other new suppliers meant that lower fares became a permanent feature of the domestic aviation market. Its high costs and the falling fares spelt the beginning of the end for Ansett. Unable to adjust its fleet of planes or other aspects of its operations sufficiently quickly, 'simple economics proved that Ansett, with its old planes, a huge staff of 15 000 and high fuel costs, could not survive' (Easdown & Wilms 2002, p. 111). Putting it more directly, Bruce Low said that Ansett's cost structure 'was the main reason for their downfall' (2002).

Costs started to matter for Ansett when it began to face extra competition from other suppliers. So it's not surprising to also find that costs matter for businesses operating in industries that are always competitive. Take the example of the mining industry. With prices for their output set on world markets, the main approach that mining businesses can take to increase profits is careful management of their costs. At times when commodity prices are falling, such as in the mid-2010s, realising ways to reduce costs – such as adopting new methods to automate production – has been paramount for the mining industry in Australia (Saunders 2015b). However, similarly to Ansett, a mining business' costs may be locked in by historical decisions about production. A review of the costs of the two major producers, BHP Billiton and Rio Tinto, noted that BHP had two significant advantages over Rio (Saunders 2015a). First, its mines were larger scale and had longer life expectancy, hence allowing it to supply higher volumes of output without needing to start new mines. Second, as its mines were located closer to the coast and to ports, its transport costs were lower.

## THEORY REFRESHER

### What are costs?

A firm is an organisation that is engaged in production. Production is the process whereby a set of inputs such as labour, capital equipment and intermediate goods are transformed into output that the firm will seek to sell to buyers. The process of production incurs costs for a firm. An economist measures these costs using the concept of the opportunity cost; that is, the costs of all the resources or inputs that the firm uses in production valued in their next best alternative uses. This measure of costs incorporates both explicit costs, such as employees' wages, and implicit costs, such as the costs of the owner's time or capital that is invested in the business. *Table 5.1.1* shows an example of annual costs for a retail fruit seller.

**Table 5.1.1** Annual costs for a retail fruit seller

| TYPE OF COST | AMOUNT $ |
|---|---|
| Explicit costs | |
| Employees' wages | 60 000 |
| Fruit bought at wholesale market | 520 000 |
| General operating expenses (electricity, etc.) | 30 000 |
| Book-keeping costs | 10 000 |
| Implicit costs | |
| Cost of owner's time (valued as wages earned working for another retailer) | 60 000 |
| Cost of capital invested in the shop (valued as the rate of interest that could be obtained on capital invested in the shop) | 40 000 |
| Economic (opportunity) costs | $720 000 |

It's not only big businesses like Ansett or mining companies where costs matter. Small business is affected by costs as well. In the market for car-repair services, it is increasingly important for mechanics to have access to repair instructions and diagnostic scanners to be able to repair our 'computer-controlled' cars, with today's new cars containing over 10 million lines of computer code (ACCC 2017, p. 61). The growing cost of repair information is having a differential effect on the costs incurred by independent garages that fix a variety of makes of cars, compared with the costs incurred by dealer garages that specialise in one type of car. Independent garages, which require access to repair information on many different types of cars, have found that their fixed costs have increased by much more than those of dealer garages which require information on only one make of car. This increase in costs for independent garages relative to their competitors seems to have affected the car repair market in Australia. A recent report by the Australian Competition and Consumer Commission suggested that nine out of 10 new car buyers had their vehicles serviced at a dealer garage (ACCC 2017, p. iv).

# KEY LESSONS

- An economist measures a firm's costs with the concept of the opportunity cost; that is, the costs of all the resources or inputs that the firm uses in production valued in their next best alternative uses.
- Costs can have a major influence on a firm's profitability. This is particularly likely to be the case when a firm operates in a competitive local market or when it faces competition from suppliers in other countries.

# SOME QUESTIONS TO THINK ABOUT

1. Think of a part-time or vacation job you have had and what service or good your employer provided its customers with. What were the main inputs used in the production of that service or good? What were the economic costs associated with production? Were all the costs explicit or were there also implicit costs that needed to be taken into account?

2. In the airline industry, a critical concept is the 'break-even load', the proportion of seats on a flight for which an airline needs to sell tickets in order to cover its opportunity costs for that flight. An aspect of early competition between Qantas and Virgin at the time the latter began operating in Australia was that Virgin chose to rent much of its infrastructure and contract with external suppliers for services such as call-centre ticket selling, whereas Qantas tended to own its infrastructure and to use employees for ticket selling. How do you think these different approaches would have affected the break-even load of each airline? How would this have affected Virgin's capacity to compete with Qantas?

3. Rent-a-Plane Inc. has agreed to charter one of its planes to take a group of tourists from Melbourne to Cairns. The tourists will return to Melbourne by car and hence they do not require the plane for the return trip. Rent-a-Plane, which needs to return its plane to Melbourne within one day of its arrival in Cairns, is then approached by a group who are interested in flying one-way from Cairns to Melbourne. The manager of Rent-a-Plane wants to charge a price to that group that will cover the opportunity cost. The cost of fuel, which does not vary with the number of passengers, is $5000 each way. The cost of pilots' wages is $1000 each way. The cost of the wages of the other flight crew is $1000 each way if there are passengers and $500 each way if there are no passengers. When passengers have travelled, the cost of cleaning the plane is $100. What minimum amount should the manager of Rent-a-Plane charge to the group who want to fly from Cairns to Melbourne?

# REFERENCES

Australian Competition and Consumer Commission (ACCC) (2017), New Car Retailing Industry – A market study by the ACCC, Draft Report, https://www.accc.gov.au/focus-areas/market-studies/new-car-retailing-industry-market-study/draft-report, viewed 24 September 2019.

Easdown, Geoff & Wilms, Peter (2002), *Ansett: the Collapse*, Lothian Books.

Low, Bruce (2002), interview with author.

Saunders, Amanda (2015a), 'BHP to accelerate cost cuts', *The Age*, 24 August, p. 21.

Saunders, Amanda (2015b), 'BHP edges Rio in costs race', *The Age*, 7 September, p. 21.

# IDEAS FOR FURTHER READING

You can read more about the history of Ansett Airlines and its collapse in Geoff Easdown and Peter Wilms' *Ansett: the Collapse* (2002, Lothian Press). The website www.australianmining.com.au has frequent news stories about recent developments in automation in the mining industry. The importance of cost management as a competitive strategy for firms is discussed in Michael Porter's *Competitive Strategy* (1980, Free Press); see chapters 1 and 2.

# CASE STUDY 5.2
## HOW MUCH DOES A UNIVERSITY EDUCATION COST?

Effective cost management is critical to the success of any organisation. Universities are no different in this regard. Keeping costs as low as possible allows a university to allocate the greatest amount of resources for teaching and research. A university will only be able to effectively manage its costs, however, if it has a thorough knowledge of those costs. Suppose, for example, that a university has to decide whether to agree to a request by the Commonwealth Government to allocate extra student places in its medical degree. Making this decision will require comparing the extra revenue offered by the government and the extra costs of supplying the medical degree to additional students; hence, the university must know how its costs will be affected by enrolling these additional students.

To understand an organisation's costs, it is necessary to understand its production method. Once we know the set of inputs an organisation uses to produce output, then this, combined with information on the cost of those inputs, allows us to determine exactly its costs of supply. This nexus between production method and costs holds for universities as much as for any other type of organisation. In fact, research on the costs of universities undertaken in the early 1990s by a group of economists at the University of Melbourne – Professor Peter Lloyd, Margaret Morgan and Professor Ross Williams – provides a nice illustration of how costs can be understood and predicted from knowledge of an organisation's production method (Lloyd et al. 1993).

In their study, the researchers examined the average costs of supplying different types of university courses across 69 tertiary institutions in Australia. The main questions they addressed were how average costs in a course varied with the number of students enrolled, and how costs varied between different types of courses. A statistical method known as regression analysis, which estimates the relation between an 'outcome' variable and a set of 'explanatory' variables, was used to calculate the relation between total costs (TC) and the number of students enrolled in each different course.*

Some findings on the average total cost of supplying undergraduate courses in Australia are displayed in *Figure 5.2.1*. It shows average total cost for two types of degree programs – commerce/law and medicine. The figure has two notable features. First, the level of average total cost is much higher for medicine than for commerce/law. Second, average total cost increases with the number of students for medicine, but decreases for commerce or law.

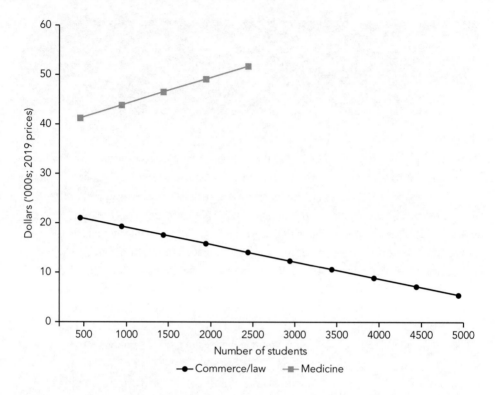

**Figure 5.2.1** Average total cost for commerce/law and medicine

What can explain these findings? Well, it all comes back to the nexus between production method and costs. To understand how the costs of a course vary depending on the number of students, and why one course appears to cost more to supply than another course, we need to examine the production method used in a university and, more specifically, the production method used in each type of course.

---

**THEORY REFRESHER**

**Measuring costs**

Economists use a variety of measures to describe different aspects of an organisation's costs of operating.

An organisation's total cost is the total opportunity cost of supplying a specified quantity of output. Total costs are divided between fixed costs and variable costs. Fixed costs are costs that do not vary with the quantity of output an organisation supplies. Variable costs are costs that do vary with the quantity of output supplied. Total cost equals fixed cost plus variable cost.

The average total cost (ATC) of supplying a specified quantity of output equals total cost divided by that quantity. It represents the total cost to an organisation per unit of output that it supplies. Average fixed cost (AFC) is similarly defined as fixed cost divided by the quantity of output supplied. Since fixed cost does not vary with the quantity of output, it follows that average fixed cost always decreases as the quantity of output supplied increases. Average variable cost (AVC) equals variable cost divided by the quantity of output supplied. The sum of average fixed cost and average variable cost equals average total cost.

Marginal cost is the addition to total cost when an organisation supplies an extra unit of output. Since the fixed cost component of total cost does not vary with the quantity of output, marginal cost is also equal to the addition to variable cost when an extra unit of output is supplied. This, in turn, implies that the variable cost of supplying some quantity of output can be calculated as the sum of the marginal costs of supplying each individual unit. For example, the variable cost of supplying three units of output is equal to the marginal cost of supplying the first unit plus the marginal cost of supplying the second unit plus the marginal cost of supplying the third unit. It also follows that there will be a close relation between marginal cost and average variable cost. For example, where marginal cost does not vary with the quantity of output, then average variable cost will also not vary with output and will be equal to marginal cost.

To illustrate how to apply these cost measures, *Table 5.2.1* gives cost data for a hypothetical firm. Fixed cost (column 2) remains constant for all quantities of output. It is assumed that the marginal cost (column 3) of producing each extra

**Table 5.2.1** Example of applying cost measures

| (1) QTY | (2) FIXED COST | (3) MARGINAL COST | (4) VARIABLE COST | (5) TOTAL COST | (6) AVERAGE FIXED COST | (7) AVERAGE VARIABLE COST | (8) AVERAGE TOTAL COST |
|---|---|---|---|---|---|---|---|
| 0 | 10 | | | | | | |
| 1 | 10 | 1 | 1 | 11 | 10 | 1 | 11 |
| 2 | 10 | 2 | 3 | 13 | 5 | 1.5 | 6.5 |
| 3 | 10 | 3 | 6 | 16 | 3.33 | 2 | 5.33 |
| 4 | 10 | 4 | 10 | 20 | 2.5 | 2.5 | 5 |
| Method | | | = Sum of MC (3) | = (2) + (4) | = (2)/(1) | = (4)/(1) | = (5)/(1) |

unit increases with the quantity of output. Variable cost (column 4) can be derived as the sum of marginal cost. For example, the variable cost of 1 unit is 1, of 2 units is 3 (1 + 2), of 3 units is 6 (1 + 2 + 3) and so on. Total cost (column 5) is the sum of fixed cost plus variable cost. Each of the average cost measures is derived by dividing that respective measure by quantity. For example, the average fixed cost of 2 units is 5, which equals 10 divided by 2. Note that average fixed cost declines continuously, whereas average variable cost increases because marginal cost is increasing with the quantity supplied.

Universities require a variety of inputs to supply undergraduate teaching: Physical capital, such as lecture theatres, laboratories, offices and other infrastructure including computers, access to online resources, books and journals; financial capital; and labour, which consists primarily of academic and administrative staff. Of these inputs, fixed costs are those that do not vary with the number of students enrolled, and variable costs are those that do vary with the number of students.

With this in mind, we can begin to think about why medical courses cost more than other courses. The answer is pretty straightforward. Supplying an undergraduate course in medicine requires a much larger amount of physical capital, such as laboratory space and hospital facilities, and requires a smaller staff-to-student ratio than the other courses. Hence, it is not at all surprising that the average total cost is higher for supplying a medicine course than for supplying the commerce and law courses.

The other issue to address is how average total cost varies with the number of students enrolled. That the average total cost of courses in commerce and law decreases with the number of students can be explained by two factors.

First, facilities such as lecture theatres, computer laboratories and library buildings, and the cost of academic staff salaries, account for a large proportion of the total costs of these courses. Increases in the numbers of students enrolled are likely to be able to be accommodated without changes in any of these inputs. Hence, these costs can be regarded as fixed. Fixed costs will therefore account for a relatively large share of the total cost of supplying courses in commerce and law. It follows that average fixed cost will make up a relatively large share of average total cost.

Second, the marginal cost of providing a course in commerce or law to an additional student is not likely to increase significantly with the number of students. The main extra costs of enrolling an additional student will be additional tutorials and grading of assessments. These costs would not be expected to vary greatly with the total number of students already enrolled. That marginal cost is relatively constant implies that average variable cost will also be relatively constant.

So, we have identified the two key aspects of the costs of supplying a commerce or law course to be the high share of fixed costs and the relatively constant marginal and average variable costs. The main influence on average total cost therefore will be average fixed cost, which always decreases with the number of students. Hence, average total cost will decrease with the number of students. This is illustrated in *Figure 5.2.2*.

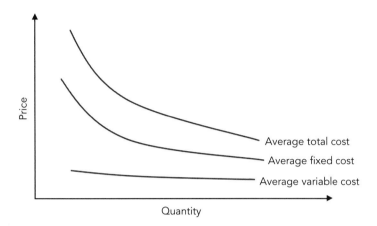

**Figure 5.2.2** Decreasing average total cost – commerce

An explanation of why the average total cost of providing medical courses increases with the number of students can be provided in a similar manner. First, for medical courses, variable costs are likely to constitute a relatively large share of total costs. This is because a large component of total costs is accounted for by infrastructure such as laboratory space and hospital facilities, and use of this infrastructure by students is sufficiently intensive that a small increase in the number of students will require extra infrastructure. Hence, average variable cost will be the largest component of average total cost. Second, the marginal cost of providing a medical course for extra students is likely to increase with the number of students enrolled. This will occur for several reasons: the increasing administrative complexity of managing small-class teaching for larger numbers of students, greater difficulty in finding clinical placements for additional students, and the rising opportunity cost of finding space for extra laboratories. Increasing marginal cost implies that average variable cost will also increase with the number of students.

In regard to the average total cost of supplying a medical course, the two key aspects of costs are therefore the high share of variable costs and the fact that marginal and average variable costs increase with the number of students enrolled. With average variable cost being the main determinant of average total cost, and increasing with the number of students, it follows that average total cost is likely to increase with the number of students. This is illustrated in *Figure 5.2.3* below.

The starting point for understanding an organisation's costs is to learn about its production method. In this case study, we've seen an illustration of this link – how

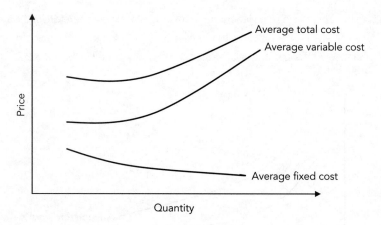

**Figure 5.2.3** Increasing average total cost – medicine

knowledge of a university's production method can be used to understand the average total costs of supplying different courses. Looking at commerce and law courses, it is the importance of inputs such as lecture theatres and library facilities in the production process, which constitute fixed costs, that explains why average costs decrease as more students are enrolled. For medicine courses, it is the use of laboratory and hospital facilities, which are variable costs, and the increasing marginal costs of obtaining these facilities for extra students, that explain why average costs increase with the number of students.

## KEY LESSONS

- Understanding an organisation's costs is always fundamentally about understanding its production method. By knowing an organisation's production method, we learn the relative magnitudes of fixed cost and variable cost, and how average variable cost will vary with the quantity of output the organisation supplies. With that information it is possible to understand and predict the organisation's average total costs.
- Supplying undergraduate teaching in different courses at a university provides an illustration of how an organisation's production method will influence costs.
- Courses such as commerce and law, which depend largely on inputs such as lecture theatres, computer laboratories and academic staff, that do not have to be varied with the number of students enrolled, have a high share of fixed cost in total cost. The dominant effect of average fixed cost on average total cost, and the fact that average fixed cost always declines with the quantity of output, explains why the average total cost of supplying commerce or law courses will decrease with the number of students taught.

- Courses such as medicine, where laboratory and hospital facilities are relatively important and need to be increased as the number of students grows, have a high share of variable cost in total cost. Together with the likelihood that average variable cost is increasing with the number of students taught, this suggests that average total cost of supplying medical courses will increase with the number of students taught.

## SOME QUESTIONS TO THINK ABOUT

1   How do you think the costs of teaching a commerce degree online would compare with the costs of a commerce degree taught at a university location?
2   How would the costs of university courses be affected by each of the following:
    a   The Australian Government specifies a maximum class size for any subject or stream of a subject.
    b   The Australian Government imposes extra safety restrictions on conditions in science laboratories.
    c   Greater competition from international universities motivates Australian universities to increase expenditure on marketing and advertising.
3   Average total cost can increase, decrease, or have a U-shaped relation with the quantity of output produced. What does each of these scenarios imply about an organisation's incentives to increase its quantity of output? What do you think are the implications from the findings on the costs of commerce and medicine courses for the likelihood of a university offering each course, and for the numbers of students it would seek to enrol in each course? Does this match what you know about the availability of commerce and medicine courses?

## EXTRA NOTE

* The regression model that was estimated for each course can be expressed in notation form as:

$$TC_i = \alpha \cdot S_i + \gamma \cdot (S_i)^2 + \varepsilon_i$$

where

- $TC_i$ = total cost of that course at university $i$
- $S_i$ = number of students in that course at university $i$
- $\varepsilon_i$ = error term for the regression model.

The regression model provides estimates of the 'parameters' $\alpha$ and $\gamma$ that describe the effect on total costs of a one-unit change in the number of students and the squared number of students, respectively. By estimating this equation for different types of courses, the economists at the University of Melbourne could examine how the total cost of any given course would vary with the number of students enrolled, and how total costs would vary between different courses.

The use of information from the regression model for total cost for a course makes it possible to represent average total cost for that particular course as:

$$ATC = \alpha + \gamma \cdot S$$

Note that this expression for the average cost per student was derived by dividing both sides of the formula for total costs by the number of students.

## REFERENCE

Lloyd, Peter, Morgan, Margaret & Williams, Ross (1993), 'Amalgamations of universities: Are there economies of scale or scope?', *Applied Economics*, vol. 25, pp. 1081–92.

## IDEAS FOR FURTHER READING

Most introductory textbooks cover how economists measure costs and the nexus between an organisation's production method and its costs. See, for example, chapter 13 in Joshua Gans, Stephen King, Martin Byford and N. Gregory Mankiw's *Principles of Microeconomics* (2018, 7th edn, Cengage Learning).

# CASE STUDY 5.3
## CUTTING COSTS BY FINDING NEW WAYS TO PRODUCE

Managing costs effectively is one of the most important tasks that any organisation must accomplish. Whether we are talking about a private sector firm or a not-for-profit organisation, a business that is a monopoly or has many competitors, a large organisation or a small one, in every case, cost management is critical.

An organisation that can lower its costs, without compromising other aspects of its activities such as the quality of its output, will almost certainly improve its overall performance. Where a firm's objective is to maximise profits, lower costs contribute directly to this objective. As well, public-sector and not-for-profit organisations, which usually operate with limited budgets, are increasingly being judged on their capacity to deliver services at the minimum possible cost.

An organisation can reduce its costs by increasing productivity. Essentially, this means producing the same amount of output using fewer inputs or, alternatively, a larger quantity of output using the same quantity or value of inputs. One way to improve productivity is for an organisation to find better ways to produce its output. This could be done using a production method that combines inputs in a different way, thereby enabling the organisation to produce output more cheaply by using a smaller total quantity of inputs, or a production method that incorporates new types of inputs that allow the organisation to use less of other types of inputs.

---

### THEORY REFRESHER

#### Productivity and the production function

Economists think of production as a process whereby an organisation converts a set of inputs into output that is supplied to buyers. For example, if you work at a takeaway food outlet, you are probably aware that the business is using inputs such as workers, shop space and equipment like ovens and cooking utensils, as well as food, to produce the output of a takeaway meal; if you work as a tutor, you are using your labour and perhaps textbooks to produce teaching services.

For any type of output, there will be many possible methods by which inputs could be combined to produce that output. These alternative production methods are likely to differ in their productivity – the amount of output that is produced from given quantities of the different inputs being used. The concept of a production function is used to represent the efficient (highest-productivity) method of producing any quantity of output. It shows the maximum amounts of output that can be produced using alternative combinations of different inputs.

# Combining inputs in a different way

A striking example of achieving higher output by finding a new way to combine inputs comes from professional baseball in the United States. The Oakland A's baseball team, despite spending much less money than other teams, won the American League West division in the US baseball competition in 2000, 2002 and 2003. This is illustrated for the 2002 season in *Table 5.3.1*.

**Table 5.3.1** Win–loss records of teams in the American League West division

|  | WINS | LOSSES | PAYROLL |
| --- | --- | --- | --- |
| Oakland | 103 | 59 | US$41 942 665 |
| Anaheim | 99 | 63 | US$62 757 041 |
| Seattle | 93 | 69 | US$86 084 710 |
| Texas | 72 | 90 | US$106 915 180 |

*Source:* Lewis (2003), p. 270.

In an entertaining book, *Moneyball*, Michael Lewis puts forward the hypothesis that the success of the Oakland A's happened because the team's manager, Billy Beane, understood much better than other managers which characteristics of players mattered for winning games in baseball. Better knowledge of the contribution different players could make to team performance meant that Beane was able to pay much less than other managers for a more successful team.

An example of where Beane thought other managers had it wrong was in valuing the contribution of individual batters to a team's likelihood of winning matches. He believed that the importance of a batter's slugging percentage was being overestimated, and that the importance of a batter's on-base percentage was being underestimated.* Both these measures of batting performance incorporate information on the batter's record of gaining bases by hitting the ball. A key difference between the measures, however, is that on-base percentage also incorporates information on the number of times at bat that a batter gets to walk to first base, whereas slugging percentage does not. Hence, knowing a batter's on-base percentage is the better measure of a batter's ability to avoid getting out. On the other hand, a batter's slugging percentage is the preferred measure of a batter's effectiveness in gaining bases from hitting the ball. Beane's analysis suggested that hiring a player with a high on-base percentage was as effective for winning matches as hiring a player with a high slugging percentage. Yet other managers were mainly concerned to hire players with a high slugging percentage. This meant that, at the time Beane became the Oakland A's manager, batters with a high slugging percentage were paid more than batters with a high on-base percentage. By focusing on hiring players with a high on-base percentage, Beane was able to put together a mix of batters who had a higher likelihood of winning matches, yet had a lower salary cost than other teams. Ultimately, Billy Beane succeeded because he had a better understanding of the 'production method' for winning matches.

Michael Lewis writes that:

> At the bottom of the Oakland experiment was a willingness to rethink baseball; how it is managed, how it is played, who is best suited to play it, and why … In what amounted to a systematic scientific investigation of their sport, the Oakland front office had re-examined everything from the market price of foot speed to the inherent difference between the average major league player and the superior Triple-A one. That's how they found their bargains. Many of the players drafted or acquired by the Oakland A's had been the victims of an unthinking prejudice rooted in baseball's traditions … A baseball team, of all things, was at the center of a story about the possibilities – and the limits – of reason in human affairs.

Source: Lewis (2003), p. xiv.

Subsequent formal statistical analysis has confirmed the main aspects of Lewis' story (Hakes & Sauer 2006). For the period 1999–2003, the Oakland A's were an 'outlier' in terms of their ratio of winning percentage to salary costs. No other team had a ratio of winning percentage to salary expenses that came near to theirs. But interestingly, after the publication of Lewis' book, the value of batters with a high on-base percentage was more widely appreciated. More teams began to compete for these players, causing a significant increase in their salaries. The Oakland A's no longer had the advantage of better understanding the production function for performance in baseball and, with a limited budget, their win–loss ratio declined.

## Incorporating new types of inputs

The application of information technology (IT) illustrates how using new inputs can increase an organisation's productivity by allowing it to use less of other inputs. New technologies for monitoring the water content of soil have enabled cotton farms to reduce water use by tailoring the amount of water used on crops to soil moisture levels (Bolt 2002). In the airline industry, the introduction of e-tickets has had a substantial impact on costs. Whereas a paper ticket cost $10 to process for each passenger, an e-ticket costs just $1. The e-ticket also reduces the costs to airlines of changing flight bookings and has allowed the introduction of self-service check-ins (*The Economist* 2008). Airlines have also benefited from using IT to optimise the routes that they fly. Qantas estimated that it was able to save $40 million a year on fuel costs by basing its flight paths on new algorithms that can incorporate the latest information on wind patterns – made possible by cloud computing (Hatch 2018). Another example of the application of IT is the role of the internet in selling. Being able to sell online involves an extra fixed cost for a supplier, such as a computer system, but replacing salespeople with online sales is likely to significantly lower marginal costs. Increasingly, it is also possible to sell online via centralised websites that provide potential customers with information about offers made by multiple suppliers, such as travel websites Trivago and TripAdvisor. Finally, there is the new kid on the block – Artificial Intelligence. AI is now being used to automate tasks as diverse as reading and analysing legal documents, constructing data sets describing what happens in sporting contests and language translation – all of which bring a substantial decrease in labour costs for the organisations applying AI (Agrawal et al. 2019).

Adopting a new production technology may also have implications for the types of output a business can supply. One example is the effect of IT on book retailing. Book sales follow what is known as a power-law distribution: a small number of books sell a very large number of copies, and there is a 'long tail' of books that sell a small number of copies. This has implications for the nature of book retailing:

> A real-world shop can only stock so many titles on its shelves, so it generally holds those most likely to sell, at the head of the curve: even the largest bookstore carries only around 130 000 titles. But an online store, with no limits on its shelf space, can offer a far wider range and open up new markets further down the long tail.

Source: *The Economist* (2005), p. 69.

In other words, the introduction of online retailing, by decreasing the cost of selling less popular items, creates a new type of supply activity from which a business can earn profits.

A general lesson from these examples is that a key task for any manager is to know their production function. Information on the production function, however, is not simply given to an organisation. Instead, it is information that the organisation's managers must discover. To make this task more difficult the production function is likely to be continually shifting; for example, technological changes may make some inputs more productive, or may even change the efficient way to combine inputs. Evaluating your organisation's method of production, and whether a better way of producing can be found, is therefore a job that never goes away for a successful manager.

# KEY LESSONS

- Organisations can reduce their costs by improving productivity. Essentially, this means producing the same amount of output using fewer inputs or, alternatively, a larger quantity of output using the same quantity or value of inputs.

- An organisation's productivity can be improved by adopting a new method of production that combines inputs in a different way, or that incorporates new types of inputs, thereby allowing the organisation to reduce its use of other inputs. An example is the application of IT in an organisation's production or sales activities.

# SOME QUESTIONS TO THINK ABOUT

1   An article in *The Monthly* described the method used by computer-betting king Alan Woods as follows:

> Alan and his computer team win by capitalising on bad betting by the general public … Alan's team employs a dozen or so staff to analyse and compile data for every horse running in Hong Kong … The data is then plugged into a computer program, and using a formula based on past results, a probability for every horse in the race is calculated.

Source: (Wilson 2005).

How could you interpret the 'formula' that is described in this quote?

2   The e-ticket system and paper tickets are alternative methods of providing tickets to airline passengers. Each is produced using a different production method. In the short run, an airline will be restricted to using one or other of these methods. In the long run, though, it can choose whichever method it wants.

   a   What do you think are likely to be the differences in fixed costs and short-run marginal costs between the production methods for e-tickets and paper tickets?

   b   Draw a graph showing how you think the short-run average total cost of each production method will vary with the number of passengers carried.

   c   How should a profit-maximising airline decide between the alternative methods of providing tickets to passengers?

   d   How do you think the gains from switching to an e-ticket system will vary by the size of an airline (that is, number of passengers carried)?

3   Managers often have discretion in allocating organisation expenditure between costs that are 'productive' and 'unproductive' for that organisation. For example,

productive expenditure might involve investing in R&D for new product development, while unproductive expenditure might involve buying new furniture for managers' offices. 'X-inefficiency' is the idea that managers may allocate too much expenditure to unproductive uses. How is the idea of X-inefficiency related to an organisation's production efficiency? Can you think of examples of X-inefficiency?

## EXTRA NOTE

\* A batter who comes up to bat in baseball can get a hit, a walk, a sacrifice, or an out. A hit is where the batter hits the ball and gains one or more bases. A walk is where the batter receives four pitches that are called balls by the umpire, in which case the batter is allowed to move to first base. A sacrifice hit is credited to a batter who advances one or more runners by bunting the ball for an out, or who would have been out but for an error by a fielder. An out occurs where a batter is deemed to have had three strikes. Slugging percentage is the total bases gained divided by at-bats. This measure only includes times a batter comes up to bat that result in a hit or an out. On-base percentage is the fraction of times a batter comes up to bat and successfully reaches a base either through a walk or hit. Hence, this measure does include times a batter comes up to bat that result in a walk. On-base percentage measure is the best way of knowing a batter's record of not getting out. Importantly, the alternative measures can rank players differently. For example, in *Table 5.3.2*, using slugging percentage, batter 1 would have a record of 0.500 and batter 2 a record of 0.400 (supposing each of the hits results in one base gained), but using on-base percentage, batter 1 has a record of 0.500, whereas batter 2 has a record of 0.700.

**Table 5.3.2** Batting examples

|  | BATTER 1 | BATTER 2 |
| --- | --- | --- |
| Hits | 5 | 2 |
| Outs | 5 | 3 |
| Walks | 0 | 5 |

## REFERENCES

Agrawal, Ajay, Gans, Joshua & Goldfarb, Avi (2019), 'Artificial Intelligence: The ambiguous labor market impact of automating prediction', *Journal of Economic Perspectives*, 33(2), pp. 31–50.

Bolt, Cathy (2002), 'Growers cotton on to efficient conservation', *Australian Financial Review*, 24 April, p. 9.

Hakes, Jahn & Sauer, Raymond (2006), 'An economic evaluation of the "Moneyball" hypothesis', *Journal of Economic Perspectives*, vol. 20, summer, pp. 173–85.

Hatch, Patrick (2018), 'Flight path changes will boost Qantas', *The Age*, 10 December, p. 20.

Lewis, Michael (2003), *Moneyball*, W.W. Norton.

*The Economist* (2005), 'Profiting from obscurity', 7 May, p. 69.

*The Economist* (2008), 'Who needs paper?', 7 June, p. 67.

Wilson, Tony (2005), 'Mr. Huge', *The Monthly*, December, https://www.themonthly.com.au/monthly-essays-tony-wilson-mr-huge-alan-woods-and-his-amazing-computer-nags-riches-story-149, viewed 3 August 2015.

# IDEAS FOR FURTHER READING

A current perspective on the role of data analytics in sport is provided by Christoph Biermann in *Football Hackers: The Science and Art of a Data Revolution* (2019, Blink Publishing). An introduction to the field of sports economics is provided by Stefan Szymanski in *Playbooks and Checkbooks* (2009, Princeton University Press). John Kelleher and Brendan Tierney provide an accessible introduction to the field in their book *Data Science* (2018, MIT Press). You can listen to an interview with the originator of the idea of the 'long tail', Chris Anderson, on the EconTalk website (www.econtalk.org/archives/2006/08/chris_anderson.html).

# CASE STUDY 5.4
## THE PATH TO MARKET POWER: WHEN CAN YOUR BUSINESS CHARGE HIGH PRICES WITHOUT LOSING ALL OF ITS CUSTOMERS?

A firm's capacity to earn sales revenue depends critically on its market power, because it is market power that determines how high a firm can set its prices. The role that market power plays in determining a firm's revenue and profits makes it a key element of competitive strategy for any business. Of course, for a business to be able to create and maintain market power, it needs to understand what is meant by market power.

### THEORY REFRESHER

#### What is market power?

A firm has market power when it can choose the price at which it supplies output. By saying the firm can choose its price, what is meant is that if a firm increases the price for its output to above the level that would exist in a perfectly competitive market, it will lose some but not all of its customers.

Firms in different markets, and even different firms within the same market, are likely to have different degrees of market power. A firm's market power is greater the larger the increase in price that it can implement for a given percentage reduction in quantity demanded by its customers. Making this connection between market power and the effect of an increase in price on quantity demanded shows that the term 'market power' is really just another way of describing the own-price elasticity of demand for the firm's output. A firm that has a low price elasticity of demand for its output will be able to increase price by a relatively large amount without losing many customers, and therefore is said to have a high degree of market power. A firm with a high price elasticity of demand can only increase price by a smaller amount for the same loss of customers (in proportionate terms) and hence is regarded as having a low degree of market power. This is illustrated in *Figure 5.4.1*.

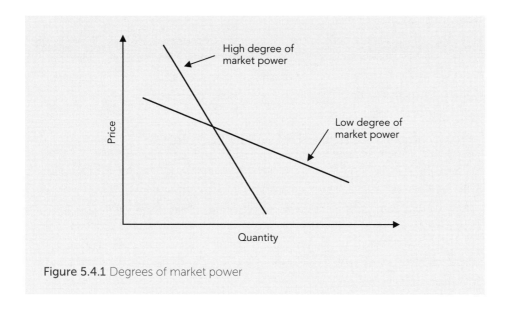

**Figure 5.4.1** Degrees of market power

A firm's market power is its ability to increase prices above the level that would exist in a perfectly competitive market. This ability can be measured or represented by the own-price elasticity of demand for the firm's output. Elasticity of demand for a firm's output, and hence its market power, will depend on two main factors: first, the price elasticity of market demand for the product being supplied by the firm; and, second, the extent of competition between suppliers in the market for that product.

To understand this definition of market power it's important to understand that we are talking about, and making a distinction between, two different measures of elasticity. Elasticity of market demand describes the responsiveness of market demand to changes in the price of the product being sold in that market. Elasticity of demand for a firm's output describes how customers or potential customers of an individual firm respond to changes in that firm's price. Price elasticity of market demand and price elasticity of demand for the output of a firm in that market will not be the same, except in a market with a single firm. It is the extent of competition in the market that will determine how different they are.

The rest of this case study provides a detailed description of the two main factors that determine a firm's market power.

## Price elasticity of market demand

An example can illustrate how the price elasticity of market demand affects the price elasticity of demand for the output of a firm within that market. Consider a comparison between markets for a life-saving drug and ice-cream. Market demand for life-saving drugs is likely to be less price elastic than market demand for ice-creams. Other things being equal, we would therefore expect that firms in a market supplying a life-saving drug should have greater market power than firms supplying ice-cream. In general, the less price elastic is market demand for the type of product being supplied, the less price elastic will be demand for the output of a firm in that market and, hence, the greater will be the firm's market power.

## Extent of competition between suppliers

The extent of competition between suppliers in a market will affect the quantity of customers that any individual firm loses when it increases its price. In general, the greater the degree of competition between firms in a market, the larger the number of customers that a firm will lose when it increases the price of its output, and therefore the more price elastic will be the firm's demand curve. This implies lower market power. Thus, there is an inverse relation between the degree of competition in a market and a firm's market power.

One way to understand the effects of competition on a firm's market power is to consider the polar cases of perfect competition and monopoly. Recall that perfect competition is our benchmark for the maximum possible degree of competition in a market. A firm in a perfectly competitive market has no influence over the price at which it sells its output, and simply accepts that it will sell any unit at the perfectly competitive market price. If it were to try to sell at above the perfectly competitive market price, it would lose all its customers. Hence, in a perfectly competitive market, a firm has zero market power. In a monopoly, with only a single supplier, the demand curve for the monopolist's output is the same as the market demand curve. Monopoly is used to represent a market with the minimum possible degree of competition. When a monopolist increases its price, there is no alternative supplier to which customers can switch. Therefore, a monopolist supplier has the highest possible degree of market power.

Other markets fall between the cases of perfect competition and monopoly in the degree of competition between suppliers. These markets are usually described as having imperfect or monopolistic competition. In this type of market, we think of there being competition between alternative suppliers selling differentiated products; that is, each supplier is selling a product that is in some way different from those of other suppliers in the market. Here are some examples:

- In the retail market for petrol, the distinct geographic location of each petrol station means that each is supplying a product that is different from any competitor.
- In the market for bread, a range of types of bread are available, distinguished by their contents (white, wholemeal, etc.) and by the brand name of the manufacturer (Sunicrust, Brumby's, Baker's Delight, etc.).
- In the market for news and information on current affairs, newspapers can be obtained from different suppliers (such as *The Age* from Nine Media and *The Australian* from News Limited) and via different media (hard copy or online).

In each of these examples, even though there is competition, each supplier is selling a differentiated product. Hence, we wouldn't expect a supplier to lose all its customers when it raises its price. Some customers may switch to another supplier, but there will still be other customers for whom the type of product being sold by the supplier is such a good match for what they want to buy that they will be prepared to pay the higher price.

To illustrate this point, we can use the example of petrol stations. Car drivers are likely to have a preference for buying from petrol stations that require the lowest cost of extra travel to buy petrol. Think of your own situation. Buying from a petrol station that you drive past on your way to and from university or work means that you spend less time on this activity. This difference in opportunity cost of travel implies that drivers should be willing to pay a higher price for petrol at a petrol station that involves little travel compared to one that requires travelling further. Hence, a petrol station can increase its price by some margin above the price that would exist in a competitive market and not lose all its customers. This is because the increase in price for customers who live nearby or travel past the petrol station on their way to work is less than the extra opportunity cost of travelling a longer distance to buy petrol. So, unlike the case of firms in a perfectly competitive market, firms in an imperfectly competitive market will have some market power. It's also important, however, to recognise that the competition between suppliers in an imperfectly competitive market means that the market power of each supplier will be less than in the case of monopoly. Due to the scope for drivers to switch to buy petrol from other suppliers, the price elasticity of demand for each firm will be higher than price elasticity at the market level. A comparison of firm-level demand for firms in an imperfectly competitive market with monopoly and a perfectly competitive market is shown in *Figure 5.4.2*.

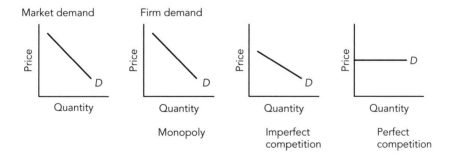

**Figure 5.4.2** Market power for firms in different types of markets

For firms in an imperfectly competitive market, there will be two main influences on the extent of competition in that market, and thus on the degree of market power possessed by each firm in the market: Barriers to entry and product differentiation.

The extent of competition in a market will depend partly on the number of firms in that market. The number of firms is likely in turn to depend on the extent of barriers to entry to the market. Barriers to entry determine the scope for new suppliers to enter a market to compete with existing suppliers. The greater the barriers to entry to a market, the fewer suppliers we would expect, and therefore the extent of competition in the market will be lower.

Barriers to entry can exist where the supply of a key input is limited, so that only those suppliers who can obtain the input are able to operate in the market; where there are legal restrictions on the capacity of firms to enter a market as suppliers; or where the nature of the costs of supplying a product mean that the average cost is minimised where there is a single supplier, a case known as natural monopoly.

One example of ownership of a key input is where there is a limited supply of some type of human capital. A report on the salaries sought by actors in the TV show *The Simpsons* provides an illustration:

> Dan Castenella, the actor who provides the voice for the star of hit cartoon series *The Simpsons*, has joined fellow cast members in a strike over pay rates … the dispute centres on a demand by each of the actors that they be paid US$360 000 an episode instead of their current US$125 000.

Source: Glaister (2004), p. 13.

That these actors can demand such high salaries is evidence of ownership of a key input: A voice associated with a character that cannot be obtained from any alternative supplier.

Control of a key input also explains China's dominance of the global market for processed cobalt. Currently, China produces four-fifths of the cobalt sulphates and oxides used to make cathodes for the lithium-ion batteries used in electric vehicles. It has been able to achieve this position by controlling the supply of raw cobalt – through ownership of mines in the Democratic Republic of Congo (the source of one-half of global output of raw cobalt); and an exclusive purchase agreement with Glencore, the world's biggest supplier of raw cobalt (*The Economist* 2018).

While some commentators have expressed concern over what might be the consequences of China's dominance in processing of cobalt, others have noted that maintaining control over the supply of a key input can be a tricky business. Just ask De Beers. Once a virtual monopolist in the wholesale supply of cut diamonds, made possible by its control of production, by 2017 it accounted for only about one-third of global sales. New discoveries of raw diamonds in the 1990s made it harder for De Beers to maintain its control over all sources of supply; and some existing members of their cartel decided to go it on their own. By 2000 De Beers admitted that it was no longer able to control the market in the way it once had (*The Economist* 2017a).

Examples of legal restrictions on the capacity to enter a market are patents and copyright. A patent confers on the originator of a product or process a legal monopoly right to supply a product. Governments have on occasion also conferred monopoly rights on some firms to act as suppliers of specific types of goods or services. For example, in the sixteenth and seventeenth centuries, the British Government gave the English East India Company the monopoly right to undertake trade between Great Britain and Asia (Ferguson 2003, pp. 18–26).

The degree of competition a firm faces from other suppliers will also depend on the extent to which those other suppliers are selling products that are close substitutes. A greater degree of substitutability between a firm's product and those of its competitors means that its customers will be more willing to switch to the other suppliers when the firm increases its price. Hence, the firm faces a greater extent of competition. The degree of substitutability between products will depend primarily on the extent of product differentiation. Sources of product differentiation between alternative suppliers could be the quality or design of the product, the location of a supplier, or the brand name.

There are probably as many examples of product differentiation as you can think of types of products. Car manufacturers try to distinguish their motor vehicles on the basis of characteristics such as fuel efficiency, exterior and interior design, safety and mechanical reliability (*The Economist* 2011). Pizzerias seek to distinguish themselves by the quality of their ingredients and the method of cooking (Cain 2014). Dating apps are introducing the scope for users to provide 'safety ratings' to differentiate themselves (Koehn 2018). Accommodation booking platforms distinguish their service from competitors by the quality of accommodation they offer (Waters 2019). Meanwhile, bottled water companies are racing to make their products seem ever more exotic (*The Economist* 2017b). The list is endless.

An interesting aspect of product differentiation is its degree of persistence. Reputations for quality differences between suppliers of products such as motor vehicles appear to persist for relatively long periods of time (think of Porsche and Mercedes). By comparison, the market power conferred by having a distinctive song or novel seems relatively short-lived. In the case of sound recordings, it has been suggested that 'in the initial release at full price there may be a certain level of demand which is fairly price inelastic. This demand is generally exhausted within twelve months of initial release as the fashion and fad nature of the product causes many consumers to move to newer material' (Prices Surveillance Authority 1990, p. 97).

## Conclusion

The amount of revenue and profits a firm earns will depend on its market power. Equipped with knowledge of what determines your firm's market power, as a manager you will be in a much better position to create and maintain that power. Bringing together the different strands of our analysis of the determinants of market power suggests that, for the most part, trying to achieve a high degree of market power will be about the product your firm chooses to supply. It is the choice of product that determines the market in which your firm will be a supplier, and hence the degree of competition you will face. An understanding of market power therefore affirms the fundamental importance of the decision a firm must make about what to produce.

## KEY LESSONS

- A firm is defined as having market power where it has the capacity to increase the price for its output to a level that is above what would exist in a perfectly competitive market, without losing all of its customers. A firm's market power is greater the larger the increase in price that it can implement for a given size of reduction in quantity demanded by its customers. Market power depends on the price elasticity of market demand for the product the firm sells, and on the degree of competition in the market.

- It is usual to distinguish two main determinants of the degree of competition between firms in a market: barriers to entry (number of competitors) and product differentiation (degree of substitutability of products sold by competitors). A firm's choice of product to supply determines the market in which it will be a supplier, and hence the price elasticity of market demand and the extent of competition it will face from other suppliers. This suggests that a firm's choice of what to produce can be thought of as the critical decision that will determine its market power.

## SOME QUESTIONS TO THINK ABOUT

1   How is the market power of a firm that produces a weekly celebrity magazine likely to be affected by the following events?
    a   the introduction of a new TV series focusing on the lives of celebrities
    b   an increase in the popularity of one of the magazine's columnists
    c   a new arrangement whereby the magazine gains the exclusive right to interview famous actors
2   Which of the following firms would have the highest market power?
    a   a car dealer that sells Volvos or a second-hand car dealer
    b   the University of Melbourne or a private high school
    c   a McDonald's restaurant or your local takeaway hamburger shop
    d   Qantas on the Melbourne–Sydney route or a bus line that runs from Melbourne to Sydney
3   What do you think are likely to be the sources of market power for the following suppliers?
    a   airports in major capital cities supplying landing rights and terminal facilities to airlines

  b private health insurers providing reimbursement to hospitals for services their members have been provided with at the hospitals

  c hotels offering free bikes, art installations and in-room gym equipment to guests

  d bicycle-sharing services providing bikes for use by cyclists at locations within capital cities

 4 An article in *The Economist* (2014) suggested that 'Online businesses [such as Amazon, Google and Alibaba] can grow very large very fast' giving them a high degree of market power. Despite competition 'being just a click away', the article noted that most customers do not seem interested in switching.

  What do you think are the sources of market power for large online suppliers?

# REFERENCES

Cain, Alexandra (2014), 'Margheritas at 10 paces as pizza war heats up', *The Age Business Day*, 28 July, p. 26.

Ferguson, Niall (2003), *Empire*, Allen Lane.

Glaister, Dan (2004), 'Simpsons actors demand bigger share', *The Guardian*, Los Angeles, 3 April.

Koehn, Emma (2018), 'Eatability founders launch safety-focused dating app', *The Age*, 4 October, p. 24.

Prices Surveillance Authority (1990), *Inquiry into the Prices of Sound Recordings*.

*The Economist* (2011), 'Economies of scale made steel', 12 November, p. 66.

*The Economist* (2014), 'Everybody wants to rule the world', 29 November, pp. 19–22.

*The Economist* (2017a), 'The future of forever', 25 February, pp. 46–8.

*The Economist* (2017b), 'Liquid gold', 25 March, p. 54.

Waters, Cara (2019), 'Far cry from blow-up mattress: Airbnb goes lux', *The Age*, 18 March, p. 29.

# IDEAS FOR FURTHER READING

Perhaps the classic analysis of the determinants of a firm's competitive environment, and of the strategies firms can use to compete in different types of markets, is Michael Porter's *Competitive Strategy* (1980, Free Press), especially chapters 1 and 2. There is also a very good treatment of this topic in chapter 2 of Preston McAfee's *Competitive Solutions* (2002, Princeton University Press). Applications of the concept of market power are provided in chapters 13 and 14 of David Anderson's *Economics by Example* (2007, Worth Publishers).

# CASE STUDY 5.5
## THE RESOURCE SUPER PROFITS TAX:
## HOW IT COULD HAVE BEEN SUPER

The attempt by the Australian Government to introduce a Resource Super Profits Tax brought down a Prime Minister, and almost the government itself. Initially proposed in general terms in a review of Australia's tax system conducted by the Commonwealth Treasury (2009), the detailed policy was sprung on the mining industry in mid-2010 by then Prime Minister Kevin Rudd. The mining industry didn't like what they saw, and they didn't like the fact that they hadn't been consulted. And so began a 'battle by advertisement' in which the government and the mining industry splurged on TV and newspaper campaigns arguing for and against the policy (Gordon & Craig 2010). Ultimately, Kevin Rudd was dispatched, and after negotiations with the mining industry, Australia ended up with a very different tax, the Minerals Resource Rent Tax.

For all the criticism of the Resource Super Profits Tax, it had one feature that was universally supported by the government, industry and independent commentators. Instead of the existing royalty scheme, where tax payments are based on the revenue earned by a mining business, the Resource Super Profits Tax would have made tax payments by mining businesses dependent on their economic profits. This shift in the basis of taxation, from revenue to economic profits, potentially had a great benefit: reducing the size of loss in social wellbeing due to taxation of the mining output.

Most tax systems cause a decrease in the level of the economic activity that is being taxed to below its efficient level. Taxation reduces the net gain from an activity and therefore less of the activity will be done. This is what happens when a royalty tax is imposed. But a tax based on economic profits will not affect the level of output of the sector being taxed and therefore does not have adverse consequences for efficiency.

How can we show that the Resource Super Profits Tax would have been good for efficiency? We'll do this in several steps. The first step is to describe a model of a firm choosing its level of output – specifically, a profit-maximising firm that operates in a perfectly competitive market. The second step is to use that model to study the effect on a firm's output of, first, a royalty tax and, second, the proposed Resource Super Profits Tax. In the final step, comparing the effects on the firm's output of introducing each of the alternative taxes, we can make inferences on how the taxes will affect society's wellbeing.

# A model

Our starting point is a firm in the mining industry. This firm engages in the production activity of extraction of minerals for sale to customers, such as steel makers wanting iron ore. The mining firm's objective is to maximise its economic profits. The prices of minerals are best thought of as being determined in a world market, and in most cases Australian suppliers will not be able to have an appreciable effect on price setting. So we can assume that the mining firm operates in a perfectly competitive market, where it takes the price at which it can sell each unit of its output as fixed.

---

### THEORY REFRESHER

#### Profit maximisation for a firm in a perfectly competitive market

A firm's economic profits equal total revenue minus total opportunity cost. Because economic profits incorporate opportunity costs, not only are explicit costs (such as wage payments to workers) included as a cost, but implicit costs are too (such as the best alternative return on capital invested in the business). By contrast, a measure of a firm's accounting profits would usually only incorporate explicit costs.

A firm with the objective of profit maximisation will want to choose a quantity of output that achieves the highest possible level of profits, and then will need to make sure that it is willing to operate at that level of profits.

To choose the quantity of output that makes it the highest level of profits, a firm should use the golden rule for profit maximisation. This rule is that a firm should produce any unit of output for which marginal revenue is greater than or equal to marginal cost, but it should not produce any unit of output for which marginal cost exceeds marginal revenue.

Why would a firm use this rule to maximise profits? The intuition is relatively straightforward. Any unit a firm supplies for which marginal revenue is greater than marginal cost, by definition, adds more to the firm's total revenue than to its total costs. Hence, the firm's profits increase. On the other hand, supplying a unit for which marginal revenue is less than marginal cost will increase total costs by more than total revenue, and hence reduce profits. The profit-maximising quantity for a firm in a perfectly competitive market can therefore be defined as the quantity at which marginal revenue equals marginal cost: $q^*$. This is shown in *Figure 5.5.1*.

When it comes to deciding whether to operate, the firm needs to look at its level of economic profits. Different levels of profit identify whether a firm will want to operate. A firm that earns *zero economic profits* is indifferent to operating or not. Earning zero economic profits means that the firm has revenue equal to the opportunity cost of being in business. Hence, the firm is earning from this business exactly what it could get by investing its resources in their next

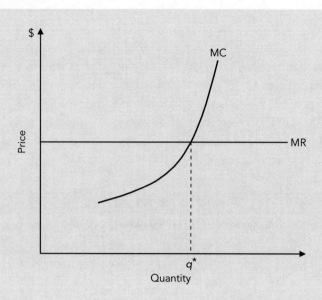

**Figure 5.5.1** The profit-maximising quantity for a firm in a perfectly competitive market

best uses, and so it will be indifferent to operating its current business. Recall that opportunity cost includes the best alternative rate of return on capital invested in the business, so a firm that is earning zero economic profits will still be getting back the market rate of return on its capital. A firm that earns *positive economic profits* strictly prefers to be operating. It is doing better than covering its opportunity costs; that is, earning a higher return from this activity than by using its resources in their next best uses. For example, the firm may be earning an above-market rate of return on the capital invested. Hence, the firm has a strict preference to be operating in this business. A firm that earns *negative economic profits* will not want to operate. Its revenue is less than opportunity cost. Hence, the firm is better off applying its resources to their best alternative uses.

By using the model of a firm in a perfectly competitive market, we are now in a position to study the effects of the alternative tax schemes. Our main concern is with the consequences for society's wellbeing; that is, the extent to which the tax schemes distort the quantity of output produced by firms in the mining sector away from the efficient level. Hence, our focus will be on how each tax affects the level of output produced by the firm, and the decision the firm makes about whether to remain in operation. We are only studying one firm, but make the assumption that what happens to this firm will be representative of how other firms in the mining industry would be affected by the taxes.

# Royalty tax scheme

A royalty tax scheme requires a firm to pay to the government a fixed percentage of each dollar of revenue it earns. For example, subjected to a royalty tax rate of 10 per cent, a firm that earns $1 million would need to pay a royalty tax of $100 000. We can therefore represent the firm's economic profits before and after tax as being (where '$t$' equals the royalty tax rate):

Economic profits before tax = Total revenue − Total opportunity cost
Economic profits after tax = (Total revenue)$(1 - t)$ − Total opportunity cost

The effect of the royalty tax is to reduce the firm's economic profits by the proportion of total revenue that is paid to the government.

There is also a direct implication of the royalty tax for the firm's marginal revenue. For every extra dollar of total revenue earned, the firm will have to pay an extra amount of taxation. This amount is the royalty taxation rate. Continuing the example from above, with a tax rate of 10 per cent, extra revenue of $1 would give rise to an extra tax payment of 10 cents; that is, the firm's marginal revenue is reduced by a fraction equal to the royalty tax rate.

Hence, the firm's after-tax marginal revenue can be represented as:

Marginal revenue after tax = (Marginal revenue before tax)$(1 - t)$

How does the imposition of a royalty tax affect the output of our firm in the mining industry? There are two effects. First, the firm will reduce its output. Second, it is possible that the firms that were only marginally profitable before the introduction of the royalty tax will go out of business.

*Figure 5.5.2* illustrates the first effect. The firm's MR is lowered by the tax, but its MC remains unchanged. Hence, the profit-maximising level of output is reduced – from $q^*$ to $q_{tax}$.

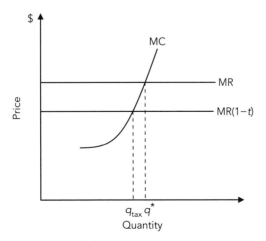

**Figure 5.5.2** How a royalty tax affects a firm's profit-maximising quantity of output

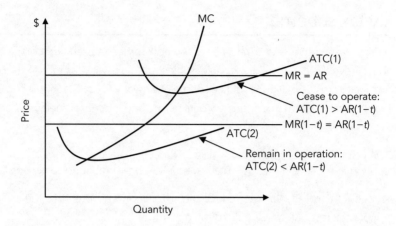

**Figure 5.5.3** How a royalty tax affects the firm's decision of whether to operate

*Figure 5.5.3* illustrates the second effect. A firm with average total cost of ATC(1) will earn positive economic profits prior to introduction of the tax. This is because its average revenue from each unit of output, AR, is greater than ATC(1). But following the imposition of the tax, this firm now earns average revenue on each unit it supplies, AR(1 − t), that is below its average cost of producing those units. This implies negative economic profits, so the firm is better off ceasing operation. Of course, the tax will not affect all firms in this way. A firm with average total cost of ATC(2) would be making positive economic profits both before and after the tax.

## Resource Super Profits Tax

The Resource Super Profits Tax can be expressed as a requirement for the firm to pay to the government a proportion of its economic profits (Commonwealth Treasury of Australia 2010). Hence, the firm's economic profits before and after tax can be represented as (where 's' represents the rate of the Super Profits Tax):

Economic profits before tax = Total revenue − Total opportunity cost
Economic profits after tax = (Total revenue − Total opportunity cost)(1 − s)

The Resource Super Profits Tax reduces the firm's economic profits by the proportion of profits that are paid to the government.

Notice that there is one major difference between the royalty tax and the Resource Super Profits Tax. Whereas the royalty tax is imposed only on revenue, the Resource Super Profits Tax can be thought of as 'taxing' both total revenue and total opportunity cost. The Resource Super Profits Tax reduces a firm's revenue, but it also reimburses the firm at the same rate for its opportunity cost.

Suppose a firm begins with total revenue of $1 million and total opportunity costs of $500 000. With a tax rate on economic profits of 10 per cent, the firm would therefore pay $50 000 as tax. What if the firm's total revenue increases to $1.5 million? Now it would pay a higher amount of tax, $100 000. Equally, however, the firm's tax payment will also change if its total opportunity cost changes. Suppose, for example, that the total opportunity cost increases to $750 000. Now the firm will pay only $25 000 in tax.

Introducing a Resource Super Profits Tax has the same effect on the firm's marginal revenue as a royalty tax. It scales down the marginal revenue by a fraction equal to the rate of Resource Super Profits Tax. In addition, however, there is a similar effect on the firm's marginal cost. It is scaled down by the same fraction, equal to the rate of Resource Super Profits Tax.

What, then, is the overall effect on output of the mining industry from imposing a Resource Super Profits Tax? The answer is that there should be no effect. This is shown graphically in **Figure 5.5.4** below. Because the firm's MR and MC are scaled down by the same fraction, it follows that there will be no effect on the profit-maximising quantity of output produced by the mining firm. Moreover, if it was profitable for the firm to produce before the tax is imposed, it will always be profitable after. The Resource Super Profits Tax will reduce a firm's amount of economic profits by a fraction that is equal to the rate of tax, but it can never turn the firm from earning positive to negative economic profits.

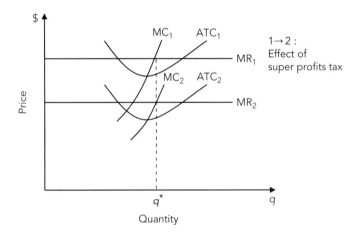

Figure 5.5.4 The effect of the Resource Super Profits Tax on a firm's quantity of output and the decision whether to operate

## Comparison of the taxes

We have reached the stage where we can summarise our findings on the effects of a royalty tax and the proposed Resource Super Profits Tax. A royalty tax does distort the amount of output produced and hence has adverse consequences for society's wellbeing. This distortion occurs because the royalty tax causes a profit-maximising firm to reduce its level of output, and may make it unprofitable for some firms to continue operating. The Resource Super Profits Tax, by contrast, does not distort how much output is produced, and therefore would not have adverse consequences for efficiency. The neutrality of the tax derives from it being imposed on economic profits, implying that there are offsetting effects on a firm's revenue and costs that leave its decision on the profit-maximisation quantity of output unchanged.

In light of the Resource Super Profits Tax having this major advantage over a royalty tax, you might be wondering why its introduction was opposed. Part of the explanation is that having a more efficient tax system was only one of the government's objectives. The introduction of the Resource Super Profits Tax was also engineered as a way of collecting more tax from the mining industry. So while the industry supported having a more efficient tax, it wasn't as keen on paying more tax. The other key part of the explanation concerns problems with the details of the proposed tax. Many commentators who supported the principle of shifting to a tax based on economic profits thought that there were aspects of the Resource Super Profits Tax that needed revision (see, for example, Parmenter et al. 2010). An initial (and frequent) criticism of the Resource Super Profits Tax was that it had set the allowable rate of return on capital too low. Working out economic profits requires estimating opportunity cost, which in turn depends on the rate of return on capital invested in the business. By only allowing mining companies to deduct for a return on capital calculated using the (essentially risk-free) rate of interest on long-term government bonds, it was argued that insufficient account was being taken of the risky nature of many mining ventures. Another objection was that it was unfair to apply the Resource Super Profits Tax to existing projects that were making positive profits, while ignoring failed projects that commenced at the same time.

Some critics also argued that an entirely different policy, involving the auctioning of the rights to seek and then obtain minerals from the deposits discovered, would be more easily implemented and would also be more successful in gaining an increased share of the returns from the mining boom for Australia.

In the end, therefore, the Resource Super Profits Tax went to the policy graveyard. It remains a useful lesson, however, in how governments can go about raising taxes in ways that are better or worse for the economy. It's also worth reiterating that we have done this analysis of the effects of taxes on society's wellbeing using a model of a firm operating in a perfectly competitive market. It's an excellent example of how far the basic concepts in microeconomics can take you. The debate over the Resource Super Profits Tax was high-stakes policymaking, yet the very first approach to studying firms that is taught in economics can be used to study its consequences.

# A numerical example: How a Resource Super Profits Tax would work

Big Mining Co. is a gold-mining firm. In the year 2011–12, it earned revenue of $2 million. Its operating costs and depreciation on capital for tax purposes amounted to $500 000.

One possible scenario is that Big Mining Co. is only required to pay company tax, which is set at 30 per cent of accounting profits. Then, as company tax, Big Mining Co. would pay 0.3($2 million − $500 000) = $450 000. Its after-tax accounting profits would be $1.05 million ($2 million − $500 000 − $450 000).

A second possible scenario is that, as well as the requirement to pay company tax, Big Mining Co. must pay a royalty of 5 per cent of its revenue to the government. The royalty payment made by Big Mining Co. to the government will be 0.05($2 million) = $100 000. This royalty payment is taken into account when calculating Big Mining Co.'s company tax obligation, which becomes 0.3($2 million − $500 000 − $100 000) = $420 000. So when it pays both company tax and the royalty payment, Big Mining Co.'s total payment to the government is $520 000; and its after-tax accounting profit is $980 000 (= $2 million − $500 000 − $420 000 − $100 000).

A third scenario to consider is one in which Big Mining Co. must pay a Resource Super Profits Tax in addition to company tax. Suppose the rate of the Resource Super Profits Tax is set at 40 per cent. To implement this tax, it is also necessary to define 'super profits'. Here, it is assumed that:

Super profits = Revenue − Operating expenses/depreciation − Normal rate of return on debt and equity capital

The normal rate of return on capital is assumed to be $500 000. Hence, the Resource Super Profits Tax paid by Big Mining Co. will be 0.4($2 million − $500 000 − $500 000) = $400 000. Company tax is then calculated taking into account the amount of Resource Super Profits Tax paid as 0.3($2 million − $500 000 − $400 000) = $330 000. The total tax paid by Big Mining Co. is therefore $730 000, and its after-tax accounting profit is $770 000 (= $2 million − $500 000 − $730 000).

(Note that this example assumes that it is known that Big Mining Co. will make positive super profits. In general, it would be necessary to take into account the possibility that Big Mining Co. might make negative super profits. This is important because the Resource Super Profits Tax made allowance for the government to make payments to mining companies when such losses occurred, equal to the tax rate multiplied by the loss amount. For a more detailed numerical example that incorporates this broader scenario, see Parmenter et al. 2010, p. 282.)

## KEY LESSONS

- By reducing the net gain from an activity, taxation generally results in less of the activity being done. Taxation therefore can be regarded as distorting economic activity away from its efficient level.
- The proposed Resource Super Profits Tax, by taxing mining firms on the basis of their economic profits, would have avoided any distortionary effect on industry output. By contrast, a royalty tax, based on revenue earned, reduces the output of firms and may cause some firms to cease operating.

## SOME QUESTIONS TO THINK ABOUT

1   The economic consultant Never Wrong Ltd seeks your advice on what would be a profit-maximising strategy for two of its clients. These clients are firms that operate in perfectly competitive markets. The marginal cost of both firms increases with the quantity of output they supply. ATC for both firms is U-shaped with the quantity of output. MC intersects ATC at the minimum point of ATC. Further information regarding the firms' costs and revenues, at current levels of output, is presented in the following table:

|  | FIRM 1 | FIRM 2 |
| --- | --- | --- |
| Price | 10 | 10 |
| MR | 10 | 10 |
| MC | 15 | 5 |
| ATC | 5 | 10 |

What would you advise each firm to do:

a   increase output

b   decrease output

c   shut down operations in the long run

d   seek new cost and price data due to measurement error in the original data

2   An article in *The Age* (Ker 2014) states that in 2013 the coal producer Yancoal operated at a loss (of $832 million). It is also described how Yancoal had committed to long-term contracts for access to railway and port facilities for transporting its coal; and that it was required to make large payments for those facilities regardless of whether it used them.

Is it possible that – despite making a loss – it was still profit-maximising for Yancoal to remain in operation in 2013?

# REFERENCES

Commonwealth Treasury of Australia (2009), 'Australia's future tax system', http://www.treasury.gov.au, viewed 3 May 2012.

Commonwealth Treasury of Australia (2010), 'The Resource Super Profits Tax: a fair return to the nation', http://taxwatch.org.au/, viewed 3 August 2015.

Gordon, Josh & Craig, Natalie (2010), 'PM, miners splurge on tit-for-tat ads war', *The Age*, 30 May, p. 5.

Ker, Peter (2014), 'Take-or-pay contracts hurting Yancoal as coal prices slump', *The Age Business Day*, 15 April, p. 25.

Parmenter, Brian, Breckenridge, Amar & Gray, Stephen (2010), 'Economic analysis of the government's recent mining tax proposals', *Economic Papers*, vol. 29, pp. 279–91.

# IDEAS FOR FURTHER READING

The marginal revenue/marginal cost rule for profit maximisation is generally attributed to the economist Augustin Cournot. You can read more about him, together with a review of the rule, in Steven Pressman's *Fifty Major Economists* (1999, Routledge, pp. 40–4). Excellent reviews of the Resource Super Profits Tax, as well as discussions of possible objections to the tax, are provided by Ross Garnaut (2010, 'The new Australian Resource Rent Tax', lecture presented at the University of Melbourne, 20 May, www.rossgarnaut. com.au/files/2016/01/The-New-Australian-Resource-Rent-Tax-200510-v5-10n7s0g.pdf) and Brian Parmenter and colleagues (2010, 'Economic analysis of the government's recent mining tax proposals', *Economic Papers*, vol. 29, pp. 279–91). Prior to the 2019 Federal election in Australia, the Greens Party made a new proposal for a super tax on mining companies – see the article by Katherine Murphy (2018, 'Super profits tax for miners and 'Buffett rule' on Greens' tax agenda', *The Guardian*, 2 May, https://www.theguardian.com/australia-news/2018/may/02/super-profits-tax-for-miners-and-buffett-rule-on-greens-tax-agenda).

Brendan Nelson was on the warpath. As then Federal Minister for Education, Science and Training, he was campaigning in the mid-2000s to prohibit universities from compelling students to join a student union. In the course of the campaign, one of Nelson's arguments for voluntary student unionism attracted the attention of journalist Jason Koutsoukis:

> The key to Nelson's argument is that it makes sausage rolls more expensive … According to Nelson: 'If you turn up at the cafeteria [at Sydney University] you will pay $2 for a sausage roll, but if you go across the road … to the Crispy Inn Bakery in King Street, Newtown, you will pay $1.70 for a sausage roll'.

Source: Koutsoukis (2005), p. 4.

Koutsoukis' newspaper article went on to make light of Brendan Nelson's claim, and certainly few people would be expected to support voluntary student unionism if making sausage rolls cheaper was its biggest benefit. Nelson's argument, however, does raise a puzzling question: How can suppliers of a seemingly identical product operating in the same market be charging different prices? This question may initially seem perplexing, but it becomes easy to answer once you know the right economic theory.

Explaining why suppliers in the same market might choose different prices is an application of the economic theory of price setting by a profit-maximising firm with market power. The theory gives us a way to evaluate any argument about why firms choose the prices they do, such as Brendan Nelson's claim that student unions make sausage rolls more expensive.

### THEORY REFRESHER

#### The profit-maximising price for a firm with market power

The golden rule for profit maximisation is for a firm to choose a price or quantity at which its marginal revenue equals its marginal cost of supply. For the case of a firm with market power, *Figure 5.6.1* provides a graphical representation of how a firm maximises its profits at the quantity at which marginal revenue equals marginal cost. Once the profit-maximising quantity is known, the profit-maximising price can be worked out. This is done using the firm's demand curve to find the price

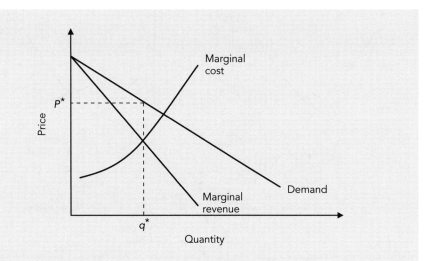

**Figure 5.6.1** Profit-maximising price and quantity for a firm with market power

that corresponds to the profit-maximising quantity. In **Figure 5.6.1**, having found that the profit-maximising quantity is $q^*$, the profit-maximising price, $P^*$, can be read off the demand curve at that quantity. Choosing either the profit-maximising quantity or the profit-maximising price will give the firm exactly the same level of profits, and hence we can think of a firm with market power as choosing either price or quantity to maximise its profits.

Suppose that both the University of Sydney cafeteria and the Crispy Inn Bakery are selling identical sausage rolls. The fact that the suppliers' sausage rolls are identical has two implications for our analysis. First, it means we will think of the cost of supplying a sausage roll as being the same for each business. Second, the main way in which the two suppliers are differentiated is by their locations – on-campus for the university cafeteria and off-campus in a retail shopping area for the Crispy Inn Bakery.

With this model of the market for sausage rolls in mind, we can analyse why the two suppliers might set different prices. The answer comes straight from the economic theory of how a profit-maximising firm sets its price. The profit-maximising price for each firm depends on its marginal revenue and marginal cost of supplying different quantities. We are assuming that the marginal costs are the same for both suppliers, so the only possible cause of a difference in price must be a difference in demand and marginal revenue. Differences in demand between firms reflect differences in their market power. A firm with high market power faces demand for its product that is less price elastic – it loses fewer customers when it raises its price above the competitive level – compared to a firm with low market power. Hence, the profit-maximising price set by a firm will be higher, the greater its degree of market power. This is shown graphically in **Figure 5.6.2**.

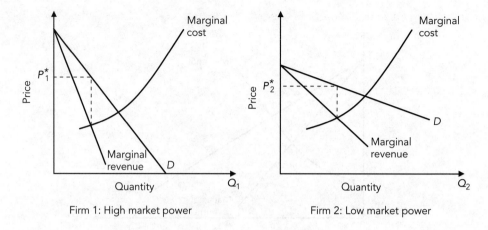

**Figure 5.6.2** Profit-maximising prices for firms with different degrees of market power (and identical costs)

Hence, for the economic theory to explain why sausage roll prices differ between suppliers, it must be that the university cafeteria has a higher degree of market power than the Crispy Inn Bakery. Does this seem likely? In fact, it does seem quite reasonable to think that this would be the case. A greater concentration of potential customers in its vicinity, and more substantial barriers to prevent new competitors entering the market and being able to locate very close to it, are both reasons to expect that the university cafeteria will have greater market power than the Crispy Inn Bakery.

The University of Sydney campus provides a large concentration of potential customers for bakery food, and for these customers there is less distance to walk or travel to buy food on-campus than off-campus. Therefore, other things being equal, they would prefer to buy from the university cafeteria. In contrast, there is probably not such a significant concentration of potential customers within the same distance of the Crispy Inn Bakery. As well, there are likely to be limits on the total number of food outlets on-campus at the university, whereas off-campus any new supplier would only need to obtain premises in the retail shopping area to be able to start up a bakery business near to the Crispy Inn Bakery. Barriers to entry to the university campus will mean that the university cafeteria faces a smaller number of competitors in close proximity than the Crispy Inn Bakery.

Now that we understand how differences in market power can explain the difference in sausage roll prices between the university café and Crispy Inn Bakery, it's possible to go back to the original question. Could it be that compulsory student unionism has anything to do with the higher price at the university cafeteria? To answer this question in a definitive manner we would need more information. It is possible, however, to say how an economist would go about trying to answer it. To an economist, it is differences in market power that cause the difference in prices between suppliers. It follows that only if compulsory student unionism is a source of differences in market power could it explain the discrepancy in sausage roll prices. It is difficult to think how student unionism would be responsible for a concentration of potential customers in the vicinity of the university cafeteria. But perhaps it might be possible to argue that compulsory student unionism had some effect on the number of food outlets on campus. To make this argument, it would be necessary to find evidence that having compulsory student unionism caused the number of food outlets on campus to be lower than otherwise.

Beyond sausage rolls, you'll find that it's possible to apply the same economic theory of price setting to understand many other examples of markets where suppliers charge different prices. Brand-name compared to generic pharmaceuticals, courses in the same discipline areas at different universities and petrol prices at service stations in different regions – in each case, differences in market power can explain the price differences that exist between these products.

## Pain-relieving drugs

Have you ever compared the prices of different pain-relieving drugs at the supermarket? If you haven't, *Table 5.6.1* may surprise you. Prices for the brand-name versions of the drugs are significantly higher, even though each of the brand-name paracetamol and brand-name aspirin products contains exactly the same active chemical constituents as the no-brand products. The explanation for these price differences is the greater market power of the brand-name products compared to the no-brand-name products. Strategies associated with developing the brand name, such as advertising, are likely to have created an impression among consumers that the brand-name products are of higher quality and meet more stringent safety standards. Hence, demand by consumers is less price-sensitive for the brand-name than for the no-brand-name products and, accordingly, the brand-name products have greater market power.

**Table 5.6.1** Prices of alternative pain-relieving drugs

| BRAND | PARACETAMOL (20 TABLETS) | ASPIRIN (24 TABLETS) |
| --- | --- | --- |
| Panadol | $3.70 | |
| Herron Gold | $3.99 | |
| Coles | $0.70 | $0.95 |
| Aspro | | $4.00 |
| Disprin tablets | | $4.50 |

*Source:* Based on data from Coles Supermarkets Australia Pty Ltd, www.shop.coles.au/online/, viewed 22 September 2019.

## University courses

Different universities teach courses that are often very similar; for example, qualifying graduates in accounting at different universities have exactly the same level of eligibility for membership in professional associations such as CPA Australia. This suggests that the costs of providing degrees at those different universities should be similar. Yet universities often set different prices for these courses. *Table 5.6.2* shows the prices charged by three universities in Melbourne for full-fee-paying places for international students in courses in 2019. The prices charged by the university with the highest fees, the University of Melbourne, are up to 30 per cent higher than the prices charged by the university with the lowest fees, La Trobe University.

**Table 5.6.2** Prices for full fee-paying international students in undergraduate courses, 2019

| UNIVERSITY | COMMERCE | ARTS | SCIENCE |
| --- | --- | --- | --- |
| University of Melbourne | $42 784 | $32 512 | $43 808 |
| Monash University | $43 400 | $31 500 | $41 600 |
| La Trobe University | $32 800 | $29 800 | $36 400 |

*Source:* http://futurestudents.unimelb.edu.au/admissions/fees; http://monash.edu/fees/; http://www.latrobe.edu.au/study/costs/international

Differences in market power again seem the most likely explanation for these price differences. Some evidence that differences in market power do exist between the universities can be obtained by examining the demand for Higher Education Contribution Scheme (HECS) places at each university. Due to government regulation, the price of HECS places can only vary by a small amount between the universities; instead, it is differences in the required entry score for admission to each university that reveal differences in demand. These required entry scores for commerce and arts courses have the same pattern as the price differences for full-fee-paying places, being higher at the University of Melbourne than at Monash University, and higher at Monash University than at La Trobe University. We can therefore infer that the ordering of the prices of full-fee-paying places between the universities does reflect differences in the relative strength of demand for these courses and in the market power of each university. Differences in market power could be explained by a variety of characteristics of the universities, including age and prestige, geographic location and closeness to the central business district, the reputation of staff and teaching programs, and the employment outcomes achieved by graduates.

## Petrol prices

The price of a litre of unleaded petrol varies significantly between different locations in Australia. Generally, prices in country regions are higher than in cities. As one example, from 2012–13 to 2016–17 the price per litre of petrol was on average 8 cents higher in Cairns than in the capital city in the same state, Brisbane (ACCC 2017, p. 2). What explained this difference? Partly it was higher costs of supply. The Australian Competition and Consumer Commission (ACCC) estimated that about 5 cents per litre of the higher price in Cairns was explained by higher transport costs and higher costs of wholesale and retail supply due to the size of the market in Cairns being smaller than in Brisbane and hence there not being the same scope for economies of scale in supply. The remaining 3 cents per litre of the price difference between the locations appears to have been due to the capacity for retail petrol suppliers in Cairns to exercise a higher degree of market power than in Brisbane. The ACCC attributed the difference in market power to a lower degree of competition in Cairns than in Brisbane – with over one-half of the retail outlets and 60 per cent of sales controlled by BP, Coles Plus and Caltex in Cairns; and there being a limited presence of independent retailers who might drive price competition in Cairns (ACCC 2017, pp. 14–15).

## KEY LESSONS

- Suppliers competing in the same market may choose different profit-maximising prices. One explanation for why this occurs is that these suppliers have different degrees of market power. The economic theory of price setting by a profit-maximising firm predicts that a firm with a higher degree of market power will choose a higher price.
- Differences in market power seem a likely explanation for price differences between brand-name and generic versions of products, such as pharmaceutical drugs, between different universities supplying similar courses, and between the retail prices of petrol in different regions. It can even explain why sausage rolls are more expensive at the University of Sydney cafeteria than at the Crispy Inn Bakery.
- The economic theory of profit-maximising price setting by firms provides a general framework that can be applied to evaluate a range of potential influences on prices in any market where firms have market power.

## SOME QUESTIONS TO THINK ABOUT

1   Mike's Mechanical Toy Co. is the sole producer of battery-operated robots in Funville. It faces the following daily demand for robots:

| PRICE ($) | QUANTITY DEMANDED |
|-----------|-------------------|
| 50 | 0 |
| 45 | 1 |
| 40 | 2 |
| 35 | 3 |
| 30 | 4 |
| 25 | 5 |
| 20 | 6 |
| 15 | 7 |
| 10 | 8 |
| 5 | 9 |
| 0 | 10 |

The cost of production for Mike's business is FC = 50, and the MC of each additional unit is three times the number of units supplied (for example, MC of the first unit = 3, MC of the second unit = 6 and so on).

a What are the MR and MC for Mike's Mechanical Toy Co. to supply from one to 10 units; that is, the MR and MC of supplying the first unit, the MR and MC of supplying the second unit ...)?

b What will be the profit-maximising quantity for Mike's Mechanical Toy Co. to supply? What profits will the business earn?

2 In January 2014 Qantas raised fuel surcharges on flights to Europe, parts of Asia and the Middle East. The fare rises varied by passenger class. The price for a one-way economy ticket to destinations in Europe and North Africa was increased by $15 to $270 (6 per cent), the fare for premium economy increased by $30 to $355 (9 per cent), and business and first-class travellers had fare rises of $50 to $495 (11 per cent) (O'Sullivan 2014).

Explain why Qantas (as a profit-maximising firm with market power) would choose to increase the price more for first-class passengers than for economy passengers when there is an increase in its costs.

3 In 2018 the Australian Competition and Consumer Commission (2018) reported on differences in average prices set for petrol by the major retailers in Australia

across the five largest capital cities. The report noted that: (i) Independent chains were the lowest priced major retailers in each of the five cities (for example, United in Melbourne) (ii) Coles Express was on average the highest priced major retailer in all five cities; and (iii) the remaining retailers varied between being generally below the market average price in most cities (Woolworths) and generally above it (BP COCO and Caltex).

Use the concept of market power to explain why there might be these price differentials between the retail suppliers of petrol.

# REFERENCES

Australian Competition and Consumer Commission (ACCC) (2017), *Report on the Cairns petrol market*, https://www.accc.gov.au/system/files/1203_ACCC%20Petrol%20Report_Cairns_FA.pdf, viewed 18 September 2019.

Australian Competition and Consumer Commission (2018), *Petrol Prices Are Not the Same: Report on Petrol Prices by Major Retailer in 2017*, https://www.accc.gov.au/system/files/1411_Report%20on%20petrol%20prices%20in%202017_FA.pdf, viewed 18 September 2019.

Koutsoukis, Jason (2005), 'Sausage rolls', *The Age*, 17 March, p. 4.

O'Sullivan, Matt (2014), 'Fuel costs and dollar force Qantas to pump up surcharges', *The Age Business Day*, 16 January, p. 23.

# IDEAS FOR FURTHER READING

A good introduction to the theory of profit-maximising price setting for firms with market power is provided in chapter 8 of Joshua Gans' *Core Economics for Managers* (2006, Cengage Learning). Some extra examples of how market power can affect pricing can be found in chapters 13 and 14 of David Anderson's *Economics by Example* (2007, Worth Publishers).

# CASE STUDY 5.7
## INNOVATION AND IMITATION: DYNAMICS IN A COMPETITIVE MARKET

In competitive markets, the battle between firms for profits can be fierce, and it is generally never-ending. A weapon of choice in this battle is the decision each firm makes about what to produce. Making the right choice about the products it is going to sell is a large part of what a firm in a competitive market must do to make money. Indeed, pondering on the dynamics of competitive markets, the economist Joseph Schumpeter wrote: 'the competitive weapon that counts is not lower prices, but newer commodities and techniques' (quoted in *The Economist* 2006, p. 74).

*Innovation* occurs when a firm introduces a new product that is differentiated from other products in a market. When the new product is not easily substituted by other available products and can attract a sufficiently large number of customers, a firm will be able to earn positive profits. In markets that are highly competitive, it is likely that firms will be engaged in a continuous process of product innovation. An approach that economists use to analyse how a firm might go about product innovation is known as the 'characteristics approach'. The idea is that any product can be thought of as a bundle of characteristics, and it is these characteristics that determine the value of a product to consumers. For example, a package holiday could be thought of as being composed of the characteristics of relaxation and new experiences. Different types of holidays will include different amounts of these characteristics. Consumers are likely to have different preferences concerning the alternative types of holidays. Some will prefer a holiday that primarily provides relaxation, whereas others will prefer a holiday that primarily provides new experiences. Hence, a firm that supplies a holiday that is mainly intended to provide relaxation will attract consumers who prefer that type of holiday, and similarly for firms that supply a holiday that provides mainly new experiences.

A graphical representation of the characteristics approach is presented in *Figure 5.7.1*. Different points in the diagram can be thought of as holidays that incorporate different quantities of relaxation and new experiences. Firm A is supplying a holiday that provides relatively more relaxation (perhaps lying by the pool on an exotic island) and Firm B is supplying a holiday with relatively more new experiences (maybe kayaking up a river filled with piranha).

Product innovation occurs when a firm introduces a product with a bundle of characteristics that differs from any existing product. When a profit-maximising firm engages in product innovation it should try to supply a new product with a bundle of characteristics that is a better match for the preferences of potential customers.

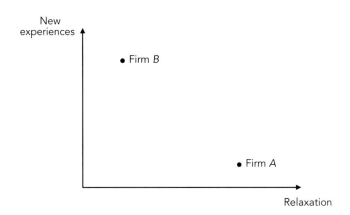

**Figure 5.7.1** The characteristics approach to product differentiation: holidays

This way of thinking about product innovation can be illustrated with many examples. One is the ride-sharing services such as Uber and Lyft which aim to provide greater convenience and comfort than taxi services (*The Economist* 2015a). New online suppliers are taking on Amazon by seeking to provide clothing and household products that are more closely tailored to the preferences of local consumers (*The Economist* 2019a); and Lego is following a similar approach by launching new sets specifically for the Chinese market (*The Economist*, 2019b). In the world of accounting software, Xero has sought to differentiate itself from its main competitor, MYOB, by locating on the cloud, which has allowed it to automate aspects of the bookkeeping process – increasing reliability of the system (McDuling 2018). Increased competition between rail firms in Europe has spurred innovations such as integrating rail travel with other travel services required by travellers – even to the extent of offering e-bike hire (*The Economist* 2018a). The market for beverages has also been a focal point for innovation in recent years, with coffee capsules designed to improve convenience for consumers, and sellers of prestige bottled water seeking to develop new 'healthy' flavours (*The Economist* 2017, 2018b).

So now we have firms that have successfully innovated. They have created new products that customers like, and they are making positive profits. What happens next? Well, the other side of competition is *imitation*: whereby new entrants are attracted to the market by the lure of positive profits. Firms in the market making positive economic profits are earning a return on their assets that is above the market rate or the next best alternative investment. Hence, there is an incentive for new suppliers to enter the market and imitate the existing firms – supplying the same type of product in order to earn the same profits.

---

### THEORY REFRESHER

#### Competition and competitive market dynamics

Competition occurs when there is more than one supplier seeking to sell to a group of buyers in a market. Those suppliers are then said to compete for the business of the buyers. The extent of competition in the market will depend on the number of other suppliers, and on the degree of substitutability of the products they are selling.

An important aspect of competitive markets is the scope for new firms to enter and to compete with existing suppliers. In competitive markets, where existing suppliers are making positive economic profits, new suppliers will have an incentive to enter the market. Positive economic profits imply that firms are earning a rate of return on the resources they are using to supply output that is above what is available from pursuing any alternative activity. It is the opportunity to earn this above-market rate of return that attracts new suppliers. Entry by new firms will create extra competition and decrease the profits earned by incumbent suppliers. Only when firms in the market (or when the last firm to enter the market) are earning zero economic profits does the incentive for entry by new suppliers disappear. The scope for entry by new firms into competitive markets therefore implies that there is a natural dynamic in these markets which is towards firms earning zero economic profits. (The scope for exit from competitive markets means that the same argument can also be made when firms in a competitive market are earning negative economic profits.)

---

The process of entry into a market by new suppliers will change the nature of competition in the market. New entrants will supply products that are closer substitutes to existing products than were previously available. This will cause the demand for products of incumbent suppliers to lessen and to become more price-sensitive. The ultimate effect will be that prices and profits of the incumbent suppliers will decrease.

An illustration of this process of imitation and entry by new firms is the history of the wine grape market in Australia in the 1990s and 2000s. During the 1990s, exports of Australian wine soared from 50 million litres to 450 million litres (Evans 2003), and with the growth in demand for wine, wine grapes were selling for as much as $3000 a tonne. Higher prices and profits caused a rapid increase in the supply of wine grapes, commencing from the mid-1990s. The 10 years to the mid-2000s saw the areas in Australia planted with grapevines more than double, and over 100 new wineries opened each year (Walquist 2005). The effect of this expansion in supply on the prices of wine grapes was dramatic, with the price of a tonne of grapes declining to around $1000 by 2005, and then falling further to only $300 a tonne by the end of the decade (Walquist 2005; Hunt 2009). At one stage, a newspaper article reported that it was now 'cheaper to drink wine than water', with a major retailer selling a 750-ml bottle of chardonnay for $1.99 compared with a price of $2.05 for the same-sized bottle of water (*The Age* 2006).

There are many other illustrations of imitation in competitive markets. Ted Hopkins, founder of Champion Data, Australia's original sports data business, recounted (2011, pp. 155–6) how once his success became evident, a competitor quickly entered the market: '... if something you have created has merit and potential value someone will find a way to copy it'. With increases in demand for cruise travel, new suppliers entered the market seeking to cater to the Asian market, eroding what incumbent suppliers had seen as a potential source of future profits (*The Economist* 2014). Perceived growth in the returns to strategy consulting induced the big four accounting firms in the US to move into that space (*The Economist* 2013a). Increased demand for influenza vaccinations in Australia has induced pharmacies to expand the flu shot services they offer, thereby increasing competition with medical practitioners providing the same service (Dow 2018).

A final example was the flurry of activity to find new sources of supply of rare earth elements in the early 2000s. A decision by the world's major supplier, China, to reduce exports caused the price to increase six-fold in 2010. The consequence was that 'announcements of rare earth projects around the world have accelerated' (*The Economist* 2010).

Firms innovate and make positive profits. Other firms imitate, which drives down profits. What occurs next? Probably more innovation. Existing suppliers, whose profits are being eroded by imitation, will seek to innovate again in order to maintain their profits. McDonald's fought back against greater competition from Burger King by expanding its menu (*The Economist* 2015b), Korean and Singaporean shipmakers responded to new competition from Chinese suppliers by focusing on manufacturing highly complex ships (*The Economist* 2013b), and Netflix, which pioneered DVD rentals via the post, went on to provide a streaming service and now commissions films and mini-series for its platform (Stone 2019). And so it goes on, with more imitation, and then innovation. In this way, the story of competitive markets and the battle for profits is the story of a race between innovation and imitation – a race that has no end.

## KEY LESSONS

- Firms' choices about what to produce are an important aspect of competition in many markets. The decisions firms make can be characterised as either innovation or imitation.
- By innovating, producing new products that are successful in attracting customers, firms can earn positive economic profits in a competitive market.
- The existence of firms that are earning positive economic profits will cause new entrants to enter that market and to seek to imitate those suppliers to also earn positive profits themselves. Imitation by new entrants is likely to decrease the

profits of existing firms. This will in turn promote further innovation as existing firms seek to maintain their positive profits.

■ The dynamic process of innovation and imitation by firms is a fundamental characteristic of competitive markets.

## SOME QUESTIONS TO THINK ABOUT

1   Think about the market for movies. What have been the main innovations in the ways in which it is possible to view movies? What do you think has been the motivation for each of these innovations?

2   Music services such as Spotify and Apple offer streaming of full-length content via the internet. Prior to these services, in order to be able to listen to the same music, it was necessary to purchase a file of the music content for download.

   a   Think about consumers who like to listen to music. What do you think are the main characteristics of time spent listening to music that matter for these consumers?

   b   Use the characteristics approach to say how you think that music streaming services such as Spotify and Apple are differentiated from other ways of listening to music.

3   In the wine grape market in Australia, high profits caused many new suppliers to enter the market. Prices and profits then fell, which is what would be predicted by economic models of competitive markets. However, the increase in supply was so large that prices decreased by an amount that caused some wine grape suppliers to become unprofitable and to exit the market. This is not something that would be predicted by economic theory – supply should only have increased by a sufficient amount to decrease the profits of existing suppliers towards zero, but not to below that level. What do you think the economic theory of competitive markets is missing that is needed to explain why supply increased so much?

## REFERENCES

Dow, Aisha (2018), 'Pharmacists and doctors trade jabs over flu shot', *The Age*, 30 March, p. 16.

Evans, Simon (2003), 'Tipsy times in topsy-turvy wine market', *Australian Financial Review*, 15 May, p. 3.

Hopkins, Ted (2011), *The Stats Revolution*, Slattery Media Group.

Hunt, Peter (2009), 'Makers blame world market', *Weekly Times*, 13 April.

McDuling, John (2018), 'KKR, Xero make boring world of accounting software exciting', *The Age*, 13 October, Business, p. 9.

Stone, Lucy (2019), 'Why Netflix annihilated Blockbuster', *The Age*, 9 July, p. 25.

*The Age* (2006), 'Now cheaper than water, wine works its gluts out', 5 August, p. 3.

*The Economist* (2006), 'Searching for the invisible man', 11 March, p. 74.

*The Economist* (2010), 'Digging in', 4 September, p. 78.

*The Economist* (2013a), 'Strategic moves', 9 November, p. 68.

*The Economist* (2013b), 'The deeper the better', 23 November, p. 67.

*The Economist* (2014), 'Sailing into headwinds', 11 January, p. 56.

*The Economist* (2015a), 'A tale of two cities', 15 August, p. 33.

*The Economist* (2015b), 'When the chips are down', 10 January, p. 53.

*The Economist* (2017), 'Liquid gold', 25 March, p. 54.

*The Economist* (2018a), 'New kids on the track', 30 June, pp. 51–2.

*The Economist* (2018b), 'Full of beans', 13 October, p. 65.

*The Economist* (2019a), 'How to beat Bezos', 3 August, pp. 53–4.

*The Economist* (2019b), 'Brick by brick', 27 July, p. 50.

Walquist, Asa (2005), 'Cheap wine and too much growth', *The Age, 27* April, p. 11.

# IDEAS FOR FURTHER READING

There is a useful discussion of a firm's choice of what to produce, including an introduction to the characteristics approach, in chapter 7 of Timothy Fisher and Robert Wasschik's *Managerial Economics* (2002, Routledge). The way that markets promote product innovation is discussed in chapters 2 and 3 of John McMillan's wonderful book *Reinventing the Bazaar: a Natural History of Markets* (2002, W.W. Norton). You can read more about the economist Joseph Schumpeter and his ideas in Steven Pressman's *Fifty Major Economists* (1999, Routledge, pp. 105–9).

Setting prices is one of the most important and difficult decisions a firm makes. Ideally, any firm would like to be told how much each of its customers is willing to pay for the product it is selling. With this information, life would be easy. By setting a separate price for each customer equal to the amount they are willing to pay, the firm will know that every customer is paying the maximum amount possible. It follows that the firm's revenue will be as high as it could possibly be. In reality, however, things are not so simple. Customers aren't going to tell a firm the truth about how much they are willing to pay. Knowing that the firm would use the information to set the maximum possible price, customers have an incentive to understate their willingness to pay. So, the firm needs to get smart.

Here's one way to think about the firm's problem. It knows that different customers are willing to pay different amounts for its output. It knows that if it can set prices for these different customers that reflect their willingness to pay, it will be able to make the maximum amount of revenue possible. But customers are not going to admit how much they are willing to pay. So what should the firm do? Well, one approach would be to try to guess willingness to pay. Perhaps the firm decides that all people with professional occupations have a high willingness to pay and should be charged a high price, and everyone else has a low willingness to pay and thus should be charged a low price. Unfortunately, this isn't likely to be very successful. Not only is it an imprecise way of targeting price at customers' willingness to pay, but it may also be illegal.

Let's consider another idea. Maybe the firm can get customers to reveal their willingness to pay, without directly asking them for this information. Surely this is impossible, though. How can the firm find out information that only a customer knows, if the customer won't tell it? Well, suppose the firm is able to sell alternative versions of the same product at different prices. A firm might, for example, make available a high-quality version of a product that it sells at a high price and a low-quality version that it sells at a low price. Customers with high willingness to pay may prefer to buy the high-price/high-quality version, while customers with low willingness to pay can buy the low-price/low-quality version. If customers with different willingness to pay do buy different versions, the firm will have induced them to reveal information about their willingness to pay. At the same time, the firm can then use this information to charge those customers different prices.

## THEORY REFRESHER

### What is price discrimination?

Price discrimination occurs when a supplier sells the same product to different customers for different prices, and those price differences do not relate to differences in the cost of supply. For example, if Hoyts Cinema charges a lower price for movie admission on Tuesday compared with other days of the week, or where a hotel owner sets higher prices during schoolies week than at other times of the year, then this would be price discrimination. By contrast, when a service station in rural Victoria sets a higher price per litre of petrol than a service station in Melbourne, one that reflects the higher costs of transporting petrol from the refinery to rural Victoria than to Melbourne, this would not be price discrimination.

The motivation for price discrimination is straightforward. Charging different prices to different customers can be a strategy that allows firms to better target prices at what their customers are willing to pay, compared with the situation where the same price is charged to all customers. Therefore, by using price discrimination, a firm can earn higher revenue and profits.

For a firm to be able to engage in price discrimination it is essential that (a) the firm has market power, (b) willingness to pay differs between customers, and (c) the firm can prevent resale between customers. Conditions (a) and (b) are necessary for price discrimination to be feasible and for the firm to achieve higher profits than it would by setting the same price for all customers. Condition (c) is necessary to prevent price discrimination being undone by customers avoiding payment of a 'high' price by instead buying from customers who have bought from the firm at a 'low' price.

Several types of price discrimination can be distinguished. First-degree (perfect) discrimination is where each unit of a product is sold at a price equal to the willingness to pay of the customer who buys that unit. With this type of price discrimination, a firm extracts the largest possible payments from its customers. Hence, it provides a benchmark against which other types of price discrimination can be assessed. Second-degree discrimination encompasses a variety of pricing methods, such as bundling, quantity discounts, product quality differentiation and two-part tariffs that are intended to achieve higher profits. Third-degree price discrimination is where customers are segregated into submarkets on the basis of some observable characteristic, likely to be associated with willingness to pay, and a separate profit-maximising price is charged in each submarket. An example is a cinema charging different movie admission prices for adults and children.

Now that you are aware of this approach that firms use in pricing, no doubt you will be able to think of many examples. One that will probably come to mind is where airlines offer different categories of travel, such as economy, business and first class, and charge different ticket prices for each category. Essentially, each passenger is getting the same product, transport by air from one destination to another. Airlines are, however, able to create versions of the product that differ in quality by providing different levels of comfort and service between the categories. *Table 5.8.1* shows some examples of the prices you would have paid for return trips in different flight classes on Qantas Airways between Melbourne and a variety of other destinations in September 2019.

**Table 5.8.1** Cost of full-fare one-way trips from Melbourne on Qantas Airways

| DESTINATION (EX-MELBOURNE) | ECONOMY (RED E-DEAL/SUPER-SAVER) | ECONOMY (FULLY FLEXIBLE) | BUSINESS | FIRST CLASS |
|---|---|---|---|---|
| Canberra | $262–$357 | $455–$704 | $873–$1 199 | |
| Perth | $338–$409 | $762–$1108 | $1 265 | |
| London | | $2079 | $10 596 | $16 790 |
| New York | | $2207 | $11 814 | $14 625 |

*Source:* Based on data from www.qantas.com.au; information viewed on 17 September 2019.

The costs of a higher quality of service and the opportunity cost of the extra space for passengers do make it reasonable to think that first-class and business-class travel would cost more than economy. However, the cost differentials would certainly not be as large as the price differences shown in *Table 5.8.1* – with a business-class fare being two to five times higher than economy, and first-class being six to eight times greater. Instead, what is happening is that Qantas is trying to use the different flight classes to allow it to better target price at customers' willingness to pay.

With only a single class of flight the airline has no way of distinguishing between the different groups, and hence no way of charging them different prices. So Qantas has created multiple classes of passengers – for example, business class for business travellers who, because travel is necessary for their work and with their frequency of travel making greater comfort more valuable, are likely to have a relatively high willingness to pay. It is the introduction of different price–quality combinations that makes it possible for Qantas to get business customers to pay more and to still have other customers travelling.

To see how this can happen, it is useful to work through a numerical example. Suppose there are two types of passengers: holiday-makers and business travellers.

The willingness to pay for a trip to London is $2000 for a holiday maker and $5000 for a business traveller, and there are 500 holiday makers and 100 business travellers. If Qantas is restricted to setting a single price for all customers, it can either charge a low price ($2000), in which case both groups of customers will choose to fly but Qantas will not be obtaining as much revenue as it could from business travellers; or it can charge a high price ($5000), which will capture as much revenue as possible from business travellers, but at the cost of holiday-makers choosing not to travel. The revenue consequences of these alternative scenarios with a single class of flight are shown in **Figure 5.8.1**.

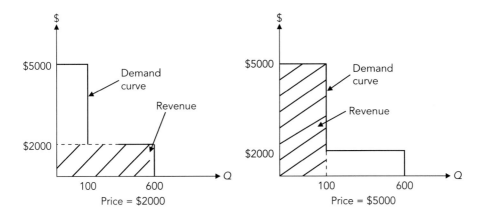

**Figure 5.8.1** Revenue outcomes from a single class of flight

Now consider what happens if Qantas is able to introduce an additional class of flight, which it labels business class, that provides a higher quality of service than the other class, which it labels as economy. Qantas is also able to charge a different price for each class. Suppose that the willingness of holiday and business travellers to pay for each class are as shown in **Table 5.8.2**. Business travellers are assumed to value the extra quality of service provided by business class more highly than holiday travellers. There is also assumed to be a slightly higher cost of providing a business-class seat than an economy seat; for example, due to more seating space, and more flight attendants per passenger.

**Table 5.8.2** Valuations and costs of different flight classes for a trip to London

|  | ECONOMY CLASS | BUSINESS CLASS |
| --- | --- | --- |
| Willingness to pay – holiday travellers | $2 000 | $2 500 |
| Willingness to pay – business travellers | $5 000 | $10 000 |
| Marginal cost per passenger | $1 000 | $1 500 |

The profit-maximising prices for Qantas to set are $2000 for an economy-class ticket and $7000 for a business-class ticket. At these prices, all holiday travellers will prefer economy class and will be charged the highest price possible for that class. Business travellers are indifferent when it comes to choosing between economy and business class as the net gain they make from travelling by business class ($10 000 – $7000) is exactly the same net gain as they would make by buying an economy seat ($5000 – $2000). Hence, we can assume that business travellers will choose to buy business-class tickets. Note that this means Qantas is charging the highest possible price for business class at which business travellers will be willing to purchase this class of flight. At any higher price than $7000, business travellers will prefer to buy an economy-class ticket.

How does having two classes of flight affect Qantas' profits? If holiday travellers choose economy seating and business travellers choose business class, Qantas will make profits of $1.05 million (equal to 500 × [$2000 – $1000] + 100 × [$7000 – $1500]). This compares with where Qantas offers only the economy class of flight, in which case it maximises its profits by setting a price of $2000 and makes profits of $0.6 million (equal to 600 × [$2000 – $1000]); and where it offers only the business class of flight, in which case it maximises its profits by setting a price of $10 000 and makes profits of $0.85 million (equal to 100 × [$10 000 – $1500]). (These profit calculations exclude any fixed costs.)

Hence, Qantas has succeeded in targeting price at the willingness to pay of each group of customers, thereby allowing it to earn more revenue and profits. Creating different classes of flights means the customers have told Qantas how much they are willing to pay without even being asked!

Exactly the same idea of using different versions of a product to distinguish between customers who differ in their willingness to pay can be easily extended to cases where a firm believes that it has more than two groups of customers. In fact, from the information on Qantas' prices, potentially the airline is trying to distinguish between passengers with willingness to pay at several different levels: with very cheap (but restricted-condition) economy tickets, more expensive (but flexible) economy tickets, business class and first-class tickets.

Implementing price discrimination using alternative versions of the same product also happens with the sale of radio broadcast rights for Australian Football League (AFL) matches. Packages for 2007 to 2009 are shown in *Table 5.8.3*. The AFL created two versions of broadcast rights: 'first-division' rights that provided a radio station with priority in the choice of matches to broadcast, and 'second-division' rights that essentially provided for a radio station to broadcast matches not being covered by stations with first-division rights. First-division rights are believed to have been priced at about $1 million per season, whereas second-division rights had a price of $150 000 to $500 000 (Wilson 2006).

**Table 5.8.3** AFL broadcast rights packages, 2007–09

| FIRST DIVISION | SECOND DIVISION |
|---|---|
| About $1 million per season | $150 000 to $500 000 per season |
| Four games per round: Friday night, Saturday afternoon (first choice), Saturday night (first choice), Sunday 2.10 p.m. match | Five games per round: Friday night, Saturday afternoon (second choice), Saturday night (interstate), Sunday 1.10 p.m. match, Sunday twilight match |

*Source:* Adapted from Wilson (2006), p. 1.

This two-tier system of broadcast rights can also be explained as an attempt by a seller, in this case the AFL, to better target price at the willingness to pay of buyers. High-rating commercial radio stations such as 3AW and Triple M, which earn large amounts of advertising revenue, were believed to have much higher willingness to pay for football broadcast rights than smaller commercial or public radio stations such as SEN and ABC. Of course, those stations with high willingness to pay are not going to agree to pay more when, as was the case previously, they get exactly the same broadcast rights as other stations. The AFL realised, though, that this situation could be changed by creating alternative packages of radio broadcast rights. Having a first-division package of broadcast rights that was most valuable to radio stations with a high willingness to pay induced those stations to agree to pay more in return for obtaining this higher-quality package. Radio stations with a lower willingness to pay were able to purchase the lower-quality second-division package of rights with a smaller payment. Similar to when Qantas introduces business and economy classes with different prices, by having these different-quality packages of broadcast rights, the AFL is able to do much better than offering the same package to all radio stations. Extra revenue is extracted from radio stations with a high willingness to pay, and at the same time stations with lower willingness to pay continue to purchase broadcast rights.

## KEY LESSONS

- Price discrimination occurs when a supplier sells the same product to different customers for different prices, and those price differences do not relate to differences in costs of production.
- Charging different prices to different customers can be a strategy that allows firms to better target prices at customers' willingness to pay, compared with the situation where the same price is charged to all customers, and therefore to earn higher profits.

■ One example of price discrimination is when a firm is able to sell alternative versions of the same product at different prices, in a way that causes customers to sort themselves into groups according to willingness to pay. By having a high-price/high-quality product that is preferred by customers with a high willingness to pay, and a low-price/low-quality product that is preferred by customers with a low willingness to pay, a firm can earn revenues from both groups of customers that capture most of their willingness to pay. Examples include the different classes of flights that are available to airline passengers and the sale of different-quality packages of radio broadcast rights for AFL matches.

## SOME QUESTIONS TO THINK ABOUT

1 Peta the Publisher must decide on a publication strategy for the new economics blockbuster book *Maxxing Your Profit*. She can publish only a hardback version, only a paperback version, or both hardback and paperback versions (with the paperback version being published six months after the hardback version). Peta believes there are two types of customers – 'Economics enthusiasts' (of whom there are 10) and 'Others' (of whom there are 40). Information on the willingness to pay of each type of customer for each version of the book, as well as the MC of producing each version of the book, are shown below:

| | HARDBACK VERSION | PAPERBACK VERSION |
| --- | --- | --- |
| Economics enthusiasts – Willingness to pay | $60 | $30 |
| Others – Willingness to pay | $30 | $25 |
| MC of supply | $10 | $5 |

a What is the profit-maximising publication strategy for Peta to adopt, and what price(s) will she charge for the version(s) of the book she sells?

b Explain why this is the profit-maximising strategy.

2 An article in *The Economist* (2010) described how a hot issue for movie studios in Hollywood was whether to sell DVDs of new movies to cheap rental suppliers, such as Netflix and Redbox, on the same day as they made them available for sale to the general public. (At that time, Netflix sent DVDs through the post, and Redbox rented them to customers from kiosks for $1 per day.) And the studios made different choices. Fox, Time Warner and Universal made Redbox wait 28 days before making the DVDs available to them, believing that cheap rentals

would undermine more profitable DVD sales and rental-on-demand; whereas Disney, Paramount and Sony made them available immediately. The article suggested that the choice the movie studios were making is whether to earn a lot of revenue from a small number of customers, or a small amount of revenue from a large number of customers.

a How does the choice that movie studios make relate to the trade-off a firm faces when it can only choose a single price for its output? How does price discrimination allow a firm to relax this trade-off?

b How does the choice of whether to sell DVDs of new movies to the cheap rental services on the same day as making them available for public sale relate to the concepts of price discrimination and versioning? What must be Disney, Paramount and Sony's beliefs about consumers' preferences for them to decide it is not worth making Netflix and Redbox wait 28 days to obtain DVDs of new movies?

# REFERENCES

*The Economist* (2010), 'Media's two tribes: charging for content', 3 July, p. 61.

Wilson, Caroline (2006), 'ABC relegated to second tier in football radio deal', *The Age*, 27 September, p. 1.

# IDEAS FOR FURTHER READING

Developments in airline pricing are described in *The Economist* ('Phantom flights', 17 January 2015, p. 60). Introductions to how firms can engage in price discrimination are provided in chapter 2 of Tim Harford's *The Undercover Economist* (2006, Little, Brown and Co.) and in chapter 4 of Robert Frank's *The Economic Naturalist* (2007, Basic Books). A thoroughgoing coverage of the strategy of pricing is provided by Hermann Simon and Martin Fassnacht in *Price Management: Strategy, Analysis, Decision, Implementation* (2018, Springer). William Poundstone's book *Priceless* (2010, Scribe) is an excellent introduction to how businesses go about pricing, and in particular how they seek to take advantage of psychological biases in consumer decision making.

It is not often that a government regulation is described as 'ingenious'. The honour of this description has, however, been bestowed on one piece of regulation in Australia. This is the Pharmaceutical Benefits Scheme (PBS), the policy framework that is used to regulate the prices of pharmaceutical drugs (Johnston & Zeckhauser 1991). The great achievement of the PBS is to undo what would otherwise be the adverse welfare consequences of monopoly supply of pharmaceutical drugs, and thereby significantly improve wellbeing in Australian society.

In Australia, new pharmaceutical drugs can be licensed under patents. The owner of a patent for a pharmaceutical drug has the exclusive right to supply that drug in the Australian market. The effective life of the patent for pharmaceutical drugs in Australia has been estimated to be about 10 years (Bureau of Industry Economics 1985). Hence, although substitute products may be developed in the intervening period, it is likely that the manufacturer of a new drug will have a degree of monopoly power for a significant proportion of the time that a drug will be used.

Pharmaceutical drugs are an important component of the treatment of many illnesses and can account for a large share of a family's expenditure on health care. The outcomes that occur in markets for pharmaceutical drugs are therefore of concern to any government. It is well known that having a monopoly supplier in a market, such as for a new drug, will lower overall wellbeing in a society. Hence, an important objective for any government is to find a policy that can deal with this problem. In Australia, this is where the PBS comes in.

### THEORY REFRESHER

#### The welfare costs of monopoly

Having a market that is supplied by a monopolist has consequences for efficiency and equity in society. A monopolist supplier will maximise profits by using its bargaining power to increase price above the level that would exist in a perfectly competitive market. It can achieve this higher price by selling a smaller quantity compared to the quantity that would be traded in a perfectly competitive market.

Therefore, in a market with a monopoly supplier, the supplier's profits are higher than in perfect competition, whereas consumers are made worse off by paying a higher price and consuming a smaller quantity. Since the loss in

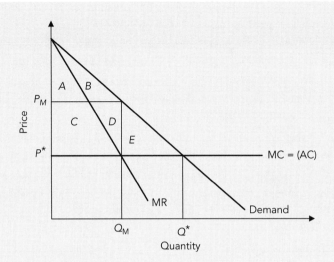

**Figure 5.9.1** The efficiency consequence of a monopoly

consumer surplus is larger than the gain in profits, there is a decline in overall wellbeing in society due to monopoly.

These consequences are illustrated in **Figure 5.9.1** for the case of a market where any supplier would have zero fixed costs and a constant marginal cost, implying that marginal cost equals average cost. (These assumptions are not essential. They just make the example simpler.) In a perfectly competitive market, the equilibrium outcome is at price $P*$ and quantity traded $Q*$. Hence, the whole area above the MC curve and below the demand curve (A + B + C + D + E) is consumer surplus. Profits of firms are zero, which is the usual equilibrium condition for perfect competition. In contrast, a monopolist supplier will choose a price and quantity where MR = MC such that price equals $P_M$ and quantity is $Q_M$. Now profits are equal to the area C + D and consumer surplus has been reduced to A + B. Compared to the efficient outcome under perfect competition, there is a reduction in total surplus caused by monopoly equal to the area E. This decrease in surplus is referred to as 'deadweight loss'. These effects are summarised in **Table 5.9.1**.

**Table 5.9.1** Effects of monopoly of surplus

|  | PERFECT COMPETITION | MONOPOLY | CHANGE |
|---|---|---|---|
| Consumer surplus | A + B + C + D + E | A + B | − C − D − E |
| Profits |  | C + D | +C + D |
| Total surplus | A + B + C + D + E | A + B + C + D | − E |

The PBS provides for pharmaceutical drugs that are listed as 'pharmaceutical benefits' to be available at a subsidised price to consumers. For most consumers in 2019, the maximum price to be paid for any listed pharmaceutical drug was $40.30, and after a consumer's total expenditure in that year reached $1550.70, the payment per item was $6.50. Pharmaceutical drugs subsidised under the PBS can only be obtained with a prescription from a medical practitioner. For a drug to be listed under the PBS, it must be recommended by the Pharmaceutical Benefits Advisory Committee (PBAC). In making its recommendation, the PBAC will consider issues such as the additional therapeutic benefits gained from listing the product, but also, importantly, the cost of the drug. A drug will generally not be listed under the PBS until a satisfactory price is negotiated between the drug manufacturer and the Pharmaceutical Benefits Pricing Authority (PBPA) (Commonwealth Department of Health 2019).

The subsidy provided to drugs listed on the PBS means doctors are more likely to prescribe a PBS-listed drug than a substitute that is not listed. In fact, about 70 per cent of the sales of drugs prescribed by doctors are made through the PBS. Therefore, achieving listing on the PBS can yield a large increase in a drug's sales. For this reason, manufacturers are keen to have their products listed, and the PBPA has significant bargaining power in its negotiations with drug manufacturers over the price at which drugs will sell.

How does the PBS affect outcomes in the market for a pharmaceutical drug compared with the situation where the market is unregulated and the supplier has monopoly power? Suppose we think of there being a monopoly supplier with zero fixed costs and a constant marginal cost of supplying each unit of the drug – this makes it easier for us to calculate the firm's profits because the average cost of any number of units is also now just equal to the marginal cost. The demand for pharmaceutical drugs comes both from the doctors who choose which drug to prescribe to a patient and from the patients who ultimately will pay for and consume the drug. So, we will think of a market demand curve for the monopolist that incorporates both parties' preferences, and make the usual assumption that the quantity demanded is inversely related to price.

In the absence of government regulation, the monopolist will choose a price and quantity such that marginal revenue equals marginal cost. In *Figure 5.9.2*, the outcome in a market with a monopolist is represented as $P_M$ and $Q_M$. To maximise its profits, the monopolist uses its bargaining power (as the sole supplier in the market) to force a price that is higher than the equilibrium price in a perfectly competitive market. To achieve the higher selling price, the monopolist restricts the quantity that is traded compared with the competitive market outcome. Hence, in the market for a pharmaceutical drug with a monopoly supplier, the quantity traded will be less than the efficient quantity.

Now think about what happens with the PBS. Let's suppose that the government's bargaining power allows it to set the price that will be paid to the drug manufacturer if it agrees to have its drug listed on the PBS. Of course, the manufacturer is able to decide not to have its drug listed, and if this happens then we assume that the manufacturer

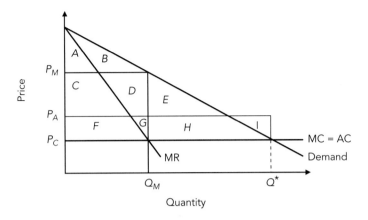

**Figure 5.9.2** The effect of the PBS on market outcome and wellbeing

makes the monopoly level of profits. Therefore, we'll assume that to agree to have its product listed on the PBS, the manufacturer must earn at least the same level of profits as the monopoly level. The government is also able to choose the price that consumers will pay under the PBS. If it chooses a price for consumers that is less than the price paid to the manufacturer, any difference will be made up by a subsidy.

To see in more detail how the PBS works, one scenario might be as follows. First, the government chooses a price for consumers, $P_C$, that is equal to marginal cost. Hence, in *Figure 5.9.2*, which shows the effect of the PBS, the quantity demanded of the drug will be $Q^*$. Consumers are made better off by having the PBS as they pay a lower price and consume a larger quantity of the drug. In fact, the quantity $Q^*$ is efficient since it is where willingness to pay equals the marginal (opportunity) cost of supply. Second, the government chooses a price for manufacturers equal to $P_A$. Now the drug manufacturer will make a profit of $(P_A − MC)$ on each unit it sells if it is listed in the PBS. This price has been chosen so that the manufacturer will make exactly the same profits as from being a monopolist; that is, $Q^* (P_A − MC) = Q_M (P_M − MC)$, or in *Figure 5.9.2* the areas $(C + D + F + G)$ and $(F + G + H + I)$ are equivalent. Hence, the drug manufacturer should agree to participate in the PBS. Third, because the government has chosen a price for consumers that is below the price paid to the manufacturer, it is effectively paying a subsidy equal to $(P_A − P_C)$ for each unit of the drug that is consumed.

The overall welfare consequences of the PBS will depend on the relative magnitudes of the gain to consumers and the cost of the subsidy to the government. We can work this out by studying the effect of the PBS on total surplus. Using the labelled areas in *Figure 5.9.2*, this is done in *Table 5.9.2*. The table confirms the previous discussion of the effects of the PBS. Consumers are made better off, the manufacturer earns the same level of profits and government pays a subsidy. Overall, total surplus for society is increased because the PBS increases the quantity of the drug traded from $Q_M$ to the efficient quantity $Q^*$. The size of the increase in total surplus is equal to the amount of

**Table 5.9.2** Effect of the PBS on total surplus

| | MONOPOLY | PBS | CHANGE |
|---|---|---|---|
| Consumer surplus | A + B | A + B + C + D + E + F + G + H | +C + D + E + F + G + H |
| Profits | C + D + F + G | F + G + H + I | H + I − C − D (equals zero) |
| Government revenue | | −F − G − H − I | −F − G − H − I |
| Total surplus | A + B + C + D + F + G | A + B + C + D + E + F + G + H | +E + H |

deadweight loss that would have existed if there was a monopoly supplier and no regulation. Hence, the PBS achieves the efficient or socially optimal outcome.

So, in theory, the PBS makes Australia much better off. But does this actually happen? Well, it seems that the answer is a resounding 'yes'. Evidence on international pharmaceutical drug prices suggests that the PBS has had exactly the effect that would be predicted. For example, a cross-country comparison of prices paid to manufacturers for pharmaceutical drugs found that in 2010 the average price was about 50 per cent lower in Australia than in countries such as the United States, Germany and France (Kanavos et al. 2013). Lower prices also appear to have translated into a gain in overall wellbeing. One study has estimated that the gain in total surplus to Australia is about 15 per cent compared with a situation where the PBS did not exist (Johnston & Zeckhauser 1991).

The PBS does, however, have its critics. Some have argued that the subsidy to drugs in the PBS induces doctors to overuse drug therapy in treating illness, and that having drug prices set by the government has caused manufacturers to engage in wasteful non-price competition for their drugs, such as advertising and promotions for doctors. It has also been suggested that by forcing a lower price for drugs, Australia is reducing the return to drug manufacturers from investing in research and development to find new drugs, and hence the rate of discovery of new drugs may be compromised. For a country that is as small a part of the world market as Australia, this does not seem likely, although the PBS did become a major sticking point in negotiations for the Australia–United States Free Trade Agreement (*The Economist* 2004). None of this should make us think, though, that the PBS is unworthy of the title of 'ingenious'. Its success in lowering prices and increasing access to pharmaceutical drugs makes it an exemplar of how clever government regulation that deals effectively with market failure can make a society better off.

## KEY LESSONS

- Having a market that is supplied by a monopolist will have consequences for efficiency and equity in society. By increasing price and reducing the quantity sold, a monopolist makes higher profits than any firm in a perfectly competitive market, but consumers are made worse off. Since the loss in consumer surplus is larger than the gain in profits, there is a decline in overall wellbeing in society.

- Due to patent regulations, manufacturers of new types of pharmaceutical drugs are likely to have a monopoly on the supply of those drugs. The PBS is an attempt by the Australian Government to overcome this source of market failure. The PBS provides the government with significant bargaining power that it can use to negotiate a lower price with drug manufacturers, and by paying a subsidy for pharmaceutical drugs, consumption can be increased to the efficient level. Hence, in theory, the PBS should achieve a significant increase in wellbeing for Australian society.

- International comparisons of the prices of pharmaceutical drugs suggest that the PBS allows Australia to purchase drugs from manufacturers at much lower prices than occurs in countries such as the United States.

## SOME QUESTIONS TO THINK ABOUT

1. Suppose that a monopoly supplier of a pharmaceutical drug faces a market demand curve $Q = 50 - P$ and has zero fixed costs and a constant MC of production equal to 10.

   a. What price and quantity will a profit-maximising monopolist choose? What is consumer surplus? What are the monopolist's profits?

   b. Suppose the government decides to regulate the market for the pharmaceutical drug. It offers a subsidy of $s$ per unit to the manufacturer if it allows the government to set the price to consumers equal to 10. What value of $s$ should the government choose? What would be the equilibrium quantity of the drug sold with government intervention? What changes occur in consumer surplus and the manufacturer's profits? How is the overall surplus affected?

2. The Durr government has made a law that makes Artslet Co. the monopoly supplier of telephone services in Ozland. Alan Accountant and Edwina Economist are discussing how government intervention may therefore be required to correct for market failure in the market for telephone services in Ozland. Alan says: 'Because Artslet Co. is a monopolist, it will supply less than the efficient quantity of services. Hence, the government could improve the wellbeing of society in Ozland by paying Artslet Co. a subsidy that will induce it to increase its quantity supplied'. Edwina replies: 'I agree that a subsidy will increase the quantity

of services provided, which will therefore improve society's wellbeing. But this policy means that most of the surplus from trade goes to Artslet Co. A better policy – which will mean that most of the surplus from trade will go to buyers – is to force Artslet Co. to set a price equal to the competitive equilibrium price'.

Consider the statements made by Alan Accountant and Edwina Economist. Say whether you believe each statement to be correct or incorrect.

# REFERENCES

Bureau of Industry Economics (1985), Submission to the IAC Inquiry into the Pharmaceutical Products Industry, mimeo.

Commonwealth Department of Health (2019), 'About the PBS', www.pbs.gov.au/info/about-the-pbs, viewed 17 September 2019.

Johnston, Mark & Zeckhauser, Richard (1991), The Australian Pharmaceutical Subsidy Gambit: Transmuting Deadweight Loss and Oligopoly Rents to Consumer Surplus, National Bureau of Economic Research, working paper no. 3783.

Kanavos, Panos, Ferrario, Alessandra, Vandoros, Sotiris & Anderson, Gerard (2013), 'Higher US branded drug prices and spending compared to other countries may stem partly from quick uptake of new drugs', Health Affairs, 32, pp. 753–61.

The Economist (2004), 'Aussie rules', 21 August, pp. 50–1, 54.

# IDEAS FOR FURTHER READING

The PBS website (www.pbs.gov.au/pbs/home) provides a large amount of information about the scheme. The prices of pharmaceutical drugs and government regulation of health care are examples of the topics studied in the field of health economics. A good textbook introduction to this field can be found in Charles Phelps' Health Economics (2017, Addison-Wesley, 6th edition).

# VI

## Game theory

Studying economics 30 years ago, it's most unlikely game theory would have got a mention in your classes. At that time, game theory was hardly used. In the period since then, in a virtual revolution, it has come to be seen as one of the most valuable tools available to economists.

Game theory is used to study strategic situations. A strategic situation is where there is an interdependency between decision makers. Interdependency means that a decision maker needs to anticipate the decisions others will make, or how they will react, in order to be able to work out his or her own best decision.

Economists have increasingly recognised the importance of strategic situations and hence the role that game theory can play in economic analysis. Competition between firms like Woolworths and Coles, auctions of houses, bargaining between employers and trade unions over wages, governments' choices about macroeconomic policy – these are just a few of the areas to which game theory has been applied.

It's not only economists who find game theory useful. The original impetus for its development was to guide decisions that the US Government had to make about the production and stockpiling of nuclear weapons during the Cold War with the former Soviet Union. As well as having continuing importance in the field of international relations, game theory is also applied today to areas such as political science, psychology and mathematics. Wherever human society and the interaction of individuals or groups in that society are being studied, it is almost certain that game theory will be used.

So, let the games begin! In the case studies in this section, you'll see that game theory is applied in two ways. First, it can be used to help us make decisions when we are involved as participants in a strategic situation. Using game theory, we are able to develop general rules to guide behaviour, or in some cases figure out the optimal strategy to follow in a game. Second, game theory assists us in studying and predicting the outcomes of strategic situations. By providing a framework for working out what rational players would choose to do in any strategic situation, it enables us to predict what is likely to happen in those situations.

There are two steps to applying game theory. First, it's necessary to develop a model of the strategic situation. The model must describe the participants, the strategies available to each participant and the 'pay-off' for each participant from each possible combination of strategies that might happen in the game. Pay-offs summarise the total effect of an outcome of the game on a participant's wellbeing. Second, the model is applied to advise on the best choice of strategy for a player in the game, or to predict the outcome of the game. Any method of predicting the outcome of a game uses the concept of an equilibrium: An outcome in which all players are choosing strategies that are best for them. The exact equilibrium concept that is used to predict the outcome will vary with the specific type of game being studied.

Games can be classified as simultaneous or sequential. A simultaneous game occurs where every player makes a choice of strategy without observing the strategy choice of any other player. A sequential game occurs where at least one player observes an action chosen by another player prior to choosing his or her own strategy. Case studies 6.1 and 6.2 describe examples of simultaneous games, and Case studies 6.3 and 6.4 are about sequential games.

Case study 6.1 uses auctions to illustrate how game theory can be applied to guide decision making in simultaneous games. Today, auctions are used for selling many different items, such as flowers, paintings and houses. In auctions that are second price (that is, where the winning bidder pays a price equal to the amount bid by the second-highest bidder), game theory provides strong advice on how you should bid. Bidders in this type of auction have what game theorists call a (weak) dominant strategy, a strategy that always does at least as well as, and sometimes better than, any alternative strategy that is available. Despite our predisposition to dissimulate in front of an auctioneer, the optimal strategy in the second-price auction is shown to be to bid how much the item being sold is worth to you.

Case study 6.2 changes tack to show how game theory can help us understand what happens in markets, specifically why governments in the United States and Europe persist in making huge payments to support their passenger jet manufacturers, Boeing and Airbus, even though these payments don't end up improving the competitive position of either business. In this example, you'll learn about an important method of predicting outcomes of simultaneous games, the Nash equilibrium.

Case study 6.3 presents a rather different application of game theory. In many countries, corruption in government and among public officials is a major impediment to economic progress. Measuring and understanding the sources of corruption are an important part of solving this problem, and in this case study you'll see how one group of researchers has tried to help in this task using game theory. They devised a 'corruption game' that has participants make decisions about whether to engage in and punish corrupt behaviour. By having the game played in different countries around the world, the researchers were able to obtain new insights into why corruption occurs. Our analysis of the corruption game will also illustrate how the model of a sequential game can be represented using a game tree, and how the equilibrium concept of subgame perfect Nash equilibrium and the idea of backward induction can be applied to predict the outcomes of sequential games.

In Case study 6.4, you'll get a deeper appreciation of sequential games and learn the important lesson that the order in which you get to make your choices in a sequential game can matter a lot for your pay-off from the game. Sometimes, such as in the example of competition between Boeing and Airbus that is analysed, there may be a 'first-mover' advantage. A firm that can commit to how much it is going to produce before its competitor decides how much to produce can cause the competitor to reduce its output compared with when both firms choose their output quantities simultaneously, and hence earn higher profits. In other games, as in an example of bidding for the TV broadcast rights to Australian Rules football, it may be much better to make your choice of strategy after your competitors – this is known as a 'second-mover' advantage.

Have you ever bid to buy something on eBay? If you have, you will know the competitive thrill of being involved in an auction. No doubt you will also have thought about how you should bid. When should you start bidding? How high should you make your first bid? When should you stop bidding?

You might also have observed that auctions similar to the one you participated in are taking place everywhere around us. From flowers in the Netherlands to spectrum in the United States, fish in Tokyo, fine art in London and wool in Australia – all of these items, with sales in the billions of dollars, are nowadays sold by auction.

The growing importance of auctions as a method of trade has meant that economists have taken a great interest in them, and in the same questions that you would have contemplated while bidding on eBay. For an economist, an auction is an example of a strategic situation. Any bidder, to work out his or her best strategy, will generally need to think about how other bidders will choose to bid in an auction. So, an economist approaches the task of thinking about auctions using game theory.

### THEORY REFRESHER

#### Game theory, simultaneous games and dominant strategy equilibrium

Game theory is the study of strategic situations. A strategic situation is a situation where there is an interdependency between decision makers. To work out what choices will best serve their own interests, decision makers need to anticipate the decisions of other parties or how those parties will react to their decisions.

A simultaneous game occurs where every player in that game makes a choice of strategy without observing the strategy choice of any other player. Note that what we call a simultaneous game may actually involve players choosing strategies at different times, but so long as no player observes the choice of any other player prior to making their own choice of strategy, it will still be as if they were choosing simultaneously.

Simultaneous games can be represented using a game table. In a two-player game, there is a 'Row player' and a 'Column player'. Strategies for the 'Row player' are represented as different rows on the table, and strategies for the 'Column player' as different columns. Pay-offs, which represent the effect of an outcome on the players' wellbeing, are written within sections of the table corresponding to each combination of strategies, where the convention is to write the pay-off to the 'Row player' first and to the 'Column player' second.

An example of a simultaneous game is shown in **Table 6.1.1**. In this game, 'Row player' chooses between 'Up' and 'Down', and 'Column player' chooses between 'Left' and 'Right'. Where, for example, 'Row player' chooses 'Up' and 'Column player' chooses 'Left', the pay-offs are 5 to 'Row player' and 2 to 'Column player'.

**Table 6.1.1** Example of a simultaneous game

|  |  | COLUMN PLAYER | |
| --- | --- | --- | --- |
|  |  | Left | Right |
| Row player | Up | 5, 2 | 4, 2 |
|  | Down | 6, 4 | 4, 5 |

One way to predict players' choices in a simultaneous game, or to advise those players on strategy, is to use the concept of dominant strategy.

A player has a (weak) dominant strategy where there is a strategy that always gives at least as high a pay-off as any other strategy available, and gives a strictly greater pay-off for at least one possible combination of strategies that could be chosen by other players. A rational player would always choose to play a (weak) dominant strategy. This is because there is no other strategy that could ever do strictly better for the player.

Where all players in a game have (weak) dominant strategies, following the assumption that they are rational, we should expect them to choose those strategies. This combination of strategies is then described as a weak dominant strategy equilibrium.

The simultaneous game in **Table 6.1.1** can be used to illustrate a weak dominant strategy equilibrium. In this game, each player has a (weak) dominant strategy. First, for 'Row player', 'Down' is a (weak) dominant strategy. If 'Column player' chooses 'Left', 'Row player' will get a pay-off of 5 from choosing 'Up' and 6 from choosing 'Down'. If 'Column player' chooses 'Right', 'Row player' obtains the same pay-off of 4 from choosing either 'Up' or 'Down'. Hence, by choosing 'Down', 'Row player' always does at least as well, and sometimes better, than choosing 'Up'. Second, for 'Column player', choosing 'Right' always gives at least as high a pay-off and sometimes a higher pay-off than choosing 'Left'. Hence, the weak dominant strategy equilibrium would be for 'Row player' to choose 'Down' and 'Column player' to choose 'Right'.

It is also possible to define a strict dominant strategy equilibrium where all players choose a (strict) dominant strategy. This is where each player has a strategy that, regardless of the strategies chosen by other players, always gives them a strictly higher pay-off than any other strategy available.

In this case study, our main objective is to demonstrate how game theory can be applied to advise on an optimal bidding strategy to use in an auction. To do this, we will focus on a type of auction where game theory can give particularly strong guidance on an optimal bidding strategy, known as a 'second-price' auction. In a second-price auction the winning bidder, who makes the highest bid, pays a price equal to the bid made by the second-highest bidder. For example, suppose there is an auction with three bidders, who submit bids of $10 million, $15 million and $20 million. In a second-price auction, the participant who bids $20 million will win and will pay $15 million (the amount of the second-highest bid) to the seller.

There are many examples of second-price auctions (see McMillan 2002, chapter 7; Ashenfelter 1989). Art, wine and postage stamps are sold in second-price auctions, as are the publication rights to high-profile books. In Australia, many residential and commercial property sales occur through a second-price auction. And, of course, there is also the example of the eBay auction.

We'll begin our analysis by thinking about a particular type of second-price auction, a sealed-bid second-price auction. 'Sealed bid' means that the auction process involves all bidders submitting a single bid for the item being sold, and doing so without knowing anything about the bids submitted by the other bidders. As each bidder does not observe other bids, this auction is an example of a simultaneous game.*

In this type of auction, it turns out that the optimal bidding strategy is straightforward: *always bid how much the item is worth to you.* To illustrate why bidding your true value is the best strategy, consider the following example. Suppose you are a housing developer participating in a second-price sealed-bid auction for a tract of land. Your valuation of the land is $100 million. If the optimal strategy is to bid how much the item being sold is worth to you, this implies that you should bid your valuation of the land: $100 million.

Think about what happens if you do bid $100 million. What matters for the outcome of the auction is how your bid compares to the highest bid made by any other bidder. There are three possibilities. First, maybe there is a higher bid, say $105 million. In this case you don't win the land and make zero profits. Second, there may be another bid equal to $100 million. If this happens, then even if you win the item, you are going to pay $100 million (since the second-highest bid is also for this amount), so again you would make zero profits. Third, your bid could be the highest, beating the next highest bid, which might be $95 million. In this case you win the item and make a profit equal to the difference between your value and the second-highest bid; that is, $5 million. *Table 6.1.2* summarises your possible profits when you choose to bid $100 million.

Table 6.1.2 Your profits from alternative bidding strategies (1)

|  | BID $100 MILLION |
| --- | --- |
| Highest bid by other bidders is $105 million | Zero |
| Highest bid by other bidders is $100 million | Zero |
| Highest bid by other bidders is $95 million | $5 million |

Next, suppose you consider bidding less than $100 million. For example, you might try $90 million. This doesn't change anything if there is another bidder who bids $100 million or $105 million. You don't win the auction and you make zero profits, just like if you bid $100 million. But the outcome does change if the highest bid by any other bidder is $95 million. Now that you have lowered your bid to $90 million, this other bidder will beat your bid. You miss out on the item and make zero profits. This is worse than if you had bid $100 million. So, we've shown that by bidding less than your valuation, you can never do better, and will in fact sometimes do worse than if you had followed the strategy of bidding what the land was worth to you. *Table 6.1.3* shows the comparison of profits from bidding $90 million and $100 million.

Table 6.1.3 Your profits from alternative bidding strategies (2)

|  | BID $90 MILLION | BID $100 MILLION |
| --- | --- | --- |
| Highest bid by other bidders is $105 million | Zero | Zero |
| Highest bid by other bidders is $100 million | Zero | Zero |
| Highest bid by other bidders is $95 million | Zero | $5 million |

Finally, you can consider bidding a higher amount than the value you attach to the land, say $110 million. In this case, you are in trouble if the higher bid means you win the land and there is someone else who has bid more than $100 million. For example, when the highest bid by any other bidder is $105 million and you have bid $110 million, you win the land and are going to have to pay the amount of the second-highest bid, $105 million. So, you lose $5 million because you have paid this amount more than the land is worth to you. You would have been better off bidding $100 million, in which case you don't win the land and end up with zero profits. If the highest bid by any other bidder is $100 million or less, the outcome will be just the same as if you had bid $100 million. So, we're able to reach the same conclusion about bidding more for the land than your value as for bidding less. Compared to bidding your valuation, choosing a different strategy will never make you better off, and sometimes will make you worse off. *Table 6.1.4* summarises this information on profits from the alternative bidding strategies you might choose.

**Table 6.1.4** Your profits from alternative bidding strategies (3)

|  | BID $90 MILLION | BID $100 MILLION | BID $110 MILLION |
|---|---|---|---|
| Highest bid by other bidders is $105 million | Zero | Zero | −$5 million |
| Highest bid by other bidders is $100 million | Zero | Zero | Zero |
| Highest bid by other bidders is $95 million | Zero | $5 million | $5 million |

The optimal bidding strategy that we've just characterised has a very special property. It is known as a dominant strategy. Using the formal language of game theory, a player is said to have a (weak) dominant strategy where there is a strategy that always gives at least as high a pay-off as any other strategy available, and gives a strictly greater pay-off for at least one possible combination of strategies that could be chosen by other players. This is exactly what has been shown to hold for the strategy of bidding your valuation of $100 million for the land. So, we can designate that strategy as a (weak) dominant strategy.

Having a dominant strategy dictates how a player should behave in a game. Simply put, the player would always want to choose that strategy. No alternative strategy can ever do better for the player, so it is unambiguously the best choice to make. This holds regardless of the strategies chosen by other players in the game. As the developer in the land auction, you would always want to bid $100 million.

Bidding your valuation also has a broader application than just to the specific example of a second-price sealed-bid auction. A closely related type of auction is the second-price open auction. In this auction, bidders make 'open' bids that are observed by other bidders. At any stage in the auction there will be a highest bid that has been made by some bidder. Another bidder is able to take over as the highest bidder by offering a higher amount to the seller. When no bidder wants to make an offer above the current highest bid, the item being auctioned is sold to the highest bidder for the amount they have bid. This type of auction is also known as 'second-price' since the winner need only have bid a small amount above the second-highest bidder in order to win the item.**

In a second-price open auction, the optimal bidding strategy is very similar to that used in the sealed-bid auction. It is to be willing to bid up to, but no more than, what the item being sold is worth to you. Let's show why this is optimal. Suppose again that you are a developer interested in buying a tract of land that you value at $100 million. It's easy to see that you should never bid more than the land is worth to you. If you do bid more, say $110 million, and you end up winning the land, then you have to pay $110 million and make a loss of $10 million. You'd have been better off not making the bid. Equally, bidding less than your value, when bidding more might have given you a chance of winning the auction, is not a good idea. If the current highest bid is any amount less than $100 million – for example, $95 million – you should definitely bid more. Not being the highest bidder, you have no chance of getting the land, but if you enter a bid above $95 million, maybe $96 million, that makes you the highest bidder, and if no other bidder improves on your offer, you will win the land and make a profit of $4 million.

So, whenever you are involved in a second-price auction, such as for a house or some item you just can't resist on eBay, game theory is able to give precise and unambiguous guidance on how you should bid. Of course, there are many other types of auctions. In these situations, it turns out that game theory can still be used to work out an optimal bidding strategy. It just becomes more difficult to do this (for one thing, you need to know a lot more game theory), and the optimal strategy is likely to be more complex. Nothing changes, however, in regard to the essential usefulness of game theory as a tool for guiding your behaviour.

## KEY LESSONS

- Auctions are a strategic situation; for example, each bidder's optimal bid can depend on bids made by other bidders. Hence, economists use game theory to study auctions and to suggest rules for optimal decision making in auctions.
- An important type of auction is known as a second-price sealed-bid auction. This is an example of a simultaneous game. For this type of auction, game theory provides precise and unambiguous advice on what constitutes an optimal bidding strategy. The optimal strategy is for each bidder to make a bid equal to their valuation of the item being sold. It is shown that any other bidding strategy can never achieve a higher pay-off and will sometimes result in a lower pay-off. This is therefore an example of a (weak) dominant strategy.
- A similar approach to bidding is the optimal strategy for any bidder in a second-price open auction: that is, bidding up to, but no more than, the value that the bidder attaches to the item being sold.

# SOME QUESTIONS TO THINK ABOUT

1   Four students who have studied game theory – Al, Byung, Chris and Dawei – plan to bid in a second-price auction for a complete set of Australian Rules grand final programs. Their respective valuations for the set are $100, $150, $75 and $400. Who would you expect to win the programs in a second-price sealed-bid auction? What about a second-price open auction? What would you expect to be the selling price for the programs in each of these auctions?

2   The market for cigarettes in a country is dominated completely by two firms, Chokoe Ltd and Fumed Lungs Ltd. The market size is fixed at $8 billion. Each firm can choose whether to advertise or not. Advertising costs $1 billion for each firm that advertises. If one firm advertises and the other does not, then the firm advertising captures the whole market. If both firms advertise, they split the market 50:50 and pay for their respective advertising. If neither advertises, they split the market 50:50 but without the expense of advertising.
    a   Draw a game table to describe this game.
    b   What strategy would you advise Fumed Lungs Ltd to follow?
    c   What would you predict will be the strategy chosen by each firm?
    d   Is there an outcome that would make both firms better off? Why aren't they able to achieve this outcome?

3   Qantas Airways has announced a new scheme for frequent flyers to upgrade to business class seats (Freed 2015). Under the previous system, passengers with a specified amount of frequent flyer points were allowed to upgrade to available business class seats, Now selected frequent flyers can also bid a mix of frequent flyer points and cash for upgrades. A minimum dollar amount of cash will be required, and Qantas will give guidelines on the likelihood that a proposed bid will be successful.
    a   Could Qantas' new scheme be considered as an auction?
    b   Why would Qantas believe that its profits will be increased by the new scheme?
    c   Why would Qantas give a guide to whether the cash bid made by a passenger for an upgrade will be successful?

# EXTRA NOTES

\* The other assumption that will be implicit in our analysis is that bidders have valuations for the item being sold that are independent, so that each bidder's valuation is unrelated to any other bidder's valuation.

\*\* Since each bidder gets to observe bids made by other bidders, the second-price open auction is an example of a sequential game (see Case study 6.3 for a more thorough treatment of this type of game). Generally, a different approach is used to work out optimal strategies in a sequential game than in a simultaneous game. For this example of a sequential game, however, the optimal bidding strategy can be derived in a similar way to the optimal strategy for the simultaneous version of the second-price auction. This extra version of the second-price auction, although it is a different type of game, is discussed to show that the strategy of bidding the amount an item is worth to you has a wider application than just to the second-price sealed-bid auction.

# REFERENCES

Ashenfelter, Orley (1989), 'How auctions work for wine and art', *Journal of Economic Perspectives*, vol. 3, summer, pp. 23–36.

Freed, Jamie (2015), 'Qantas offers auctions for upgrades', *The Age Business Day*, 10 February, p. 23.

McMillan, John (2002), *Reinventing the Bazaar*, W.W. Norton and Co.

# IDEAS FOR FURTHER READING

Avinash Dixit and Barry Nalebuff's book *Thinking Strategically: the Competitive Edge in Business, Politics and Everyday Life* (1992, W.W. Norton) is an excellent introduction to many of the main ideas in game theory. Good introductory textbook treatments of game theory are Avinash Dixit and Susan Skeath's *Games of Strategy* (1999, W.W. Norton) and Prajit Dutta's *Strategies and Games* (1999, MIT Press). A very good history of the early development of game theory is provided by William Poundstone's *Prisoner's Dilemma* (1992, Anchor Books). Introductions to the economic analysis of auctions are provided in chapter 7 of Tim Harford's *The Undercover Economist* (2007, Oxford University Press) and chapters 6 and 7 of John McMillan's *Reinventing the Bazaar* (2002, W.W. Norton).

Developing a new model of passenger jet is an expensive business. Boeing, for example, is estimated to have spent $32 billion on its new 787 Dreamliner (*The Economist* 2016). Not surprisingly, then, it is also pretty expensive to buy a jet – the Dreamliner will set you back US$250 million (Auslick 2014). Another notably big number associated with the passenger jet market is the amount of government support that the major manufacturers such as Airbus and Boeing receive. In mid-2018 the World Trade Organization ruled that the European manufacturer Airbus had received US$9 billion in illegal government subsidies. If this seems an unfair advantage for the European producer, at the same time Airbus was claiming to the World Trade Organization that the US producer Boeing had received tax breaks worth US$11.7 billion (*The Economist* 2018, p. 62). These are very large amounts of money; for example, the support to Boeing means that, in about 10 years, a single firm received as much support from government as the whole of the farming sector in the United States receives each year.

Why did governments in the United States and Europe commit so much money to support Boeing and Airbus? Initially, the answer to this question may seem simple. Surely each government is providing a subsidy to give the manufacturer in its country or region a competitive advantage. By being able to set lower prices or produce a better-quality plane, the manufacturer should get more business and this will benefit the country. This sounds plausible. Recall, however, that both the US and European governments are paying similar subsidies. If only one government pays a subsidy it may provide a competitive advantage, but if both manufacturers are getting subsidies, aren't they just in the same position as if there were no subsidies? In which case, we come back to our original question – Why are governments paying the subsidies?

The amount of money that is involved makes these questions important. For an economist, the way to go about answering them is to use game theory. With only two main manufacturers in the passenger jet market, we should certainly think of those manufacturers as competing strategically. For example, any decision Airbus might make about whether to develop a new jet is likely to depend on what product development it believes Boeing is undertaking and on how it thinks Boeing will respond to its decision. So, this makes game theory the appropriate method for studying competition in the passenger jet market (see, for example, Spencer & Brander 2008).

In this case study, we'll start off by using game theory to study competition between Boeing and Airbus. In particular, we'll focus on how the firms' behaviour will be changed by receiving subsidies from their respective governments. The next step is to think about the question of why governments in the United States and Europe are willing to pay subsidies. Once again, we will use game theory to do this, treating the choice each government makes about whether to pay a subsidy as a strategic situation. The application of game theory to answer the questions we have posed about the passenger jet market will illustrate for you why economists find game theory such a valuable method of analysis.

---

### THEORY REFRESHER

#### Simultaneous games and the Nash equilibrium

A simultaneous game occurs where every player makes a choice of strategy without observing the strategy choice of any other player. Note that what we call a simultaneous game may actually involve players choosing strategies at different times. But so long as no player observes the choice of any other player prior to making their own choice of strategy, it will still be as if they were choosing simultaneously.

Simultaneous games can be represented using a game table. In a two-player game there is a 'Row player' and a 'Column player' and, for example, strategies for the 'Row player' are represented as different rows on the table. Pay-offs, which represent the effect of an outcome on the players' wellbeing, are written within sections of the table corresponding to each combination of strategies, where the convention is to write the pay-off to the 'Row player' first and to the 'Column player' second.

The most commonly used method to predict the outcome of a simultaneous game is Nash equilibrium. This approach to predicting outcomes is named after the Nobel prize-winning economist John Nash, who invented the concept. A set of strategies, one for each player, is defined to be a Nash equilibrium where each player is choosing a strategy that achieves the best possible outcome for him or her given the strategy choices of all the other players. Another way of putting this is to say that a Nash equilibrium is a set of strategies such that for each player, taking as given the strategies of all other players, it is not possible to obtain a strictly better outcome by switching to a different strategy.

Any Nash equilibrium in a game can be found using what is known as the 'cell-by-cell' inspection method. This involves checking each possible strategy combination of players in the game to see if it satisfies the definition of a Nash equilibrium. For each possible strategy combination, the following question is asked for each player: Given the choices of other players, can this player obtain a strictly higher pay-off by switching to another strategy? If the answer to this question is 'no' for all players, then that strategy combination is a Nash equilibrium.

If the answer to the question is 'yes' for any player, then the strategy combination is not a Nash equilibrium.

**Table 6.2.1** Game table showing that a Nash equilibrium is for player 1 to choose 'Down' and player 2 to choose 'Left'

|  |  | PLAYER 2 | |
| --- | --- | --- | --- |
|  |  | Left | Right |
| Player 1 | Up | $0, $6 | $1, $2 |
|  | Down | $2, $8 | $0, $5 |

In the game table (*Table 6.2.1*), the Nash equilibrium is for player 1 to choose 'Down' and player 2 to choose 'Left'. This is because: (a) given that player 2 chooses 'Left', player 1 cannot obtain a higher pay-off by switching from 'Down'; and (b) given that player 1 chooses 'Down', player 2 cannot obtain a higher pay-off by switching from 'Left'. It is possible to check the other three possible strategy combinations ([Up; Right], [Up; Left], [Down; Right]) and use the same approach to show that since at least one player always has an incentive to switch to a different strategy, none of these strategy combinations is a Nash equilibrium.

The justification for using a Nash equilibrium to predict the outcome of a game is that it is a 'stable' outcome. Players in a simultaneous game do not observe the choices of strategies of other players prior to making their own choices.

However, suppose that after choosing their strategies, but prior to them being carried out, those strategies were revealed and each player given the opportunity to change. Where the strategies they have chosen are a Nash equilibrium, no player would want to switch. In this sense, the Nash equilibrium can be regarded as a stable outcome.

A difficulty with using a Nash equilibrium as a way of predicting the outcome of a game is that it is possible to have more than one Nash equilibrium in the same game. Without extra information that allows us to distinguish between those equilibria, therefore, it is not possible to make a unique prediction of the outcome of the game.

To decide how we should represent competition in the passenger jet market, we need to identify the main features of the market. Arguably, the most important feature is 'a tendency towards natural monopoly' (*The Economist* 2005). This tendency can be explained by the high fixed costs of developing a new type of aircraft, and the significant reductions in marginal costs as the quantity of an aircraft produced increases. Decreases in marginal cost come from the extra knowledge about the best way to produce that develops when a higher quantity is produced. It has been estimated, for example, that every doubling of the number of any type of jet that is produced decreases the marginal cost of production by 20 per cent. Together, high fixed costs and decreasing marginal costs imply that average cost will fall rapidly as the quantity produced increases. A single producer will therefore always be able to supply the whole market more cheaply than any group of suppliers; hence, the tendency to monopoly.

From this description, we might (in very simple terms) represent the strategic situation involving the decision each firm makes about whether to produce a new generation of passenger jet as a simultaneous game in the way shown in the game table in *Table 6.2.2*.

**Table 6.2.2** Game table for Boeing and Airbus to produce or not produce a new generation of passenger jet

| | | BOEING | |
|---|---|---|---|
| | | Produce | Not produce |
| Airbus | Produce | −$10 billion, −$10 billion | $100 billion, $0 |
| | Not produce | $0, $100 billion | $0, $0 |

A tendency to natural monopoly suggests that the market will end up with just one supplier. But where Boeing and Airbus begin from the same position, it's difficult to predict which will end up as the monopolist. The game table captures this idea by having two Nash equilibrium outcomes. In both outcomes, one of the firms chooses 'Produce' and the other firm chooses 'Not produce'. Each outcome is a Nash equilibrium because given that one firm chooses 'Produce', the other cannot do better than by choosing 'Not produce', and vice versa. The existence of two Nash equilibrium outcomes represents the idea that the market outcome is indeterminate. In other words, we can identify two scenarios involving natural monopoly that we think are reasonable predictions of what the market outcome will be, but we cannot say which is more likely to occur.

Now suppose that European governments have the idea of paying a subsidy of $15 billion to Airbus provided that it chooses to 'Produce' a new generation of jet plane. With this offer of a subsidy to Airbus, the strategic situation involving the choice of whether to develop the new jet changes the game table to what is shown in *Table 6.2.3*.

**Table 6.2.3** Game table for Boeing and Airbus with a subsidy from European governments

|  |  | BOEING | |
| --- | --- | --- | --- |
|  |  | Produce | Not produce |
| Airbus | Produce | $5 billion, −$10 billion | $115 billion, $0 |
|  | Not produce | $0, $100 billion | $0, $0 |

The offer of the subsidy has a dramatic effect on the outcome we would predict to occur. In the revised game, Airbus has a (strict) dominant strategy to choose 'Produce'; that is, regardless of the choice made by Boeing, Airbus is always strictly better off choosing 'Produce'. Given that Boeing will know that Airbus has a dominant strategy to choose 'Produce', it should therefore choose 'Not produce'. Hence, there is now a unique Nash equilibrium prediction of the outcome of the game: for Airbus to 'Produce' and Boeing to 'Not produce'. The subsidy from the European governments has given Airbus a competitive advantage. Originally, Airbus was evenly matched with Boeing and it was difficult to predict which firm would win out. With the subsidy, Airbus will clearly be the winner in the battle for monopoly.

The idea that the European governments might provide a subsidy to support Airbus in its competition with Boeing is an example of what is known as strategic trade policy, an approach to thinking about international trade policy that is usually attributed to two economists from the University of British Columbia, Professor Barbara Spencer and Professor Jim Brander, and to Professor Paul Krugman from Princeton University. Strategic trade policy is defined as 'trade policy that affects the outcome of strategic interactions between firms in an actual or potential international oligopoly' (Spencer & Brander 2008). The idea of international oligopoly is that there is a small number of firms, located in different countries, which compete strategically. Having firms that are located in different countries means that a government in one country can use trade policy to seek to raise the profits of local firms at the expense of firms in other countries.

Strategic trade policy is notable as an example of a situation where government intervention in international trade may improve a country's wellbeing. Consider our game between Airbus and Boeing. In the absence of any subsidy from European governments, it seems plausible to think that there is a one-half chance that Airbus will end up winning out as the monopolist supplier and therefore make $100 million, and a one-half chance that it will be Boeing, in which case Airbus will make zero profits. Hence, the expected surplus for Europe from the passenger jet market would be $50 billion. What about with a subsidy? Now, with the equilibrium outcome certain to have Airbus as the monopoly supplier, the surplus for Europe is $100 billion. (We need to subtract the subsidy of $15 billion from the total pay-off to Airbus of $115 billion, as this amount was taken from taxpayers in Europe.) Supporting Airbus with a subsidy has made Europe better off. The reason that this can happen is that we are dealing with a situation where government support can allow its supplier to become a monopolist.

So far, we have seen that Europe can be made better off by using strategic trade policy to support Airbus. Perhaps, though, you are thinking that it is a bit strange just to give governments in Europe this opportunity. Can't the US Government also work out that it can assist Boeing by offering it a subsidy to choose 'Produce'? This is exactly right. We should also give the US Government the opportunity to provide a subsidy to Boeing. With both governments able to offer a subsidy (again assume $15 billion), the game table changes to be as shown in *Table 6.2.4*.

**Table 6.2.4** Game table for Boeing and Airbus with subsidies from both European and US governments

|  |  | BOEING | |
| --- | --- | --- | --- |
|  |  | Produce | Not produce |
| Airbus | Produce | $5 billion, $5 billion | $115 billion, $0 |
|  | Not produce | $0, $115 billion | $0, $0 |

In this game, both firms have a (strict) dominant strategy to choose 'Produce'. By paying a subsidy to Boeing, the US Government can induce it to choose 'Produce'. Hence, the predicted outcome using either the Nash equilibrium or dominant strategy equilibrium is for both Boeing and Airbus to choose 'Produce'. Notice, however, that the outcome is not so good for either the United States or Europe. Both countries are losing an amount of −$10 billion. (This is equal to the outcome for Boeing and Airbus, $5 billion, minus the cost of the subsidy, $15 billion.)

Whereas when only one country provides a subsidy it can make itself better off, when both provide a subsidy, they are both made worse off. This may seem strange. Both governments are paying subsidies even though they are made worse off. How can this happen?

To answer this question, an economist thinks about there being another game happening, one where each of the governments of the United States and Europe is simultaneously deciding whether to 'Give subsidy' or 'Not give subsidy'. This game might be represented in a game table as shown in *Table 6.2.5*.

**Table 6.2.5** Game table for the United States and Europe to give subsidy or not give subsidy

|  |  | UNITED STATES | |
| --- | --- | --- | --- |
|  |  | Give subsidy | Not give subsidy |
| Europe | Give subsidy | −$10 billion, −$10 billion | $100 billion, $0 |
|  | Not give subsidy | $0, $100 billion | $50 billion, $50 billion |

The pay-offs in **Table 6.2.5** represent the amount of surplus accruing to each country from each outcome. If Europe gives a subsidy and the United States does not, then Airbus will become the monopoly supplier, and therefore Europe will get $100 billion surplus and the United States gets zero. The opposite applies where the United States gives a subsidy and Europe does not. If both do not give a subsidy, then there is a one-half probability that either will become the monopoly supplier, so that the expected outcome is for each to get a surplus of $50 billion. Where both countries give a subsidy, then both firms end up producing and each country gets −$10 billion surplus.

In this game, using the Nash equilibrium to predict the outcome, we again have two possibilities – one Nash equilibrium where the United States pays a subsidy and Europe does not, and another Nash equilibrium where Europe pays a subsidy and the United States does not. These equilibria, however, don't seem to explain what actually happens, since we know that both governments pay a subsidy. What might we be missing in our description of the game between the governments? One possible explanation is that any government that chose not to give a subsidy might suffer significant political costs. For example, suppose the US Government did not give a subsidy. In that case, Boeing will not engage in new product development and will close down, with the loss of many jobs. A government that allowed this to happen would most likely experience a major adverse reaction from voters, especially in locations where Boeing plants are located. The same argument could be made for Europe. These political costs can be taken into account in our analysis of the game involving the US and European governments by assuming that a government that does not give a subsidy has a loss of votes that we can value in monetary terms, say at $15 billion. This means we would need to modify the game table to be as shown in **Table 6.2.6**.

**Table 6.2.6** Game table for the United States and Europe to give subsidy or not give subsidy accounting for political costs

|  |  | UNITED STATES | |
|---|---|---|---|
|  |  | Give subsidy | Not give subsidy |
| Europe | Give subsidy | −$10 billion, −$10 billion | $100 billion, −$15 billion |
|  | Not give subsidy | −$15 billion, $100 billion | $35 billion, $35 billion |

Taking account of political costs has changed our story. Both governments have a (strict) dominant strategy to choose to pay a subsidy, and therefore the predicted outcome, using either Nash equilibrium or dominant strategy equilibrium, is for both governments to choose 'Give subsidy'. So, we've explained how both governments can come to be paying a subsidy. You would be right, though, to still be a bit puzzled about this outcome. Although both governments are choosing 'Give subsidy', they could do much better by agreeing to both choose 'Not give subsidy'. This doesn't happen, however. Neither government would abide by such an agreement since each has a dominant strategy to choose 'Give subsidy'. The governments are engaged in what is known as a prisoners' dilemma game, where they know there is an outcome they both prefer to the equilibrium, but which they cannot attain.

---

### THEORY REFRESHER

#### The prisoners' dilemma game

There may be no better-known game than the prisoners' dilemma. The game has become an important part of economics because it describes a strategic situation that is similar to many aspects of competition in markets with few firms, as well as a variety of other situations in which economists are interested.

The prisoners' dilemma game can be described as follows. Two suspects for a crime have been arrested and are being interrogated separately by the police. The police officer in charge of the case offers each prisoner the same deal:

1 If you confess and the other prisoner does not, we'll go easy on you and you'll only get two years in jail.
2 If you don't confess and the other prisoner does, you are in trouble and will get 20 years in jail.

Each prisoner also knows that if they both confess they will each get 10 years in jail, whereas if neither of them confesses they are still likely to be found guilty but will just get five years in jail. Each prisoner must tell the police officer whether they confess or not confess without knowing the other prisoner's choice.

This prisoners' dilemma game is a simultaneous game and can be represented using a game table, as shown in **Table 6.2.7**. In the game table, each year spent in jail is assumed to contribute a pay-off of $-1$ to a player, so that more years in jail are associated with a worse pay-off.

**Table 6.2.7** The prisoners' dilemma game

|  |  | PRISONER 2 | |
|---|---|---|---|
|  |  | Confess | Not confess |
| Prisoner 1 | Confess | $-10, -10$ | $-2, -20$ |
|  | Not confess | $-20, -2$ | $-5, -5$ |

In the prisoners' dilemma game, each prisoner has a (strict) dominant strategy to choose 'Confess'. Regardless of the choice made by the other prisoner, choosing to confess always gives a player strictly fewer years in jail. For example, where prisoner 2 chooses 'Confess', then prisoner 1 will get 10 years in jail if he also chooses 'Confess', whereas choosing 'Not confess' brings a sentence of 20 years. And if prisoner 2 chooses 'Not confess', then prisoner 1 gets two years by choosing 'Confess' but five years by choosing 'Not confess'.

As both players have a dominant strategy to choose 'Confess', we'd predict that the outcome in the game will be that both players will choose 'Confess'. Notice, however, that there is another outcome, where both players choose 'Not confess', that would make them both better off. If the prisoners could somehow agree to both choose to 'Not confess', they would each spend five years in jail instead of 10 years. The dilemma is that this is not going to happen. Even if the players were able to communicate with each other prior to making their choices, and they agreed to choose 'Not confess', once they went back to their cells, if each really believed that the other was going to choose 'Not confess', he would be better off by switching to 'Confess' and thereby get two years in jail instead of five years. If both players are rational, they will both think this way, and the outcome is back to both players choosing to 'Confess'. The dilemma is that it is not individually rational for each player to choose the strategy that is best for them jointly.

Now we have an explanation for why governments in both Europe and the United States pay huge subsidies to their passenger jet firms. A government's decision not to pay a subsidy would, because of the market being a natural monopoly, spell the death knell for its firm. Provided the political costs of either Airbus or Boeing going out of business are sufficiently large, each government will then prefer to pay a subsidy. This is despite the subsidies cancelling each other out and leaving both firms in the same position as if no subsidies had been paid. We have also explained why both Airbus and Boeing remain in operation, even though we think the market is a natural monopoly. Once each government chooses to pay a subsidy, both Airbus and Boeing will choose to produce, even though they may earn relatively low profits.

## KEY LESSONS

- Models of simultaneous games, and the dominant strategy equilibrium and Nash equilibrium methods of predicting outcomes in simultaneous games, can be used to study competition between Airbus and Boeing in the passenger jet market.
- The passenger jet market in recent years has been characterised by ongoing competition between Airbus and Boeing, and large subsidies paid to these firms by governments in Europe and the United States, respectively. Game theory can be used to demonstrate how this market outcome could arise through strategic competition between governments and between the firms. The tendency for the passenger jet market to be a natural monopoly, together with the likely political costs for governments in the United States or Europe were their local firm to go out of business, appears to be critical to explaining the current market outcome.

## SOME QUESTIONS TO THINK ABOUT

1  Suppose the game between Airbus and Boeing was as depicted below:

|  |  | BOEING | |
| --- | --- | --- | --- |
|  |  | Produce | Not produce |
| Airbus | Produce | $25 billion, $25 billion | $100 billion, $0 |
|  | Not produce | $0, $100 billion | $0, $0 |

a  What is the Nash equilibrium of this game?
b  Would there be any role for strategic trade policy in this game?
c  Would the governments of the United States and Europe have an incentive to apply strategic trade policy?

2   Two players are involved in a game. Each player begins with $10 and must simultaneously decide how much of the $10 to allocate between two accounts: a 'private' account, and a 'public' account. Money allocated to the private account by a player is kept by that player. Money allocated to the public account is multiplied by 1.5 and then distributed back equally to each of the two players. Each player has three possible choices: (i) allocate $0 to the public account, (ii) allocate $5 to the public account, and (iii) allocate $10 to the public account.

   a   Draw a game table to represent this game.

   b   Do players have a strict dominant strategy in this game?

   c   What is the Nash equilibrium of the game?

   d   Does the Nash equilibrium outcome maximise the total pay-off to players? How can you explain this result?

3   A recent article on Qantas (Hatch 2018) has described how CEO Alan Joyce committed that the airline would resist the temptation to add more capacity into its domestic network, with an absence of growth in total seats available in Australia having helped propel the airline to a record half-year profit. Qantas recorded a 14 per cent jump in net profit, supported by cutting domestic capacity 3 per cent and increasing fares by about 8 per cent. According to the Bureau of Infrastructure, Transport and Regional Economics, this reflected 'an on-going truce from the damaging capacity war, that has let both Qantas and Virgin improve their earnings' (Hatch 2018).

   a   Why would Qantas and Virgin want to constrain the total amount of capacity for air travel in Australia?

   b   Would such behaviour be expected to arise if each firm was separately competing to maximise its profits, or is it likely to require some coordination between the airlines?

# REFERENCES

Auslick, Paul (2014), 'Why a Boeing 787-9 Dreamliner Costs $250 Million', https://247wallst.com/aerospace-defense/2014/06/17/why-a-boeing-787-9-dreamliner-costs-250-million/, viewed 31 May 2019.

Freedman, Jennifer (2011), 'Boeing subsidies illegal, WTO rules', *The Age*, business section, 5 December, p. 5.

Hatch, Patrick (2018), 'Qantas vows to keep seat numbers down, fares up', *The Age*, 23 February, pp. 22–3.

Spencer, Barbara & Brander, James (2008), 'Strategic trade policy', in Steve Durlauf & Lawrence Blume (eds), *The New Palgrave Dictionary of Economics*, Macmillan, can be accessed at: http://blogs.ubc.ca/barbaraspencer/files/2016/02/2008-strategic-trade-policy-Palgrave.pdf, viewed 30 June 2012.

*The Economist* (2005), 'Nose to nose', 25 June, pp. 67–9.

*The Economist* (2016), 'The eye of the storm', 14 May, pp. 54–5.

*The Economist* (2017), 'Flying blind', 19 May, pp. 62–3.

# IDEAS FOR FURTHER READING

Adam Brandenburger and Barry Nalebuff attempt to distil the main lessons of game theory for business in *Co-opetition* (1996, Currency Doubleday). You can read more about John Nash in Sylvia Nasar's exceptional biography *A Beautiful Mind* (1998, Simon and Schuster).

# CASE STUDY 6.3
## THE CORRUPTION GAME

No country is immune from corruption among its government and bureaucracy. Giving and accepting bribes, stealing public funds, even interfering with supposedly democratic elections – you can find examples in pretty much any country you might name. In countries such as Australia, although the corruption that occurs (for example, deals between developers and local councils over rezoning of land or political appointments to government jobs) may be ethically objectionable, it does not have much effect on the average citizen. Unfortunately, in many countries the story is very different, the scale of corruption being so great as to constitute a major impediment to economic development.

A common way in which corruption can affect development is through its influence on the amount of investment that occurs in a country. Where high levels of corruption exist, incentives for private entrepreneurs to make investments will be reduced by the need to pay bribes or by the possibility of having one's business or profits expropriated, and public funds that would otherwise be spent on infrastructure and government services are often diverted to the pockets of politicians or used to pay government supporters. A recent IMF study (2016, p. 10) has estimated that the efficiency of investment is about 30 per cent lower in countries with high levels of corruption than countries with low levels of corruption. The lower levels of investment caused by corruption will inevitably lead to lower rates of economic growth.

Many countries, then, could be made better off by implementing policies that address corruption. To deal with a problem, of course, we first need to understand it. To manage corruption, we need to know the answer to questions like: In which countries is corruption worst? What are the main sections of society that are engaged in corruption? What gives these individuals or groups an incentive to engage in corrupt practices?

One way of learning about corruption is from the opinions of analysts and business people who deal regularly with a country. An organisation called Transparency International compiles ratings of the perceived extent of corruption among politicians and public officials in different countries from exactly this type of expert data. In the organisation's 2018 Corruption Perceptions Index, Denmark is ranked as the least corrupt country, with a score of 88/100. At the other end of the scale Somalia was ranked as the most corrupt country with a score of 10/100. Australia comes out of the assessment relatively well, being ranked 13th with a score of 77/100 (Transparency International 2018). These rankings are certainly useful as an indicator of countries where there is the greatest scope to improve development by reducing corruption. Like any measure, however, the Corruption Perceptions Index is not perfect. It is based on perceptions rather than actual behaviour, and although it provides an indication of how much corruption exists in each country, it doesn't tell us much about why corruption occurs.

Some years ago, researchers at the University of Melbourne and University of Auckland set out to find a new way of thinking about corruption to complement information from the Corruption Perceptions Index. Dr Nisvan Erkal and Associate Professors Lisa Cameron, Ananish Chaudhri and Lata Gangadharan turned to game theory and experimental economics. They designed a clever game that, played in experiments in different countries, added to our understanding of why corruption occurs (Cameron et al. 2009).

---

### THEORY REFRESHER

#### Sequential games and subgame perfect Nash equilibrium

In a sequential game, at least one player observes the choice of action by another player prior to choosing his or her own strategy.

Sequential games can be represented using a game tree. A game tree consists of decision nodes, which are points in the tree at which a player must make a choice of action, branches that show the choices of action available to a player, and terminal nodes that are points at the end of the game tree. Each terminal node corresponds to a possible outcome of the game, and pay-offs associated with the outcome are then written at that terminal node, with the convention of writing the pay-off to the first-moving player first, the second-moving player second and so on.

In the example given in **Figure 6.3.1**, player 1 makes a choice of 'Up' or 'Down', after which player 2, having observed player 1's choice, must decide to move 'Top' or 'Bottom'. Where, for example, player 1 moves 'Up' and player 2 moves 'Top', the pay-offs to those players are respectively 10 and 5.

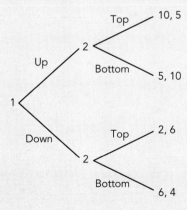

**Figure 6.3.1** Possible outcomes in a sequential game

The outcome in a sequential game can be predicted using the concept of subgame perfect Nash equilibrium (sometimes referred to as roll-back equilibrium). A subgame perfect Nash equilibrium is a choice of strategy for each player that involves making an optimal choice of action at each decision node given that all other players will choose optimal actions at all subsequent decision nodes in the game tree.

The subgame perfect Nash equilibrium can be found using the principle of 'backward induction'. Backward induction requires starting at the final decision nodes in the game tree and working out the optimal actions for the players at those nodes. Then the information on pay-offs from those optimal choices of actions is 'rolled back' in the tree to become the pay-offs for choices of actions at decision nodes at the previous stage in the game. This is repeated until all choices of actions in the tree have been predicted.

In the example in *Figure 6.3.1*, we would begin at the decision nodes for player 2. At the upper decision node, player 2 would choose 'Bottom', which provides a pay-off of 10 rather than 5 from choosing 'Top'. At the lower decision node, player 2 would choose 'Top', which provides a pay-off of 6 rather than 4 from choosing 'Bottom'. We then 'roll back' to the choice of player 1. Player 1 knows that if 'Up' is chosen, then player 2 will choose 'Bottom' and hence player 1 will get 5, whereas if 'Down' is chosen, player 2 will choose 'Top' so that player 1 will get 2. Hence, player 1 chooses 'Up'. This process is depicted in *Figure 6.3.2*. We say that the subgame perfect Nash equilibrium is for player 1 to choose 'Up' and for player 2 to choose ['Bottom', 'Top'] at the upper and lower decision nodes respectively.

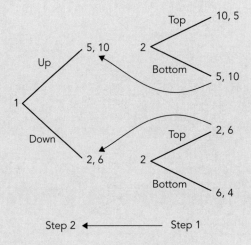

Figure 6.3.2 The subgame perfect Nash equilibrium

The subgame perfect Nash equilibrium of a sequential game is the outcome that we would expect to occur if all players in the game are rational and believe that other players will also make rational choices.

The 'corruption game' that the researchers developed had three players and involved several stages. In the first stage, a player designated as a 'Firm' chooses whether to 'Offer' or 'Not offer' a bribe to a public official. If the firm does not offer a bribe, the game ends; otherwise, the game proceeds to a second stage where a player designated as an 'Official' must decide whether to 'Reject' or 'Accept' the bribe. If the official decides to reject the bribe, the game ends; otherwise, it proceeds to a third stage where a player designated as a 'Citizen' makes a choice of whether to 'Punish' or 'Not punish' the firm and official. Pay-offs are assumed to be such that the firm and official are made better off by offering and accepting a bribe so long as the citizen does not punish them, but are worse off if they are punished. The citizen suffers a cost from the bribe being offered and accepted compared with when no bribe is offered, and then loses an extra amount by making the choice to punish the firm and official.

This game, together with a slightly simplified version of the pay-offs the researchers used in their experiments, is represented in *Figure 6.3.3*. As the game is sequential, a game tree is used.

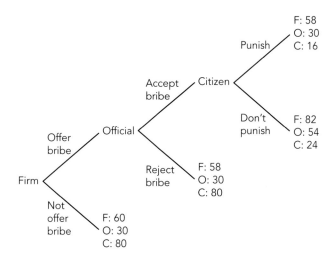

**Figure 6.3.3** The corruption game

Having developed this game, the researchers took it to several countries and ran experiments where human subjects were given the roles of the firm, official and citizen. The subjects received monetary pay-offs from participating in the experiments that corresponded to the pay-offs in the game tree. By comparing the choices made by the subjects in different countries, it was hoped that a new perspective on the extent of corruption in each of the countries would be provided. Moreover, by separating the choices to engage in and punish corruption, the game provided a way of studying the sources of corruption.

To interpret the results of the experiments, we need to step back for a moment and think more deeply about the corruption game. What would we expect the outcome of the game to be? To answer this question, we can apply the equilibrium concept of the subgame perfect Nash equilibrium (SGPNE).

Solving for the SGPNE involves backward induction. We begin at the end of the game tree and work out the optimal action for the player making the choice at that point in the tree. Knowing what choice is made at the last stage of the game provides us with information about the players' pay-offs that can be rolled back to the second-last stage of the game. It's then possible to determine the optimal action for the player making the choice at that second-last stage. The same process is followed until we get to the start of the game tree. The set of optimal actions that we have found throughout the game tree constitutes the SGPNE of the game.

The way to solve for the SGPNE in the corruption game using this process of backward induction is shown in **Figure 6.3.4**. We first see that the citizen's optimal choice is to choose 'Not punish', since doing this gives a pay-off of 24 compared with 16 from punishing. Given that the citizen will not punish, when we roll back to the previous stage, the optimal action for the official is to 'Accept' the bribe, as this gives a pay-off of 54, whereas choosing to reject the bribe gives a pay-off of only 30. Finally, when we roll back to the first stage of the game, taking into account the fact that the official will accept the bribe and that the citizen will choose not to punish, the best action for the firm

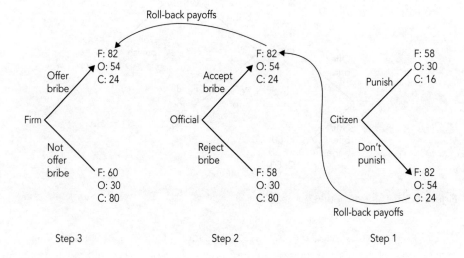

**Figure 6.3.4** Working out the SGPNE in the corruption game

is to choose to 'Offer' the bribe, which gives a pay-off of 82 compared with 60 when no bribe is offered. Hence, the SGPNE is for the firm to offer a bribe, for the official to accept the bribe and for the citizen to choose to not punish the corruption.

Experiments involving the corruption game were run in four countries: Australia, Singapore, India and Indonesia. The results, it has to be said, were fascinating. In all countries, the subjects doing the experiments in the role of the firm and official conformed fairly closely to predictions of their behaviour in the SGPNE. Almost 90 per cent of firms chose to offer a bribe and a similar proportion of officials accepted those bribes. These proportions did not vary significantly between countries. In contrast, subjects playing the role of citizens diverged markedly in their behaviour from the SGPNE prediction. Only about 50 per cent chose to not punish the bribery; or putting this the other way around, about 50 per cent chose to punish the bribery even though this lowered their monetary pay-off from the experiment. For this choice, there were significant differences between the subjects in different countries. Citizens in India were much less likely to punish than those in Australia or Singapore, who in turn were slightly less likely to punish than citizens in Indonesia.

What can we learn about corruption from these results? Primarily, they tell us that there is no great difference between the countries in the likelihood that members of society will be willing to engage in corrupt practices when presented with a sufficient financial incentive to act in that way; rather, it is differences in the social acceptance of corruption that seem more important in explaining why the incidence of corruption differs between countries. In India, which is generally perceived to have high levels of corruption, most subjects in the role of citizens chose not to punish the bribery. By contrast, in Australia and Singapore, which are regarded as countries with low levels of corruption, a much higher proportion of the population chose to punish the bribery, despite being financially worse off by doing this.

A puzzle that resulted from the experiments was Indonesia. Although Indonesia is usually rated as having high levels of corruption, it was the country with the highest proportion of citizens choosing to punish the bribery. An explanation that the researchers suggested is that corruption in Indonesia has been centralised (for example, among the ruling family and military leaders) and has therefore existed without general social acceptance, whereas in India, where corruption is more diffused throughout the operations of government, it has required widespread social acceptance to survive. So, the results also strongly suggest the need to distinguish the level at which corruption occurs in a society and its extent of diffusion throughout government.

New ways are constantly being found in which game theory can be applied to improve our understanding of the economy and society. This is illustrated by the experimental corruption game, which has provided novel insights into how corruption occurs. In this particular application, the value of being able to use game theory to predict the outcome in a strategic situation is also demonstrated. The SGPNE of the corruption game sets a benchmark from which it has been possible to make inferences on the strength of incentives to engage in and punish corruption in different countries.

## KEY LESSONS

- Corruption is a major barrier to material progress in many countries. A prerequisite for dealing with corruption is to understand it, especially issues such as how its incidence differs between countries and the main sources of incentives to engage in corruption.

- Recent research has sought to develop our understanding of corruption by having experimental subjects in different countries play a corruption game, where they must choose whether to engage in or to punish corrupt behaviour.

- The corruption game is an example of a sequential game and therefore we use the equilibrium concept of SGPNE to predict the outcome. The extent to which experimental subjects make choices consistent with SGPNE can be used as the basis for making inferences about the sources of corruption. The social acceptance of corruption emerges from the experimental research as an important source of incentives to engage in corruption.

## SOME QUESTIONS TO THINK ABOUT

1   In the Envelope game there are two players and two envelopes. One of the envelopes is marked 'player 1' and the other is marked 'player 2'. At the beginning of the game, each envelope contains $1. The game has three stages. In the first stage, player 1 must decide whether to 'Stop' or 'Continue'. If he chooses 'Stop', then each player receives the money in their own envelope and the game stops. If he chooses 'Continue', then the $1 is removed from his envelope, and $2 is added to player 2's envelope. In the second stage, player 2 must decide whether to 'Stop' or 'Continue'. If she chooses 'Stop', then each player receives the money in their own envelope and the game stops. If she chooses 'Continue', then $1 is removed from her envelope, and $2 is added to player 1's envelope. In the third stage, player 1 must again decide whether to 'Stop' or 'Continue'. If he chooses 'Stop', then each player receives the money in their own envelope and the game stops. If he chooses 'Continue', then $1 is removed from his envelope, and $2 is added to player 2's envelope. After this the game ends.

a   Draw the game tree that represents the Envelope game.

b   What is the roll-back equilibrium of the game?

2   Suppose there is an incumbent monopolist in a market. A potential entrant is deciding whether to 'enter' or 'not enter' the market. If the potential entrant chooses 'enter', then the incumbent can choose to either 'lobby' or 'not lobby' the government to impose a tax on the potential entrant. If the incumbent chooses to 'lobby', this imposes a cost on it of $20, but as a result, the government passes a law that places a tax of $60 on the potential entrant. If the potential entrant chooses to not enter the market, it makes zero profit and the incumbent firm makes a monopoly profit equal to $100. If the potential entrant enters the market, it earns a duopoly profit of $50, minus any tax, and the incumbent earns a duopoly profit of $50, minus any lobbying costs.

a   Use a game tree to represent this game.

b   What is the subgame perfect Nash equilibrium of this game?

3   Consider the statements made by Alan Accountant and Edwina Economist. Say whether you believe each statement is correct or incorrect. Briefly explain your answer. Note that most of the marks will be given for your explanation.

Alan Accountant and Edwina Economist are deciding whether to donate to a charity organisation that wants to build a new library in a remote area of Ozland. They also need to decide whether to make their decisions on donations simultaneously or sequentially. They know that only if they both donate can the library be built. For each of them, their payoff depends on whether the project is completed (zero if not completed, and 100 if completed); and whether they donate (zero if no donation, and −50 if donate). Hence the game table for the simultaneous version of the game is:

|  |  | ALAN | |
| --- | --- | --- | --- |
|  |  | Not donate | Donate |
| Edwina | Not donate | 0,0 | 0,−50 |
|  | Donate | −50,0 | 50,50 |

Alan Accountant says: 'It doesn't matter what process we use for making donations. The outcome will always involve us both deciding to "Donate".'
Edwina Economist says: 'I disagree. If we make our decisions simultaneously a possible outcome is for us both to choose to "Not donate". Whereas if we make our choices sequentially then, regardless of who makes the first and second choices, the outcome should involve us both choosing to "Donate".'

# REFERENCES

Cameron, Lisa, Chaudhuri, Ananish, Erkal, Nisvan & Gangadharan, Lata (2009), 'Do attitudes to corruption differ across countries?', *Journal of Public Economics*, vol. 93, pp. 843–51.

International Monetary Fund (2016), *Corruption: Costs and Mitigating Strategies*, Staff Discussion Note 16/05.

Transparency International (2018), https://www.transparency.org/cpi2018, viewed 31 May 2019.

# IDEAS FOR FURTHER READING

Tim Harford presents a great discussion of why corruption is bad for economic development in chapter 8 of *The Undercover Economist* (2006, Oxford University Press). *Experimental Methods: a Primer for Economists* by Daniel Friedman and Shyman Sunder (1994, Cambridge University Press) and *Experiments in Economics* by Ananish Chaudhuri (2009, Routledge) each provide a very good introduction to the methods of experimental economics, and some of the key findings obtained.

Most likely you will know of the game 'Rock, paper, scissors'. Two players simultaneously announce a choice out of rock, paper, or scissors. If one player selects 'scissors' and the other 'paper', whoever chooses 'scissors' wins. Otherwise, rock beats scissors, paper beats rock, or if both players choose the same option it's a draw. (If you're not familiar with this game, the idea is that scissors can cut the paper, rock can blunt the scissors, and paper can smother the rock.)

You may only have played this game in the schoolyard, but in some places it is taken very seriously. In the early 2000s the World Rock Paper Scissors Society developed standardised rules for international play. It has declared 27 August as World Rock Paper Scissors day, and there are now annual US, Canadian and European championships.

How could you become national champion? Well, there is some strategy in trying to guess what your opponent will choose, but mainly you'll need a lot of luck. Think of the difference it would make, though, if you got to observe your opponent's choice before having to commit to your own choice. Your opponent chooses rock, so you choose paper. Or if they choose scissors, you choose rock. You will never lose, and the national championship will be yours.

A game of 'Rock, paper, scissors' in which one player gets to observe the opponent's choice prior to choosing his or her own strategy is, of course, not going to be very interesting to play (or indeed to watch on TV). Once we know who gets to go second, then we know the winner. For this reason, it is not a version of the game that is ever likely to be played much. But imagining how such a game would work does illustrate an important point about strategic situations – that in sequential games, the order in which players choose their actions can matter a great deal to the outcome.

---

### THEORY REFRESHER

For a 'Theory refresher' on 'Sequential games and subgame perfect Nash equilibrium', see Case study 6.3.

Studying strategic interactions between businesses provides many examples of how order can matter. Sometimes it turns out that firms can do best by getting to commit to a choice of action before other firms make their choices. This is known as 'first-mover advantage'. Moving first can benefit a firm when it enables it to commit to a strategy and thereby force another firm to adjust its behaviour in a way that is advantageous. In other circumstances, it can be best to move second. This is known as 'second-mover advantage'. For example, by moving second, a firm learns information about its competitor's strategy that allows it to choose a more profitable strategy. This is the same rationale behind why it would be good to be able to move second in 'Rock, paper, scissors'.

# First-mover advantage

Competition between the two main manufacturers of large passenger jets, Boeing and Airbus, is intense; it's been described in a report on the industry as 'a dog fight' (*The Economist* 2004, p. 57). Despite generally sluggish growth in demand for commercial jets at the time of the report, it described how Airbus had just made the 'bold statement ... that production will expand by a huge 25% next year' (*The Economist* 2004, p. 57).

Increasing supply at the same time as market demand is growing slowly might seem a curious strategy. But pre-committing to higher production levels may be optimal for Airbus if it is a way of inducing Boeing to reduce its quantity of output or its production capacity.

How Airbus might get a first-mover advantage by committing to its production strategy can be illustrated with a numerical example. Suppose that Boeing and Airbus are the only firms in the market for commercial passenger jets, both have zero fixed costs and a marginal cost of $5 million per jet, and each firm can only vary the number of jets it supplies in multiples of five. (Nothing depends on these assumptions about costs and varying supply. They are just used to simplify the numerical example.) Suppose that market demand for passenger jets is as shown in *Table 6.4.1*.

**Table 6.4.1** Market demand for passenger jets

| MARKET QUANTITY DEMANDED | PRICE ($ MILLION) |
|:---:|:---:|
| 10 | 70 |
| 15 | 65 |
| 20 | 60 |
| 25 | 55 |
| 30 | 50 |
| 35 | 45 |
| 40 | 40 |
| 45 | 35 |
| 50 | 30 |
| 55 | 25 |
| 60 | 20 |
| 65 | 15 |
| 70 | 10 |

What happens if the two firms compete by simultaneously choosing a quantity to supply? Using the concept of the Nash equilibrium, we would predict the outcome to be a choice of quantity by each firm which maximises its profits given the quantity chosen by the other firm. This Nash equilibrium will involve each firm choosing to supply a quantity of 25 jets. Hence, combined output in the market by the two firms is 50 jets. Reading from the market demand information in **Table 6.4.1**, the market price is therefore $30 million. It follows that profits to each firm equal 25 × ($30 million − $5 million) = $625 million.

Working out that each firm supplying a quantity of 25 jets is a Nash equilibrium is a process of trial and error. It requires checking all the different possible combinations of output that the two firms could produce to find the combination that meets the conditions for an equilibrium. Here, we won't go into details about all the possible outcomes that are not an equilibrium. We can, however, demonstrate that it is a Nash equilibrium for each firm to produce 25 jets. We will do this by showing that neither firm has an incentive to switch to supply either a lower or higher quantity, given that the other firm supplies 25 jets. Suppose that a firm considers switching to a lower output of 20 jets. This makes the market output 45 jets and hence the market price is $35 million. Thus, the firm that switches will earn profits equal to 20 × ($35 million − $5 million) = $600 million. This is less than the profits from supplying 25 jets. Alternatively, suppose a firm considers switching to a higher output of 30 jets. This would make the market output 55 jets and hence the market price is $25 million. In this case, the firm that switches will earn profits equal to 30 × ($25 million − $5 million) = $600 million. This is again less than the profits from supplying 25 jets. Hence, neither Boeing nor Airbus has an incentive to switch from supplying 25 jets, given that the other firm adopts this strategy.

Now think about the alternative situation where Airbus can pre-commit to a quantity of jets to supply, and then, having observed this choice made by Airbus, Boeing must choose a quantity to supply. How will this affect the outcome for both firms? Suppose Airbus chooses a quantity of 30 jets. Boeing must now take this as given in choosing its own quantity. Hence, the optimal quantity for Boeing to choose is 20 jets. This is because, by choosing to supply 20 jets, Boeing earns profits equal to 20 × ($30 million − $5 million) = $500 million. By choosing a lower quantity of 15 jets, and with Airbus supplying 30 jets, Boeing would earn profits of only 15 × ($35 million − $5 million) = $450 million, and by choosing a higher quantity of 25 jets it would earn profits of 25 × ($25 million − $5 million) = $500 million. Hence, Boeing cannot earn higher profits by switching from supplying 20 jets. By committing to supply 30 jets, Airbus has therefore been able to force Boeing to reduce the quantity of jets it supplies, compared with when both firms choose their quantity of output simultaneously. With Airbus supplying 30 jets and Boeing supplying 20 jets, the market output is 50 jets. Therefore, the market price is $30 million. We can then calculate that Airbus will earn profits of 30 × ($30 million − $5 million) = $750 million. Thus, Airbus has higher profits than in the situation where both firms choose their output levels simultaneously. Airbus is better off from having the opportunity to commit to its quantity of output prior to Boeing making its choice of quantity.

In this example, Airbus has benefited from a first-mover advantage. By committing to the strategy of a higher production level, it induces Boeing to reduce its output compared with the situation where the firms make simultaneous choices, and hence it earns higher profits. Of course, for the strategy of pre-committing to a production level to be successful, Airbus must be able to make it credible to Boeing that it has made this commitment. Otherwise, Boeing, knowing that Airbus has not made a commitment, will choose its quantity as if both firms were making simultaneous choices. Airbus might be able to make the commitment seem credible by, for example, making public the number of orders it has received, or by investing in new plant and equipment that will only be profitable if it expands its output.

# Second-mover advantage

During 2005, the Australian Football League (AFL) sold the TV broadcast rights to AFL football for the five years from 2007 to 2011. The sale process, which involved two bidders (consortia of Channel 9/Foxtel and Channel 7/Channel 10) making offers for the TV rights, had one special feature. The consortium of Channel 7/Channel 10 had the right to make the last bid. Channel 7 had bought this right for $20 million in the late 1990s, on the previous occasion that the AFL TV rights were sold.

In the type of auction or tender process by which the AFL TV rights were sold, having the right to make the last bid can be extremely valuable. Essentially, it means that whenever you would be able to make a positive profit by winning the item being sold, you can do this. We can demonstrate this point using a numerical example. Suppose that the team of Channel 9 and Foxtel have made a bid for the TV rights of $500 million. Conditional on this bid, there are two possible scenarios. One is that Channels 7 and 10 believe the rights would be worth less to them than $500 million. In this case, they would not exercise the right to make the last bid since they cannot profitably beat the bid made by Channel 9/Foxtel. The other possibility is that Channels 7 and 10 believe the TV rights are worth more than $500 million, say $520 million. In this case, all they need to do is make a bid slightly above $500 million, and since it is the last bid, they will win. By having the right to make the last bid, and thereby being able to observe the final bid made by Channel 9/Foxtel, Channels 7 and 10 are guaranteed a win whenever they can make a profit.

In the bidding that actually occurred for the AFL rights in 2005, Channels 7 and 10 made an initial bid which was topped by Channel 9/Foxtel. But Channels 7 and 10 then won the AFL TV rights for 2007 to 2011 by making a last bid of $780 million. In an environment of intense competition between the two bidders, it does seem that the right to make the last bid was valuable for Channels 7 and 10. Observing Channel 9/Foxtel's bid before they made their own last bid gave Channels 7 and 10 a second-mover advantage. Of course, to decide whether this was a good strategy overall, we would need to compare the size of the payment Channel 7 made for the right to be the last bidder against the value that it derived from having the last bid. Perhaps we can infer that Channel 7 thought it had made a good investment by its interest in buying the same right to the last bid for the next auction for the AFL TV rights, which was to be held in 2010. This time, however, the AFL refused to sell this right (Wilson 2006).

Knowing that your order of move in a strategic situation can have a big effect on your pay-off is an important lesson from game theory. To be able to also take advantage of this knowledge, however, you will have to do some extra work. You'll need to distinguish between situations where it is likely to be better for you to move first or to move second, and then you need to make sure you get to choose your move at the preferred time. Manoeuvring to be able to make your choice at the time you want will often mean that there's a role for more game theory!

# KEY LESSONS

- In sequential games, the order in which players make choices can affect their pay-offs.
- A player can obtain a higher pay-off by moving first in a sequential game where this allows that player to force another player to change their choice of strategy in a way that is advantageous to the player moving first. This is known as a 'first-mover advantage'.
- A player can obtain a higher pay-off by moving second in a sequential game where it is valuable to be able to choose a strategy using information on the strategy of the other player. This is known as a 'second-mover advantage'.

# EXTRA NOTE

In these examples, competition between Boeing and Airbus or between Channel 7/Channel 10 and Channel 9/Foxtel hasn't been represented in a formal way by drawing a game tree or working out the equilibria of these games. It isn't necessary to go into this amount of detail to make the point that there could be a first-mover or second-mover advantage in sequential games. It would certainly be possible, however, to work out the subgame perfect Nash equilibria of these games using the concept of backward induction. For example, consider the game involving competition between Airbus and Boeing. As a first step, it would be necessary to derive the profit-maximising quantity for Boeing for each possible quantity choice Airbus might have made. The second step would then be for Airbus to choose its profit-maximising quantity, taking into account the response that it knows Boeing will make to each possible quantity it could choose. These two steps will characterise the choices that Airbus and Boeing will make, from which we can predict what will happen in the game.

# SOME QUESTIONS TO THINK ABOUT

1   The market for bananas in Ozland is an oligopoly with two profit-maximising suppliers – Bongo Bananas and Bendy Bananas. These suppliers compete strategically by choosing a quantity of bananas to supply to the market. Each supplier is able to choose either 50 megatonnes or 100 megatonnes of bananas. Market demand for bananas in Ozland is represented by the following schedule:

| QUANTITY (MEGATONNES) | PRICE ($ PER MEGATONNE) |
|---|---|
| 100 | 100 |
| 150 | 75 |
| 200 | 50 |

For each supplier, the marginal cost of producing a megatonne of bananas is constant and equal to $40 per megatonne, and there are zero fixed costs.

Suppose that Bongo Bananas and Bendy Bananas must simultaneously choose a quantity of bananas to supply.

a   Draw the game table that represents this strategic situation.

b   Does either player have a (strict) dominant strategy? Is there a (strict) dominant strategy equilibrium?

c   What is the set of Nash equilibria in the game?

d   Suppose that Bongo Bananas has the option of committing to a choice of quantity prior to Bendy Bananas making its choice of quantity, and that Bendy Bananas observes Bongo Bananas' quantity choice prior to making its choice. Would you advise Bongo Bananas to accept the option of choosing its quantity first?

2   A report on Qantas Airlines described how:

> Qantas has finally blinked in a vicious capacity battle with Virgin Australia … Qantas will freeze domestic capacity in the first three months of the financial year because of weak consumer confidence and a slowdown in the mining sector that have hit at a time when capacity has outstripped demand. It marks the formal abandonment of a strategy of maintaining a line in the sand at 65 per cent domestic market share …

Source: (Freed 2014).

a   Why might Qantas have adopted the strategy of committing to supply 65 per cent of the passenger seats required for the domestic Australian market?

b   Why do you think that Qantas decided that it should cease its strategy of committing to supply 65 per cent of the market?

3   An article in *The Economist* (2008) describes negotiations between China and its main foreign suppliers of iron ore. Early in the process, China's largest steelmaker, Baosteel, had struck a deal with Vale, a Brazilian iron ore producer. However, at the time the article was written, a deal was yet to be reached with the two major Australian suppliers of iron ore, Rio Tinto and BHP. At the same time, the Australian suppliers were finding themselves unable to obtain import licences necessary to sell iron ore onto China's spot market, where iron ore was trading at a price two to three times above the contract price. Yet, shipments from Brazil were having no trouble obtaining import licences.

a   Consider the bargaining over iron-ore prices between Australian suppliers and Chinese steel producers as a strategic situation. Who would you say are the main players in the game? What are the main choices of actions that each of the players must take? How would you represent the order of actions?

b   What would the Chinese Government be seeking to achieve by preventing Australian iron ore suppliers from selling in China's spot market? What are the main costs to them of restricting supply in this way? How might the slowdown in industrial demand for iron ore in China affect this trade-off?

# REFERENCES

Freed, Jamie (2014), 'Qantas blinks first in Virgin battle, with domestic capacity freeze', *The Age Business Day*, 22 May, p. 21. The use of this work has been licensed by Copyright Agency except as permitted by the Copyright Act, you must not re-use this work without the permission of the copyright owner or Copyright Agency.

*The Economist* (2004), 'Opening the throttles', 10 July, p. 57.

*The Economist* (2008), 'Pile up', 29 March, pp. 68–9.

Wilson, Caroline (2006), 'Devil is in the detail for TV rights', *The Sunday Age*, sport section, 3 December, p. 8.

# IDEAS FOR FURTHER READING

You can find more information about the World Rock Paper Scissors Association at https://www.wrpsa.com/about/. Adam Brandenburger and Barry Nalebuff attempt to distil the main lessons of game theory for business in *Co-opetition* (1996, Currency Doubleday).

## Economics of information

Economists are often criticised for oversimplifying their descriptions of how the world works. Simple theories can be a good thing, when they allow a more straightforward and transparent explanation of economic activity. But simplicity can become a shortcoming when it means excluding features of economic activity that really matter. New techniques and approaches that enable economists to develop richer representations of economic activity are therefore always welcome. Among the main technical advances in microeconomics in the past several decades have been approaches used to study situations where decision makers have limits on the information available to them.

Decision makers are often missing some piece of information they would like to know before making a choice. Failing to take this lack of information into account in describing the decision makers' behaviour will give an incomplete understanding of why they make the choices they do. For example, without acknowledging the limits on the information possessed by decision makers, it is not possible to explain the existence of insurance or futures markets, why financial advisers recommend to their clients that they diversify their investments, or the role of brand reputation and warranties in product markets.

The field of studying how limits on information affect economic activity is known as the economics of information. Economists who work on topics to do with information have examined two main types of situations. The first situation is where there is *uncertainty*. Uncertainty implies that the consequence of a choice to be made by a decision maker is not known. The range of outcomes that might occur is known, but rather than being informed about which of the outcomes will happen, instead decision makers just know the probability of each outcome. Importantly, in this environment it is assumed that all decision makers in the economy have the same limits on their information; that is, ignorance is symmetric. Here are some examples of situations involving uncertainty:

- If we buy a lottery ticket, we don't know the outcome of the lottery at the time we buy the ticket. All we know is that at a future date we might win a prize or we might not.
- If we install a new heating system in our house, at the time we buy the system we don't know exactly how much benefit we'll get from it. This will depend on the temperature in winter in future years.
- If we buy a house in a rural area, we cannot be sure whether there will be a bushfire in the area in future years that will threaten the house.

In each of these examples there is information the decision maker does not know. It also seems reasonable to think that the same uncertainty would be shared by all decision makers. Just as I don't know whether I will win a prize in a lottery, others who buy tickets will also not know this information. All that any of us knows is the probability of winning each of the prizes.

The second situation is where there is *asymmetric information*. An information asymmetry occurs when decision makers in the economy have different information available to them.

Examples of situations involving asymmetric information are:

- The seller of a used car has better information on the quality of the car than a potential buyer. While the seller may know the exact quality of the car, the buyer is likely to know only the range of possible qualities.
- A legal firm that is hired by a client to undertake legal work will have much better information than the client about its abilities in that area of law and about how much effort is going to be put into the case.
- A tenant farmer has information about soil and weather conditions that will affect output from the land which is not available to the landowner.

Economists became interested in situations where decision makers experience limits on the information available to them for one main reason: Limits on information can be a source of inefficiency in the economy. Having decision makers in society face uncertainty or asymmetric information means that their wellbeing is reduced, compared with a situation where everything is known. The fact that limits on decision makers' information have this effect on wellbeing has been the motivation for most of the research undertaken by economists who work on topics related to the economics of information. These economists have sought to identify ways in which decision makers, or governments, might alleviate the adverse consequences to wellbeing when there are limits on information.

This is the theme that is taken up in the case studies in this section. Case study 7.1 considers situations involving uncertainty and shows how insurance can remedy inefficiency that would otherwise exist due to uncertainty. We'll see how insurance can be thought of as a means of transferring risk – from members of society with a lower tolerance for risk to organisations such as insurance firms that are more willing to bear risk. By enabling this transfer to occur, insurance increases society's total wellbeing. Case study 7.2 looks at a situation involving an information asymmetry, where a business cannot monitor the efforts its employees are making. Being unable to monitor employee effort can make it difficult for a business to get its employees to work as hard as it wants. It is suggested that one way in which business can overcome this problem is to introduce a pay-for-performance scheme in order to motivate its employees to exert the appropriate amount of effort.

These days, it seems you can buy insurance against just about any event that might befall you. No doubt you will be familiar with the idea of buying house or car insurance, which will cover most of the costs incurred if your house or motor vehicle were to be damaged. If you have some experience in a workplace, you might have heard of disability insurance, which protects against loss of income from becoming disabled and unable to work, or professional indemnity insurance, intended to cover against claims of malpractice or negligence made against you by clients. This is just the start of the list of types of insurance that can be bought today, the most inventive of which are typically being created for businesses.

Take the example of political risk insurance. Globalisation has created new opportunities for businesses in the United States and Europe to trade with, or to set themselves up as producers in, countries where they did not previously operate, such as in Africa and Latin America. Political instability and weak legal systems in many of the countries in these regions, however, means that there is greater uncertainty involved than the businesses are used to dealing with. A mining business may have negotiated a contract with the ruler of a country to extract minerals, only to have that agreement overturned when the next ruler decides to nationalise the industry. Or events, such as civil wars or wars with a neighbouring country, may seriously disrupt production and trade. To protect themselves against these risks, many businesses have turned to political risk insurance, which provides a payout when the activities being undertaken by a business are adversely affected by political developments in the countries where they are operating. *The Economist* (2007) described how the Berne Union, a group of the 30 biggest public and private insurers, had over $113 billion in insurance policies covering companies against political violence, nationalisation and expropriation of assets, and currency inconvertibility.

Covering your business against political risk is not the only exotic type of insurance policy that is available. Suppose you are planning to use a well-known sportsperson as the 'face' of the product your company sells. You have chosen a sportsperson who has a reputation that matches the image you want for your product. But you also worry that all too often reputations of sportspeople can get tarnished, with collateral damage for the image of the business that sponsors them. In this case, maybe you should consider getting death and disgrace insurance to cover you in the event of any nasty surprises. It's been said that buying this insurance 'can limit damage from appalling behaviour (or worse) ... [It is] available for a fee of roughly 0.5 to 1% of the designated payout' (*The Economist* 2006).

Then there is cyber-insurance. Businesses are increasingly seeking to protect themselves against the fall-out should their computer systems be hacked – including the costs of restoring their IT systems, loss of reputation and revenue when they are unable to operate due to hacking, or legal action from customers whose personal information has been stolen. As one example, the Danish shipping company, Maersk, reported in 2017 that it had cost $300 million to restore its IT systems after being infected by a malware program. At present, the global cyber-insurance market is still small, with an estimated $4 billion in contracts being written in 2018. As more and more businesses become dependent on IT, however, rapid growth in the next decade is forecast (*The Economist* 2019). Clearly, there are many types of insurance policies that a business can buy, and they all share a common purpose – to transfer risk from a party who is less willing to bear that risk to a party who is more willing to bear the risk. That the parties have different attitudes towards risk means that there are potential gains to trade from making the transfer. Society can therefore be made better off via insurance.

---

## THEORY REFRESHER

### Risk preferences

Decision makers are likely to differ in their attitudes towards risk. Economists distinguish between these different attitudes by classifying decision makers as either risk averse, risk neutral, or risk lovers.

To define these categories of attitudes towards risk, we need to introduce several concepts. First, a *gamble* is defined as a situation where a consumer can receive different wealth outcomes. Second, an *actuarily fair* gamble is defined as a gamble which has an expected value of zero. For example, a lottery for which I pay $10 for a ticket and can win $20 with a probability of one-half and get zero with a probability of one-half, is actuarily fair: $(1/2)(\$20 - \$10) + (1/2)-\$10) = 0$. Third, we refer to the situation where a consumer receives the expected value of a gamble with certainty as the *certainty equivalent*.

#### Risk averse

A decision maker who is never willing to accept an actuarily fair gamble is defined as *risk* averse. An alternative definition is that a decision maker is risk averse when they prefer to receive the certainty equivalent of a gamble (the expected value of a gamble with certainty) rather than accept the gamble.

For example, suppose I am offered a gamble that involves winning $5 with a probability of one-half and winning $15 with a probability of one-half. If I am risk averse, then I would prefer to receive $10 with certainty rather than accept the gamble.

A corollary of a decision maker being risk averse is that if they are offered two gambles, both with the same expected value but with different variances, the decision maker will strictly prefer the gamble with the lower variance.

### Risk neutral

A decision maker who is indifferent to either accepting or not accepting an actuarily fair gamble is defined as *risk neutral*. An alternative definition is that a decision maker is risk neutral when they are indifferent to receiving either the certainty equivalent of a gamble or accepting the gamble. A corollary of a decision maker being risk neutral is that if they are offered two gambles, both with the same expected value but with different variances, the decision maker will be indifferent to the gambles.

### Risk lover

A decision maker who prefers to accept an actuarily fair gamble is a *risk lover*. An alternative definition is that a decision maker is a risk lover when they prefer to accept a gamble rather than receive the certainty equivalent. A corollary of a decision maker being a risk lover is that if they are offered two gambles, both with the same expected value but with different variances, the decision maker will strictly prefer the gamble with the higher variance.

To explore this explanation of the role of insurance in more detail, let's think about a specific example. Suppose that a business, OzMine Co., is risk averse and is seeking to purchase political risk insurance from a risk-neutral insurance firm, RisksRUs. OzMine Co. has just started a new mine in Transylvania. It is known that there are two outcomes that can occur for OzMine Co. in regard to its new mine – either there is no civil war in Transylvania, in which case OzMine Co. will make a profit of $10 million, or there is a civil war, in which case OzMine Co. makes zero profits.

We're going to use the example of OzMine Co. and RisksRUs to understand the role of insurance. As background to doing this, it is useful to step back and consider a situation with a risk-averse decision maker and a risk-neutral decision maker.

Suppose that the risk-averse party is endowed with a gamble. The gamble gives a one-half chance of winning $10 and a one-half chance of winning zero. At the same time, the risk-neutral party is endowed with $5 with certainty. By endowed, what is meant is that this is how things start out for each decision maker.

Now, introduce the possibility for the risk-averse and risk-neutral decision makers to swap their endowments. After making the swap the risk-averse decision maker is guaranteed $5 and the risk-neutral decision maker has an equal probability of winning zero or $10. This transfer of the gamble from the risk-averse decision maker to the risk-neutral decision maker will increase the total wellbeing in society. The risk-averse decision maker is better off getting $5 with certainty, rather than being forced to accept the gamble. Given a choice between two gambles, both with the same expected value but having different variances, a risk-averse decision maker will always strictly prefer the gamble with the smaller variance. The risk-neutral decision maker has the same level of wellbeing as they originally had. Being indifferent to gambles that have the same expected value, the risk-neutral party will be indifferent to taking the gamble or being guaranteed $5. Since the risk-averse decision maker is better off and the risk-neutral decision maker has the same level of wellbeing, we can conclude that transferring the gamble has made society better off.

The point of working through this example is that insurance works in much the same way as the transfer of the gamble. Let's go back to our example of the risk-averse mining firm OzMine Co. and the risk-neutral insurance firm RisksRUs. In this example, the gamble is the risky situation for OzMine Co. It can make either zero profits or $10 million profits. In what way could we think of OzMine Co. transferring this uncertainty associated with its profit outcome to RisksRUs? Well, we could consider the following deal. OzMine Co. offers to pay $5 million to RisksRUs if its profits turn out to be $10 million, in return for getting $5 million from RisksRUs if it earns zero profits. This deal will do exactly what the transfer of the gamble achieved. First, OzMine Co. is guaranteed to get $5 million whatever its level of profits. This makes it better off. It has the same expected outcome, $5 million, but now gets this outcome with certainty. Because it is risk averse, it prefers the certain outcome. Second, RisksRUs has the same expected outcome as before the deal. It pays out $5 million with probability one-half and gets $5 million with probability one-half. With a 50/50 chance of getting or having to pay $5 million, its expected outcome is zero, just the same as if it did not enter into the deal. Although the outcome for RisksRUs is subject to uncertainty, because it is risk neutral its wellbeing is not affected by taking on this extra risk. So, the deal has succeeded in transferring risk from OzMine Co. to RisksRUs. Moreover, as we've demonstrated that there are gains from trade in making the deal, it is also possible to conclude that the deal will increase society's total wellbeing.

There's one point, however, that might still be worrying you. The deal that has been suggested may not sound much like the sort of insurance contract you are familiar with. This point is easily addressed. The deal can simply be re-expressed to give it the same structure as an insurance contract: (i) OzMine Co. pays RisksRUs an upfront insurance premium of $5 million, and (ii) RisksRUs must pay OzMine Co. $10 million if there is a civil war. This insurance contract gives outcomes for OzMine Co. and RisksRUs that are identical to the outcomes from the deal. For example, if it buys the insurance contract, OzMine Co. is effectively guaranteed a fixed amount that is equal to $10 million minus the $5 million insurance premium it pays to RisksRUs.

Another concern you might have is that we are assuming that RisksRUs is willing to enter into the deal, even though it ends up in the same position as before the deal. If it's indifferent, might not RisksRUs equally choose not to trade with OzMine Co.? This point can also be easily dealt with. We know that the deal makes OzMine Co. strictly better off. So, there will always be some extra amount that it is willing to pay RisksRUs to do the deal. For example, perhaps OzMine Co. offers RisksRUs an extra $10 000 premium on top of the $5 million payment. This now makes RisksRUs strictly prefer to do the deal, as it will always be better off because of the $10 000. Provided the $10 000 is less than the value OzMine Co. attaches to being insured, it is also better off. (We can't say exactly how much extra premium OzMine Co. could offer without knowing more about its attitude to risk. All we can say is that the more risk averse is OzMine Co., the larger is the extra premium it will be willing to offer to obtain insurance.)

The general lesson, therefore, is that introducing the scope for insurance has made society better off. Insurance has allowed OzMine Co. to transfer the risk involved in the uncertainty about its profit outcomes to RisksRUs. Because RisksRUs has a greater tolerance for risk than OzMine Co., making this transfer can be done in a way that increases the wellbeing of both parties, and hence of society.

There is just one final loose thread to tie up. Everything in this story about the role of insurance depends on there being parties who have different attitudes towards risk; specifically, that there is an insurance firm, RisksRUs, that is risk neutral. But why does it make sense to think that the insurance firm would be risk neutral when we are assuming that OzMine Co. is risk averse? The justification for this assumption is an idea called the 'Law of large numbers'.

Even if the owner of RisksRUs is risk averse, if it takes on enough insurance contracts from firms like OzMine Co., then it can effectively be treated as if it was risk neutral. Suppose that OzMine Co. is the only client of RisksRUs. By selling insurance to OzMine Co., we know that RisksRUs will end up either gaining or losing $5 million. Now think of an alternative scenario where RisksRUs has 1000 clients, each facing exactly the same uncertain outcomes as OzMine Co., and to each of which it sells the same insurance contract. Let's assume (and this is important) that the outcome that actually occurs for each of the clients is independent of what happens for the other clients. Whether OzMine Co. makes zero profits or $10 million therefore has no effect on the outcome for the other clients of RisksRUs. With outcomes for its 1000 clients being independent of each other, we might guess that about half of them will end up making zero profits and half will finish with $10 million. This is in fact the message of the 'Law of large numbers' – that with a sufficiently large sample of independent events with uncertain outcomes, the overall distribution of outcomes will be close to the probability with which each outcome occurs. So, thinking that half of RisksRUs' clients will make zero profits and the other half will make $10 million is a reasonable assumption. With 1000 clients to whom it offers the insurance contract, the expected outcome for RisksRUs is to earn zero. It loses from paying out to the half of its clients who make zero profits, but it gains an equal amount from the premium payments made by the other half of its clients who make $10 million profits. What has changed, however, is that the variance in outcomes for RisksRUs is substantially reduced. By pooling the risks from all of its clients, RisksRUs can be sure of making pretty close to the outcome of zero. This is the sense in which we can think of RisksRUs as being risk neutral. Because it is pooling risks across many clients, taking over the risk of one extra client has very little effect on the extent of uncertainty it faces, and so it can be treated as being indifferent to that risk.

If you think that this process of balancing risks sounds interesting, then the actuarial profession might be made for you. Actuaries are experts in evaluating risks and recommending how to deal with their financial impact, and so are heavily employed in insurance firms and the banking sector. Actuaries are an essential part of making sure that we have insurance, and in this case study we've seen how valuable insurance is to society.

## KEY LESSONS

- Individual decision makers are likely to differ in their attitudes towards risk. Economists classify decision makers as risk averse, risk neutral or risk loving, depending on their attitude.
- Insurance is a means of transferring risk between decision makers – from the party being insured to the party providing the insurance contract. Society will be made better off where this transfer shifts risk from a decision maker with a lower tolerance for risk to a decision maker with a high tolerance for risk.

## SOME QUESTIONS TO THINK ABOUT

1   Lucky Pierre is a risk-averse prospector in Ballarat who has struck it rich. He has $W worth of gold – his only wealth – safely hidden away on his mining claim. He wants to get his gold away from the claim to the bank in Melbourne. His friend, Mr Cobb, will transport the gold for him free of charge. With probability $p$, all the gold transported on a given trip will be stolen, and with probability $(1 - p)$, none of the gold will be stolen. Two options are available to Pierre: To attempt to transport the gold in one trip, or to attempt to transport the gold in two trips (one-half of the gold in each trip). The probability that the gold being transported on one trip will be stolen is independent of the probability that the gold being transported on the other trip will be stolen.

    a   For each option (one or two trips), explain what are the sets of possible outcomes? What is the probability of each outcome occurring? What is Lucky Pierre's wealth in each outcome?

    b   Show that Lucky's expected utility is larger if half the gold is transferred in each of two trips than if all the gold is transferred in a single trip.

2   Reforms to the health insurance system in Australia introduced in 2019 mean that insurers are able to offer discounts to under-30s for private hospital coverage and

can offer them lower premiums if they are willing to accept higher excess payments (Gartrell 2017). (Note: The excess payment is the amount of a patient's health care treatment costs that they must pay for themselves, with the insurer then paying the difference between the total cost of treatment and the excess payment.) A few years earlier, the insurer MLC commenced a trial where its customers were offered a discount on their health insurance if they were willing to wear a smart watch which monitored their heart rate, sleep patterns and physical activity – with the offer of further discounts if they were found to have a healthy lifestyle (Liew 2015).

a   Why would a health insurance business want to be able to offer insurance policies with premiums varying by the age of customer?

b   Why might a health insurance business prefer to offer an insurance policy with premiums depending on data on lifestyle from a smartwatch compared to a policy with premiums varying by a characteristic such as age?

# REFERENCES

Gartrell, Adam (2017), 'Under-30s discounts in insurance reforms', *The Age*, 13 October, p. 4.

Liew, Ruth (2015), 'Your insurer likes to watch', *The Age*, 10 November, p. 25.

*The Economist* (2006), 'Reputational risk', 15 July, p. 66.

*The Economist* (2007), 'Of coups and coverage', 7 April, pp. 68–9.

*The Economist* (2019), 'Black swans and fat tails', 26 January, pp. 65–6.

# IDEAS FOR FURTHER READING

Walter Nicholson and Christopher Snyder provide an introduction to decision making with uncertainty in *Intermediate Microeconomics and Its Applications* (2015, 12th edn, Thomson Learning, chapter 5). Ian Ayres' book *Super Crunchers* (2007, John Murray) is a very readable introduction to prediction and data analysis, including the statistical concept of independence.

# CASE STUDY 7.2
## DOES PAY FOR PERFORMANCE WORK?

'We lacked motivation today'. This is something you have probably heard on TV, as the coach of a football team or one of the players tried to explain why their side lost a match. In the highly competitive world of professional sport, putting in the right amount of effort is essential to winning. It is not only in the sporting arena, however, that motivation and effort matter. In your studies and in other pursuits you engage in, such as art or music or volunteering, your success will depend on the amount of effort you put in. With this in mind, in evaluating your performance in your studies and other activities, your level of effort is something you will have thought about. Of course, once you move into the workplace, you are likely to have to worry about effort even more – not only your own effort, but the efforts of your co-workers and workers you are supervising.

A common way of characterising what happens in the workplace is the idea of a principal–agent relation. A principal–agent relation exists where one party, designated as the principal, delegates the responsibility for performing some task to another party, designated as the agent. In an owner-operated business, the principal can be thought of as the owner and the employees of the business as agents. For example, an owner might employ workers to undertake production jobs or sales and marketing tasks for the business. In a listed company, there is a series of principal–agent relations: shareholders delegate responsibility for running the business they own to the board of directors; the board delegates responsibility for managing the business to the CEO; the CEO delegates responsibility for various aspects of management to deputy CEOs; and so on.

Whatever is a principal's objective in running a business, once an agent is hired to undertake tasks for the business, achieving the objective will depend in part on the agent's performance. The principal therefore needs to determine how well the agent is performing the assigned tasks. That performance is likely to depend to a large degree on the amount of effort exerted by the agent. For example, the business owner who hires salespeople needs them to contact enough potential buyers so that a sufficient level of sales is generated, and the shareholders need their board of directors to spend sufficient time monitoring the company's performance to ensure that it is being well managed. So, a big concern of the principal will be motivating the agent to exert the appropriate effort.

In many circumstances, motivating employees to make the required effort will not be a problem. Most of us want to feel we are doing a good job and so we work hard for our own satisfaction. Moreover, when our employer can monitor our effort, there is an extra incentive to work hard. But not everyone wants to work hard, and even when we feel we are working hard, we may not be doing quite as much as the owner of the business would like us to do. Furthermore, it is usually going to be difficult for a business owner to monitor how much effort workers are exerting. When this is the case, it is more difficult for the owner to motivate employees to work hard.

## THEORY REFRESHER

### Adverse selection and moral hazard

Economic analysis is fundamentally concerned with those relations in a society involving trade or exchange. In any exchange, there will be a buyer and a seller. For instance, a consumer who buys a newspaper is a buyer and the newsagent where the newspaper is obtained is a seller. Students are buyers of educational services and universities are the sellers of those services.

In some examples of exchange, both parties will have the same information. In other exchange relations, however, there will be an information asymmetry between the buyer and seller, where one party has information not available to the other.

In any exchange, there will be a date or point in time at which a buyer and seller agree to a 'contract' which specifies the terms on which exchange will occur (for example, price, quantity to be supplied, quality, etc.). This point in time is important for classifying information asymmetries (see *Figure 7.2.1*). A key distinction is made between information asymmetries which:

- exist between a buyer and seller prior to the contract date, known as precontractual information asymmetry or adverse selection
- exist after the contract date, known as postcontractual information asymmetry or moral hazard.

Examples of precontractual information asymmetries are when the seller of a used car has better information about the quality of the car than a potential

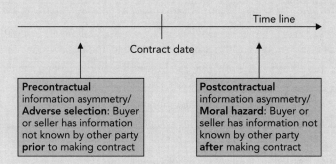

**Figure 7.2.1** Types of information asymmetry

buyer, and where potential employees of a firm have better information about their abilities than the firm which is making the hiring decision.

Examples of postcontractual information asymmetries are when an individual purchases car insurance and subsequently has better information than the insurance firm about how carefully or safely the car is driven; when a firm which employs a door-to-door salesperson cannot observe how many houses that salesperson visits; and when a tenant farmer learns information about soil and weather conditions which is not available to the landowner.

Take the example of a pay-TV supplier which hires numerous door-to-door salespeople to sell subscriptions to its service. It will not be possible for the business owner or manager to monitor how much effort each salesperson is putting in, such as how many houses they visit or the extent to which they try to get a sale. So, what can the business owner do to motivate their salespeople to put in the appropriate level of effort? One idea is to make the salespeople's pay depend on performance, the number of subscriptions they sell.

To see how this might work, let's begin by thinking about what happens if a salesperson's pay doesn't depend on performance. Salespeople would simply be paid a fixed wage regardless of how many subscriptions they sell. It's not difficult to see that this isn't going to provide much motivation for effort. Whether you sell a little or a lot, you get paid the same. And you can always claim that your low sales are explained by bad luck in the region where you were assigned to do the door-to-door selling.

Now consider the alternative, that salespeople are paid according to how many subscriptions they sell. Suppose, for example, that the payment is $50 per subscription sold. Making pay conditional on performance in this way introduces an incentive for salespeople to exert effort. The more effort a salesperson puts in, the more sales that are likely to be made, and hence the more the salesperson gets paid. Tying how much the salesperson gets paid to a performance measure that depends on their effort therefore provides an incentive to exert more effort.

The decision as to whether a pay-TV business should introduce a pay-for-performance scheme for its salespeople seems pretty straightforward. But there is still work for the business to do. It has to decide on the details of the scheme. In doing this, two important issues are, first, to what performance measure should pay be tied and, second, how much should pay depend on performance?

In the example of the pay-TV salespeople, we would probably expect that their pay will be tied to the number of subscriptions they sell, and most likely this is what the business will choose to do. We should be careful, however, about jumping to the conclusion that this is the performance measure that would be chosen. An important principle in designing a pay-for-performance scheme is that the performance measure should be responsive to an employee's effort. Employees need to believe that their pay will increase if they work harder, and this requires that the performance measure varies with the amount of effort they put in. Where this does not occur and pay is made conditional on a performance measure that is unrelated to an employee's effort, there is no incentive to exert extra effort. So, in the pay-TV example the business would need to believe that the number of subscriptions sold will mainly depend on the effort of its salespeople, in order for it to be chosen as the performance measure.

Let's suppose that after some consideration, the pay-TV business does decide that the number of subscriptions sold by its salespeople is the right measure to use in a pay-for-performance scheme. The next issue it must think about is the amount to pay for each extra subscription sold. This matters because the size of payment per subscription will determine how much incentive there is to exert extra effort. A payment of $1 per subscription is unlikely to provide an incentive to put in much effort in making sales, whereas a payment of $50 per subscription will give a much stronger incentive. The pay-TV business has several issues to balance: It must pay enough to give an incentive to its salespeople to put in more effort, but not so much that it is unnecessarily reducing its profits.

## CEOs

Does the pay-for-performance idea actually work? These days, there are many situations in which we can observe employees being paid in this way. Studying these situations gives us the opportunity to evaluate the outcomes of pay-for-performance initiatives. One prominent and intensively researched example is performance-related pay for CEOs.

The rationale for performance-related pay for CEOs is to align their incentives with those of the firm's owners – its shareholders. By relating the CEO's pay to the firm's objective, such as a measure of profits, pay-for-performance is intended to force the CEO to direct effort to that objective. Performance-related pay may provide incentives for a CEO to exert effort and to make decisions in the best interests of the firm.

Despite there being plenty of reasons to expect to see pay-for-performance initiatives in the compensation of CEOs, some early empirical research in the United States concluded that the relation between CEO pay and performance was not especially strong. Using a sample of 1668 CEOs assessed between 1974 and 1986 (from listings in *Forbes*), Michael Jensen and Kevin Murphy found that 'each $1000 change in shareholder wealth corresponds to an average increase in this year's and next year's salary and bonus of about two cents', and that 'our final all-inclusive estimate of pay-performance sensitivity – including compensation, dismissal and stockholdings – is about $3.25 per $1000 change in shareholder wealth' (1990, p. 226).

So, the pay of CEOs did seem to depend on performance, just not very much. Why might boards choose to make CEOs' pay depend only to a minimal degree on their firm's performance? One explanation is that CEOs may be risk averse. CEOs will then dislike the variability in compensation induced by performance-related pay. This means that a firm must pay a risk premium in the form of a higher average wage to its CEO, to compensate the CEO for bearing extra risk. Other explanations are that a performance-based pay scheme may focus a CEO's attention on particular tasks in their job which are reflected in the performance measure, with the consequence that other tasks are neglected; or that performance-based pay may induce a CEO to seek to manipulate the performance measure that is used to calculate pay, with adverse consequences for a firm when that performance measure does not represent the firm's overall objective. For example, if a CEO is compensated on the basis of short-term movements in their firm's share price, they may have an incentive to take actions to raise that short-term share price, even where it lowers the firm's long-run profits.

The questioning of pay-for-performance schemes for CEOs that followed the research by Michael Jensen and Kevin Murphy was valuable in identifying potential problems that could arise from their use. Nevertheless, it's important to finish this discussion by noting that subsequent research on CEO compensation has indicated that CEOs are in fact being paid in a way that makes their pay highly sensitive to firm performance. Using data on the compensation of CEOs in the United States from 1980 to 1994, Brian Hall and Jeffrey Liebman (1998) found evidence that differences in firm performance can be related to total compensation differences between CEOs amounting to millions of dollars. For example, being the CEO of a company with share returns in the 30th percentile compared with the 70th percentile would be associated with a difference in compensation of $4 million. Part of the explanation for the different findings from the earlier research is that the use of stock options, which provide very high-powered incentives, increased significantly in the 1980s and 1990s, so that the elasticity of CEO compensation to firm market value tripled between 1980 and 1994.*

## In the classroom

Most of the discussion thus far has been about how to use the pay-for-performance idea in the workplace. There are many other environments in which we worry about motivating extra effort and good performance by people for whom we are responsible, and hence where the idea of pay-for-performance also has been applied. One situation where you might not have expected to hear about pay-for-performance being used is in getting students to work hard and perform well on tests. Yet this is exactly what was done in an experiment involving 38 000 students in state-run schools in New York, Chicago, Dallas and Washington DC, and undertaken by Harvard economist Ronald Fryer (Fryer 2011).

Professor Fryer set out to test the effect of a pay-for-performance scheme on student academic performance using a randomised trial. Schools in each geographic area were randomly divided into treatment and control groups, with treatment schools being where pay-for-performance was introduced and with control schools being where financial incentives were absent. A variety of pay-for-performance schemes were tested across students at different year levels. In New York, fourth- and seventh-grade students in treatment schools could earn up to US$25 and US$50, respectively, depending on their score on each of 10 standard maths and reading tests. In Chicago, ninth-grade students in treatment schools were rewarded on a sliding scale for good grades in five courses, including English, maths and science. Earning an A-grade was rewarded with US$50, while no payment was made for a D-grade. The total amount of money students could earn was sizeable, up to $2000 a year.

Think about your own study habits. Would you have been motivated to work harder by these financial incentives? If you are like the students in the experiment, you will be answering, 'No'. As a report in *The Economist* (2010, p. 76) described: 'Plenty of money was paid out, but Mr Fryer found absolutely no evidence that paying students led them to do better than their peers in the control schools. Neither girls nor boys gained, and it did not seem to matter how students had previously performed.'

What explains this disappointing result? Well, it seems to stem from an issue concerning pay-for-performance schemes that we have already discussed – that people need to believe they can affect the performance measure. Professor Fryer's explanation for his results is that students at the schools in his trial didn't know how to improve their test results. They understood that they could earn a reward for good performance, but they didn't believe that putting more effort into studying would get them better results. Instead, Professor Fryer's trial found that an alternative approach was much more effective in improving test results: Paying students for completing tasks over which they feel they have control. Second-grade students in Dallas were paid US$2 for every book they read for which they could pass a computerised comprehension text, and the results were promising: 'this spurred them to read more books and improved their vocabularies. But it also improved their school grades substantially, although this is not what they were paid for' (*The Economist* 2010, p. 76).

## Conclusion

An examination of the use of pay-for-performance schemes for CEOs and for students reveals that they are not a panacea. The pay-for-performance model can be a source of motivation; for example, it can prompt employees to exert extra effort. To have this effect, however, requires the right circumstances – such as when employees believe that they can influence the performance measure, and where the scheme has been carefully designed to provide sufficient incentive to exert effort.

# KEY LESSONS

- How well a business performs is likely to depend in large part on the effort put in by its employees. Motivating employees to exert the appropriate amount of effort is, therefore, a major management task for every business.
- If the business owner or manager cannot observe or infer how much effort is being exerted by employees, it will not be possible to directly regulate employees' efforts. Instead, the business can use pay-for-performance schemes to try to induce the employees to exert effort. The idea of pay-for-performance is that by tying how much employees get paid to a performance measure that depends on their efforts, there will be greater incentive for them to exert effort.
- For a pay-for-performance scheme to be effective, it is important to get the design right; for example, by choosing an appropriate performance measure on which pay will depend, and ensuring that the extent of variation of pay based on performance gives sufficient incentive for employees to exert effort.

# SOME QUESTIONS TO THINK ABOUT

1   A new chain store called ToysToysToys Co. is looking to rent a number of sites for new stores. In addition to wanting to pay the minimum possible rental per site, the company has very particular requirements that each site must satisfy – a location on a main road and in an area with population concentrations in the company's target demographic group; the availability of at least 100 car parking spaces; and building space and shape that are suitable for the toy store format. Due to its own lack of expertise, ToysToysToys Co. has decided to hire an external property consultant to locate the sites. The compensation paid to the consultant is to be specified in a contract.

   a   Identify possible sources of asymmetric information in the relationship between ToysToysToys Co. and the external property consultant.

   b   Describe the likely outcome under each of the following types of contracts for the property consultant. How likely are they to achieve the objectives of ToysToysToys Co.?

      i    a fixed fee paid to the consultant for locating a specified number of potential sites

      ii   a fixed fee paid to the consultant for each site found with floor space above a specified level and with rental price below a specified level

      iii  a fixed fee paid to the consultant for each site located which ToysToysToys Co. decides to rent

   c   What type of contract would you recommend to ToysToysToys Co.?

2   An article written during the early days of Australia's Royal Commission into Banking described problems with the role of mortgage brokers – going so far as

to describe the payment of mortgage brokers as '...the most glaring instance of incentives gone wrong in the mortgage market' (Irvine 2018). A mortgage broker's role is to assist a borrower to decide how much to borrow and the best lender to borrow from. At the time of the Royal Commission, about half of the home loans written each year in Australia were organised through a mortgage broker. For providing this service, mortgage brokers were paid by lenders (such as banks) – receiving a commission based on the value of loans they directed to lenders. Lenders would also pay brokers bonuses where they directed above a certain value of loans to them. Mortgage broking services were initially supplied in Australia by independent businesses such as Aussie Home Loans. But today most are owned by the big banks. For example, the Commonwealth Bank of Australia bought Aussie Home Loans and part of Mortgage Choice.

a   Do you think there are potential information asymmetries between mortgage brokers and borrowers?

b   How is the takeover of mortgage brokers by major lenders [banks] likely to have affected the alignment of objectives of mortgage brokers and borrowers? (Note: By alignment of objectives, what is meant is the extent to which mortgage brokers act in a way that is in the interests of borrowers.)

c   Do you think that the current payment system for borrowers is likely to improve or exacerbate any misalignment between the objectives of mortgage brokers and borrowers?

# EXTRA NOTE

* Stock options grant the holder the ability to buy shares at a pre-specified price. If the market price of a share rises, option holders will benefit because they can buy the stock at less than the market price (and potentially then resell it, thus making a profit). Dollar-for-dollar, share options provide stronger incentives to a CEO than would a simple granting of shares. For example, it would cost a firm $1 million to grant 10 000 shares of $100 stock to a CEO. The CEO would gain $100 000 from a 10 per cent increase in the firm's value. If the CEO was instead given 100 000 options to buy the stock at $100, they would gain 10 times more ($1 million) from a 10 per cent increase in the firm's value and the firm's payout is again just $1 million.

# REFERENCES

Fryer, Roland Jr (2011), 'Financial incentives and student achievement: Evidence from randomized trials', *Quarterly Journal of Economics*, vol. 126, pp. 1755–98.

Hall, Brian & Liebman, Jeffrey (1998), 'Are CEOs really paid like bureaucrats?', *Quarterly Journal of Economics*, vol. 113, pp. 653–91.

Irvine, Jessica (2018), 'Broker system is broken', *The Age*, 19 March, p. 18.

Jensen, Michael & Murphy, Kevin J. (1990), 'Performance pay and top-management incentives', *Journal of Political Economy*, vol. 98, pp. 225–64.

*The Economist* (2010), 'Satchel, uniform, bonus', 22 May, p. 76.

# IDEAS FOR FURTHER READING

An (old but still) excellent introduction to the pay-for-performance model is provided by Haig Nalbantian in 'Incentive compensation in practice' (1987, in Haig Nalbantian (ed.), *Incentives, Cooperation and Risk Sharing*, Rowman and Littlefield, chapter 1). Slightly more technical introductions appear in Paul Milgrom and John Roberts' *Economics, Organization and Management* (1992, Prentice Hall, chapters 6 & 7) and Walter Nicholson and Christopher Snyder's *Intermediate Microeconomics and Its Applications* (2015, 12th edn, Thomson Learning, chapter 17). For a recent review of the literature on executive pay, see Alex Edmans, Xavier Gabaix and Dirk Jenter (2017), 'Executive compensation: A survey of theory and evidence', National Bureau of Economic Research Working Paper no. 23596. A different application of the pay-for-performance model in education – paying teachers based on their students' performances – is reviewed in Derek Neal's *The Design of Performance Pay in Education* (2011, National Bureau of Economic Research, working paper no. 16710).

# Index